New Zealand Cinema

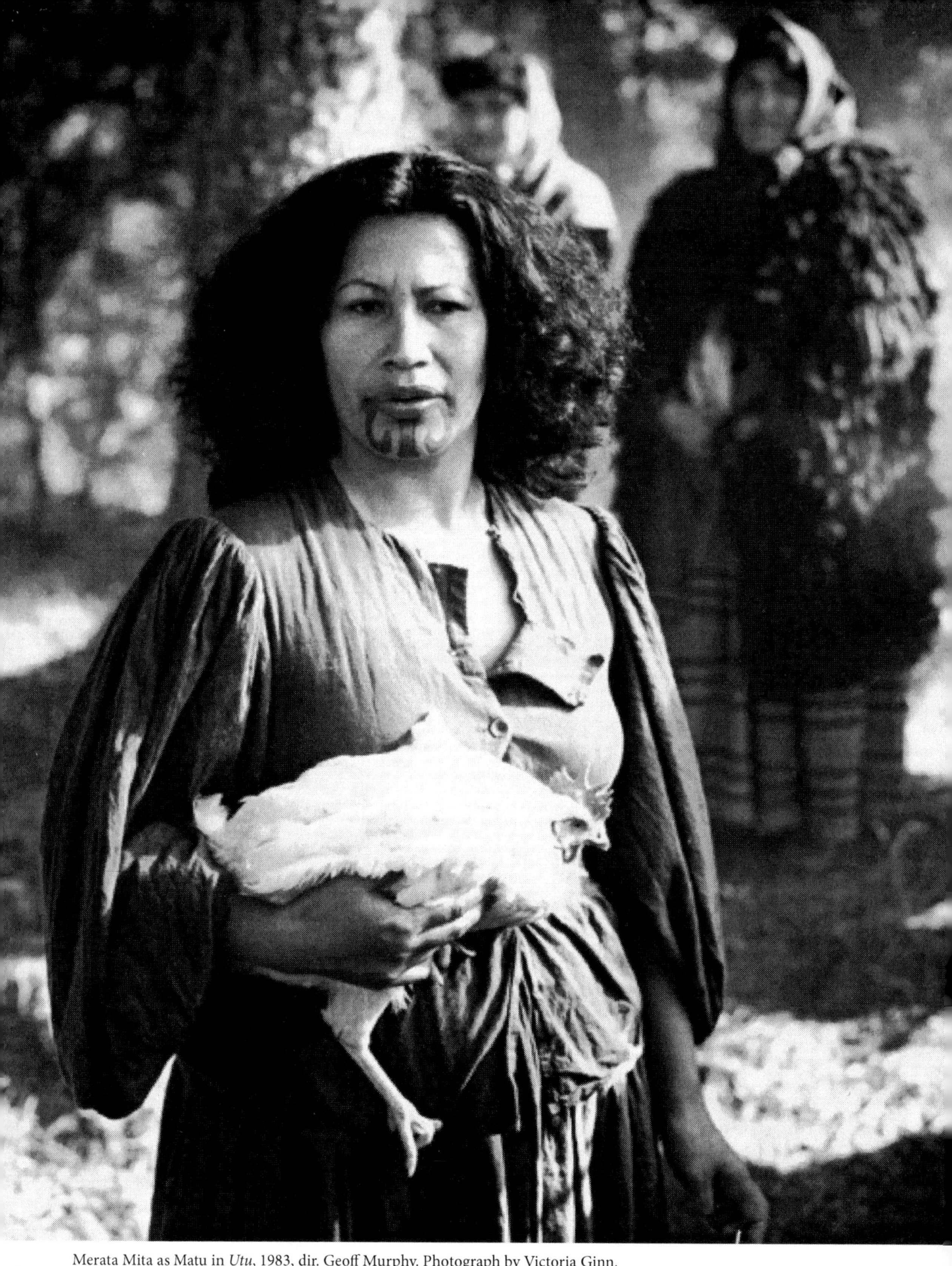

Merata Mita as Matu in *Utu*, 1983, dir. Geoff Murphy. Photograph by Victoria Ginn.

New Zealand Cinema

Interpreting the Past

Edited by Alistair Fox, Barry Keith Grant and Hilary Radner

intellect Bristol, UK / Chicago, USA

First published in the UK in 2011 by
Intellect, The Mill, Parnall Road, Fishponds, Bristol, BS16 3JG, UK

First published in the USA in 2011 by
Intellect, The University of Chicago Press, 1427 E. 60th Street,
Chicago, IL 60637, USA

A catalogue record for this book is available from the
British Library.

Cover designer: Holly Rose
Copy-editor: Integra Software Services
Typesetting: Mac Style, Beverley, E. Yorkshire

ISBN 978-1-84150-425-4

Printed and bound by Gutenberg Press, Malta.

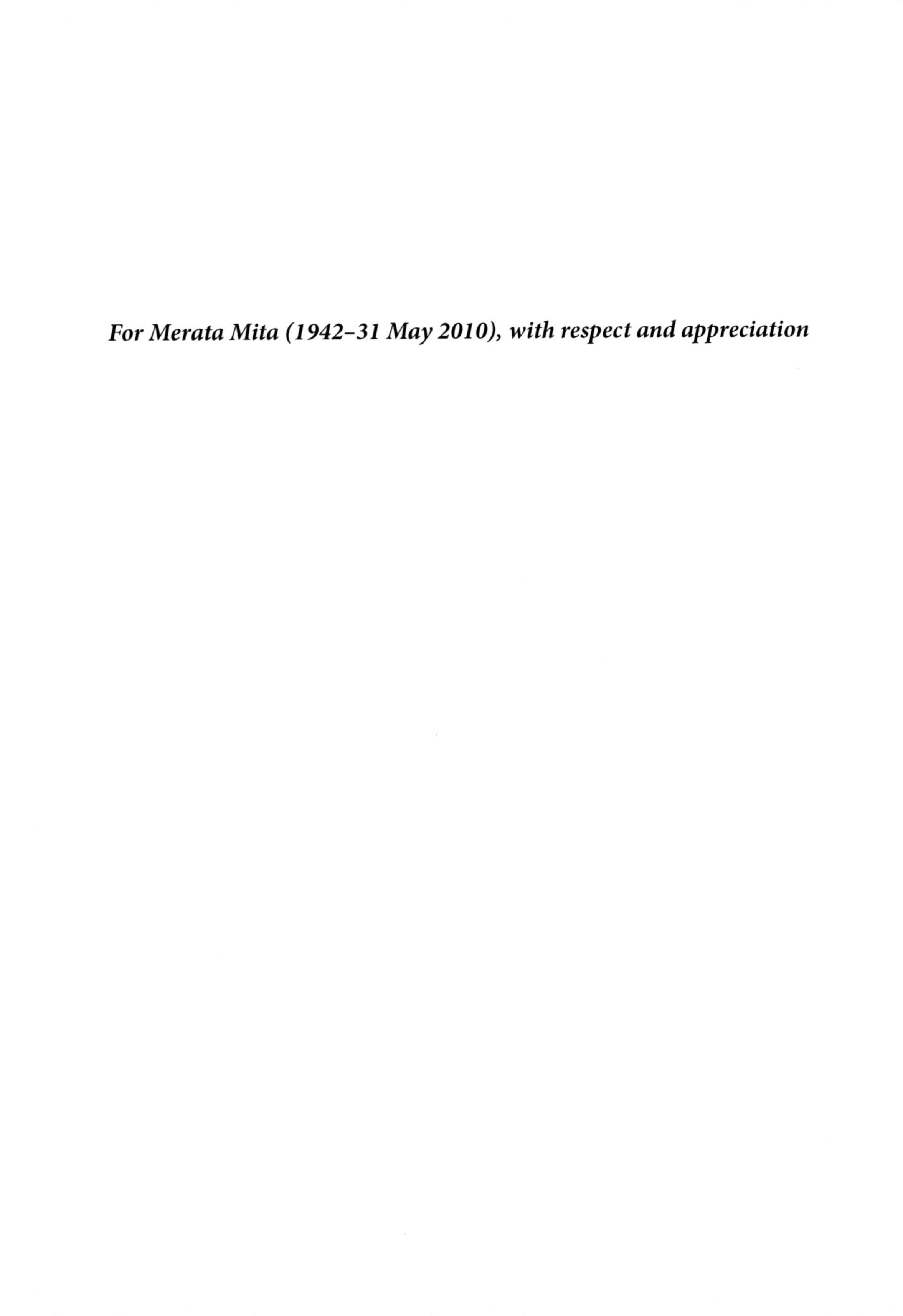

For Merata Mita (1942–31 May 2010), with respect and appreciation

Contents

Acknowledgements

The seeds for this volume were sown at the biennial meeting of the Film and History Association of Australia held at the University of Otago in November–December 2008, when the possibility of a book-length study of the New Zealand historical film first became apparent. We therefore owe a debt of gratitude to all those who participated in this conference, including those who offered comments and advice on the idea of the project – in particular, Russell Campbell and Michael Walsh who, as long standing members of this organisation, offered support in the planning stages that was much appreciated.

The editors would also like to acknowledge the financial support provided by the University of Otago generally, and the various forms of support offered by the Centre for Research on National Identity, the Cultures, Histories and Identities in Film, Media and Literature Research Network, the Department of Media, Film and Communication, the Department of English and the Division of Humanities. Erica Todd, Lisa Marr and Delyn Day provided editorial assistance. We would like to thank staff in The New Zealand Film Commission/Te Tumu Whakaata Taonga, the Hocken Library/Te Uare Taoka o Hākena, Archives New Zealand/Te Rua Mahara o te Kāwanatanga and the New Zealand Film Archive/Ngā Kaitiaki O Ngā Taonga Whitiāhua for assisting us in locating illustrations for this book.

The difficulty of accessing some of the earlier New Zealand films made it important that some photographic images were included in the book. We are therefore grateful to the whānau of Tina Hunt and Patiti Warbrick for permission to reproduce images of them; to Ramai Te Miha for permission to reproduce the production still from *Rewi's Last Stand*; and to Victoria Ginn for giving us access to her stills from the productions of *Utu* and *Mauri*.

Finally, we would like to express out sincere thanks to Jelena Stanovnik at Intellect, for the exemplary care with which she steered this book through the various states of its production.

Alistair Fox
Barry Keith Grant
Hilary Radner

I believe that history itself, the passage of people, is connected. The past influences the present, which influences the future, for better or worse [...]. We need to fight for something a little bit beyond ourselves.

(Barry Barclay, commenting on his film, *The Feathers of Peace*)

Tomorrow is the harvest of our yesterdays.

(Advertising slogan for *Pictures*, 1981, dir. Michael Black)

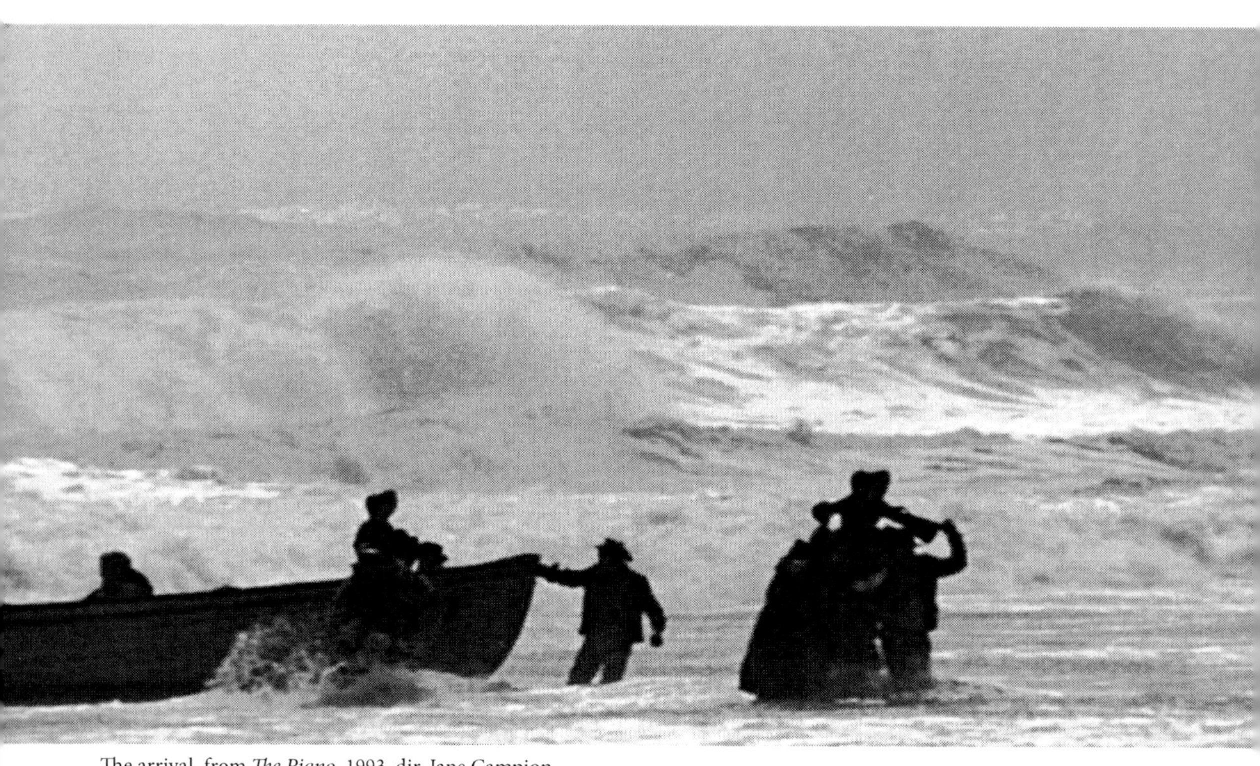

The arrival, from *The Piano*, 1993, dir. Jane Campion.

Introduction

The Historical Film in New Zealand Cinema

Alistair Fox, Barry Keith Grant, and Hilary Radner

From the time filmmakers first began to make fiction features, cinema has been preoccupied with historical subject matter. By 1911, the historical film already constituted a major genre in French cinema, with single-reel movies like *Marie Stuart* (1908) and *Le Roi s'amuse* (1909),[1] while in the United States the historical blockbuster film had found its prototype as early as 1915, with D. W. Griffith's monumental epic, *The Birth of a Nation*. The popularity of the historical film is not hard to see; as scholars like Marcia Landy have argued, historicising of one sort or another has always played a key part in determining "how individuals and groups inherit and understand their social and cultural milieu."[2] Yet, at the same time, writes Landy, "history and memory have also played a part in destabilising conceptions of the nation"[3] as "filmmakers have engaged in the centuries-old tradition of grappling with the present by writing about the past."[4] The dramatisation of history can be used to celebrate and propagate dominant institutions and ideologies; equally, it can elaborate a counter-history or counter-narrative for the sake of debunking prevailing myths.[5] This means that the historical film may be viewed as one of the most important ways in which social experience and collective consciousness is formulated, transformed, and transmitted. As Robert Burgoyne puts it, cinema has an unequalled ability to "re-create the past in a sensual, mimetic form" that, on one hand, establishes "an emotional connection to the past that can awaken a powerful sense of national belonging," while, on the other it can activate "a probing sense of national self-scrutiny."[6] For Burgoyne, the historical film thus constitutes "a privileged discursive site in which anxiety, ambivalence, and expectation about the nation, its history, and its future are played out in narrative form."[7]

To a large degree, the unique capacity of cinematic representation to articulate a nation's emergent or evolving sense of identity derives from cinema's ability to draw upon the expressive devices of a wide range of cinematic genres. The eclecticism of the historical film is reflected in Burgoyne's identification of five distinct subtypes within the larger category: the war film, the epic film, the biographical film, the metahistorical film, and the topical historical film.[8] Furthermore, one often finds that elements from other cinematic genres (for example, comedy, melodrama, the western, the romance, and so on) are combined within the same sub-genre (as in the case of Rudall Hayward's war epics, discussed in Chapter 1). Such generic fluidity, together with the admixture of perspectives from the present with material that relates to, and is often derived from, the past, inevitably predisposes the historical film towards pastiche – here defined in its general sense as the combining of elements from disparate sources, often involving the adaptation or localisation of an existing work.

This kind of pastiche, as Andrew Higson, following Pam Cook, has argued, is particularly evident in the historical costume drama, in which the creation of a story based on events imported from another time opens up a space in which to explore "the *hybrid* qualities of national identity." In Higson's words:

> Pastiche can enable the story-teller to establish a sense of location in history, in a real setting, by invoking the conventional signs for representing that historical location. But once the location is imagined, pastiche can then enable the story-teller to weave a narrative that can explore concerns that may have nothing to do with the implied historical setting, but everything to do with the moment in which the telling of the story unfolds. That is, it can enable the story-teller to explore concerns that may have everything to do with the present. Pastiche thus enables the anomalous and the perverse to be inserted into the apparently authentic historical location, it enables the past to be mixed with the present, it enables the fantastic to mingle with the realist.[9]

It is precisely this ability to bring the past into dialogue with the present that makes the historical film an invaluable marker of the process of cultural change in a nation's evolving identity.[10]

While much work has been done in the past two decades to illuminate this crucial role of the historical film with respect to the major cinemas of the northern hemisphere,[11] far less attention has been paid to historical films in the emergent national cinemas of former settler societies, or those of nations that are in a process of decolonisation after the imperial project of the nineteenth and early twentieth centuries. Most of the writing that does exist on this topic focuses on Australian cinema.[12] By contrast, with respect to New Zealand cinema, as Reid Perkins observed in 1996, "the space in which historical and cinematic narratives intersect remains an insufficiently examined but potentially fecund area of study."[13] Over a decade later, this observation remains true.

Astonishingly, there has been to date no focused investigation of the historical film in New Zealand, despite its prominence and persistence in the rapidly expanding body of feature fiction films being produced by this country. Indeed, at the time of writing, out of fewer than 200 fiction features made by New Zealanders in New Zealand, no less than 40 of them (over 20 per cent) have been historical films.[14] The purpose of this book, therefore, is to explore significant works within this general category, with the aim being to establish what contributions they have made to the project of formulating, interrogating, understanding, and representing New Zealand identities. Concomitantly, the book will examine the motivations of directors and producers who have been involved in the making of historical films, and more importantly, the uses to which subject matter drawn from New Zealand history has been put.

Following various definitions suggested by previous scholars, the "historical film" will be understood here as any fiction film that has "a meaningful relationship to historical events,"[15] either by dealing with "actual historical events or real historical persons,"[16] or which are "set in 'the past' – recent or distant, actual or imagined."[17] Such a definition is broader than that proposed by Burgoyne, who adheres to Natalie Zemon Davis's definition of the genre as "composed of dramatic feature films in which the primary plot is based on actual historical events, or in which an imagined plot unfolds in such a way that actual historical events are central and intrinsic to the story."[18] In the case of New Zealand cinema, this definition seems unnecessarily limiting, in that it would exclude from consideration films by indigenous filmmakers, such as Barry Barclay's *Ngati* (1987) and Merata Mita's *Mauri* (1988), which are set in the past in order to juxtapose a traditional, rural Māori lifestyle against the forces of modernity and the Pākehā world that are threatening to impinge upon, and destroy it (see the discussions by Janet Wilson and Bruce Harding in Chapters 9 and 10). Equally, it would exclude woman's films like David Blyth's *It's Lizzie to Those Close* (1983), discussed by Hilary Radner in Chapter 12, or Jane Campion's *The Piano* (1993), discussed by Estella Tincknell in Chapter 13, which, rather than re-enacting specific historical events, choose instead to evoke the general repressive conditions of settler experience in colonial New Zealand brought about by the combination of puritanism and patriarchy in order to explore the desire of women (both the heroines of the films themselves, and also, by extension, women at the time of the film's production) to be liberated from them.

In addition, several of the chapters in this book (by Jeanette Hoorn and Michelle Smith, Simon Sigley, and Barbara Brookes) will deal with films that address contemporary history, to the extent that, in Geoffrey Barraclough's sense, they are concerned with topics that reflect an attempt – as in Rudall Hayward's community comedies of the late 1920s and 1930s, the National Film Unit's *Journey for Three* (1950), and John O'Shea's *Broken Barrier* (1952) – to explore forces in the contemporary world that are identified as being responsible for the "visible shape" it is assuming.[19] Rather than defining the historical film in terms of plot and event, therefore, this book will adopt a broader definition in which the defining characteristic of a historical film will be the presence in it of a historical way of thinking – that is, of a concern to understand the forces in the world at large that are determining the conditions of society as a whole, or of particular groups within it, whether or not such forces are shown to be located in the past, or operating in the present.

"Fiction feature film," within this broad definition of the historical film, will include docudramas – a favoured form in New Zealand – that include significant or extensive dramatised re-enactments of historical events, as in Barry Barclay's *The Feathers of Peace* (2000), dealing with the destruction of the Moriori people in the Chatham Islands (see Janet Wilson's discussion in Chapter 9), or Vincent Ward's *Rain of the Children* (2007), which shows the suppression of the prophet Rua Kēnana and his Tūhoe followers at Maungapōhatu in the Ureweras, in 1916. (Both films are discussed towards the end of this introduction.) Here, we offer an overview of New Zealand historical films, including both feature fiction films and docudramas, and providing historical and aesthetic contexts for the analyses of the individual films in the chapters that follow.

The earliest New Zealand historical features

From the very outset of filmmaking in New Zealand during the 1910s, filmmakers were fascinated by the exoticism of the antipodean islands of Aotearoa and their inhabitants, the indigenous Māori. Somewhat earlier, this fascination of "Pākehā" (European New Zealanders of predominantly British descent) with the exotic had been expressed in romanticised tales of "Maoriland" – fantasised accounts that depict Māori as noble savages inhabiting a mythological pre-European past, or else early encounters between European explorers and fierce Māori tribes, usually centring around a cross-cultural romance between the white hero and a beautiful dusky maiden.[20] Such were the very first features made in New Zealand, the three films shot by the visiting Frenchman Gaston Méliès (the older brother of the more famous Georges) with a team of fifteen assistants on location in the thermal area of Rotorua, and in the Whanganui area during his sojourn in the North Island in late 1912: *Hinemoa*, *How Chief Te Ponga Won His Bride*, and *Loved by a Maori Chieftess* – all released in 1913, and all of which are now lost. Another version of *Hinemoa*, also lost, was made about the same time by the New Zealander George Tarr, being screened locally in 1914.

Even though these earliest features set in the colonial or pre-colonial past are no longer extant, the synopses that survive of Méliès' three films suggest the range of functions they were designed to serve.[21] The plot of *Loved by a Maori Chieftess* incorporates motifs that can be found in any number of the literary "Maoriland" romances written from the 1870s onwards, such as Alfred Domett's *Ranolf and Amohia*, Augustus Grace's *Maoriland Stories*, and Elan Westerwood's *Maoriana*. Characteristically, these romances involve a pioneer who falls into the company of a Māori tribe, and either becomes enamoured of, or is loved by, a Māori maiden. Méliès' film presents the story of a handsome white man, Chadwick, who is taken prisoner and condemned to be killed and eaten, but is saved by a Māori princess, Wena, who falls in love with him and helps him to escape. After surviving various dangers and vicissitudes, the two are united and Chadwick is made a chief of the tribe. In his otherwise excellent examination of images of Māori in New Zealand cinema, Martin Blythe distinguishes between these earliest films shot in New Zealand by foreigners, which he categorises as "imperial romances of Maoriland" set in "the timeless eternal," as against "national romances" produced by New Zealand filmmakers, which he sees, in contradistinction, as being "timebound within history" and flirting with "cross-racial miscegenation in order to produce national unity." But the presence of this kind of cross-cultural encounter in *Loved by a Maori Chieftess* means that Blythe's distinction cannot be maintained.[22]

While it is unlikely that Méliès himself knew these Maoriland tales at first hand, he contracted James Cowan, a national "authority on Māori legend and custom," as "general adviser and interpreter," and Cowan clearly did.[23] It is the presence of his vision in both Méliès' "imperial romances" and Hayward's later "national romances" that weakens any sharp distinction between Blythe's categories. At the time when he joined Méliès as his advisor on things Māori, Cowan had recently published several accounts of Māori life,

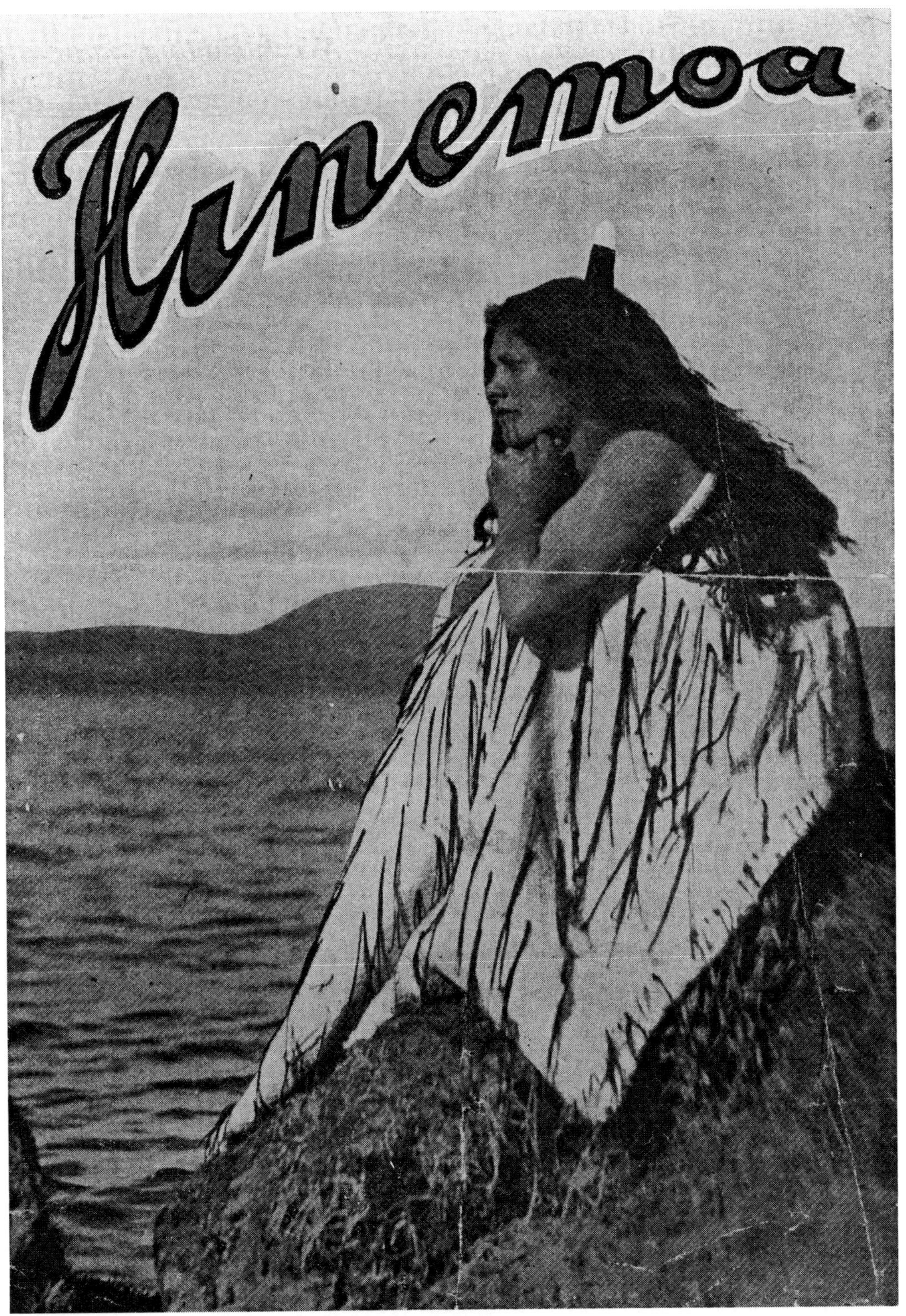

Hera Tawhai Rogers as Hinemoa in *Hinemoa*, 1914, dir. George Tarr. Original programme from Henry Gore Collection, New Zealand Film Archive Ngā Kaitiaki O Ngā Taonga Whitiāhua.

including *The Adventures of Kimble Bent: A Story of Wild Life in the New Zealand Bush* (1911), describing the exploits of an American deserter who lived with the Māori during the Taranaki campaign. Cowan would later write *The New Zealand Wars: A History of the Maori Campaigns and the Pioneering Period*, a definitive history of the Anglo-Māori Wars published by the Government Printer in 1922–23, which Hayward, who also had been inspired by *The Adventures of Kimble Bent*, would use as his main source for *Rewi's Last Stand* (1925) and *The Te Kooti Trail* (1927).[24] Méliès also brought with him as a screenwriter Edmund Mitchell, described in press releases at the time as "a well-known novelist and journalist" who had been on the staff of the *Melbourne Age*, and who had been for some time past resident at Los Angeles, California.[25]

Through the mediation of these two, therefore, with Cowan acting as source and Mitchell converting the material supplied by Cowan into a screenplay, Méliès was able to make three historical romances that reflected the popular perceptions of the day. At a superficial level, a film like *Loved by a Maori Chieftess* is obviously designed to appeal to the contemporary audience's taste for melodrama and the exotic in order simply to entertain. At a deeper level, however, one can detect a metonymically displaced, symbolic representation of a deep desire on the part of the white colonisers to be accepted by the native inhabitants of the land – to have the enmity so fiercely displayed against them during the Land Wars 50 years earlier replaced by reconciliation. Méliès' other two films, *Hinemoa* and *How Chief Te Ponga Won His Bride*, have a simpler purpose: they each take a pair of star-crossed Māori lovers – Hinemoa and Tūtānekai in the former, and Puhuhu and Te Ponga in the latter – and show how, in spite of adversity, love conquers all. The use of generic conventions characteristic of European romance serves to render the Māori subjects sympathetic, sentimentalising them on one hand, while ennobling them on the other. Such a strategy renders the indigenous Other "safe," as well as imparting a sense of ownership on the part of the Pākehā. By generating these effects, the way in which the subject matter is historicised in these two films at the level of wish-fulfilment fantasy achieves the same end as the first one: that is, an appropriation of the idea of the Other in order to master and control it, thus ultimately furthering the project of colonisation itself. In Chapter 6, Annabel Cooper provides a reading of the Pākehā–Māori relationship in several texts, from Cowan's work to Vincent Ward's film *River Queen* (2005), seeing them as markers of evolving values and sense of national identity, as well as emphasising the "continuity of Pākehā fascination with a figure who summons both the warrior as savage cannibal and the warrior as far-seeing military leader and prophet of his people."

Rudall Hayward's New Zealand wars epics and the founding of a nation

The next phase in the evolution of the historical film in New Zealand occurred during the 1920s and extended through to 1940, the year marking the centenary of the signing of the Treaty of Waitangi. During this period, some filmmakers continued to make Maoriland romances of the sort initiated by Méliès, with the Danish filmmaker Gustav Pauli making yet another version of the Hinemoa story, released as *The Romance of Hine-moa* in 1926 (United Kingdom) and 1927 (New Zealand), and the American Alexander Marky presenting in *Hei Tiki* (1935), a mish-mash of Maoriland romance motifs and extraneous imported material that, in the words of Māori filmmaker Merata Mita, is "culturally insensitive and in some cases downright offensive."[26] Despite a recent claim that *Hei Tiki* exemplifies "settler cinema,"[27] its remoteness from the perspectives found in films produced from New Zealand by New Zealanders during the first half of the twentieth century means that it is to Rudall Hayward that one must turn in order to perceive the preoccupations and representational strategies that are truly characteristic of settler cinema in this country.

It is not without justification that Rudall Hayward is widely considered to be the "father of New Zealand filmmaking." Taking the fiction feature in new directions, Hayward's major innovation was to make films that focused explicitly on the process and consequences of colonisation rather than concentrating on the romanticisation of an imaginary and exotic indigenous past. To do so, he produced and directed two settler romances – *My Lady of the Cave* (1922), set in the aftermath of the Māori-Pākehā wars of the preceding century, and *The Bush Cinderella* (1928), the action of which begins at the time of the 1901 Boer War, "when the Dominion sent its finest contingents to answer the call of the Mother-land," as the opening Prologue proclaims. Both films present narratives of dispossession and surprise inheritance that symbolically figure Hayward's sense of the pattern inherent in the historical experience of the fledgling New Zealand colony.[28] Whereas *My Lady of the Cave* presents an allegory of colonisation itself, *The Bush Cinderella* presents a myth of sacrifice at a later period in the colony's history, occasioned by a war fought on behalf of a distant mother country that leads to the frustration of a happiness and fulfilment that the nubile young heroine would otherwise have enjoyed, and which can only be put right by the restoration to a child of the next generation of the inheritance – symbolised in a literal legacy – that rightfully should have been hers. In both these romances, the respective heroines can be read as stand-ins for New Zealand herself, and, in the case of *The Bush Cinderella*, although it is the Boer War that is presented as causing the loss, it is really the First World War that Hayward has in his sights, with the earlier South African conflict being chosen mainly to provide the right age for the heroine, Mary, whose middle name is "Makepeace," in the romance plot.

At the same time as he was making these settler romances, Hayward also made a number of epic films that dramatise key episodes from the New Zealand Wars of the 1860s, with the aim of showing the sacrifice and achievements of the pioneers that had made possible the creation of the flourishing civil society of his own day. These remarkable films, which were heavily influenced by the westerns of D. W. Griffith, as well as his epic *The Birth of a Nation* (1915),[29] comprise two silent features, *Rewi's Last Stand* (1925), which presents Rewi Maniapoto's heroic defiance of the British at Ōrākau (in the Waikato region), and *The Te Kooti Trail* (1927), which re-creates the attack by the warriors of the guerrilla leader Te Kooti Arikirangi Te Turuki on the mill of Jean Guerrin near Ōpōtiki in the Bay of Plenty.

In preparation for the centenary commemoration in 1940 of the Treaty of Waitangi, the historic agreement between Māori and the British that laid the foundations of the new nation, Hayward prepared a new talking version of the events leading to the siege at Ōrākau, variously titled *Rewi's Last Stand/The Last Stand.*

Systematic settlement in New Zealand had been made possible by this Treaty, whereby Māori tribes had ceded to the British Crown *kāwanatanga* – literally meaning "governorship" in Māori, but understood as "sovereignty" by the British (a semantic distinction that has caused trouble ever since) – in exchange for the Queen's protection, the rights and privileges of British citizens, and a guarantee that Māori would continue to enjoy full possession of their lands, estates, forests, fisheries, and *taonga* (treasures). In the event, under the pressure of ever-escalating demand for land by immigrants who flooded to the new colony, the Treaty was almost immediately broken, with successive governments unscrupulously appropriating lands not actually occupied by Māori, dropping the pre-emption clause in Article 2 of the Treaty that prevented private sales, and ignoring the other guarantees that had been offered by the Crown. Inevitably, Māori grievances boiled over into a protracted series of wars with the British that took place through most of the 1860s.

Eventually, after many bloody battles, sieges, guerrilla raids, and retaliations, either Māori resistance was broken (with further land confiscations exacted as punishment), or else, in certain parts of the country, the two sides fought each other to a standstill, eventuating in an exhausted stalemate. To break the deadlock, the colonial government granted pardons to a number of undefeated Māori rebel leaders, such as Te Kooti in the Urewera mountains of the east of the country, or the even more feared Tītokowaru in Taranaki, in the west. Despite these concessions, however, the overall effect on Māori of the attrition wrought by the wars was a deep-seated cultural depression – so profound that, by the end of the century, Māori were widely perceived by Pākehā to be "a dying race." This was the reality that the fanciful depictions of Méliès and Tarr, like other exercises in Maoriland mythology, occluded: to romanticise Māori as noble savages living a pre-European existence allowed for the actual history of fierce resentment, violent contention, and ongoing grievance to be overlooked. In this way, any lingering guilt on the part of the Pākehā who had stolen their land could be palliated, at the same time as the descendants of the settlers could congratulate themselves on the superiority of the "civilisation" that their ancestors had brought with them.

By the 1920s, however, the situation had changed. There had been a determined effort by Māori leaders like Sir Āpirana Ngata, with his advocacy of Māori culture, and effective political interventions on behalf of Māori, to restore Māori pride and self-confidence. Moreover, Māori and Pākehā had recently fought beside one another against a common foe during the First World War – an experience that was felt to have deepened the mutual respect between these former antagonists into a permanent bond, sealed by the blood shed in a common cause. The time was ripe, therefore, for cinema to give expression to this new sense of a nation emerging from the violent experiences of the past.

Hayward was the filmmaker who rose to the challenge, and his three civil war epics provide a revealing insight into the myth that prevailed as the country prepared to celebrate its centenary. In them, New Zealand had been made into a "cleaner, brighter world,"[30] in which Māori and Pākehā lived in amiable harmony – in short, a pastoral paradise that was "God's Own Country," in the words of a popular catch-cry of the time. However, as Alistair Fox shows in Chapter 1, Hayward's epic films, while manifestly celebrating the achievements of the pioneers in preparing the way for this purported utopia, also contain a latent counter-narrative that is intimated through the incorporation of elements from other genres, whereby the harm to Māori wrought by the colonising process is acknowledged, and lamented.[31] For Fox, Hayward's work was responsive to both the imperialist discourse in James Cowan's influential history as well as the counter-discourse that accompanied it.

Significantly, at the same time Hayward was acknowledging the existence of this counter-narrative in his historical epics, he was also making an extraordinary and unique series of community comedies designed to reinforce the message that white colonisation had been "a good thing." These community comedies – two-reel films such as *A Daughter of Dunedin* (1928), *Winifred of Wanganui* (1928), and *Patsy of Palmerston* (1928) – are structured around a love plot which provides the pretext for a display of the achievements of the white colonial enterprise. As discussed by Jeanette Hoorn and Michelle Smith in Chapter 2, the films celebrate New Zealand's urban locations as a modern and civilised society, homogenous in its racial identity with the striking absence of Māori. The fact that these films were made in the year following *The Te Kooti Trail* is significant, suggesting that they were meant to complement Hayward's New Zealand War epics, with the two categories of film providing a before-and-after glimpse into the forging of a nation.

The same impulse that motivated Hayward is evident in another film made during this period – *The Birth of New Zealand*, released in 1922. Unfortunately, only fragments of this silent film remain, but we can gather from a surviving poster that it consisted of a series of dramatised enactments of key episodes in New Zealand's colonial history, from the landing of Captain Cook to "the present day," including the annexation of New Zealand by Governor Hobson; ancient Māori wars; the burning and sacking of Kororāreka by Hone Heke; the signing of the Treaty of Waitangi; and the gold rush in Gabriel's Gully in Otago.[32] As the film's title indicates, its purpose was similar to the twin motives of Hayward: to acknowledge the formative events that had contributed to the forging of a nation, and to celebrate the identity that was felt by the 1920s to be emerging from it.

Following the release of *Rewi's Last Stand* in 1940, there was a lull in the making of historical films and, indeed, in New Zealand filmmaking generally, until the "New Wave" of the late 1970s. The exceptions are to be found in several docudramas, including *Journey for Three*, released by the National Film Unit in 1950, and John O'Shea's *Broken Barrier* (1952). Discussing the former, Simon Sigley considers in Chapter 7 *Journey for Three's* weaving of entertainment and ideology, its presentation of the difficulties of immigration from the mother country, while at the same time constructing a sense of the colony's national identity bound up with notions of gender difference. The latter film, which Barbara Brookes in Chapter 8 historicises in the context of the social problem film, made explicit the counter-narrative that had been only implicit in Hayward's epic films – that is, that far from being marked by mutual respect and acceptance, the relationship between the two races has been marred by barriers of misunderstanding and prejudice that had severely disadvantaged Māori in actual fact as distinct from the kind of wish-fulfilment fantasy that had appeared heretofore in New Zealand cinema. The ageing Hayward himself would acknowledge the same obstacle to the achievement of his earlier vision of harmonious racial blending in a similar docudrama, *To Love a Maori* (1972) – a film that was undoubtedly informed by insights derived from his second wife, Ramai Te Miha, a Māori actress whom he had married in 1943, and who co-directed and co-wrote the script for the film. Both *Journey for Three* and *Broken Barrier* pointed to underlying tensions in New Zealand's race relations that would be explored in all their complexity when the New Wave directors turned their attention to the making of historical films.

The New Zealand New Wave, 1977–89

"The New Zealand New Wave" was marked by a sudden explosion of creative energy on the part of a group of young filmmakers, all born within a few years of each other between 1945 and 1948, who were active in the late 1970s and 1980s. The first fiction feature to emerge from this group was Roger Donaldson's *Sleeping Dogs* (1977), an updated adaptation of C. K. Stead's novel *Smith's Dream*, which was soon to be followed by features directed by Geoff Murphy, Vincent Ward, John Laing, Michael Black, Sam Pillsbury, John Reid, and Michael Firth, among others.

Significant stimulus for the advent of the New Wave was the financial encouragement provided by the establishment of an interim New Zealand Film Commission in 1977, followed by the creation of a permanent New Zealand Film Commission by Act of Parliament in 1978, with a statutory responsibility "To encourage and also to participate and assist in the making, promotion, distribution, and exhibition of films" with "a significant New Zealand content."[33] For a brief period in the early 1980s there were also tax loopholes that encouraged filmmaking.[34] This enhancement of the material conditions of film production coincided with the effects of Great Britain's decision to join the European Economic Community in 1973, meaning that the financial means to support filmmaking came into being at the same time as a major shock to the national psyche provided a powerful incentive for doing so.

The consternation and dismay felt by New Zealanders at Britain's decision to enter the EEC cannot be overestimated.[35] For a country that had regarded itself as a far-flung province of England, had fought without hesitation for Britain in two world wars, and whose economy depended on primary produce grown for the mother country, this sudden abandonment seemed like a betrayal of breathtaking proportions. Concomitantly, it pulled the rug out from under any settled assumptions on the part of New Zealanders as to what their identity was. In the face of this uncertainty, New Zealanders needed not only to work out what their new identity and destiny might be, but also to subject themselves to thorough self-examination in order to understand what aspects of the colonial legacy they might wish to retain, modify, or abandon. Inevitably, fictive representation played a major part in this process of self-exploration, and in the domain of cinema the historical film became one of the prime vehicles for pursuing it.

Films set during the New Zealand Wars make a reappearance with Michael Black's *Pictures*, released in 1981, which dramatises the contrasting approaches of two Dunedin photographers, the Burton Brothers, to the pictorial representation of Māori at this time, and Geoff Murphy's *Utu* (1983), which was based on the exploits of the Pai Mārire leader Kereopa Te Rau in the Bay of Plenty during 1864. In *Pictures*, the effects of scepticism on the part of New Zealanders about the ethical status of Britain's colonial ambitions that had set in following its entry into the European Economic Community in 1973 are vividly apparent. The film aggressively exposes the complacent hypocrisy of colonialist assumptions by presenting the idea of "photography" itself as a trope for the power of representation to control perception through omission or suppression. As discussed by Cherie Lacey in Chapter 4, antithetical attitudes towards this issue are explored through the divergent approaches of the two brothers, Walter and Alfred, raising significant questions about the role of propaganda, especially as it is conducted through the control of images (and, by extension, cultural capital) regarding indigenous people who have been colonised. The movie also exposes the role of images in the propagations of discourses that are instrumental in furthering the interests of a colonising hegemony, turning it not only into a self-reflexive interrogation of its own practices of representation, and those of the historical films that had preceded it, but also into an interrogation of the treatment of Māori by the white colonising intruders at large, with a suggestion that the reality of colonisation has, in fact, been occluded and suppressed by the propaganda disseminated by the colonial authorities.

Geoff Murphy's *Utu* – an updated version of the epic Māori westerns made by Hayward half a century earlier – similarly attests to a transformation that had occurred in the way New Zealanders were interpreting the Anglo-Māori Wars by the 1980s. Made shortly after *Pictures*, *Utu* confirms how far the deconstruction of colonialist optimism and self-congratulation had swung in the opposite direction, while at the same time undermining the claims of Māori radicalism to any moral high ground. On the Pākehā side, the myth of the civilising British is undercut by the portrayal of Colonel Elliot, the leader of the colonial troops, who is revealed to be a racist butcher. The myth of Christianity as a civilising force is also satirised in the depiction of the vicar at Ōpōtiki (based on the historical missionary Carl Volkner), who is portrayed as a fanatical, inhuman bigot rather than a beneficent missionary, and far from offering the protection of the Crown, Queen Victoria is described as "a fat German woman on distant shores." On the Māori side, the myth of the noble savage is destroyed by the representation of the progressive Macbeth-like degeneration whereby Te Wheke (based on the historical Kereopa Te Rau) turns into a ruthless monster in his search for revenge. Equally, the myth of the pioneering "Man Alone" – recurrently portrayed as heroic in the national literature[36] – is debunked in the characterisation of Williamson, the Pākehā hero, as a crazed madman who becomes equated with Te Wheke in his quest for revenge, while the film also destroys certain cherished discourses of redemption, such as

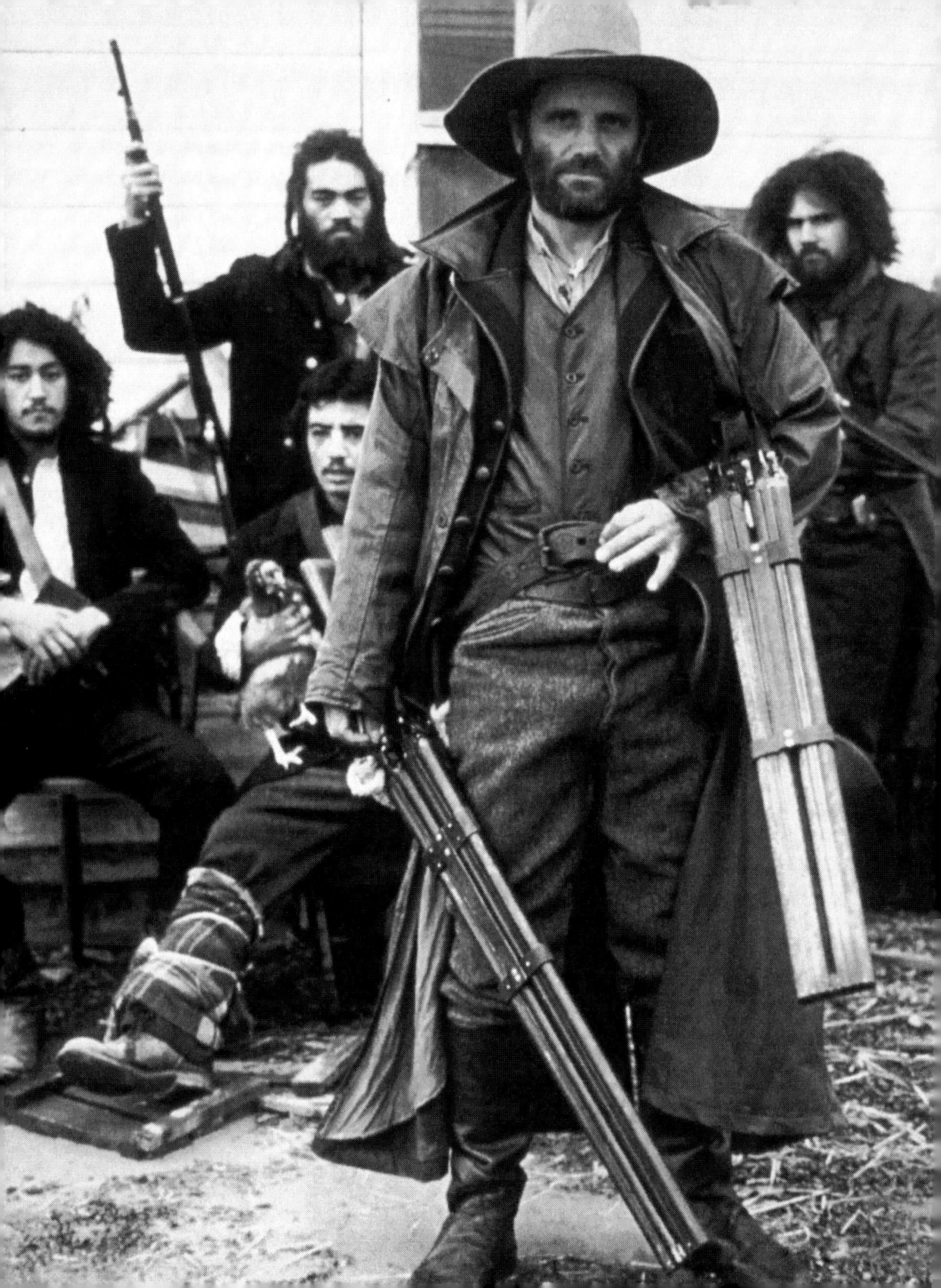

the idea that love can transcend racial barriers, or the idea that redemption can reside in tribal loyalty.

Discussing *Utu* as well as Hayward's earlier *The Te Kooti Trail* (1927) and Sam Pillsbury's later *Crooked Earth* (2001) in the context of the western genre, particularly its representation of landscape in relation to character, Harriet Margolis in Chapter 3 considers the depiction of Māori in each as a measure of the changing prevailing attitudes towards race in New Zealand.

Viewed as a metonymic displacement for concerns that really pertain to the circumstances of the 1980s, *Utu* attests to a deep anxiety at forms of extremism in the contemporary world that were perceived as being in danger of leading New Zealand society towards a dog-eat-dog mutual destruction. As Merata Mita, who played a supporting role in *Utu*, subsequently observed, "[w]hat's manifest in this film is what's happening today – we have Māori fighting Māori, we have Māori fighting Pākehā, we have Pākehā fighting Pākehā in New Zealand."[37] Zac Wallace, the Māori actor who played the vengeful Te Wheke, put it even more succinctly:

That fight of then, that's being portrayed in this movie, is happening today – it's real bad, where the young people, the young people are going through that same thing again – the defiance, eh, and the fights with Pākehā, an enemy that they didn't know who exists. They know that there's an enemy, but they can't put their finger on a policeman, or a Pākehā, or another Māori, or different tribes, different areas – they can't put their finger on it.[38]

What these statements attest to is an acute malaise in New Zealand's race relations which, having been merely papered over in earlier decades, had emerged with a vengeance by the early 1980s, once the scales of colonising rectitude had been lifted from the eyes of Pākehā New Zealanders by the realisation that they were now on their own. Inevitably, the historical films of the time express this dawning realisation.

Biographical films about historical figures are also strongly represented in the New Wave, and express, through metonymical displacement, a comparable malaise. Prominent among these films are crime dramas that focus on an outsider, or Man Alone, who is shown to be at odds with society because of its repressive or persecutory institutions. Films in this category include John Laing's *Beyond Reasonable Doubt* (1980), which recreates events leading up to the unjust conviction and imprisonment of Arthur Allan Thomas during the 1960s, and Mike Newell's *Bad Blood* (1982), depicting the paranoid breakdown of Stan Graham in the small, isolated town of Koiterangi on the West Coast of the South Island in 1941, which led to Graham's shooting of twelve policemen when an attempt was made to confiscate his rifle, followed by a massive manhunt in which the wounded Graham was hunted through the bush like an animal until he was finally shot.

Utu, 1983, dir. Geoff Murphy. Image courtesy of Kino/Photofest.

One particularly striking variety of biographical films that appears at this time consists of "filmic transpositions of the literary biography of women" – in sufficient numbers to constitute, according to Gordon Collier, "a direction in film that [...] is relatively unrepresented in, say, Canadian or Australian cinema."[39] Films in this group include Tony Isaac's *Iris* (1984), dealing with the troubled life and eventual suicide of Iris Wilkinson, a New Zealand writer active in the 1930s, known more commonly under her literary pseudonym, Robin Hyde; John Reid's *Leave All Fair* (1985), which deals with "the poetically speculative reconstruction of [Katherine] Mansfield's personality via phantom readings of her own writings;"[40] and Michael Firth's *Sylvia* (1985), which draws upon Sylvia Ashton-Warner's autobiographical novel *Spinster* and her memoir, *I Passed This Way* (1979), to recreate her attempts to introduce an innovative method of teaching against the repressive rigidities of the New Zealand state education system that existed during the late 1940s.

A further type of New Wave historical film consists of those dealing with suppressed histories that had become occluded as a result of Anglo-centrism. Chief among these suppressed histories is that of the Māori people in the post-colonial period as seen from their own perspective, in films by Māori presenting images of Māori to their own people in accordance with a culturally informed self-sense, rather than being mediated through the projective assumptions of an alien culture. The first Māori filmmaker to depict Māori life as it had been in the recent past, in the rural homelands of the traditional Māori tribes, was Barry Barclay, whose *Ngati*, released in 1987, is set in Kapua, a fictional village on the East Coast, during the 1940s. Barclay's nostalgic recreation of rural life was followed by Merata Mita's *Mauri* (1988), which is similarly set in a remote East Coast Māori settlement, and is also displaced backwards in time to the 1950s. As discussed by Bruce Harding in Chapter 10, it nevertheless attempts to return a voice to a people marginalised by colonialism. Both films emphasise the historic values of *whānautanga* (tribal birthright informed by custom) and *manaakitanga* (the practice of caring for kin, especially when sick) as a curative psychic and social remedy for the fragmentation of identity that is being suffered by modern urban-dwelling Māori who have become severed from their roots.

A second kind of suppressed history that finds its first cinematic expression is that pertaining to immigrant ethnic minorities. Groundbreaking in this regard is Leon Narbey's *Illustrious Energy* (1988), which dramatises the experience of two Chinese goldminers who come to seek their fortune in Central Otago during the gold rush of the 1860s. Its approach foreshadows later attempts to explore the experience of non-British immigrants, such as Gregor Nicholas's *Broken English* (1996), which depicts the efforts of Croatian immigrants to negotiate the stresses of moving to a new life in New Zealand. In Chapter 14, Bruce Babington considers *Illustrious Energy*'s depiction of the loneliness and sense of alienation experienced by the Chinese in the face of white prejudice. Although much of the film is dominated by old Kim's dream of a return home to China after 27 years in New Zealand, the ironies of the plot underline the fact that such a return is impossible; a sounder dream is that pursued by Chan, Kim's son-in-law, of a future in the new country that will bring him a wealth that is "better than gold" – figured symbolically in the success of the orchardist Wong,

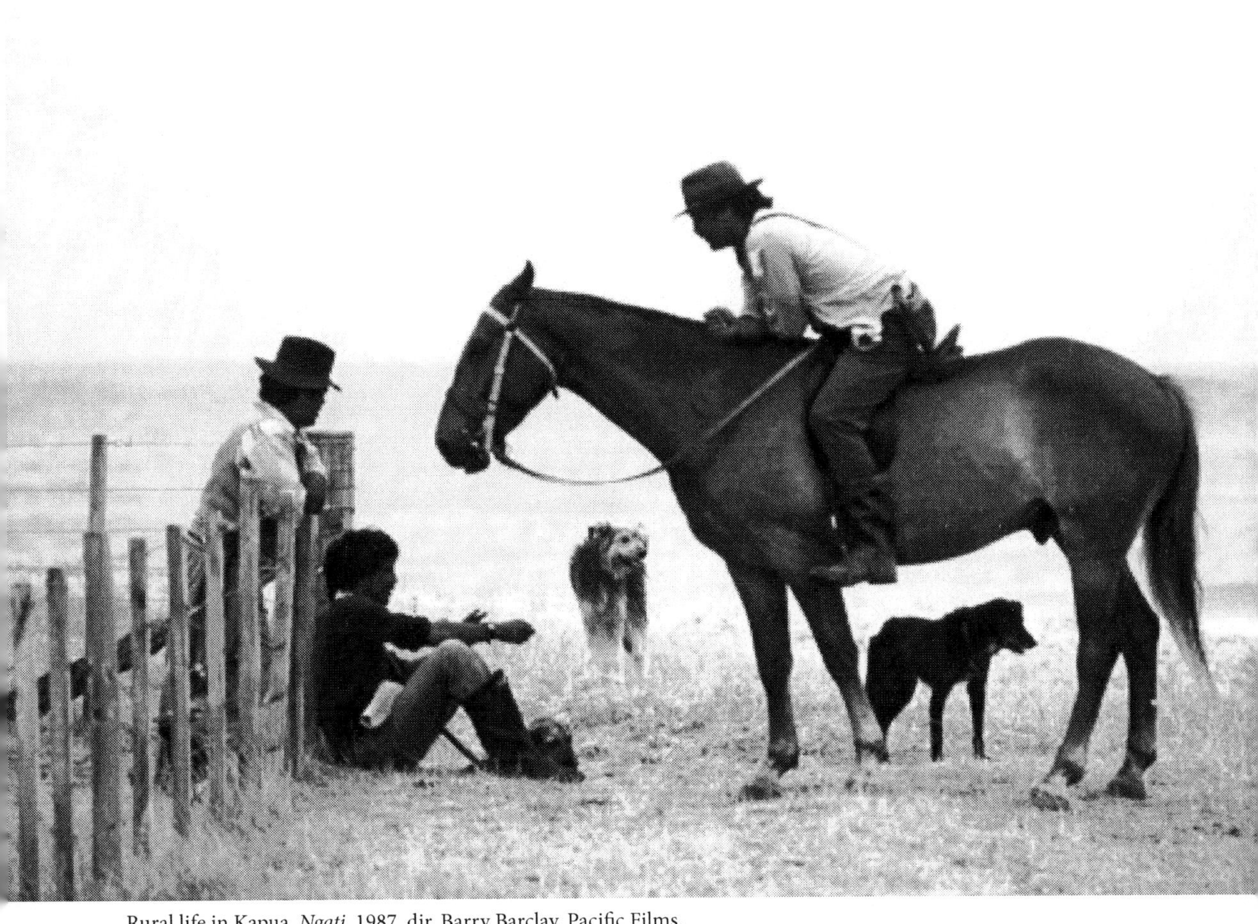

Rural life in Kapua, *Ngati*, 1987, dir. Barry Barclay, Pacific Films.

with his Scottish wife, who is discovering a different kind of gold in the growing of apricots. By ending with the sight of the younger son-in-law Chan abandoning the gold claim they have been working in order to make a new life with an Australian-Asian girl, Narbey's film affirms the desirability of a future in which immigrants enter into a world of hybridised possibility in the new land, rather than remaining wedded to the myth of cultural purity and the idea of a return to a homeland that has already, in their imaginary, been rendered inaccessible as a result of their experience in the new country. Once again, this film seems to reflect a new openness to the possibility of a more inclusive future for New Zealanders, following the abandonment of the country by Britain, that entails a recognition that settlers from ethnicities other than English, Scottish or Irish – or, indeed, other Europeans – have contributed to the formation of the new nation and have shared in its evolving experience.

A final category of New Wave historical films consists of those that explore the perennial theme of individuals who long to escape from the restrictions and repression of New Zealand life, either by taking to the road, such as the young teenager Kate and the returned serviceman Patrick do in the 1920s of Sam Pillsbury's *Starlight Hotel* (1987), or else by seeking to enact a fantasy-life constructed in accordance with images derived from stage and screen, such as the heroine does in Bruce Morrison's *Constance* (1984), set during the 1940s and 1950s. Such films build upon the prior legacy of the New Zealand novel, with its countless iterations of the itinerant Man Alone, such as Johnson in John Mulgan's novel of that name (1939), or the Woman Alone, as in Robin Hyde's *The Godwits Fly* (1938), all of which represent the psychic unease caused by feelings of alienation experienced by their protagonists at sensing themselves in a society that affords them no space in which to realise the desired idiom of their being.

Viewed as a group, the historical films of the New Wave attest to an intermittent, but persistent, concern among New Zealand filmmakers to use the recreation of history to re-examine the myths, value-systems, and interpellated assumptions that had become embedded in New Zealand life as a legacy of colonialism, but which had been placed under suspicion by the actions of a "perfidious Albion" that had betrayed a people who had believed they were still children of the Motherland, but who had discovered, to their consternation, that they had been left on their own in a displaced context in which they had not yet, at an emotional level, come to feel comfortably and naturally located.[41] This invests the New Zealand historical film with a quality that is very different from that of the British historical film, which more often than not, as Pam Cook notes, conveys "a sense of longing for something that is known to be irretrievable," and from the postmodern reconstructions of filmmakers like Wong Kar Wai, whose recreation of 1960s Hong Kong in *In the Mood for Love* (2000) strikes Cook as "less concerned with exploring colonial history than in taking a self-indulgent, backward look at an idealised, lost culture and way of life."[42] In contradistinction, New Zealand historical films seem energetically, almost desperately, engaged in the project of forging a new national identity out of the assemblage of constituents that are only now, in the second decade of the twenty-first century, at the beginning of a process that will lead to their being recognised, retrieved, and fully appreciated.

Continuities and innovations in historical films of the 1990s

By the end of the 1980s, filmmakers of the New Wave, with the assistance of the New Zealand Film Commission, had demonstrated that a sustainable local industry based on New Zealand content was well and truly viable. The example they set, together with the thematic preoccupations they inaugurated, would continue into the 1990s and beyond, but with a number of significant developments as far as the New Zealand historical film was concerned. Moreover, the 1990s saw the advent of a new set of directors who displayed an excellence in filmmaking that attracted worldwide attention to New Zealand films to an unprecedented degree. Acknowledging their distinctiveness, Ian Conrich has described films from this decade as constituting a "Second Wave."[43] Generally speaking, historical films made in New Zealand during the 1990s attest to the escalation of a trend – already visible in the New Wave films of the 1970s and 1980s – towards recreating "history from below." This trend, which extends into literature as well, has been aptly described by Trevor Bentley, who, noting "the remarkable expansion of writing about culture-crossing Pākehā," observes that writers and readers have become "less concerned with political, economic and social elites and more interested in the lives of ordinary men and women."[44]

One sign of this new development was the appearance of a significant number of women filmmakers, who quickly converted what had been a male-dominated industry[45] into one that could offer a more nuanced insight into the experience and self-sense of New Zealand women. Their contribution is strikingly evident in forms that had been inaugurated by the directors of the New Wave. The cinematic transposition of women's literary biography is compellingly extended in Jane Campion's *An Angel at My Table* (1990), based on the *Autobiography* of the celebrated New Zealand author Janet Frame – depicted as yet another outsider who has to struggle against the injustice and oppression of a social system that appears unable to accommodate her – and Gaylene Preston's *Bread and Roses* (1993), made as a series for television (as *An Angel at My Table* originally had been), which is adapted from the autobiography of Sonja Davies, an independent woman who flouted convention in her personal life and took up political cudgels first as a Trade Unionist, and then as a Member of Parliament. Campion would also depict her own fictionalised version of the colonial woman oppressed by the puritanism of a transplanted British culture in *The Piano*, based loosely, but in a way that creatively transforms the source, on Jane Mander's 1920 novel, *The Story of a New Zealand River*.[46] In all cases, these films articulate a plea for a liberation from the strictures and prejudices of a puritanical respectability that privileged a tyrannical patriarchy – whether expressed through the assumptions of a husband like Alisdair Stewart in *The Piano*, or the punitive codes enforced through the family in *Bread and Roses*, or the containment and marginalisation of the non-normative individual woman so powerfully exposed in *An Angel at My Table*. In their discussions of Campion's films, Hilary Radner in Chapter 12 considers Campion's treatment of her female protagonists in the context of the female "biopic" in New Zealand, the heritage film, and the woman's film, while in Chapter 13 Estella Tincknell examines how Campion uses details of apparent historical verisimilitude not only to evoke particular historical moments, but also to express the entrapment of his unconventional heroines.

Comparable to this deepening interest in historical films about women by women was another innovation: the appearance of the first major feature film dealing with the experience of gay men and women in colonial New Zealand – another occluded history. While the German film director Rolf Haedrich had tentatively broached homosexual themes by making a cinematic adaptation of Maurice Shadbolt's coming of age novel *Among the Cinders* in 1983, it was not submitted to the New Zealand censor until 1987 – following the legalisation of homosexuality in 1986 – and has not had a New Zealand theatrical release.[47] To all intent and purpose, therefore, *Desperate Remedies*, directed by Peter Wells and Stewart Main, broke new ground when it appeared in 1993.

The overt purpose of this singular film is to uncover in history an alternative reality capable of validating the world in which members of the gay community live. According to Wells (the prime mover behind this movie), his aim was to make

> the real, hostile world into one that is controllable and safe, by taking a well-known cinematic genre – the heritage film – in order to mock expectations by substituting a counter-cultural, gay discourse for the anticipated middle-class, heterosexual one that is conventional in the heritage film.[48]

As Wells himself has said, "[i]t was possible to read the script and believe that you might end up with the dire tedium of a BBC realisation of past and period." By naming his heroine Dorothea Brook, he deliberately intended to provide a corrective to "pasty-faced Dorothea Brook in the recent BBC adaptation of George Eliot's *Middlemarch*."[49]

The means whereby this basically conventional story is co-opted to another purpose is through the use of pastiche and the imposition of a camp style, in which excess décor and artifice work to convert what is "normal" and "natural" into the opposite of those things. Stylistic excess is evident in all aspects of the mise-en-scène: in the use of a set that looks like a modern avant-garde opera production in its surrealism (such as the use of scaffolding); in a preponderance of dark interior scenes lit by flames of various sorts (gaslight, candles, torches, chandeliers); and in a recurrent visual contrast between rich red and blue hues and the use of costumes that are outrageously flamboyant or obscene. Predictably, the camera also focuses on sexualised male bodies, especially that of the hypermasculine hero, Lawrence Hayes, played by Kevin Smith, and that of the androgynous, "dirty boy, have-anyone, fuck-everyone" Fraser, played by Cliff Curtis.[50] To top off the excess, the whole story is invested with a heightened melodramatic effect through the repeated iteration on the soundtrack of passages from Giuseppe Verdi's opera, *La Forza del Destino*.

The end effect of these stylistic strategies – unique among New Zealand historical films – is to activate a different framework of perception, one based on "the male homosexual gaze."[51] The "look" that defines the intentionality and aim of sight is thus fundamentally altered by the director in order to embed a new set of codes that the genre would not normally entertain.[52]

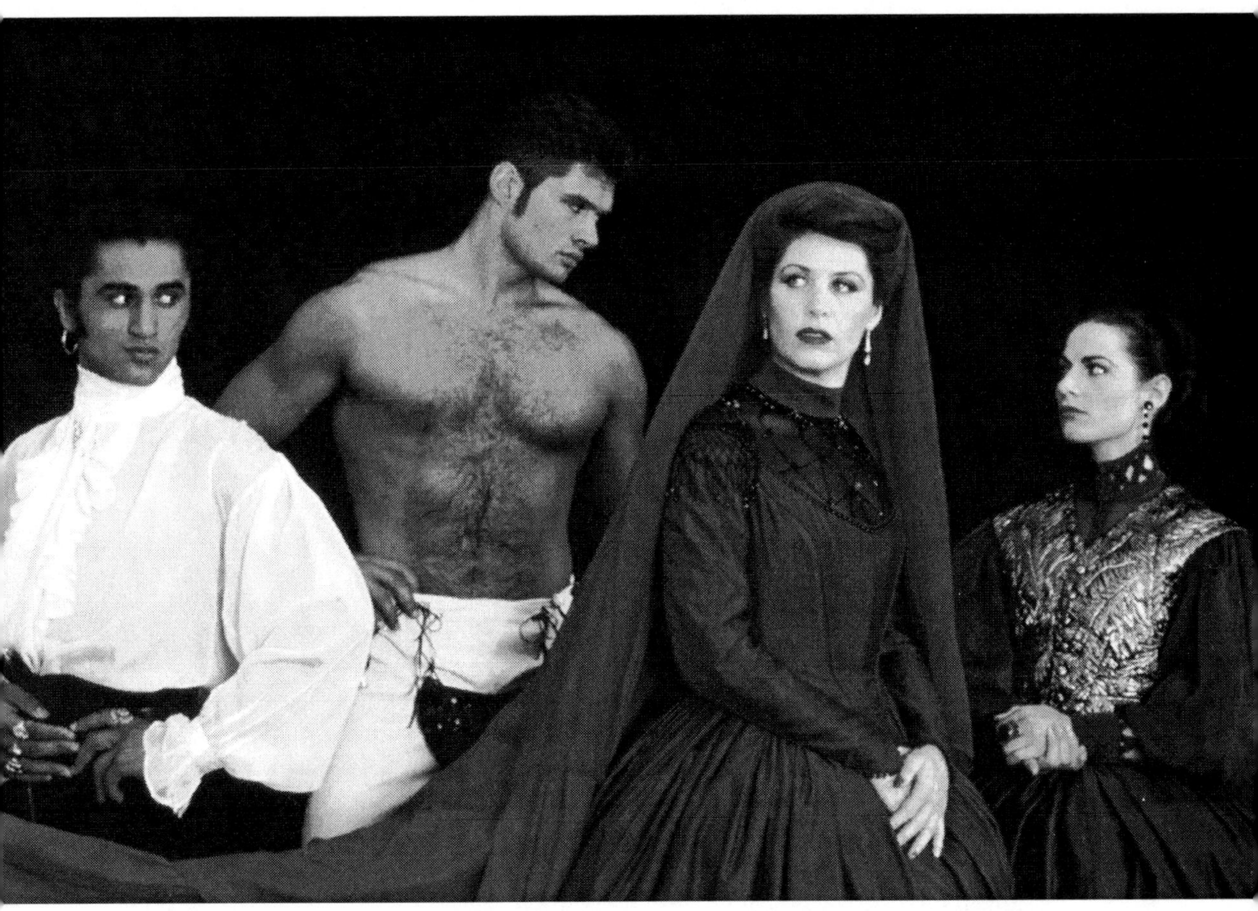

Desperate Remedies, 1993, dir. Peter Wells and Steward Mains. Image courtesy of New Zealand Film Commission.

This, in turn, generates "a system of signs" constituting "a private language for members of the gay subculture who intuit that public language has gone wrong."[53] In other words, the representation of history is used in the film as a pretext for generating a subversive counter-discourse that displaces the discourse of normative heterosexuality, releasing another world concealed beneath the surface appearance of things, the former of which, in Wells's words, is "trapped miraculously in the warp of time."[54] *Desperate Remedies* functions like an "ideogram," in that it represents an idea rather than the thing it actually appears to denote, confirming the deeper function of the historical film as pertaining to the present as much as to the past.[55] Indeed, this film perfectly illustrates how, as Higson has argued, pastiche in the historical film mixes the past with the present, enabling "the anomalous and the perverse to be inserted into the apparently authentic historical location."[56]

A further development in this same decade was the appearance of films that have a commemorative function distinctly different from the commemorative intent of earlier films like those of Rudall Hayward, the purpose of which was to celebrate the imperial project by showing the advancement of civilisation as a result of colonisation. In contrast, the commemorative films of the 1990s often seem designed to awaken in New Zealanders an awareness that their identity rests upon a history that has recurrently involved trauma – trauma that has been occasioned precisely by their colonial ties to Britain, usually as a result of wars fought to advance the interests of others. This new tendency is apparent in films dealing with the heroic, but often pointless, self-sacrifice of New Zealanders in the two world wars of the twentieth century. Notable among these is Dale G. Bradley's *Chunuk Bair* (1991), adapted from a play by Maurice Shadbolt, which depicts the tragic loss of life on both sides involved in the capture of a strategic hill by New Zealand troops during the Gallipoli campaign. The film's deeper symbolic function is suggested in its representation of how the New Zealanders, having captured the summit against all odds, find themselves being shelled by a British ship – another powerful image of the heedless perfidy of the former mother country. Other films, such as John Reid's *The Last Tattoo* (1994) and Preston's *Bread and Roses,* record the experience of New Zealand women during the Second World War, when American soldiers were stationed in New Zealand, inviting fraternisation that led to pregnancy, heartbreak, or worse.

Apart from the new preoccupations described earlier, filmmakers of the Second Wave continued to make films on topics that had absorbed the New Wave directors. The fascination with outcasts or misfits who suffer psychic disease as a result of the rigidities and repressive strictures of New Zealand society is apparent in Peter Jackson's *Heavenly Creatures* (1994), which recreates the murder in 1950s Christchurch by two schoolgirls, Juliet Hulme and Pauline Parker, of Parker's mother ostensibly to avoid being separated – an event that profoundly shocked a nation that privileged respectability and gentility. As Alison L. McKee argues in Chapter 11, Jackson's film deliberately invokes multiple readings of the notorious case's significance, especially in its association of postcolonialism with the depiction of matricide. Indeed, Jackson's film seemed designed to confront New Zealanders – as *Bad Blood* had sought to do in the 1980s – with the darker side of what they are capable of when the repression enforced by secular puritanism becomes intolerable for some.

Historical films in the new millennium: 2000 to the present

The perennial purpose of the historical film, at least in New Zealand, seems to have been twofold. On one hand, it has served to dramatise historical events for the sake of objectifying an emergent self-sense, whether subjectively individual or collectively national; on the other, it has provided an imaginative response to the forces in New Zealand society that threaten to impede progress towards a condition of personal or social being which is strongly desired as an alternative to frustrating realities in the contemporary present. Both functions are rendered more complicated by a tendency to use the historical film as a means of interrogating the validity of specific social practices that are in force or being promoted at the time when the film is made, or which are being entertained as a solution for the future. The New Zealand historical film can thus be seen as participating in the wider phenomenon identified by Robert Burgoyne, who notes that one of the main contributions of cinematic historical representations in the late twentieth and early twenty-first centuries has been their participation in an "ongoing revisionary enterprise" as nations adjust to the sea-changes that have been taking place in the post-imperial, post-colonial era.[57]

This is nowhere more apparent than in Vincent Ward's timely resurrection of the New Zealand civil war epic in *River Queen*, released in 2005. It would seem that dramatisation of the Anglo-Māori Wars of the 1860s has become an essential investigative tool for filmmakers to explore the forces that they sense are shaping the present at any particular moment, especially with respect to race relations. In Ward's case, the fictive recreation of the British troops' siege of the stronghold of Tītokowaru (Te Kai Pō in the film) in the hinterland of Whanganui in 1868 provided a displaced means of investigating the ideology of "biculturalism" that has been fostered by successive governments from the 1980s onwards in an attempt to find a mode of coexistence capable of reconciling the two races without obliterating the identity of either. By focusing on a story that involves "culture-crossing," the film is part of a wider phenomenon – especially evident in New Zealand literature in historical accounts of Pākehā-Māori and captive white women who live with Māori – wherein an acknowledgement of "an intercultural past" is meant, in Trevor Bentley's words, to "signal the possibilities for cross-cultural co-operation and accommodation in modern New Zealand."[58] The fact that it is latently informed by this commitment to a biculturalist ideology makes *River Queen* very different from either Hayward's New Zealand War epics or Murphy's *Utu*, which, in retrospect, seem even more clearly to mirror the singularly different perspectives and intentions of their own times. In Ward's updated version of the New Zealand civil war epic, biculturalism itself, while being ostensibly promoted, is simultaneously put under the microscope, with the problematic inherent in this notion being dramatised in the difficulty experienced by the heroine, Sarah, in locating a secure sense of "home" when faced by alternative possibilities that seem incompatible. For Olivia Macassey in Chapter 5, *River Queen*'s clash between this reflexive view of biculturalism and its reliance on the traditional generic tropes of the historical costume film mirrors its revisionist struggles.

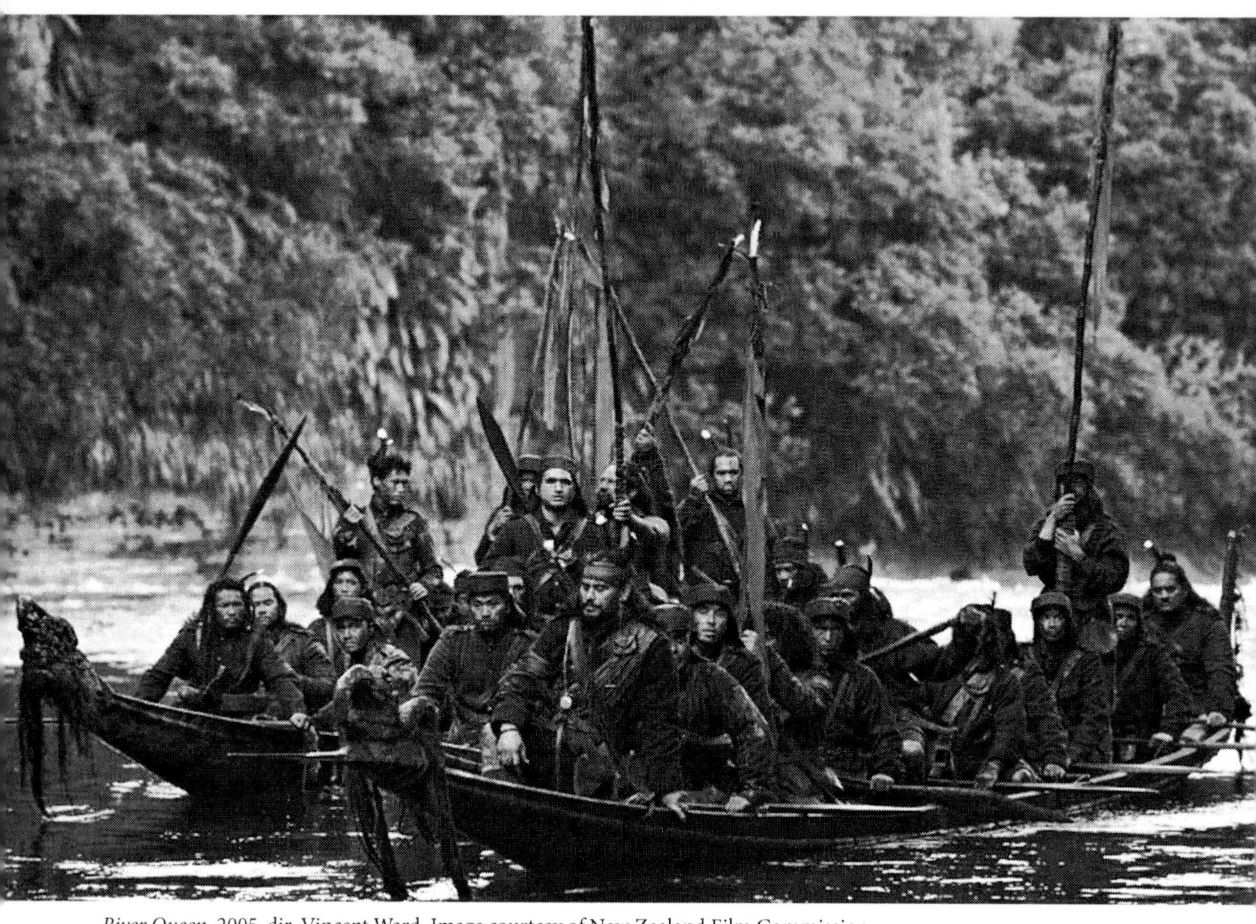

River Queen, 2005, dir. Vincent Ward. Image courtesy of New Zealand Film Commission.

A similar ambivalence is to be found in Ward's next film, *Rain of the Children* (2007), a docudrama that explores the complexities of right and wrong on both sides in the events that led up to the police raid on the religious community of the millenarian Māori prophet, Rua Kēnana Hepetipa, at Maungapōhatu in 1916. This event left the real-life protagonist of the film, an aged Tūhoe woman named Puhi, believing that she is the victim of a curse. Clearly, at some deep level, there would appear to be a profoundly condensed degree of symbolic displacement informing this representation. For this reason, *Rain of the Children* may be seen as being closely complementary to *River Queen* as a comment on contemporary issues pertaining to race relations in New Zealand.

One further indication of a significant new movement in the perspectives and understandings being activated through the cinematic representation of historical events is another extraordinary docudrama, *The Feathers of Peace* (2000), by the late Māori filmmaker, Barry Barclay. What is remarkable about this film is its uncompromising exposure of the genocidal atrocities perpetrated by Māori against the Moriori inhabitants of the Chatham Islands, a group of small islands in the Pacific Ocean approximately 800 kilometres southeast of southern New Zealand. The film recounts how the Ngāti Mutunga tribe from the North Island, themselves in flight from an aggressing enemy tribe, the Ngāti Toa, invaded the Chatham Islands in 1835. Finding a people who lived in accordance with a customary code of non-violence (the law of *Nunuku*), and hence offered no resistance, the invading Ngāti Mutunga enslaved and systematically exterminated the Moriori, leaving over 1000 dead, not counting the children killed and eaten. By the time the Māori moved back to Taranaki in 1868, leaving only twenty of their number to occupy the islands, there were only 100 Moriori left. To compound the injustice, when the surviving Moriori appealed to the New Zealand Native Land Court to recover their stolen land, a Pākehā judge ruled that, because the court operates under the native custom of the mainland, Māori were the rightful owners. On the grounds that in traditional Māori practice the "conqueror takes all," the judge declares to the Moriori plaintiffs that "meekness [is] a sign that you had no hold on the land, and therefore no right to it."

This dramatisation of a disturbing episode in New Zealand's history in which, in Barclay's own words, "we all colluded, Māori and Pākehā," not only in the destruction of a people, but also in the wiping out of such a horrific event from national consciousness, is redolent with implication. For Barclay, "it was a powerful metaphor as a story that's been buried and as a story I don't think we can fully read yet." Barclay intended the pacifism of the Moriori to be seen as a "special gift" against which "we can all measure our conduct in the past and present."[59] Viewed in this light, the film offers a reproach to the "invasions" perpetrated by *both* Pākehā *and* Māori, with an implied warning to Māori that if the same principles were applied that legitimated the Māori seizure of Moriori land, then the fact that Māori had been unable to hold their land in the face of a more determined and powerful aggressor would prove that they had no right it. Alternatively, by depicting the tragic outcome of pacifism for the Moriori, the film may equally be construed as a warning to Māori against being similarly passive and pacific, thus constituting a call to resistance. The film thus provides an image that problematises the boundaries between right and wrong in the determination of justice as the basis for the relationship between the two races, while reminding both sides that neither can claim to have entirely clean hands.

Apart from these strikingly original films exploring race relations, other historical films of the 2000s display the ongoing life of tropes and motifs inaugurated in the preceding two decades. One such film is *The World's Fastest Indian* (2005), which marks the return from overseas of Roger Donaldson to shoot a film that he had been wanting to make for 30 years – on the amazing land speed records for motorcycles set by Burt Munro, from Invercargill, at Bonneville Salt Flats in Utah during the 1950s, using an Indian Scout motorcycle unorthodoxly modified through his own tinkering. *The World's Fastest Indian* gives expression to one of the most cherished New Zealand myths: the idea that the unassuming Kiwi "bloke" can "do it himself," without pomp or pretension.[60] Donaldson's film also picks up on the trend, inaugurated by Michael Firth's *Sylvia,* of celebrating the home-grown genius, as distinct from the opposing New Zealand tradition of cutting down the "tall poppy" – that is, anyone whose achievements threaten to transgress the assumption that a commitment to equality and humility should be the markers of the national temperament.

The fascination with outsiders who cannot survive the codes and expectations of New Zealand society, but explode into homicidal violence after a psychotic breakdown, reappears in Robert Sarkies' *Out of the Blue* (2006). Sarkies' film recreates the massacre that occurred in 1990 at the small Otago seaside town of Aramoana, when David Gray, like Stanley Graham half a century earlier, went beserk and shot every human being he encountered, including children, until, after killing thirteen people, he, too, was shot dead by police. Such a film confirms a lingering sense that, although New Zealand may be, as the popular myth proclaims, "Godzone" (a slang imitation of the Kiwi pronunciation of "God's Own Country"), when one probes beyond the surface of gentility and respectability, Satan still lurks within, as the belief system informing traditional New Zealand puritanism always implicitly, if unconsciously, asserted that it did.

As far as "Fourth Cinema" filmmaking is concerned,[61] the tradition inaugurated by Barry Barclay and Merata Mita of exploring Māori life from a Māori perspective by depicting an action in a rural setting, displaced by several decades into the past, is reactivated by Taika Waititi in *Boy* (2010), set in the East Coast region of the filmmaker's own tribe, Te Whānau a Apanui. A coming of age film, *Boy* qualifies as a historical film not only by virtue of its temporal displacement, which follows the example set by *Ngati* and *Mauri*, but also of its anatomy of the social forces that produce dysfunction in Māori families. With its revelation of the destructive consequences for children of negligence on the part of parents, *Boy*, in its own gentle way, delivers an indictment as powerful as that launched earlier with respect to urban Māori in Lee Tamahori's *Once Were Warriors* (1994).[62] In Chapter 9, Janet Wilson examines Tamahori's film, as well as Barclay's *The Feathers of Peace* and Niki Caro's *Whale Rider* (2002), as authentic expressions of indigenous heritage and an attempt to reclaim a voice in the present.

Finally, both the docudrama and the commemorative war film come together in Gaylene Preston's striking movie *Home by Christmas* (2010), based on an interview between the filmmaker and her father, shortly before his death, about his experiences in the Second World War. A dramatisation of the old man talking (with Ed Preston played by actor Tony Barry) provides a frame that is interspersed with dramatised sequences recreating the experience of young Ed and his wife Tui leading up to, and following, Ed's departure for overseas, as well as actual archival footage and stills of New Zealand soldiers fighting in the desert. The result is a film that, as one reviewer put it, perfectly captures "the mood, the ethos, the characteristic, the feeling and the flavour of a country, its people and a time," giving "a lesson in history, [and] humanity."[63]

Future projects announced by the New Zealand Film Commission suggest that the New Zealand historical film will continue to be as vital and pertinent in the years ahead as it has been in the past. The announcement that the celebrated Māori actress Rena Owen (who played Beth in *Once Were Warriors*) will produce a cinematic adaptation of Heretaunga Pat Baker's harrowing novel *Behind the Tattooed Face*, which describes the brutality of Māori inter-tribal warfare in the pre-European period, suggests that the project begun by Barry Barclay (as earlier by the Māori author Alan Duff) to bring Māori people face to face with unacknowledged realities from their own past is ongoing. Similarly, the announcement of a biopic on the exploits of Charles Upham, a soldier from Canterbury who earned the Victoria Cross twice during the Second World War, to become the most highly decorated serviceman from the Commonwealth, confirms that New Zealand has reached the point in its history where it has the confidence to celebrate the distinctiveness of its own heroes. No longer do New Zealanders need to seize upon the supposed achievements of a faux national hero like Colin McKenzie in Peter Jackson and Costa Botes' *Forgotten Silver* (1995) to celebrate the accomplishments of its national heroes.

Back to the future

What becomes apparent from this brief survey of the New Zealand historical film is the important role it has played in articulating the nation's sense of itself: how it came into being, what it has been, what it wants to become, and what it might be becoming. The chapters in this volume explore particular aspects of a select number of these historical films in each of the categories this chapter identifies, with a view to deepening understanding of the crucial functions such films play in the ongoing project of national identify-formation. The essays collected here, all original contributions, discuss films that span the history of New Zealand, from the early silents of Gaston Méliès to films made in the new millennium. Several deal with the Māori Wars as a historical flashpoint (those by Alistair Fox, Cherie Lacey, and Annabel Cooper); others look at how filmmakers have drawn on the techniques of Hollywood cinema to deal with issues in contemporary history (those by Simon Sigley and Barbara Brookes); and still others examine indigenous cinema (those by Janet Wilson and Bruce Harding). Some approach the films considered in the context of genre (those of Jeanette Hoorn and Michelle Smith, Harriet Margolis, Olivia Macassey, and Estella Tincknell), while others are focused on the representation of gender (those of Hilary Radner and Annabel Cooper). Still others are more concerned with films that are representative of the histories of racial and ethnic minorities in Aotearoa New Zealand (in particular, the essays by Bruce Babington, Janet Wilson, and Bruce Harding), while Alison McKee explores the representation of one of the episodes of horrific criminal violence that have intermittently erupted in New Zealand. Together, though, these essays engage in the very same project as the films they examine: the difficult, ongoing work of defining the national identity of New Zealand.

Notes

1. Richard Abel, *The Ciné Goes to Town: French Cinema, 1896–1914* (Berkeley and Los Angeles: University of California Press, 1998), 302.
2. Marcia Landy, "Introduction," in *The Historical Film: History and Memory in Media*, ed. Marcia Landy (New Brunswick, NJ: Rutgers University Press, 2000), 2.
3. Ibid.
4. Leger Grindon, *Shadows on the Past: Studies in the Historical Fiction Film* (Philadelphia: Temple University Press, 1994), 1.
5. See Marc Ferro, *Cinema and History*, trans. Naomi Greene (Detroit: Wayne State University Press, 1988), 163–64.
6. Robert Burgoyne, *The Hollywood Historical Film* (Malden, MA: Blackwell, 2008), 1–2.
7. Robert Burgoyne, *Film Nation: Hollywood Looks at U.S. History* (Minneapolis and London: University of Minnesota Press, 1997), 11.
8. Burgoyne, *The Hollywood Historical Film*, 2.
9. Andrew Higson, *English Cinema: Costume Drama Since 1980* (Oxford: Oxford University Press, 2003), 67; see also Pam Cook, *Fashioning the Nation: Costume and Identity in British Cinema* (London: British Film Institute, 1996), 5.
10. For further discussion on this point, see Burgoyne, *The Hollywood Historical Film*, 11.
11. See J. E. Smyth, *Reconstructing American Historical Cinema: From* Cimarron *to* Citizen Kane (Lexington: University Press of Kentucky, 2006); Claire Monk and Amy Sargeant, eds, *British Historical Cinema: The History, Heritage and Costume Film* (London and New York: Routledge, 2002); and Tana Wollen, "Over Our Shoulders: Nostalgic Screen Fictions for the 1980s," in *Enterprise and Heritage: Crosscurrents of National Culture*, ed. John Corner and Sylvia Harvey (London and New York: Routledge, 1991), 178–93. Wollen sees the resurgence of British historical films as a response to "[l]oss of empire and decline of the heavy industries accompanied by strident claims made by oppressed voices and dissatisfactions with the welfare state" (p. 181).
12. See, for example, Peter Limbrick, "The Australian Western, or A Settler Colonial Cinema par excellence," *Cinema Journal* 46, no. 4 (Summer 2007): 68–95.
13. Reid Perkins, "Imag(in)ing Our Past: Colonial New Zealand on Film from *The Birth of New Zealand* to *The Piano*: Part One," *Illusions* 25 (Winter 1996): 4–10.
14. The high proportion of New Zealand historical films was first noted by Hilary Radner, "Lettre de Dunedin: Le cinema au 'pays du long nuage blanc,'" *Trafic* 67 (2008): 122–33.

15. Grindon, *Shadows on the Past*, 2.
16. James Chapman, *Past and Present: National Identity and the British Historical Film* (London: I. B. Tauris, 2005), 2.
17. Monk and Sargeant, *British Historical Cinema*, 1.
18. Natalie Zemon Davis, *Slaves on Screen: Film and Historical Vision* (Cambridge, MA: Harvard University Press, 2000); Burgoyne, *The Hollywood Historical Film*, 2.
19. See Geoffrey Barraclough, *An Introduction to Contemporary History* (London: C. A. Watts, 1964), 12.
20. For an introduction to this literature, see Jane Stafford and Mark Williams, *Maoriland: New Zealand Literature 1872–1914* (Wellington: Victoria University Press, 2006).
21. See Helen Martin and Sam Edwards, *New Zealand Film 1912–1996* (Auckland: Oxford University Press, 1997), 20–22.
22. See Martin Blythe, *Naming the Other: Images of the Maori in New Zealand Film and Television* (Metuchen, NJ and London: Scarecrow Press, 1994), 10.
23. *Evening Post*, Volume LXXXIV, Issue 68 (17 September 1912), 7.
24. See Chapter 2.
25. *Grey River Argus*, 21 October 1912, 5. On the Méliès expedition, see also Bruce Babington, *A History of the New Zealand Fiction Feature Film* (Manchester: Manchester University Press, 2007), 32–33.
26. Merata Mita, "The Soul and the Image," in *Film in Aotearoa New Zealand*, second edition, ed. Jonathan Dennis and Jan Bieringa (Wellington: Victoria University Press, 1996), 42.
27. See Peter Limbrick, *Making Settler Cinemas: Film and Colonial Encounters in the United States, Australia, and New Zealand* (New York: Palgrave Macmillan, 2010), 131–70. Limbrick's choice of *Hei Tiki*, a film produced and directed by an eccentric visiting American, as an exemplar of settler cinema seems highly questionable, especially given that it is discussed in isolation, without any informed discussion of films produced in New Zealand by New Zealanders in the 1920s. Consequently, Limbrick's argument entails a privileging of the transnational over the local, of production over authorship, and a downplaying of the importance of local and indigenous cultures, at the same time as it also seriously underestimates the influence of the nation state in generating policies and discourses with which home-grown New Zealand films have consistently engaged. The whole sad story of Marky's dubious enterprise, in which he defrauded as well as insulted the Māori whom he hired as actors, is retold in a documentary directed by Geoff Stevens, *Adventures in Maoriland: The Making of Hei Tiki* (1985), available online from NZ On Screen at http://www.nzonscreen.com/title/adventures-in-maoriland-1985. Accessed 20 October 2010.
28. For a fuller discussion, see Chapter 2.
29. On Hayward's debt to Griffith's *The Birth of a Nation*, see Babington, *A History of the New Zealand Fiction Feature Film*, 73.
30. This phrase is used in an intertitle that appears in Hayward's *The Te Kooti Trail*.
31. See Chapter 1.
32. See Martin and Edwards, *New Zealand Film*, 29.
33. New Zealand Film Commission Act 1978, No. 61, http://www.legislation.govt.nz/act/public/1978/0061/latest/DLM22640.html?search=ts_act_Film+Commission_resel&p=1&sr=1. Accessed 4 December 2009.
34. Bruce Babington notes that 29 films were made in the period 1983–85, with a sharp, but not total, falling off in the years following. *A History of the New Zealand Fiction Feature Film*, 7.
35. For further comment, see Duncan Petrie, "Cinema in a Settler Society: Brand New Zealand," in *Cinema at the Periphery*, ed. Dina Iordanova, David Martin-Jones, and Belén Vidal (Detroit: Wayne State University Press, 2010), 67–83, esp. 71.

36. For the Man Alone topos in New Zealand Literature, see Alistair Fox, "Inwardness, Insularity, and the Man Alone: Postcolonial Anxiety in the New Zealand Novel," *Postcolonial Masculinities: Essays on Postcolonial Cultures and Literatures,* ed. Stephanie Newell, *Journal of Postcolonial Writing* 45, no. 3 (2009): 263–73; Janet Wilson, "Intertextual Strategies: Reinventing the Myths of Aotearoa in Contemporary New Zealand Fiction," in *Across the Lines: Intertextuality and Transcultural Communication in the New Literatures in English,* ed. Wolfgang Kloos (Amsterdam: Rodopi, 1998), 271–90; and Lawrence Jones, "Stanley Graham and the Several Faces of Man Alone," in *Barbed Wire and Mirrors: Essays on New Zealand Prose* (Dunedin: University of Otago Press, 1990), 296–312.

37. *Making Utu* (Gaylene Preston Productions, 1982), http://www.nzonscreen.com/title/making-utu-1982. Accessed 20 October 2009.

38. Ibid.

39. Gordon Collier, "Iconic Mythography: The Mediation of Cross-Cultural and Literary Topoi in the New Zealand Film," in *Defining New Idioms and Alternative Forms of Expression,* ed. Eckhard Breitlinger (Amsterdam and Atlanta: Rodopi, 1996), 205–18, esp. 215. I am indebted to Hilary Radner for having first drawn this phenomenon in New Zealand cinema to my attention.

40. Ibid., 215.

41. "Perfidious Albion" is a pejorative epithet that has persisted from the thirteenth century to the present day. I cite it because it was a term imparted by teachers to the cohort of high school students to which I belonged in the late 1960s – reflecting a developing perception in New Zealand that Britain's commitment to its former colony had been only skin-deep, being exploitative, given that it had persisted only as long as the relationship had served to advance the United Kingdom's own economic and political interests.

42. Pam Cook, *Screening the Past: Memory and Nostalgia in Cinema* (Abingdon, Oxon. and New York: Routledge, 2005), 5–6.

43. See Ian Conrich, *Studies in New Zealand Cinema* (London: Kakapo Books, 2009), 2.

44. Trevor Bentley, *Cannibal Jack: The Life & Times of Jacky Marmon, a Pakeha-Maori* (North Shore: Penguin, 2010), 9.

45. See Stuart Murray and Ian Conrich, "Introduction," in *New Zealand Filmmakers,* ed. Ian Conrich and Stuart Murray (Detroit: Wayne State University Press, 2007), 7.

46. See Alistair Fox, "Puritanism and the Erotics of Transgression: The New Zealand Influence in Jane Campion's Thematic Imaginary," in *Jane Campion: Cinema, Nation, Identity,* ed. Hilary Radner, Alistair Fox, and Irène Bessière (Detroit: Wayne State University Press, 2009), 103–22.

47. See Martin and Edwards, *New Zealand Film 1912–1996,* 133.

48. Peter Wells, *Frock Attack! Wig Wars! Strategic Camp in Desperate Remedies* (Auckland: Centre for Film, Television and Media Studies, University of Auckland, 1997), 7.

49. Ibid., 11.

50. Ibid., 19.

51. Ibid., 13.

52. For the theory of the look, see Jacques Aumont, *The Image,* trans. Claire Pajackowska (London: British Film Institute, 1997), 38.

53. Ibid., 9.

54. Wells, *Frock Attack!,* 4.

55. For Wells's use of the metaphor of the ideogram, see *Iridescence,* 450–51.

56. Andrew Higson, *English Heritage, English Cinema: Costume Drama since 1980* (Oxford: Oxford University Press, 2003), 67.

57. Burgoyne, *Film Nation,* 6.

58. Bentley, *Cannibal Jack*, 10.
59. Lynette Read, "*Feathers of Peace*: Lynette Read Interviews Barry Barclay," *Illusions* 31 (2000/2001): 3–4.
60. For further comment on the "Kiwi bloke," see Jock Phillips, *A Man's Country? The Image of the Pakeha Male – A History* (Auckland: Penguin, 1987).
61. "Fourth Cinema" is a term advocated by Barclay to distinguish "Indigenous Cinema" from "First Cinema" (American cinema), "Second Cinema" (art-house cinema), and "Third Cinema" (cinema of the so-called Third World). See Barry Barclay, "Celebrating Fourth Cinema," *Illusions* 35 (Winter 2003): 7–11.
62. The release of Waititi's *Boy* contradicts Duncan Petrie's view that the trend since 2000 towards a more internationally oriented production environment "has arguably worked against the development of more marginal and culturally difficult work," reflected in a movement by Waititi "away from[…]more overtly Maori subject matter" because of a concern to boost international marketability (Petrie, "Cinema in a Settler Society," 80).
63. Richard Hodges, IMDb, http://www.imdb.com/title/tt1601195/. Accessed 9 May 2010.

Chapter 1

Rudall Hayward and the Cinema of Maoriland: Genre-mixing and Counter-discourses in *Rewi's Last Stand* (1925), *The Te Kooti Trail* (1927) and *Rewi's Last Stand/The Last Stand* (1940)

Alistair Fox

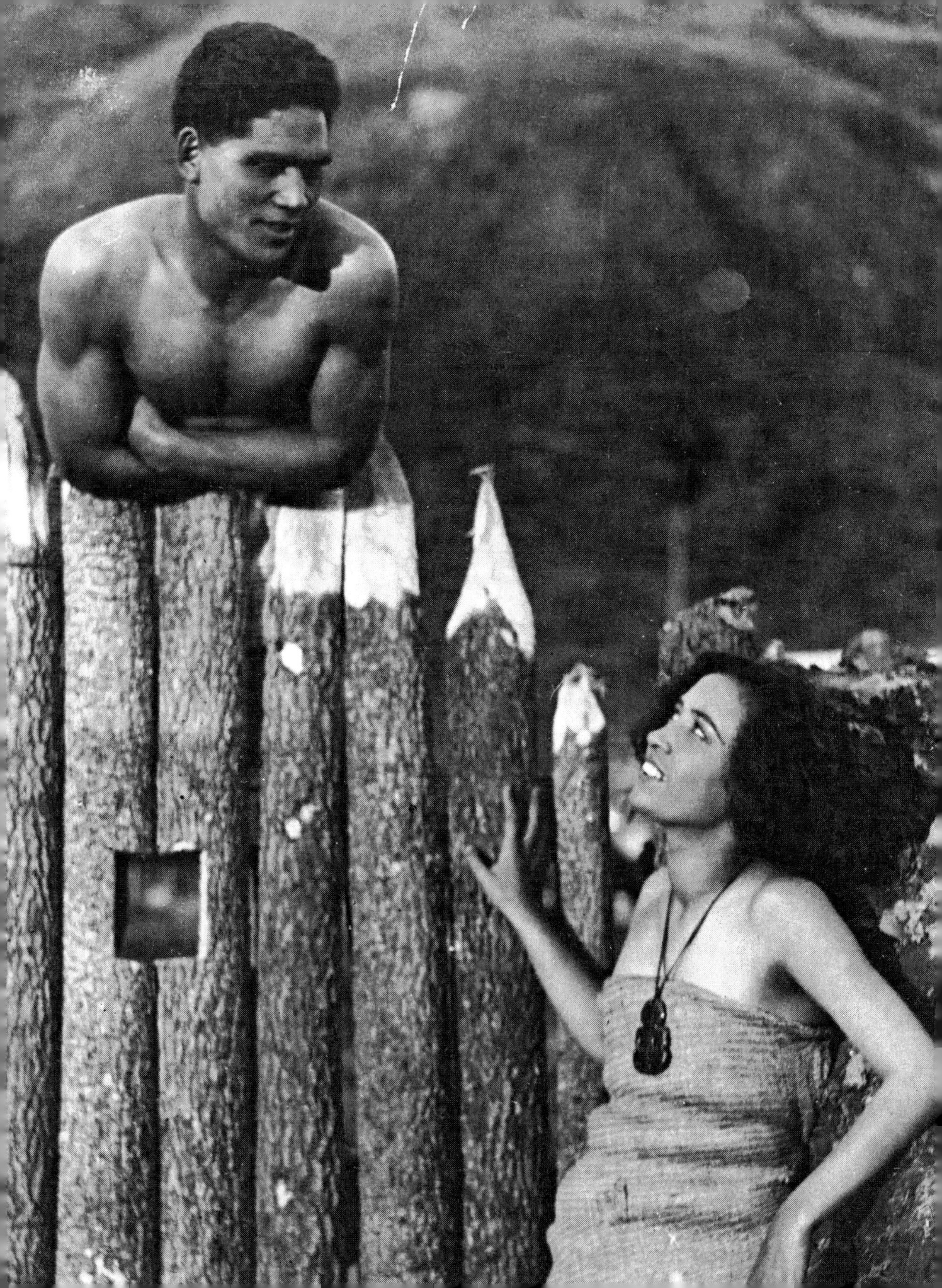

Michel Foucault and Hayden White, among others, have taught us to recognise the shaping power of discourses whenever any attempt is made to make sense of the multivariousness and apparent disorder of experience. A discourse, according to Foucault, is determined by the "group of relations established between authorities of emergence, delimitation, and specification" with respect to "objects." These "discursive relations" are necessary "to speak of this or that object, in order to deal with them, name them, analyse them, classify them, explain them, etc."[1] The problem, however, as White has argued, is that "discourse always tends to slip away from our data towards the structures of consciousness with which we are trying to grasp them." Correspondingly, "the data always resist the coherency of the image which we are trying to fashion of them."[2] In short, any attempt to assert a particular discourse as the means of interpreting experience inevitably conjures up the possibility of other, alternative ones.

These inseparably linked processes can be seen in the series of historical epics on the New Zealand Wars between Māori and Pākehā of the 1860s made by Rudall Hayward, considered the father of New Zealand filmmaking. In this chapter, I shall argue that Hayward's distinctive practice of mixing different genres resulted in films that acknowledge and animate a variety of competing discourses with the aim of correcting the simplicities of any single one. The tropes that constitute a particular genre carry with them an inherent and inherited latent meaning. For this reason, a fictive recreation of historical events that combines elements from a diverse range of genres is potentially capable of achieving a more complex, multifaceted representation than is liable to be constructed through more mono-dimensional representational means. As I shall demonstrate, Hayward's New Zealand War epics achieve this kind of complexity because of his ability to draw upon the signifying resources of a range of cinematic and literary genres that were popular at the time in order to find a new way of construing the meaning of the past. In doing so, he demonstrated the usefulness of cinema as an instrument for the interpretation of history itself.

Patiti Warbrick as Taranahi and Tina Hunt as Monika in *The Te Kooti Trail*, 1927, dir. Rudall Hayward. Image courtesy of the Hayward Collection, New Zealand Film Archive Ngā Kaitiaki O Ngā Taonga Whitiāhua.

Origins of Hayward's interest in New Zealand history

Hayward's interest in New Zealand history, as he later recalled, began when, as a schoolboy at Whanganui Collegiate College, he became fascinated by James Cowan's *The Adventures of Kimble Bent: A Story of Wild Life in the New Zealand Bush*, published by Whitcombe and Tombs in 1911.[3] This narrative, recorded by Cowan from the oral account of Kimble Bent himself, tells how Bent, a British soldier who deserted during the New Zealand Wars of the 1860s, went over to the opposing side, and lived as a Pākehā-Māori in Taranaki during the campaign of Tītokowaru, war chief of the Ngāti Ruanui iwi, and the prophet Te Ua Haumēne, founder of the Pai Mārire movement, against the colonial government.[4] The adventures described by Kimble Bent were thrilling indeed, especially in their account of Māori "primitive war-methods" that were terrifying to the Europeans, such as the revival by Pai Mārire of ancient rites, including the removal of the hearts of enemy soldiers, and cannibalism. Accordingly, his account is replete with "frightful scenes," as when one of Tītokowaru's war-parties tomahawks, cuts to pieces, cooks and eats a trooper named Smith, "who had incautiously ventured out to look for his horse beyond rifle-range of the redoubt," or when the Māori *Kūpapa* (Māori troops fighting on the government side), "mad with the lust of killing," decapitate and savagely mutilate the bodies of their Hauhau enemies.[5] Cowan's vivid rendition of these events, Hayward recalls, started him thinking about putting New Zealand history on the screen, because he realised that intercultural wars of the nineteenth century provided material as fascinating as any to be found in the American westerns that had been made popular by D. W. Griffith and his contemporaries.[6]

Hayward also appreciated that Māori subject matter, including myths and legends, could exert a powerful appeal at the box office on account of its exoticism and ethnographic interest. From the 1870s onwards, literary works began to appear that combined elevated or lyrical descriptions of New Zealand's sublime and picturesque landscapes with stories that presented the Māori as variously noble, ferocious and romantic. Dusky Māori maidens were depicted as seductive in their beauty and "wantonness," while Māori warriors were presented as matchless in their valour and martial pride. This was the literature of "Maoriland," the alternative name for New Zealand that was popular up until the 1930s.[7] It included works such as Alfred Domett's gigantic epic poem, *Ranolf and Amohia* (1872), Alfred A. Grace's *Maoriland Stories* (1895) and Elan Westerwood's romantic epic, *Maoriana*, written in 1880 and published in Dunedin by Whitcombe and Tombs circa 1916.

As explained in the previous chapter, such literature had already provided New Zealand cinema with the subject matter of its earliest feature films, in the Maoriland films made by Gaston Méliès in 1913: *Loved by a Maori Chieftess* (1913) and *How Chief Te Ponga Won His Bride* (1913). Hayward had also been influenced by the succession of films depicting the legend of Hinemoa and Tūtānekai, a kind of Māori *Romeo and Juliet*, including the version made by Méliès in 1912, although Hayward had not actually seen it; George Tarr's *Hinemoa* (1914), which Hayward thought was "a beautiful film"; and Gustav Pauli's *The Romance of Hinemoa* (1925/1927), which Hayward considered to be "by far the most advanced."[8] He declares himself to have been particularly thrilled with Tarr's shots of Māori canoes on Lake Rotorua.[9] Hayward's interest in these two sources of local subject matter – the conflicts of the New Zealand Wars on the one hand, and the exoticism of "Maoriland" romance on the other – meant that when he came to make fiction feature films himself, he would attempt to combine them.

The germs of this approach can be seen in his first feature film, the settler romance, *My Lady of the Cave* (1922), which takes aspects of the Māori idyll – a romance between the hero and heroine in a remote, exotic location (although in this instance, the beauteous maiden is white, as dictated by Hayward's allegorical purpose) – and blends them with scenes, presented in flashback, showing the earlier strife between settlers and the Māori. Set in 1890, the film presents the "dreaming soul" of an adventurous youth in "uncharted isles," and thus functions as a trope for the colonising enterprise itself. Beryl Trite, the heroine, is described in an intertitle as a "sea-nymph beauteous," implying that she may be a personification of Zealandia herself. This figure, with her Grecian attire, makes frequent appearances in late nineteenth- and early twentieth-century New Zealand as a southern Britannia. Zealandia appears, for example, on the New Zealand coat of arms, on the New Zealand Penny Universal stamp of 1901, and in literature, as the symbolic embodiment of the colony, and later the dominion, of New Zealand.[10] In Hayward's romantic fantasy, Beryl, in her role as Zealandia, waits to be liberated, at a metaphorical level, from her sequestered existence under the guardianship of the Māori Rau. Although loyal and devoted to Beryl, Rau, because he is mute and emasculated as a consequence of the warlike practices of his own people, cannot himself provide the heroine with what she needs to realise her full potential. That can only happen when she is free to marry the adventurous youth, for whom she "longs," who represents the civilising mission of the Pākehā colonists.[11]

As interesting as *My Lady of the Cave* may be, in terms of its symbolic evocativeness, and the adroitness with which Hayward deploys the emerging techniques of visual cinematic narrative, its imperialist vision is grotesquely paternalistic, conventional and simplistic. His next feature film, the first version of *Rewi's Last Stand* (1925), and his subsequent films on the New Zealand Wars would offer a much more complex view of the colonial experience. In the rest of this chapter, I shall explore how and why this more subtle and ambivalent vision was achieved.

The influence of James Cowan's The New Zealand Wars

A crucial event that occurred between the making of *My Lady of the Cave* and *Rewi's Last Stand* was the appearance of *The New Zealand Wars: A History of the Māori Campaigns and the Pioneering Period*, a magisterial account written by James Cowan – the historian whose earlier work had fired Hayward's imagination while he was still at school – and published by the Government Printer in 1922. The great value of Cowan's work was twofold: first, it provided Hayward with several heroic "episodes of the quality which makes the true romance," as Cowan put it,[12] and, second, it presented him with a discursive interplay that suggested a much more complex view of the colonial past than the one he had reproduced in *My Lady of the Cave*.

In Cowan's *The New Zealand Wars*, two rival discourses compete with one another. On one hand, he reproduces the discourse of colonial imperialism, including its Darwinian assumption that colonisation entailed an inevitable march of progress towards civilisation. On the other, he introduces a counter discourse that expresses unease about the motives of the colonisers, and about the justice of their dealing with the indigenous Maori. Noting the parallel between New Zealand's colonial history and "the white conquest in America," Cowan observes that

> [t]here was the same dual combat with wild nature and with untamed man; there was the necessity in each land for soldierly skill; the same display of all grades of human courage; much of the same tale of raid and foray, siege, trail-hunting, and ambuscade.[13]

In this discourse, Māori, like native Americans, are inscribed as primitive and barbaric, needing to be tamed in the name of civilisation and progress, and the settlers as the heroic agent of that civilising mission.

Accompanying this discourse, however, is a second discourse that subverts the assumptions and certitudes of the first. This counter-discourse is revealed in Cowan's recognition of a heroism and dignity in the Māori defence of their lands and way of life that not only questions the justice of British actions in depriving them of those things but also establishes a relation of equality between the races, rather than one marked by the superiority of the one and the subservience of the other. Indeed, as Cowan puts it, the trial of strength on the battlefield led to a situation in which "[e]ach admitted the other's pre-eminence under certain conditions, and each protagonist came to admire the primal quality of valour in his opponent."[14]

The Māori Wars ended, he concedes, "with a strong mutual respect, tinged with a real affection, which would never have existed but for this ordeal of battle."[15] By the time Cowan has finished recounting the final suppression of Kingite resistance in the Waikato, on the occasion when Rewi Maniapoto and 120 members of his tribe were overpowered by 1800 imperial troops, in what, effectually, was an act of genocide, he concludes:

> The story of the last day in Orakau imperishably remains as an inspiration to deeds of courage and fortitude. Nowhere in history did the spirit of patriotism blaze up more brightly than in that little earthwork redoubt, torn by gunfire and strewn with dead and dying.[16]

Gone is the condescension of the opening of Cowan's history – this is no longer a barbarous race of savages being described, but rather a people of immense valour who are resolute in their determination to defend their land and way of life. Not only has condescension been replaced by respect, but the terms in which Māori resistance has been described betrays the presence of a latent awareness that perhaps the violent actions of the colonial troops amounted, in reality, to a perpetration of gross injustice.

Others in the colony shared a similar unease about the actions of the Government in confiscating Māori land and suppressing resistance. One of the most telling expressions of this disquiet was a poem written by Jessie Mackay, "The Charge at Parihaka," which satirically commemorates the event in 1881 when 1600 armed government troops stormed the village to crush a non-violent campaign by Māori to reoccupy their own land, which had previously been confiscated. In verses that parody Tennyson's "Charge of the Light Brigade," Mackay mocks the false heroism of the colonial troops in order to expose the hypocritical self-interest of the whole venture:

> Children to right of them,
> Children to left of them,
> Women in front of them
> > Saw them and wondered.
>
> . . . .
>
> When can their glory fade?
> Oh! The wild charge they made,
> > New Zealand wondered
> Whether each doughty soul
> Paid for the pigs he stole:
> > Noble Twelve Hundred![17]

The very degree to which Cowan (and others) assert the heroism of the Māori defenders at Ōrākau suggests a counter-compensation that masks the feelings expressed more directly by Jessie Mackay.[18] Although the British had prevailed in their contest with the Māori, they were not proud of themselves. Thus, even though Cowan, as a historian, professes to be giving a facsimile record of the actual events of the Māori wars, the presence of these competing discourses attests to a degree of irresolution in his understanding of their significance.

The first version of *Rewi's Last Stand* (1925)

In adapting Cowan's account of Rewi Maniapoto's heroic resistance at Ōrākau for the screen in 1925 as *Rewi's Last Stand*, Hayward was responsive to both the imperialist discourse in Cowan's history, and also the counter-discourse that accompanied it.[19] Traces of the former are present in the romanticised celebration of "the beloved Von Tempsky" and his Forest Rangers, who are presented as heroes, and in a contrasting episode in which "Te Waro, the fierce old Pagan *Tohunga*, seeks to make sacrifice to Uenuke, his God of Battle, by burning the heart of the first enemy killed." The counterposing of episodes like these betrays the presence of the conventional colonial mythos equating the Pākehā with civilisation and the Māori with the primitive. Having activated this mythos, however, Hayward immediately intercepts it by having Rewi himself intervene to stop the barbaric practice his tohunga is about to commit, by asserting that "we [the Māori] are fighting under the religion of Christ." Not only does this assertion ennoble the Māori side, but it also equates Māori and Pākehā in terms of the civilised/barbarous polarity found, for example, in so many classic American westerns.

Hayward's modification of the conventional mythos was also intensified by his importation of elements drawn from a range of literary and cinematic genres that were popular at the time. In doing so, he was undoubtedly prompted by his awareness of what would appeal at the box office. The generic mix that constituted that appeal is suggested by a poster advertising *The Te Kooti Trail* (1927). Audiences can anticipate, the poster proclaims, "Red-Blooded Drama, Uproarious Comedy, Tender Romance, Whirlwind Action, amid the Glorious Scenery of the N.Z. Bush."[20] In other words, the film will combine elements from popular silent-era cinematic genres including the action/adventure film, the slapstick comedy, the historical epic and the romantic drama, along with scenic attractions.

Rewi's Last Stand (1925) embodies exactly the same mix of generic attributes. For the raw material of "Red-Blooded Drama" and "Whirlwind Action," Hayward needed to look no further than Cowan's historical account, which included the account of the perilous scouting mission conducted by Von Tempsky and Lieutenant Colonel Thomas McDonnell at Paparata, as well as a description of the siege at Ōrākau itself, both of which feature prominently in the movie. Hayward also sought to introduce "uproarious comedy" by creating a fictional *miles gloriosus* in the form of "Colonel" Dobby (Fred Mills), described as "one of Auckland's 'wags'," who claims that he is a "pussonal friend o' the Dook o' Wellington." Colonel Dobby, like his antecedents (such as Falstaff in Shakespeare's *Henry IV*), is farcical, both in appearance and actions. "Every pawn-shop in the Colony," we are told, "had contributed something to the Colonel's uniform." The fact that he is overage and has flat feet renders his bellicose military posturing merely ridiculous, while his attempts to play the gallant with the ladies are equally ludicrous.

For the element of "tender romance," Hayward drew upon the stock conventions of the literary Maoriland romance, as found in Westerwood's *Maoriana*. Characteristically, in such works, there is a framing romance in which the hero must separate from his white beloved in order to seek adventure and/or his fortune. Invariably, he is captured by the Māori and becomes embroiled in their warfare, in the course of which he falls in love with a beautiful Māori maiden. Bound by honour and the vow of constancy he has sworn to his European beloved, however, the hero is unable to yield to his desire for the dusky beauty. Eventually, the pathos attending her unrequited love for him is deepened into melodrama by her death – which, in the case of *Maoriana*, occurs when the beautiful Rahene is killed by a greenstone axe thrown at the hero, Evan, by his enemy, Te Huah, chief of the enemy tribe.[21]

Hayward imported both components of this archetype into the first version of *Rewi's Last Stand*. The hero, Kenneth Gordon (Edmund Finney), newly arrived from England, falls in love with Cecily Wake (Nola Caselli), the daughter of an Auckland surgeon. Following a quarrel with an officer in the army, which he has now joined, Kenneth is obliged to separate from his beloved when he goes to serve on the front with Von Tempsky and his rangers. Like Evan in *Maoriana*, Kenneth falls into league with a Māori maiden of high birth, Takiri (Tina Hunt), who saves his life when both are taken prisoner by a Māori war party. Tragically, however, Takiri, like Rahene, dies when she is shot while trying to escape with Kenneth from the pā at Ōrākau, and expires in his arms. Just as it is foreseen that Evan in *Maoriana* will return to Scotland and marry Minnie, his sweetheart, so, too, is Kenneth reunited with Cecily.

Even though they may have been introduced in the first instance for entertainment purposes, the addition of these elements from fictive genres to the basic historical account found in Cowan served a serious thematic purpose that enlarged the complexity of the discursive interplay already in Hayward's historical source. Colonel Dobby is not merely farcical, he is also parodic, providing a satiric image of a British soldier that deflates the idea that the colonial troops are a band of valorous heroes. As such, his presence undermines any presumption of the superiority of the British, or of the justness of their cause.

Similarly, the interracial romance between Kenneth and Takiri provides a trope that figures a relationship between the races that is much more complex than the complacent one being celebrated at the time. Cowan, at the end of *The New Zealand Wars*, proclaims that "Pakeha and Maori are now knit in such close bonds of friendship that they can contemplate without a trace of the olden enmities the long-drawn struggles of other years." "Only one thing was needed," he adds, "to cement for ever the union of the races, and that opportunity the Great War brought […] [when] Maori soldiers fought and died by the side of their *Pakeha* fellow New Zealanders."[22] Even though the footage of the film's ending has been lost, we know from a review in the *Christian Science Monitor* that Hayward followed Cowan in this conclusion:

The end of the picture is finely dramatic and symbolic. There is shown the great Sir George Grey, who loved and understood the Maori so well, dreaming in his old age of a time when the two peoples shall be one. Then there is thrown on the screen a picture of Maoris and British leaving together for service in the Great War. The troops march along to the strains of "Land of Hope and Glory" and the spectator has a catch in his throat as he remembers those days, and realises to what an extent the great Proconsul's dream came true.[23]

Despite the apparent optimism of this ending, Hayward's inclusion of the plot elements drawn from the Maoriland romances serves to undermine it by dramatising an experience in which the possibility of a "romantic" union between the races is, at a metaphorical level, contemplated, only to be thwarted first, by a prior commitment of the white hero to bond with a member of his own race, and then by the consequences of a determination of one race (the Pākehā) to gain dominance over the other. One might argue that, in Hayward's vision, this simply reflects what was not possible in 1864, had indeed become possible by 1914, but the final film Hayward made dealing with race relations, *To Love a Maori* (1972), would suggest otherwise. The picture painted in Hayward's final feature film is one in which cultural incompatibility, socio-economic disparity and racial prejudice provide apparently insuperable impediments to a union that the young couple – he a Māori, and she a Pākehā – yearn for. Already, in 1925, Hayward's imagination (perhaps at an unconscious level) had registered this lamentable fact, as his inclusion of a thwarted interracial romance attests.

The Te Kooti Trail (1927)

Comparable complexities are to be found in Hayward's next film on the New Zealand Wars, *The Te Kooti Trail* (1927), and they result from a similar strategy of genre-mixing, involving the incorporation of elements drawn from a range of fictive genres.

The basic narrative – dealing with the heroic defence of Jean Guerrin's flour mill at Te Poronou, near Whakatāne, against an attack by the guerrilla leader, Te Kooti Arikirangi, and his warriors – is, like *Rewi's Last Stand*, drawn from Cowan's *The New Zealand Wars*. A serialised version written by Frank Bodle also appeared shortly before the release of *The Te Kooti Trail*, in the *Otago Witness*, the *Auckland Weekly* and the *New Zealand Herald* in September and October 1927, thus ensuring an audience for the film. As he had done in *Rewi's Last Stand*, Hayward surrounded the historical event with a frame plot involving a love story – this time between Eric Mantell (Arthur Lord), the hero, and Alice (Billie Andreasson), the heroine, in which Eric (as is typical in Maoriland romances) leaves England for the colonies, finds himself separated from his beloved, and becomes caught up in the conflicts of the 1860s, in which he has to prove himself before he can marry Alice. For the sake of introducing some light relief, Hayward places Eric in the company of two comic characters, a Frenchman and Irishman, with the three of them forming a motley crew of soldiers of fortune reminiscent of Pistol, Nym and Bardolph in Shakespeare's *Henry V*. Most crucially, as far as its impact on the symbolic meaning of the film is concerned, Hayward added a romance plot involving the love between a young Māori maiden, Monika (Tina Hunt), and a noble young warrior, Taranahi (A.P. Warbrick).

As with his first two feature films, Hayward's ostensible and main purpose was to celebrate the achievements of the colonists. To highlight this intention, he opens the movie with a "Dedication – To that great 'Lost Legion' of British pioneers, colonists and soldiers of fortune whose nameless graves mark the paths of empire," quoting from a popular poem, "The Dwellings of Our Dead," written by Arthur H. Adams, whose *Collected Verses* had appeared in 1913:

> They came as lovers came,
>   all else forsaking
> The bonds of home and
>   kindred proudly breaking;
> They lie in splendour lone –
>   the nation of their making
> Their everlasting throne![24]

To underscore the courage of these unsung heroes, Hayward amplifies the dangers they face by magnifying the sinister aspects of their opponents. To do so, he draws upon the devices of the American western, which had become popular in New Zealand as a result of the westerns made by D. W. Griffith in his years with the Biograph Company, such as *Comata, the Sioux* (1909), a romantic melodrama, or *The Battle of Elderbush Gulch* (1913) and *The Massacre* (1914), which depict interracial conflict. Te Kooti's attack on Guerrin's mill is modelled closely on the Indian attacks in Griffith's westerns, as is the pursuit of Taranahi when he rides off to seek help, and the suspense as to whether the colonial forces (the equivalent of the cavalry) will arrive in time to rescue the besieged defenders of the mill. Hayward also imitated aspects of Griffith's civil-war epic, *The Birth of a Nation* (1915), as a means of validating and sanctifying the mission of the colonists. Just as Griffith tries to convey a sense of fear arising from the emancipation of the slaves by showing marauding Negroes dressed in the uniforms of Yankee soldiers, so too does Hayward show Te Kooti (Te Pairi Tu Terangi), dressed in "a looted uniform," aping a British army officer to suggest that he is a grotesque parody of a genuine order-enforcer. Hayward intensifies the inscription of Te Kooti as a kind of Antichrist by showing him quoting from the bible to incite his followers "to kill all white men." Finally, as Bruce Babington has noted, Hayward models his characterisation of Peka Makarini (Baker Maclean), Te Kooti's half-caste lieutenant, on that of Silas Lynch, Stoneman's evil mulatto henchman in *The Birth of a Nation*, in that both goad or deceive their masters into actions that cause tragedy to be inflicted on innocent others.[25]

Despite Hayward's commitment to the imperial vision of the colonists as enlightened agents of civilisation, charged with a mission to overcome the powers of darkness, represented by the indigenous Other as manifest in the form of Te Kooti and his evil lieutenant, the inclusion of the love story of Monika and Taranahi introduces a whole new dimension to the depiction of Māori that challenges the simplicity of the conventional mythos that Hayward invokes in the rest of the film. Monika and Taranahi, through Taranahi's flute-playing, are associated with Hinemoa and Tutanekai and thus evoke the world of Māori before contact with Europeans. Their association with the old culture is underlined in several ways. Monika wears a large tiki around her neck, whereas her sister, Erihapeti (Mary Kingi), wears an equally large Christian cross. Similarly, whereas Monika loves a Māori man, Erihapeti loves a Pākehā man (she is married to Jean Guerrin). As well, Taranahi seeks *utu* (revenge) after Monika's death, in accordance with traditional Māori practices: and in his dying moments he has a vision of Monika waiting for him on the high-point at Cape Reinga from which the

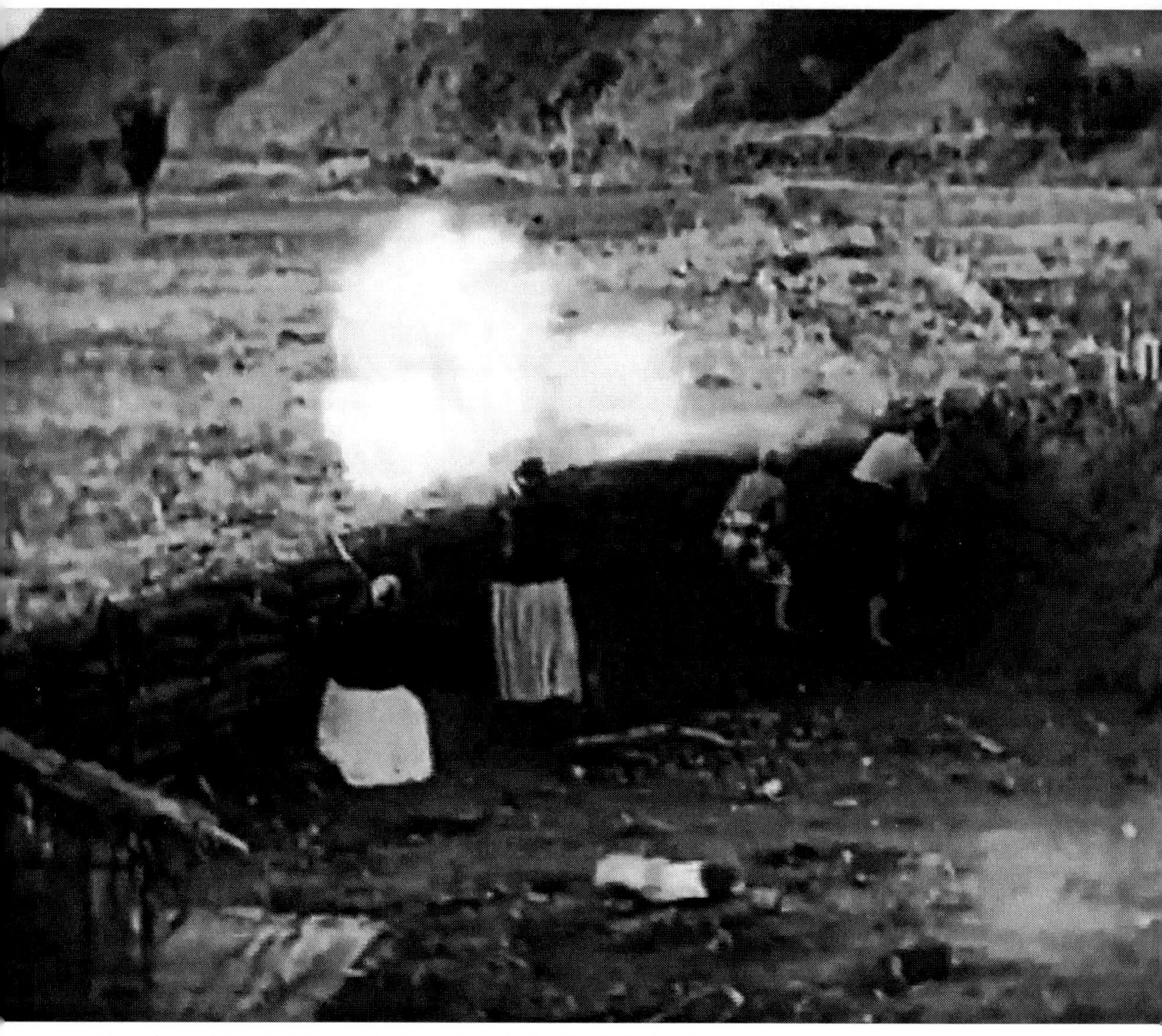

The defence of the mill at Poronou in *The Te Kooti Trail*, 1927, dir. Rudall Hayward.

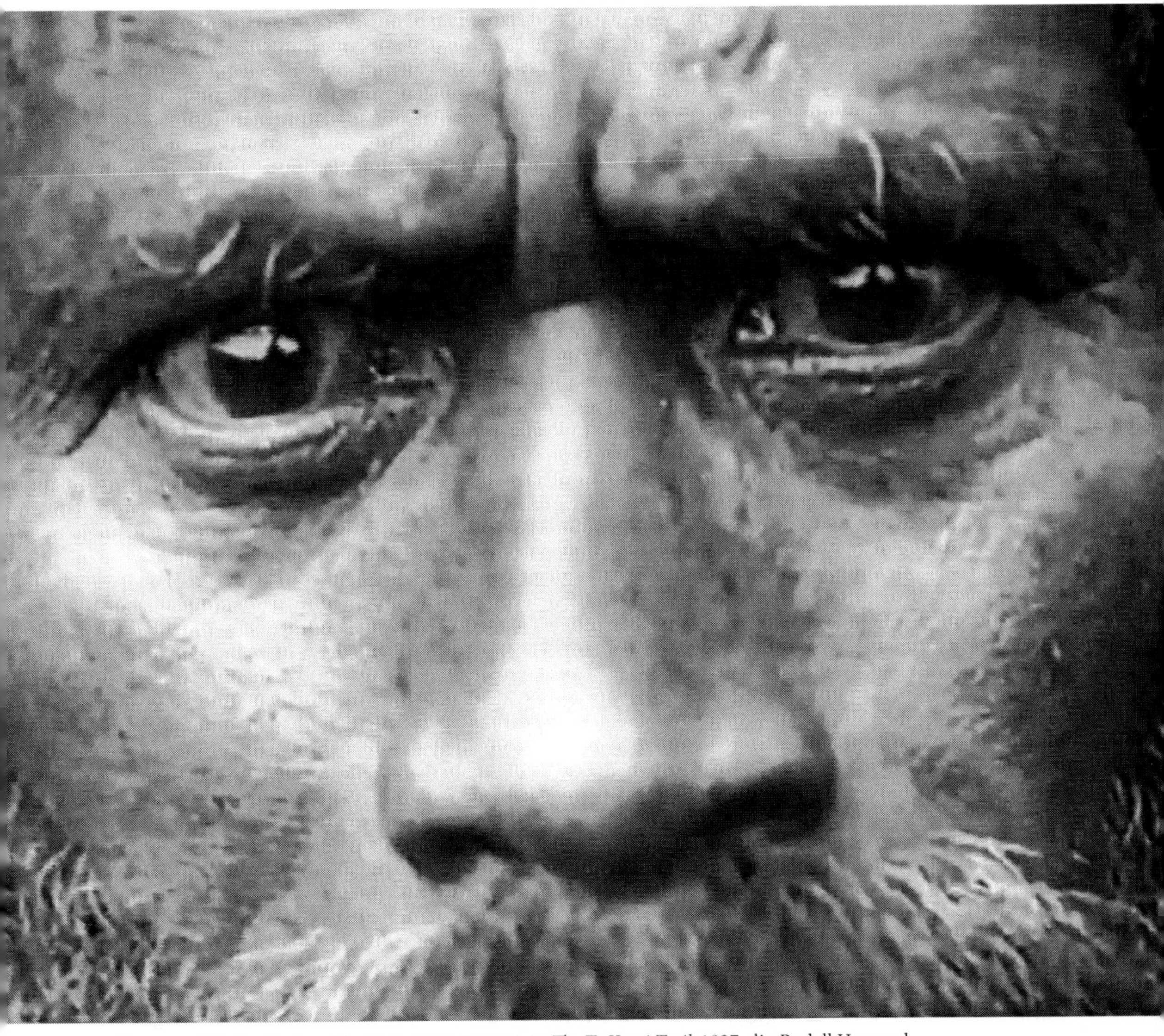

The gaze of Te Kooti, played by Te Pairi Tu Terangi, in *The Te Kooti Trail*, 1927, dir. Rudall Hayward.

spirits of the dead depart in Māori mythology, which associates him with the ancient belief system.[26]

The presence of these associations invests the most dramatic and pitiful moment in the movie – the slaying of Monika – with a tropic significance. The basic event, including the dialogue between Monika and Erihapeti, is recorded word for word by Cowan. Hayward, however, adds a detail that is not present in Cowan: the fact that it is the half-breed, Peka Makarini, who prompts Te Kooti to order the horrific act, whereby Rangihiroa, who has rescued Monika and Erihapeti from the massacre at the mill, must undertake to marry Erihapeti and kill Monika to avoid all three being killed. The pretext for this atrocity is that Monika has refused to tell Te Kooti where Guerrin hid his bullets.

The fact that Monika has been so strongly associated in the movie with pre-European culture tempts one to read the episode symbolically – as the destruction of the originary Māori culture at the hands of those who represent a hybrid fusion of the Māori and Pākehā worlds. This hybridity is represented by Te Kooti on the one hand, and by Peka Makarini on the other, both of whom incarnate a form of degeneracy resulting from a miscegenation between the races – intellectual, in Te Kooti's case (because of his marriage of Christianity with hatred and violence), and physical and moral, in Peka Makarini's case. Hayward's portrayal of this pair as degenerate was no accident. Indeed, his original conception of them had been even more damning, causing the censor to refuse to issue a certificate of release for the film until an intertitle referring to Te Kooti as "resorting to faked miracles," and another referring to Peka Makarini as "torture master" and "stage manager of miracles" had been removed.[27] Even without these more explicit cues, Hayward's presentation of the killing of Monika may, at a symbolic (and perhaps unconscious) level, articulate a deep unease at the actual consequences of colonisation that intercept and qualify the unequivocally positive affirmations with which the film begins. Even though order is eventually restored, with Taranahi and Gilbert Mair (Thomas McDermott) joining forces to kill Makarini and defeat Te Kooti's guerillas, Taranahi, like Monika, is also destroyed by the destructiveness that has been unleashed. The final vision of Taranahi joining Monika to depart for Hawaiki reinforces the metaphoric suggestion that their tragic deaths may also figure the death of the old world they represent. By acknowledging this latent unease about colonialism and its effects, Hayward anticipated critical viewpoints that would resurface with a vengeance more than half a century later.

Hayward's remake of *Rewi's Last Stand* and the Centenary of 1940

Eleven years after *The Te Kooti Trail*, Hayward shot a remake of *Rewi's Last Stand*, this time in sound, which was released in 1940, the year of the centenary of the signing of the founding Treaty of Waitangi, in which the Māori tribes conceded sovereignty to the British

Ramai Te Miha as Ariana and Leo Pilcher as Robert Beaumont in *Rewi's Last Stand*, 1940, dir. Rudall Hayward. Image courtesy of the Hayward Collection, New Zealand Film Archive Ngā Kaitiaki O Ngā Taonga Whitiāhua.

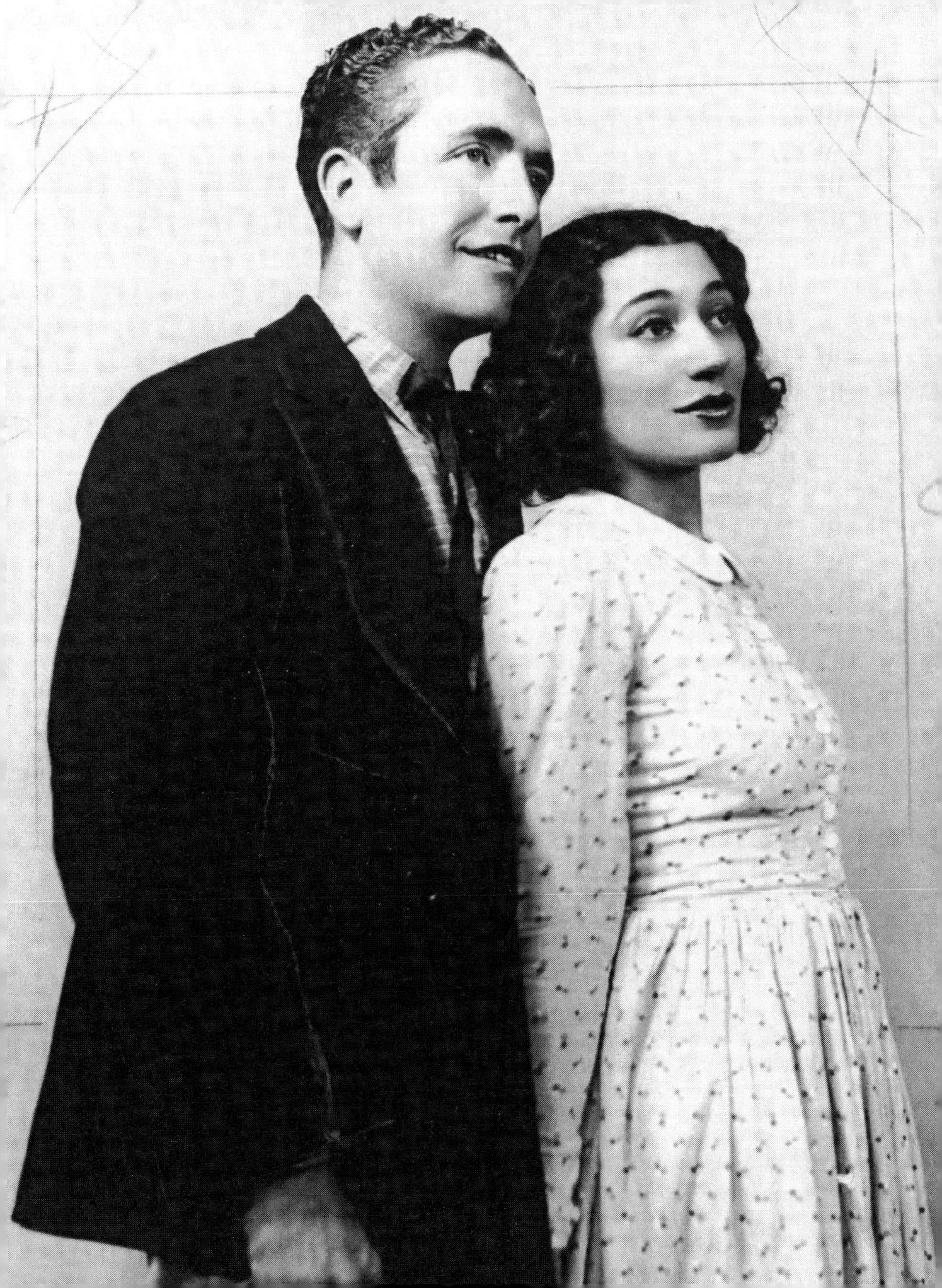

Crown in exchange for being accorded the rights of British citizens, and the protection of their customary rights and taonga (treasures). As Hayward himself pointed out, only the central part, the defence of Ōrākau Pā, was used in both films; the rest of the story was very different.[28] The differences between the two versions of *Rewi's Last Stand* are very striking, and highly instructive, telling us of a major shift that had occurred in the politics of race relations.

Behind all the changes Hayward made was an intention to replace the mixed-genre approach of the earlier *Rewi* with a more elevated treatment that enhanced both the romantic and the heroic elements of the story. Gone is the frame tale that obliges the Pākehā hero to remain constant to a woman beloved of his own race; instead, the intercultural romance between the hero and a Māori maiden that was aborted in the earlier film is not only allowed to flourish, but takes centre-stage in the love relationship between Robert Beaumont (Leo Pilcher) and Ariana (Ramai Te Miha). Correspondingly, the dyslogistic aspects in the depiction of Māori are largely removed. The only hint of a contrast between the colonists as representing civilisation and the Māori as representing the primitive and barbaric is a reference by the Reverend who runs the mission station near Te Awamutu to that fact that "twenty years ago when Mrs Morgan and I moved out here all this was virgin county – the Maoris were cannibals." In other words, the civilisation/wilderness opposition is relegated to the past, a shift that is reflected in a diminution of the devices imitated from Griffith – the evil tohunga figure in the earlier *Rewi*, for example, is entirely absent. Significantly, the comic elements are also omitted, with no farcical or parodic figure being present to provide a deflating commentary on the colonial enterprise.

The effect of all these changes is to present both the Māori and the Pākehā as commensurately noble – worthy antagonists who respect one another, even though their respective aspirations lead them into conflict. As the opening "Foreword" makes clear, it was "the struggle for possession of this land of promise" that caused the warfare between the races, not a lack of respect on the part of the Pākehā: "the Pakehas (white man) found the Maoris tough and chivalrous fighters, who were often defeated by sheer weight of arms, but never conquered." Any such contention, Hayward affirms (echoing Cowan), belongs to the past: "Today the slowly blending races of white men and brown, live in peace and equality as one [...]" Here, then, is a utopian vision of a future for New Zealand in which the two races will be assimilated, following a resolution of the conflict that had previously pitted them against each other.

It is easy enough to see what might have motivated Hayward to make these shifts in his vision. At a political level, the remake of *Rewi's Last Stand* is Hayward's response to the country's preparations for the centenary of the signing of the Treaty of Waitangi. For Pākehā, this was a time of great nationalism and patriotic fervour. The prevailing mood is captured in a speech by the Member of Parliament for Stratford when the Centennial Bill was introduced into Parliament in 1938, the year Hayward shot the film. The Bill, the speaker declares, would provide for the celebration of one hundred years of progress in this wonderful Dominion [...] the history of those hundred years is amazing, and one which has never been outshone in any other country. Ours is one of the brightest gems in the Pacific: a real pacific haven away from the troubles of a distracted older world.[29]

Hayward's film was designed, in part, to illuminate the process whereby this "progress" had come about.

Apart from his political motive for celebrating unity and reconciliation between the races, Hayward also had a more personal one: he was soon to marry as his second wife the Māori actress who was the leading lady in the remake of *Rewi* – the beauteous Ramai Te Miha. To a very real extent, therefore, the intercultural romance depicted in the film was meant to serve as a trope for the reconciliation between the races taking place both in Hayward's own life as well as at a national level.

Even though this may have been Hayward's intent, the actual mimesis suggests something rather different, as the love relationship between Robert and Ariana is shown to be fraught with difficulty. Ariana, like other Maoriland heroines such as Rahene in Westerwood's *Maoriana*, is half-Māori, half-Pākehā, having been adopted by the local white traders who raise her in Pākehā ways. When conflict breaks out and the Maniapoto Māori reclaim her as one of their own, she is presented with an agonising choice: to escape to be with her Pākehā lover when offered the opportunity, or to remain with her tribe. At a symbolic level, this choice figures that of contemporary Māori at the time of the New Zealand Centenary celebrations: should they acquiesce to the Pākehā vision for their future – that is, of assimilation to the Pākehā way of life – or should they seek to retain their lands, culture and identity?

In the film, Ariana elects to stay with her people, despite her love for Beaumont, on the grounds that "[she] can't change what is in [her]." Whether intentionally or not, this decision puts the viability of the film's opening assumptions about progress in doubt, just as in historical reality the choices of Māori were putting the viability of the optimistic vision of the future entertained by Pākehā in doubt. Significantly, many Māori leaders did not share the sanguine view of progress being proclaimed by Pākehā. Princess Te Puea and the Māori King Korokī, for example, boycotted the 1940 Waitangi celebrations on the grounds that the issue of unjust land confiscations in the nineteenth century remained unresolved. By showing Ariana's refusal to desert her people to join her Pākehā lover, Hayward's film implicitly acknowledges the impediment to assimilationist "progress" posed by the commitment of Māori to their own identity.

The ending of the remake of *Rewi's Last Stand* also underlines the existence of these latent doubts. True to the traditions of melodrama, Ariana (taking over the role of Takiri in the first version of *Rewi*) ends up being shot in the process of trying to escape among the survivors of the siege, and is shown dying pathetically in the arms of her lover as she is reunited, too late, with her lost Pākehā father. It is possible that this ending does not represent Hayward's original intention, because the novelisation by A. W. Reed, based on Hayward's scenario, does not end with Ariana dying; rather, it contains a continuation in which Robert Beaumont is allotted 50 acres of Waikato land following the end of the war against the Waikato tribes, as well as a town allotment. In this alternative ending, Ariana recovers from her wound, which turns out to have been only superficial, and Beaumont, having decided they will get married, plans to "build a house and plant roses round it."[30] From the evidence of an interview recorded between Rudall Hayward, Walter Harris and Ray Hayes held in the New Zealand Film Archive, it would appear that Hayward felt obliged to change Ariana's fate out of consideration for the box office – no doubt in response to the rapidly emerging taste for romantic drama in the cinema of the 1930s.[31]

Whether or not this change occurred for the New Zealand version, or was made subsequently for the British release, for which substantial editing was required to meet the strict requirements of the British Quota system, is impossible to say.[32] What is certain is that in the surviving version of the film – *The Last Stand*, the cut version released in Britain – the possibility of an intercultural romance, both literally at the personal level and metaphorically at the level of race relations, is arrested, rather than being allowed to blossom into the fulfilment depicted in Reed's novelisation. The changed ending attests to a reality that the happiness achieved in the novelised version may have aspired to obscure in order to conform to the celebratory spirit that the country was trying to manufacture for the 1940 centenary of the founding of the nation. In the version of the film that survives, the reconciliation between Pākehā and Māori that is symbolised in the union of Robert and Ariana is presented, by implication, as a future prospect whose time had not yet arrived in the 1860s. The probability of such an intention is strengthened by Hayward's subsequent depiction of a Māori-Pākehā romance, in his docudrama, *To Love a Maori* (1972) set in modern New Zealand, in which he shows the impediments to a happy outcome to be just as formidable as they had been a century earlier. The prospect of a marriage between the two young lover-protagonists in this film, Tama (Val Irwin), a Māori, and Penny (Marie Searell), a Pākehā, turns out to be frowned on equally by both their families. As Tama's aunt sums it up, "To love a Māori takes a lot of courage!" – even in the 1970s.

In retrospect, one can see that Hayward was well ahead of his time in anticipating a need to find a view of the relationship between Māori and Pākehā in the post-settlement context that avoided the self-privileging simplicities of the colonialist myth that was still very powerful during the provincial period when his movies were made. The ambivalence that is generated in his depictions of both the Māori and Pākehā sides in the New Zealand Wars would resurface even more explicitly in later cinematic treatments of this period by Geoff Murphy in *Utu* (1983), and Vincent Ward in *River Queen* (2005). For this reason, Hayward should be considered the father of New Zealand filmmaking not merely because he was the first to make a significant number of fiction feature films, but also because he pointed the way towards a complex, rather than reductive, view of history that later filmmakers would continue to explore.

Notes

1. Michel Foucault, *The Archaeology of Knowledge*, trans. A. M. Sheridan Smith (New York: Pantheon Books, 1972), 44, 46.
2. Hayden White, *Tropics of Discourse: Essays in Cultural Criticism* (Baltimore: Johns Hopkins University Press, 1978), 1.
3. Rudall Hayward, interview with W. B. Harris, 30 August 1961, New Zealand Film Archive, AUD 1380.
4. A convenient edition of *The Adventures of Kimble Bent* by the New Zealand Electronic Text Centre can be found online at http://www.nzetc.org/tm/scholarly/tei-CowKimb.html. Accessed 8 February 2009.
5. Ibid., 286–87.
6. Hayward, interview with W. B. Harris.
7. See Jane Stafford and Mark Williams, *Maoriland: New Zealand Literature 1872–1914* (Wellington: Victoria University Press, 2006), 10–22.
8. Hayward, interview with W. B. Harris; Rudall Hayward, interview with Ray Hayes, 1961, New Zealand Film Archive, CD AUD 1382.
9. Hayward, interview with Ray Hayes.
10. See, for example, the epic poem *Maoriana*, by Elan Westerwood, ed. David S. Westerwood (Dunedin: Whitcombe & Tombs, [c. 1916]), in which the poet refers to "Zealandia's fruitful shore […] The gem of all the southern sea […] More fair than all the Isles of Greece" (XIV, 41).
11. For another interpretation of *My Lady of the Cave* that recognizes an allegorical intent, see Sam Edwards and Stuart Murray, "A Rough Island Story: The Film Life of Rudall Charles Hayward," in *New Zealand Filmmakers*, ed. Ian Conrich and Stuart Murray (Detroit: Wayne State University Press, 2007), 35–53, esp. 39–40. My view differs from theirs, however, in that I see the Pākehā youth as a metaphor for the new settler, rather than the heroine.
12. James Cowan, *The New Zealand Wars: A History of the Maori Campaigns and the Pioneering Period*, 2 vols (1922–23; repr., Wellington: P. D. Hasselberg, Government Printer, 1983), 3.
13. Ibid., 1.
14. Ibid., 2.
15. Ibid., 3.
16. Ibid., 395.
17. Jessie Mackay, "The Charge at Parihaka," in *The New Place: The Poetry of Settlement in New Zealand 1852–1914*, ed. Harvey McQueen (Wellington: Victoria University Press, 1993), 85.
18. Cowan's view of the siege at Ōrākau is very similar to that expressed by Thomas Bracken in his poem "Orakau," published in *Musings in Maoriland* (Dunedin: Arthur T. Keirle, 1890):

> With wild, untutored chivalry the rebels scorn'd disgrace, –
> Oh, never in the annals of the most heroic race
> Was bravery recorded more noble or more high,
> Than that displayed at Orakau in Rewi's fierce reply –
> "*Ka Whawhai tonu! Akè! Akè! Akè!*" (p. 165)

19. See also Reid Perkins, "Imag(in)ing Our Past: Colonial New Zealand on Film from *The Birth of New Zealand* to *The Piano*: Part One," *Illusions* 25 (Winter 1996): 4–10. I consider that Hayward's films on the New Zealand Wars display a greater degree of inherent ambivalence than does Perkins, who subscribes to the view (advanced earlier by Russell Campbell, "In Order that They

May Become Civilized: Pakeha Ideology in *Rewi's Last Stand, Broken Barrier* and *Utu*," *Illusions* 1 (Summer 1986): 4–15), that Hayward reproduces "the pervasive dichotomising of cultural traits as representative of either 'savage' or 'civilised' states of development" (p. 8).

20. *The Te Kooti Trail* Poster [Type 1], New Zealand Film Archive.
21. Westerwood, *Maoriana*, part VI, 205 ff.
22. Cowan, *New Zealand Wars*, 502.
23. *Christian Science Monitor* (USA) [n.d.], clipping held in Rudall Hayward's Papers, New Zealand Film Archive.
24. For the complete text of this poem, see Harvey McQueen, ed., *The New Place: The Poetry of Settlement in New Zealand 1852–1914* (Wellington: Victoria University Press, 1993), 117.
25. See also Bruce Babington, *A History of the New Zealand Fiction Feature Film*, 73.
26. Noted by Babington, *History of the New Zealand Fiction Feature Film*, 74.
27. See S. R. Edwards, "Docudrama from the Twenties: Rudall Hayward, Whakatane, and the Te Kooti Trail," *Historical Review, Bay of Plenty Journal of History* 41, no. 2 (November 1993): 58–65, esp. 59.
28. Rudall Hayward, interview with Jan Bieringa, [n.d.], New Zealand Film Archive, AUD 0356.
29. "The Treaty of Waitangi," New Zealand History Online, http://www.nzhistory.net.nz/culture/centennial/the-centennial-and-the-treaty-of-waitangi. Accessed 14 February 2009.
30. A. W. Reed and Rudall C. Hayward, *Rewi's Last Stand* (Wellington: A. W. Reed and A. H. Reed, 1939), 172.
31. "Interview: Rudall Hayward talks to Walter Harris and Ray Hayes," New Zealand Film Archive, AUD 0835. Hayward records that other scenes cut in the version for British release included: a cold war in existence prior to the Māori war in the Waikato; scenes showing both sides preparing for it; the occurrence of frequent skirmishes; very bad feelings among Pākehā directed against Māori in Auckland; the bravery of Governor George Grey in riding with only one aide into the Waikato; a scene showing Morgan, who had stayed on by himself with his little family after the evacuation of other Pākehā, being harassed by Māori hotheads. Hayward also revealed that Ariana had been based on the historical figure Hariana, a Māori woman who, according to Gilbert Mair, was among the wounded after the battle, and later wished to thank a British soldier who had protected her during the final charge.
32. Diane Pivac, "Rewi's Last Stand," The New Zealand Film Archive, http://www.filmarchive.org.nz/feature-project/pages/Rewis.php. Accessed 13 May 2010.

Chapter 2

Rudall Hayward's Democratic Cinema and the "Civilising Mission" in the "Land of the Wrong White Crowd"

Jeanette Hoorn and Michelle Smith

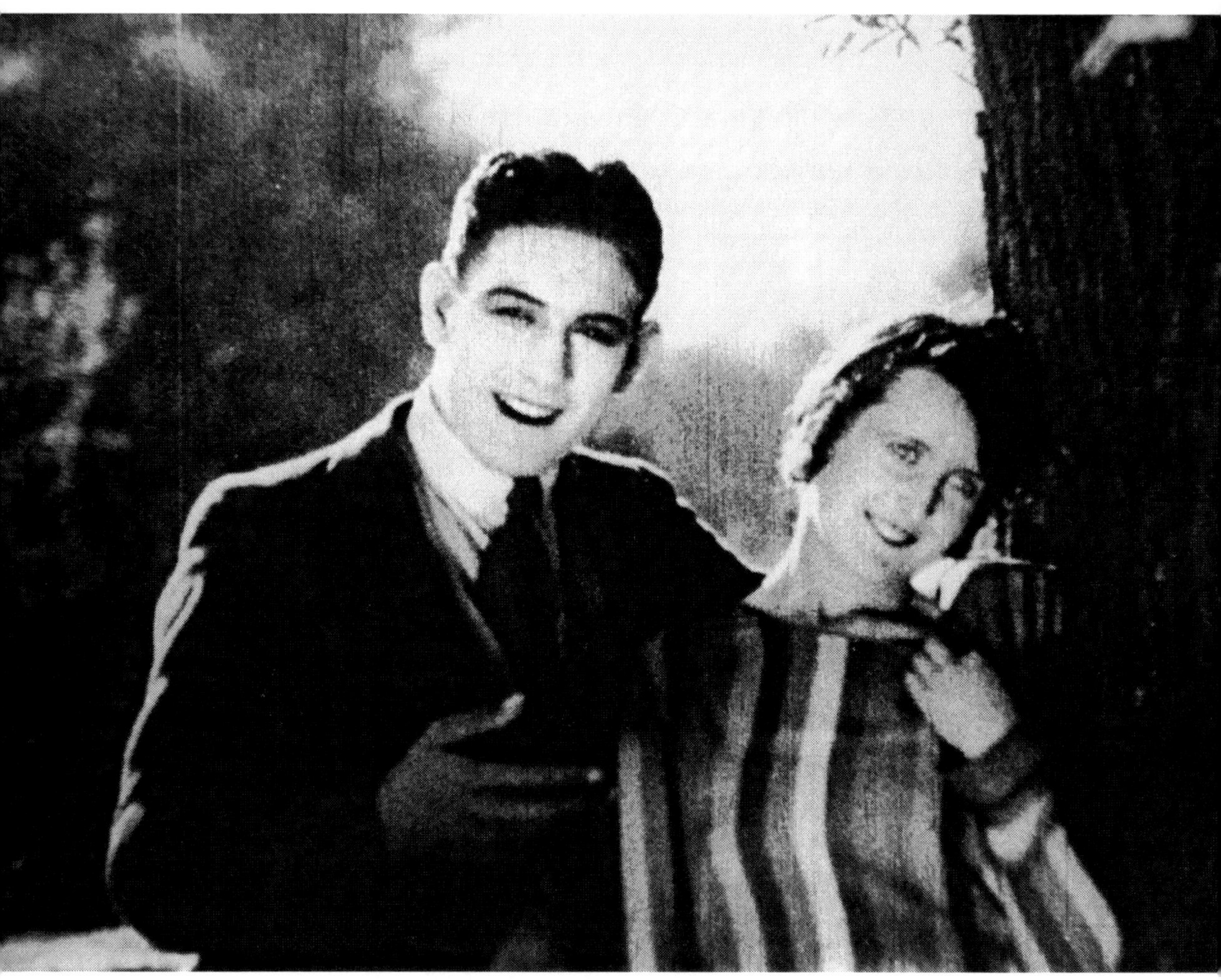

Frame enlargement from *Daughter of Dunedin*, 1928, dir. Rudall Hayward. Courtesy of the Hayward Collection, New Zealand Film Archive Ngā Kaitiaki O Ngā Taonga Whitiāhua.

Between 1928 and 1930, Rudall Hayward made 23 two-reel feature films, which now form a cycle that are referred to as his *community comedies*. These titles took full advantage of the fashion for alliteration of the day featuring *Winifred of Wanganui, Tilly of Te Aroha, Patsy of Palmerston, Natalie of Napier* and *A Daughter of Dunedin*. This chapter argues for a re-assessment of these special silent films which recognises Hayward's cycle as part of an international movement to make more populist films in which everyday people starred in the towns and cities in which they lived. We argue that these remarkable films and other Australasian and American examples constitute a unique manifestation of itinerant filmmaking because of the special ways in which the filmmakers used locality. Relying entirely on what was available in the location in which the films were shot; requiring no studios, professional actors or scriptwriters; and utilising local talent, scenes, architecture and landscape, Hayward produced an exceptional cycle in the history of New Zealand cinema. Fired by socialism and a desire to contribute to New Zealand's emerging national identity through film, he revealed what was possible for a skilful director and cameraman to achieve on a small budget, by involving ordinary people and harnessing community generosity and spirit. Each film followed an identical script, the only differences being the location and cast, which in each case was made up of the citizens of the towns in which each film was shot. Seeing them today is something like watching *Groundhog Day*, but for the viewers of the period who had been involved in making the films and who saw it with their families at the "world premiere" screening at their local theatre, it was an exciting experience.

Significantly, the films record a celebration of the cities in which they were shot as modern, white and, above all, civilised. The vision of New Zealand modernity that is presented is grounded in an image of a homogenous society. By introducing each film with scenes depicting fashionably dressed white men and women amid the hustle and bustle of city life and by foregrounding the motorcar and signs of architectural and horticultural achievement, each film's construction of New Zealand's progress depicts a prosperous white nation. Māori do not appear in any of the community comedies. This at first glance seems at odds with Hayward's career as a filmmaker, which is distinguished by a preoccupation with race relations and with Māori myth and legend, especially in his later films. When Hayward made films set in the past, he focused upon stories about the white settlement of New Zealand and did not avoid the issue of racial conflict. However, the community comedies championed a modern, sophisticated and up to date New Zealand that proudly competed with anywhere in the world when it came to innovation and industry. It followed that the modern New Zealand "self" constructed in these films, as a sign of the successful establishment of civilisation, is white, and that Māori are not part of the celebration of the cultural achievements of each New Zealand city that the films present.

In addition to examining the films' engagement with race through the absence of Māori, we will also consider their relationship with the subject of modernity in gendered terms. This cycle of films was produced at a time when modern femininity, a fascination with Hollywood stardom and the beauty contest, and the desire to send New Zealand talent to the United States collided. The films were marketed as bringing something of the US film industry to culturally isolated New Zealand, as reflected in Hayward's company name "Hollywood on Tour." Interestingly, this type of itinerant filmmaking popularised in New Zealand's community comedies and comparable Australian examples may have fed back to the United States, with the majority of similar extant American examples emerging from the mid-1930s. The potential reverse flow of the genre from Australia and New Zealand to the United States defies conventional thinking of a largely one-way transmission of cultural forms from America.

Hayward's series of comic-burlesque films were set in New Zealand's towns and cities as were those of his offsider, Lee Hill, who made four more. Hill had worked on Hayward's films and branched off on his own, making *Mary of Morton, Nellie of Nelson, Betty of Blenheim* and *Frances of Fielding* by working with exactly the same formula. All four of Hill's films have survived, whereas only four of Hayward's still exist: *A Daughter of Dunedin, A Daughter of Invercargill, A Daughter of Christchurch* and *A Daughter of Masterton* are what remain of Hayward's 23. These were prefigured by *The Bush Cinderella* (1928), which shared a number of their themes though it had aspirations to being a more serious and rounded portrait of the trials of a young woman which took on some of the interests of Raymond Longford's *The Woman Suffers* (1918).

The origins of the community comedies' storyline, in which rival suitors battle for the heroine's affection, building to a climactic kidnapping and car chase, were likely American. Chris Watson notes that school board elections, which figure among the films' stock scenes along with shots of the local fire brigade and schoolchildren, were not conducted as they are in the films in New Zealand.[1] The script may have arrived in New Zealand from the United States via Australia, given the degree of similarity between the plot of the earlier "Adventures of Dot" films, discussed later, and the community comedies. Lee Hill did work with the Australian production company prior to involvement with Hayward's itinerant films, so it is possible that he brought the script with him to New Zealand.

The presence and absence of race in Hayward's *oeuvre*

Hayward's films appealed to local values and pride that to a certain extent avoided the nationalistic rhetoric of the First World War and the inter-war years. They were, nevertheless, strictly Pākehā. Set in cities and towns throughout the country, from the top of the North Island to the bottom of the South, viewers could have no inkling of the existence of a substantial Māori minority in New Zealand by looking at them. There is no discussion of the interaction of Pākehā and Māori in the films at all, and it is hard to find any indigenous faces, even in the panning shots of crowds that appear regularly. A simple explanation for the absence of Māori from Hayward's community comedies is that they would not have been physically located in the cities and towns in this period. This prompts the question of why Māori were absent from the country's major cities, and what significance this holds for the presentation of modernity in Hayward's films.

The community comedies are, in fact, about the whitening of New Zealand and the introduction of British culture. The spoils of modern civilisation are abundantly portrayed through new motorcars, women's and men's fashion, the new woman, commerce, architecture, and civic pride witnessed through botanic gardens and well appointed public squares. But Māori are not part of this narrative. Much of what is celebrated replicates quintessentially British symbols such as *A Daughter of Christchurch's* visual focus on "punting on the Avon" and the flowing expanse of the Botanic Gardens' rose bushes. The community series operates in a white bubble that celebrates the success of the civilising mission in converting New Zealand from a southern wilderness into a prosperous European community in which commerce, fashion and the exigencies of modern life are represented in an orderly and seemly fashion and in which there is no hint of the displacement of Māori or even the existence of a powerful indigenous community. The films, unlike many of those which were to come from Hayward's stable, are shamelessly populist, designed to appeal to a broad audience and modelled on Hollywood prototypes in which race is only represented in pejorative ways.

As mentioned earlier, the absence of discussion or reference to race issues in the series is not typical of Rudall Hayward's film oeuvre. Several of his early features were taken up with race issues, including his first, *My Lady of the Cave* (1922), followed by *Rewi's Last Stand* (1925) (later remade in sound as *The Last Stand* in 1940), and *The Te Kooti Trail* (1927). The films that he made after he married his leading lady, Ramai Te Miha, who is of Māori descent and now a very senior and revered elder in the Māori community in Auckland, were very engaged with race relations. His interaction with cultural tensions in these films produced a representation of Māori that is, according to Sam Edwards and Stuart Murray, "positive," but "firmly immersed with Pakeha logic."[2] They go on to suggest that the Pākehā version of New Zealand life contained in the community comedies outlines a model of success related to the "dynamics of settlement," attaining a husband and setting up the possibility of starting a family.[3] However, an important part of the ritual of finding a partner – the central plot point of the comedies – must be considered in light of the absence of Māori visibility in the films. The romance plot unfolds within a white world in which any obvious cultural differences between Māori and Pākehā have been assimilated to a white norm, as in the casting of "Tiff" Bennett in the role of Bill Cowcocky in *A Daughter of Dunedin*. Bennett, although himself of Maori descent,[4] looks white, and embodies a stereotypical Pākehā masculine type. The universality of whiteness in the representation of each city across the cycle sets up a dynamic that Richard Dyer describes as equating whiteness with "the human condition" that therefore

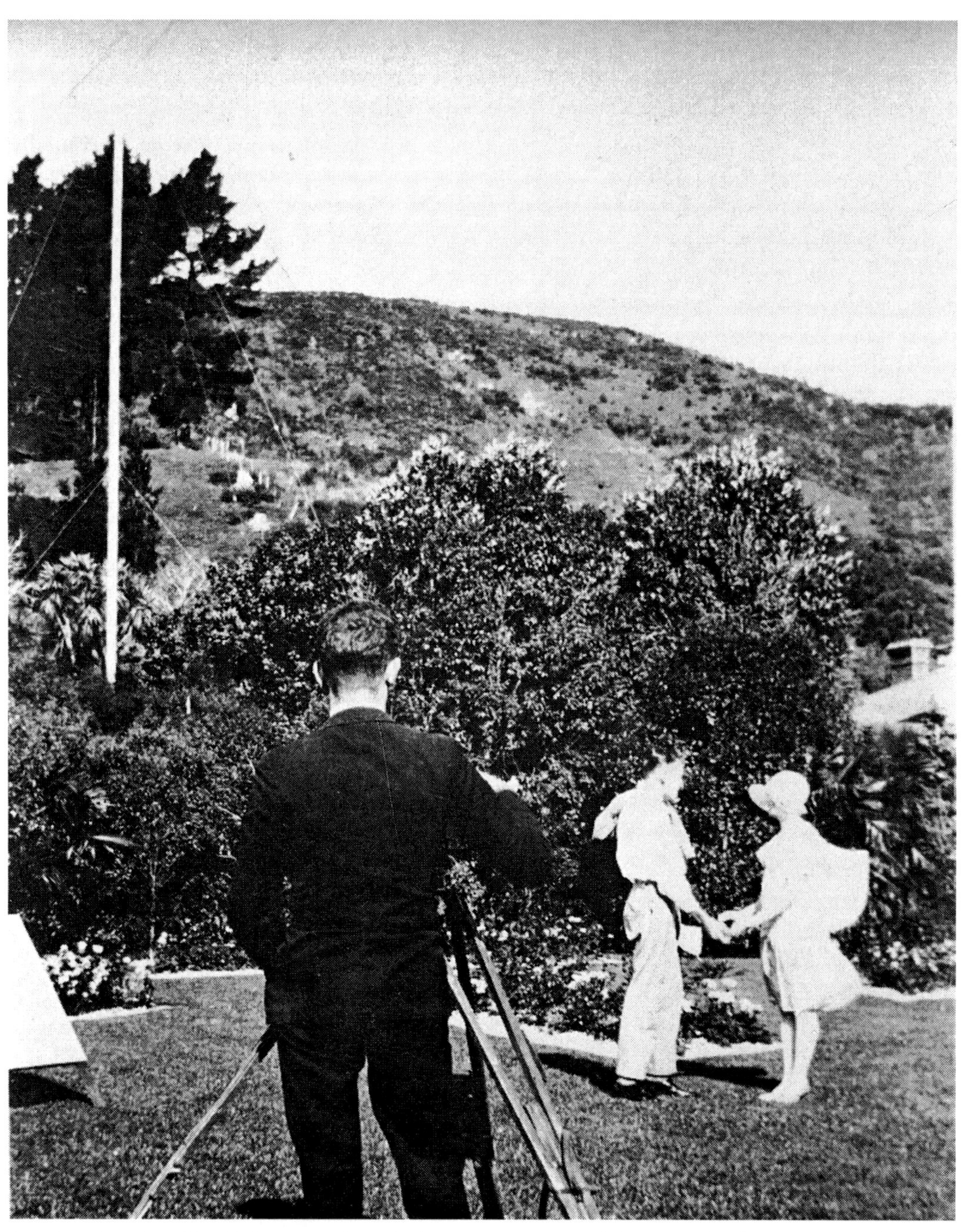

Location shoot for *Nellie of Nelson*, 1928, dir. Rudall Hayward. Courtesy of the Hayward Collection, New Zealand Film Archive Ngā Kaitiaki O Ngā Taonga Whitiāhua.

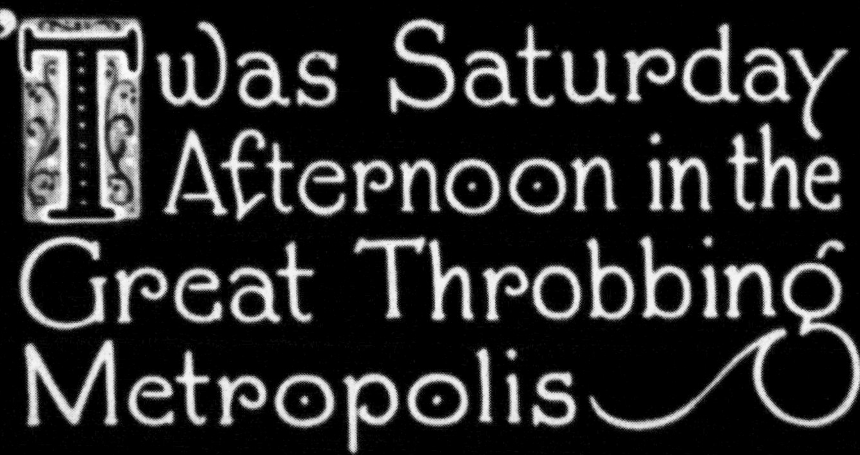

Intertitle from *Daughter of Dunedin*, 1928, dir. Rudall Hayward. Courtesy of the Hayward Collection, New Zealand Film Archive Ngā Kaitiaki O Ngā Taonga Whitiāhua.

"secures a position of power."[5] The pervasive whiteness constitutes an underlying expression of how power operated in early-twentieth century New Zealand in relation to race.

Linked to the films' showcasing of successful white settlement is their display of pride in its modernisation. In *A Daughter of Christchurch*, achievements in cultivating the environment to conform to civilised norms are emphasised through the display of "one of the finest" rose gardens "in the Southern hemisphere." New Zealand's progress and achievements are shown to be keeping pace with other former colonies and dominions. Modernisation is most obviously apparent in the cities bustling with pedestrians, coaches and motorcars. The city centre itself is viewed through sped-up footage, making the pace of life appear quicker and size of the population greater than the reality. Intertitles refer to each city as a "Great Throbbing Metropolis," which is "Getting more like New York every day." The degree of civilisation is being measured not only in contrast with British norms but also in light of the America that New Zealanders knew so well from the cinema.

Situating the community comedies within the history of itinerant filmmaking

The community comedies occupy a special place in the history of the cinema, along with other little-known or "orphan" examples of formulaic, itinerant films produced within local communities and for local audiences in two of the countries with greatest cultural influence on New Zealand. Hayward's films may have been influenced by American and Australian examples of itinerant filmmaking that were flourishing in the late-1920s. Dan Streible has written in detail about an "orphaned" 1926 silent film from Anderson, South Carolina that recreated the popular "Our Gang" comedies and showcased the town's children.[6] Closer in subject matter to the New Zealand community comedies, father and son duo Daniel B. Dorn and Daniel W. Dorn produced 35 short films in and around New Jersey from 1927 that were designed to devote screen time to local businesses, schools and churches. Roger Smither points out that the itinerant film was suited to "dispersed, largely rural communities" such as these New Jersey locations and country towns in Australia and New Zealand.[7] In the same year as the Dorns began their films, director Cyril J. Sharpe and cameraman Reginald Young produced *The Adventures of Dot*, a series of silent films shot throughout rural New South Wales, Australia. There are three surviving films, featuring the towns of Grenfell, Young and Temora, which share the community comedies' plot of a schoolteacher pursued by two suitors. The similarities between the "Dot" films and Hayward's include standard shots of groups of schoolchildren, the conduct of a municipal election, a false newspaper story designed to blacken the name of the hero, and the drama of a fire brigade call-out to extinguish a blaze. There is also another, lesser-known Australian series of local short films, none of which has survived. This series was produced as a promotional venture by production manager William R. Reed and cameraman Dal Clauson, using a script by Jack McLaughlin. The first was a three-reel film made and screened at the Capitol Theatre, Tamworth, on 5 February 1928, entitled *Tam of Tamworth*. It replicated the conventions of

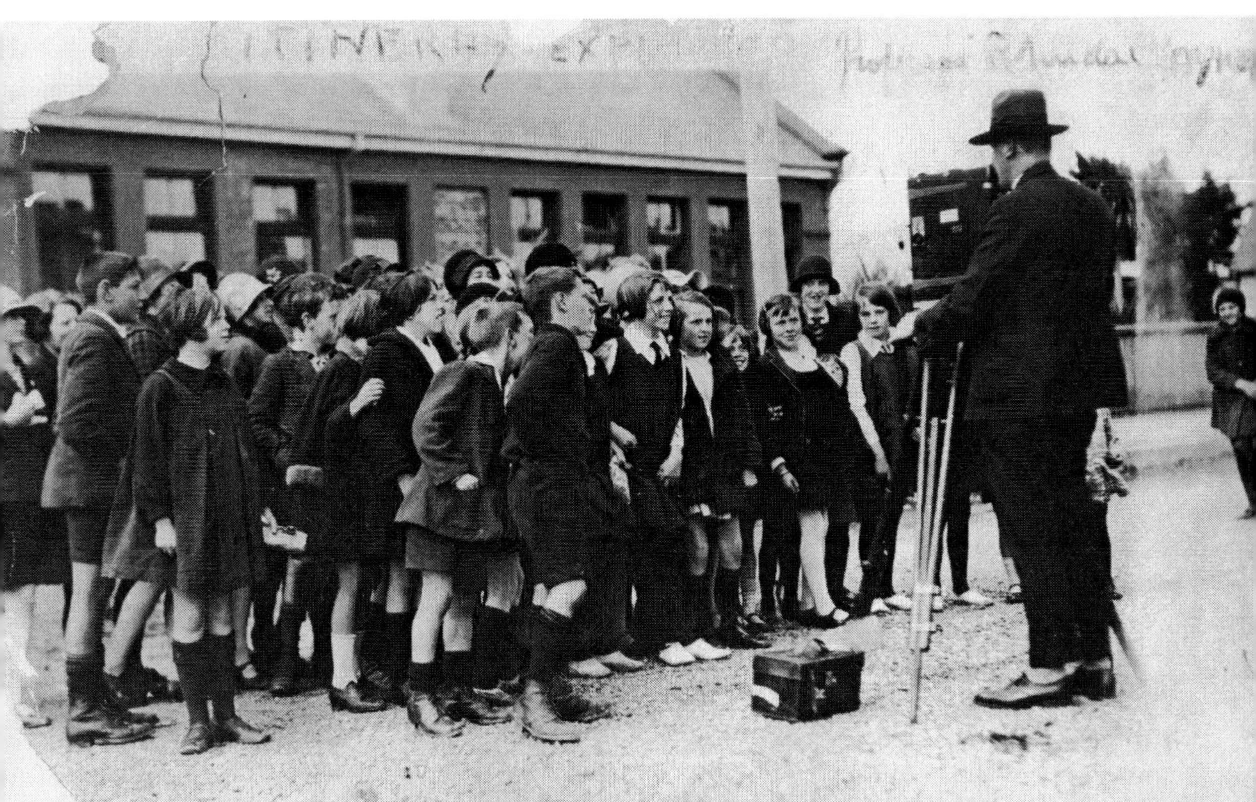

Rudall Hayward filming children during the production of *Daughter of Invercargill*, 1928, dir. Rudall Hayward. Courtesy of the Hayward Collection, New Zealand Film Archive Ngā Kaitiaki O Ngā Taonga Whitiāhua.

using a local cast and the plot also reportedly contained the stock-standard fire sequence. Other films with the same premise and alliterative titles were produced, including *Olive of Orange* and *Priscilla of Parkes* and, according to Eric Reade, locations covered a large area of New South Wales from Grafton to Wollongong.[8]

Apart from the Dorns in New Jersey, however, Hayward's community comedies constitute the largest known collection of local silent films produced in this era, being filmed in 23 different New Zealand cities and primarily designed for local consumption in the city in which they were filmed. They all followed the same formula, with similar intertitles and with the same plot and narrative structure. When a teacher arrives in town, she is courted by two suitors, one a good fellow, a farmer, called Bill Cowcocky, the other a newspaper reporter and a villain who in each film goes by the name of Freddy Fishface. In his attempts to win the heroine's affection, Freddy tries to blacken the name of the farmer by writing a false story about him in his newspaper, which turns the heroine against him. The hero spends the rest of the film trying to win the schoolteacher back, and after kidnappings and exciting chase scenes, in the end good triumphs over evil. Filmed in different locations in New Zealand, each uses the same script, which is adapted to the conditions of the city or town in which it is set so as to allow local attractions or pastimes to be featured. In addition, each film used amateur actors from the local area as well as using local talent and members of the community as extras. There are large panning shots of the primary school children from the local school, and of crowds that made up the extras for a number of scenes, as well as members of the local polo club, the fire brigade and scenes incorporating the wives of the cities' prominent men all sporting bobs and short skirts.

The films were a raging success, attracting large crowds to the screenings in the cities where they had been made. In an interview held in the New Zealand Film Archive, Hayward described their popularity: "You couldn't keep them out the theatre with iron bars."[9] The films were also very inexpensive to make. Shot over a few days, they involved principal actors recruited with well-publicised "auditions," together with many crowd scenes. Very soon, while excitement was still hot, as Chris Watson, who has written about the Lee Hill films, points out, the "world premiere" was organised in the local cinema. The obvious irony is that, at the time, any New Zealand film was unlikely to travel much further than its homeland. Hayward's community comedies generated a unique resonance given the isolation of New Zealand and its fledgling film industry so distant from Hollywood. New Zealand had a comparatively large number of theatres and relatively high attendance figures, and its largest supplier of films from 1914 onwards (excluding 1915), well ahead of Britain and Australia, was the United States.[10] The sheer mass of imported American entertainment consumed in New Zealand led journalist and eventual film censor Gordon Mirams to comment in the 1940s: "If there is any such thing as a 'New Zealand culture' it is to a large extent the creation of Hollywood."[11]

Gender, modernity and manufactured "stars"

A Daughter of Dunedin was among the most popular of the community comedies, possibly because it featured Dale Austen, the actress from Hayward's previous film, *The Bush Cinderella* (1928), in the lead. Austen had won her role in *The Bush Cinderella* as part of her prize as the reigning Miss New Zealand. The beauty quest, advertised as a "Search for a Screen Type," was sponsored by the Fuller-Hayward chain (the largest theatre circuit in New Zealand) and Metro-Goldwyn-Mayer, and Austen won her crown courtesy of the votes of 250,000 theatre patrons. This complex relationship between the cinema, the beauty queen and the public spectacle of the contest did not end there, as Austen was also awarded an acting contract including travel to Hollywood as Miss New Zealand.

The cinema constituted a crucial aspect in the formation of the modern feminine ideal of the 1920s. Brigette Søland argues that the "energetic physicality" of movie stars captivated young women internationally after the First World War: "For young women it was this combination of a healthy, active, and energetic body and an exuberant personality [embodied by the movie star] that constituted a 'modern' female style."[12] This modern femininity is clearly evident in the dress of the young women featured in the community comedies. The films reflect the revolution in the manners and dress of the middle-class that was taking place in other Western nations. Like elsewhere, the 1920s in New Zealand saw the transformation of women's and men's bodies from a formal style of dress and comportment to a more relaxed and less rigid set of parameters. All of the heroines in the community comedies are new women. All emulate the modern boyish look made famous by Coco Chanel and have their hair cut in a bob and wear cloche hats, which were also all the rage. All wear dresses either just above or just below the knee. In the scenes in which the heroine mixes with a group of upper-class women, all have bobs and all are dressed *à la mode*. The heroes also wear the latest male fashions, with white flannels and bright ties the order of the day.

During the First World War, New Zealand held provincial "Queen" carnivals to raise money for the war effort. Various districts and companies chose a queen, usually a married woman or spinster, to head their bid to raise money. While these wartime queens were celebrated for their virtuousness, by the 1920s physical appearance and youth had taken precedence. Sandra Coney notes that after the First World War, the ideal body shape became less voluptuous and thinner, and the transformation from the "matronly, mature ideal of beauty to a youth one was marked in New Zealand by a series of beauty contests and film quests in the late 1920s which provoked an astonishing level of public interest."[13] The new idealised femininity of the 1920s was wrapped up in ideas of beauty and fame. In particular, the New Zealand public was captivated by the prospect of one of its own "daughters" finding success in the American film industry it so readily ingested. When Dale Austen left for Hollywood after winning Miss Otago, thousands thronged the railway station to bid her farewell on her journey to stardom.

The audition process for the community comedies tapped into the same concept of public spectacle as beauty pageants that offered related prizes and held the allure of travel to Hollywood. Similar contests that invoked beauty, national identity and the cinema were held in Australia. Beryl Mills, the first Miss Australia in 1926, toured the United States as an advertisement for Australian girlhood and subsequently made public appearances at picture theatres in New South Wales. In her study of the way in which popular images of women were used by countries to define their relations with one another, Liz Conor suggests that "In Australia, the search for national authenticity, indeed cultural distinctiveness, was carried on by opposing the fraudulent American cinema to a naturalistic Australian cinema."[14] By contrast, New Zealand's desire for *its* own girls to become Hollywood stars, evidenced by the public interest in these competitions, speaks to its immersion in American popular culture, as does the replication of several distinctly American stock scenes in Hayward's community comedies. Nevertheless, there are elements that define a unique New Zealand identity that resist a reading of straightforward reproduction of Hollywood conventions in Hayward's films. For one, as Chris Watson suggests, the villain Freddy Fishface is portrayed as a stereotyped American figure and is costumed to resemble 1920s silent film star Harold Lloyd.[15]

Auditions for the community comedies were publicised heavily in each local area, serving to drum up interest not only among the town's aspiring actors and beauty queens but also functioning as a promotional forerunner to the screening of the finished film. A generic advertisement produced in 1929 to attract townspeople to participate in Hayward's films connected the search for movie stars with refining New Zealand's identity. Likening film to the developing nation itself, which was declared an independent dominion only 17 years earlier, the circular proclaimed that "The dominion's film industry, now rapidly emerging from the days of infancy to those of lusty childhood [...] is in need of Screen Personalities." The creation of Hayward's community comedies can be situated as part of a process in which the New Zealand film industry gradually developed its own identity. As part of this self-definition, these films importantly promised and delivered the prospect of ordinary New Zealand citizens viewing themselves and their neighbours on the screen. This idea constituted a predominant aspect of the films' marketing. *Patsy of Palmerston*, for instance, was promoted as not only featuring the three leads, but also "Charming Palmerston girls, the fire brigade, Rough-riding cowboys, and hundreds of citizens and bonny schoolchildren." Local scenery and local "gags" are also mentioned in the advertisement, enabling New Zealand surroundings, rather than the backgrounds of the cinematically familiar United States, to be highlighted. Nevertheless, the most exciting element of the films is clearly the potential to see "yourself as others see you!"

Looking at the genealogy of these films, it is clear that, in addition to American and Australian itinerant films of the same era, they owe a great deal to the adventure films involving flappers and new women that were being made in the early twentieth century, from those starring the Australian actress Fearless Nadia in Bollywood to Pearl White's *The Perils of Pauline* in Hollywood from 1914 into the 1920s. They shared in common an interest in using alliteration to full effect in their titles as well as in the names of those who starred in the productions. Films such as *Rio Rita* (1929), *Flapper Fever* (1924), *The Expert Eloper*

Have You a Screen Personality?
IF SO---NEW ZEALAND NEEDS YOU!

The Dominion's film industry, now rapidly emerging from the days of infancy to those of lusty childhood, and likely to be helped in the near future by legislation now before the New Zealand Parliament, is in need of Screen Personalities. Among the million and a-quarter people who inhabit these fair isles, there must be some within whom the spark of true screen genius lies dormant.

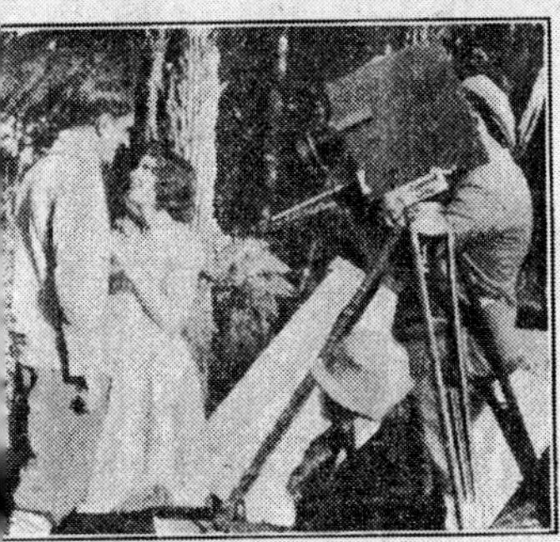

Mr. Hayward directing Dale Austen and Cecil Scott in "The Bush Cinderella."

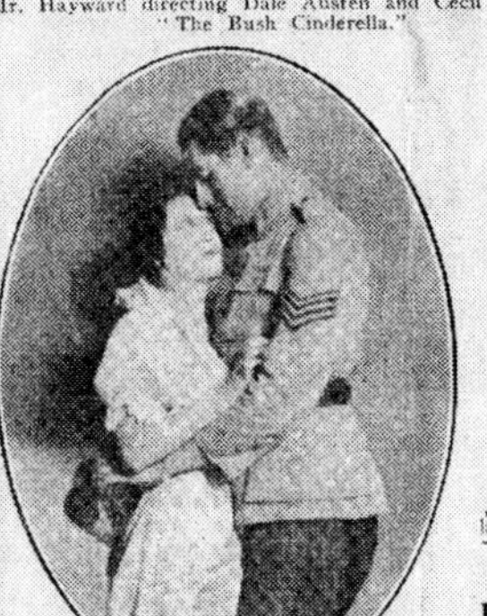

Mr. Tony Firth plays opposite Miss Dale Austen in "The Bush Cinderella," a role he earned through his performance in a local amateur film.

THE VALUE OF LOCAL COMMUNITY FILMS.

The Local Community Films Mr. Rudall Hayward is producing in the various towns throughout New Zealand are calculated to be the means of discovering many Dominion screen types.

Local amateur theatrical folk and screen aspirants will be given every opportunity to reveal their talents under skilled direction and actual studio conditions.

ORIGINATED IN NEW ZEALAND BY MR. HAYWARD.

The idea of a town making its own film production came from America, but the first community film to be made here, "Hamilton Husbands," was produced by Mr. Hayward at Hamilton last May, and proved an astonishing success. As a result of it, Mr. Tony Firth, one of the Hamilton players, was given a contract and played opposite Miss Dale Austen ("Miss New Zealand") in Mr. Hayward's latest big production "The Bush Cinderella."

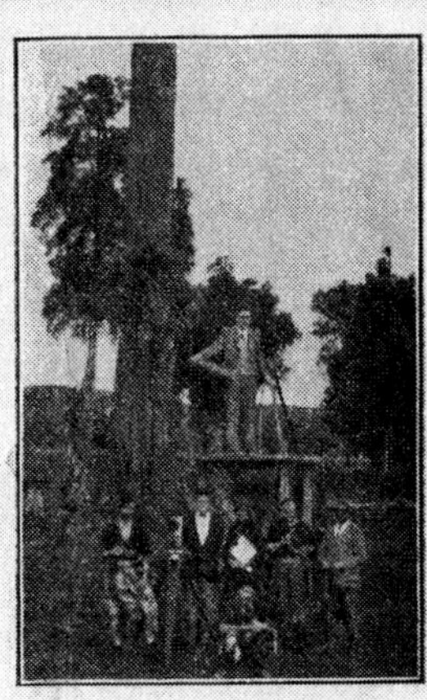

Mr. Hayward (on platform) directing some of the bush-fighting scenes in "The Te Kooti Trail."

PLAYERS SHOWING ANY PROMISE IN THE FILM BEING PRODUCED HERE WILL BE TABULATED BY THE PRODUCER FOR FUTURE REFERENCE WHEN SELECTING THE CAST OF HIS BIG PICTURES.

REMEMBER! MR. RUDALL HAYWARD IS THE ONLY PROFESSIONAL NEW ZEALAND FILM PRODUCER AT PRESENT OPERATING. FOR THE LAST EIGHT YEARS HE HAS BEEN CONTINUOUSLY ENGAGED IN MAKING DOMINION FILMS WITH MARKED SUCCESS.

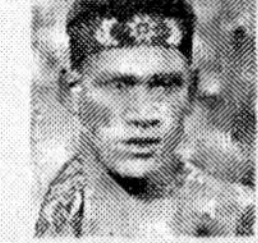

Mr. Patiti Warbrick, a Maori star discovered by Mr. Hayward, and now playing lead with the Universal Company.

Acting applicants advertising circular for Rudall Hayward's Community Comedies (1928). Courtesy of the Hayward Collection, New Zealand Film Archive Ngā Kaitiaki O Ngā Taonga Whitiāhua.

(1919), *The Mating of Marcella* (1918), *Moonshine Molly* (1913), as well as *Wild and Woolly Women* (1917) and *The Bondage of Barbara* (1919) were all part of Hollywood's response to new and sexually daring roles for women in the cinema.

But perhaps the most prominent of this series and probably the greatest influence on Hayward may well have been the *Perils of Pauline* series. These deal with the fate of a young heiress kidnapped by villains whose interest it is to prevent her from gaining the inheritance which is rightfully hers; inevitably there is a kidnapping scene in which Pauline is truly placed in peril, and in which she is famously tied to the railway tracks, rescued seconds before a locomotive looms before her. The narrative of a *Bush Cinderella*, the feature film that Hayward made before embarking on the community comedies, took from the narrative of *The Perils of Pauline*. Like Pauline, *The Bush Cinderella*, or at least her daughter (both are played by Dale Austen in the film), is left an inheritance when her wealthy uncle dies, and whose secretary attempts to prevent her from gaining her inheritance, seeking to keep it for himself. The fact that the secretaries of uncles in both the *Perils of Pauline* films and in *Bush Cinderella* are the villain cannot be a coincidence. All of the community comedies, unlike the Australian "Dot" films, involve what are supposed to be dramatic kidnapping and chase scenes. Another commonality between American silent serials like the *Perils of Pauline* and Hayward's films is the tension between celebrating and restraining modern femininity. Shelley Stamp argues that the *Perils of Pauline* films functioned as cautionary tales "in which independence is always circumscribed by the shadow of danger, the determinacy of familial ties, and the inevitability of marriage."[16] While the limitations of the itinerant filmmaking formula did not allow for the same degree of narrative subtlety, the community comedies similarly safely contain the lives of the independent female schoolteacher heroines through marriage. Distinctly, the courtship narrative is concerned not only with placing bounds around modern femininity but also about continuing to secure the modernisation and whitening of New Zealand's cities.

The impact and legacy of the silent "See Yourself in the Movies" genre

Hayward's political orientations reflected the democratic temper for which New Zealand and Australia were famous in the first decades of the twentieth century. There was a strong civic interest in popular culture in New Zealand, reflected in the enormous popularity of cinema. According to the New Zealand historians Barbara Brookes, Erik Olssen and Emma Beer in their study of women, men and modernity in Southern Dunedin, by 1916 more than a third of the population went to the movies once a week.[17] The Queens Theatre on Princess Street screened films continuously from midday until 10.30 pm, and most picture palaces had two three-hour sessions every day except Sundays. Hayward's uncle, Henry Hayward, was the largest theatre owner and film distributor in New Zealand in the 1920s. The Haywards were outspoken socialists and religious sceptics. They celebrated the values of the ordinary bloke. The socialist point of view evident in their films is later reflected in the emergence of a school of socially oriented historians, such as the prominent left-wing historian William

Pember Reeves and Keith Sinclair, whose work, as John Stenhouse has argued, promoted New Zealand as "a city upon a hill," pioneering enlightened race relations, votes for women, industrial and labour legislation, age pensions and humane and progressive politics.[18]

In this phase of Rudall Hayward's career, we might identify a peculiar cinema emerging out of the local, the popular, the communal – indeed, there seems to have been for a brief period a form of local cinema which operated in parameters defined by geographical and regional boundaries that is rare in the international history of the cinema. This was a cinema that could function on a relatively low budget because it did not require a costly professional cast of actors or scriptwriters whose task it was to produce original scripts from scratch. Itinerant filmmakers producing local films emerged at the end of the silent era, before production requirements would ostensibly have precluded such inexpensive and hastily completed films. Hayward recalled in a 1962 interview that later films produced with sound did not approach the popularity of the silents from the late 1920s.[19]

As a curious footnote, there are American silent examples that were produced long after the arrival of sound and New Zealand's community comedies. The "See Yourself in the Movies" genre proliferated in the 1930s and 1940s in the United States, much later than in New Zealand. Stephanie Elaine Stewart suggests that sound was not introduced in these films because it was unnecessary, with "audience dialogue" (upon recognition of friends and family) becoming "the primary sound accompaniment."[20] The only known American itinerant female director and cinematographer, Margaret Cram Showalter, shot a series of silent films with a 16mm camera in New England towns from 1936 to 1939. These films, such as *Bar Harbor* and *Queen* (1936), which are documented in detail by archivists Karan Sheldon and Dwight Swanson,[21] clearly connect the heroine, played by a local actress, with the idea of Hollywood fame. The actress played the part of a Hollywood star or "movie queen" who returns to her hometown, visits local stores (which may have paid for the privilege of "product placement"), and who is then kidnapped and subsequently rescued by the local hero. By 1941, the genre was still being produced in America and in colour "See Yourself in the Movies" films finally came into vogue.

Itinerant director H. Lee Waters' produced over two hundred and fifty silent "Movies of Local People" between 1936 and 1942 in the Carolinas, Virginia and Tennessee. All were shot in black and white until the final two years of his productions.[22] Like Hayward's films, Waters' movies of local people were advertised in local newspapers with taglines such as "See Yourself as Others See You." He distinctively immortalised a diverse cross-section of the communities in which he filmed, including both African Americans and white Americans in each town, despite the era of segregation in which both sections of the community could not view his films in the same theatre.[23] Notably, his multi-racial *Kannapolis N.C.* (1941) has been included in the Library of Congress Film Registry for its rare record of African American life that was otherwise excluded from the filmic archive of the first half of the twentieth century. Hayward's earlier community comedies do not achieve this same outcome, excluding non-white New Zealanders from their celebration of modernity and settlement.

More than a decade earlier, for a short period between 1928 and 1930, there emerged a third level or genre of filmmaking that complemented the international and national cinema that was already emerging in New Zealand. Its nature was indeed local; it relied entirely on what was available in the location in which it was shot. It required no studios, no professional actors or scriptwriters and utilised local talent, scenes, architecture and landscape. These films drew on American and Australian itinerant filmmaking influences and participated in a celebration of modern New Zealand and modern femininity, but did so within the context of white settlement and civilising discourse. While they are democratic reflections of modernity and depict a cross-section of the white community in each town and were produced in an egalitarian spirit, the Māori population is not evident. Given Rudall Hayward's interest in exploring race relations in many of his other films, the absence of Māori from the community comedies seems to isolate them as producing an image of a modern white cuture in which, intentionally or otherwise, a kind of apartheid is in operation. However, his employment of Tiff Bennett in "whiteface" in *A Daughter of Dunedin*, although it is a one-off case, is still a significant exception. Audiences outside of Dunedin may not have known who Tiff Bennett was, but some in the local audiences may have recognised him as Māori. In a strange way, a faux inter-racial romance, one that could be seen to operate through disguise, is nevertheless achieved in *A Daughter of Dunedin*. This prevents the cycle from being entirely about white settler progress in New Zealand – instead a role for Māori is forged through camouflage. While these community comedies are about the success of the white "civilising mission" in New Zealand, the appearance of Tiff Bennett in a role opposite Dale Austen points to the complex and complicated dynamics at work in the colonial project where "white" did not always mean white.

Notes

1. Chris Watson, "*Frances of Fielding* (Lee Hill, 1928) – A Community Comedy: New Zealand's Populist Answer to Hollywood," *Screening the Past* 8 (1999): http://www.latrobe.edu.au/screeningthepast/firstrelease/fr1199/cwfr8c.htm.
2. Sam Edwards and Stuart Murray, "A Rough Island Story: The Film Life of Rudall Charles Hayward," in *New Zealand Filmmakers*, ed. Ian Conrich and Stuart Murray (Detroit, MI: Wayne State University Press, 2007), 44.
3. Edwards and Murray, 45.
4. I am grateful to Jane Paul of the New Zealand Film Archive for drawing this to my attention.
5. Richard Dyer, *White* (London and New York: Routledge, 1997), 9.
6. Dan Streible, "Itinerant Filmmakers and Amateur Casts: A Homemade 'Our Gang', 1926," *Film History* 15 (2003): 177–92.
7. Roger Smither, "'Watch the Picture Carefully, and see if You Can Identify Anyone': Recognition in Factual Film of the First World War Period," *Film History* 14.3/4 (2002): 392.
8. Eric Reade, *History and Heartburn: The Saga of Australian Film, 1896–1978* (East Brunswick, NJ: Associated University Presses, 1981), 64.

9. "Tracking Shots: New Zealand on Film," *New Zealand Film Archive*, http://www.filmarchive.org.nz/tracking-shots/close-ups/TopTowns.html. Accessed 20 December 2008.

10. Miles Fairburn, "Is There a Good Case for New Zealand Exceptionalism," in *Disputed Histories: Imagining New Zealand's Pasts*, ed. Tony Ballantyne and Brian Moloughney (Dunedin: Otago University Press, 2006), 155.

11. Gordon Mirams, *Speaking Candidly: Films and People in New Zealand* (Hamilton, NZ: Paul's, 1945), 5.

12. Birgitte Søland, *Becoming Modern: Young Women and the Reconstruction of Womanhood in the 1920s* (Princeton and Oxford: Princeton University Press, 2000), 60.

13. Sandra Coney, *Standing in the Sunshine: A History of New Zealand Women Since They Won the Vote* (Auckland: Penguin, 1993), 146.

14. Liz Conor, *The Spectacular Modern Woman: Feminine Visibility in the 1920s* (Bloomington and Indianapolis: Indiana University Press, 2004), 89–90.

15. Watson, *"Frances of Fielding."*

16. Shelley Stamp, *Movie-Struck Girls: Women and Motion Picture Culture after the Nickelodeon* (Princeton, NJ: Princeton University Press, 2000), 126.

17. Barbara Brookes, Erick Olssen and Emma Beer, "Spare Time? Leisure, Gender and Modernity," in *Sites of Gender: Women, Men and Modernity in Southern Dunedin, 1890–1939*, ed. Barbara Lesley Brookes, Annabel Cooper and Robin Law (Auckland: Auckland University Press, 2003), 182.

18. John Stenhouse, "God, the Devil and Gender," in *Sites of Gender: Women, Men and Modernity in Southern Dunedin, 1890–1939*, ed. Barbara Lesley Brookes, Annabel Cooper and Robin Law (Auckland: Auckland University Press, 2003), 318.

19. Rudall Hayward interview with Walter Harris and Ray Hayes, 1962. Held at the New Zealand Film Archive. Reference Number A0004.

20. Stephanie Elaine Stewart, "Movies of a Local People and a Usable Past: Mill Town Treasures and Transcendent Views, 1936–1942," *The Moving Image* 7, no. 1 (2007): 57.

21. Karan Sheldon and Dwight Swanson, "The Movie Queen: Northeast Historic Film," in *Mining the Home Movie: Excavations in Histories and Memories*, ed. Karen L. Ishizuka and Patricia R. Zimmerman (Berkeley: University of California Press, 2008), 185–90.

22. Stewart, "Movies of a Local People," 52.

23. Waters also produced some films exclusively in African American sections of towns for screening in black theatres.

24. "Tiff" Bennett is likely to have been Frederick Te Tiwha (Tiff) Bennett (b. 1906 in Rotorua), who studied at the University of Orago, graduating as Bachelor of Dental Surgery (http://teaohou.natlib.govt.nz/journals/teaohou/issue/mao60TeA/c1.html).

Chapter 3

The Western, New Zealand History and Commercial Exploitation:
The Te Kooti Trail, *Utu* and *Crooked Earth*[1]

Harriet Margolis

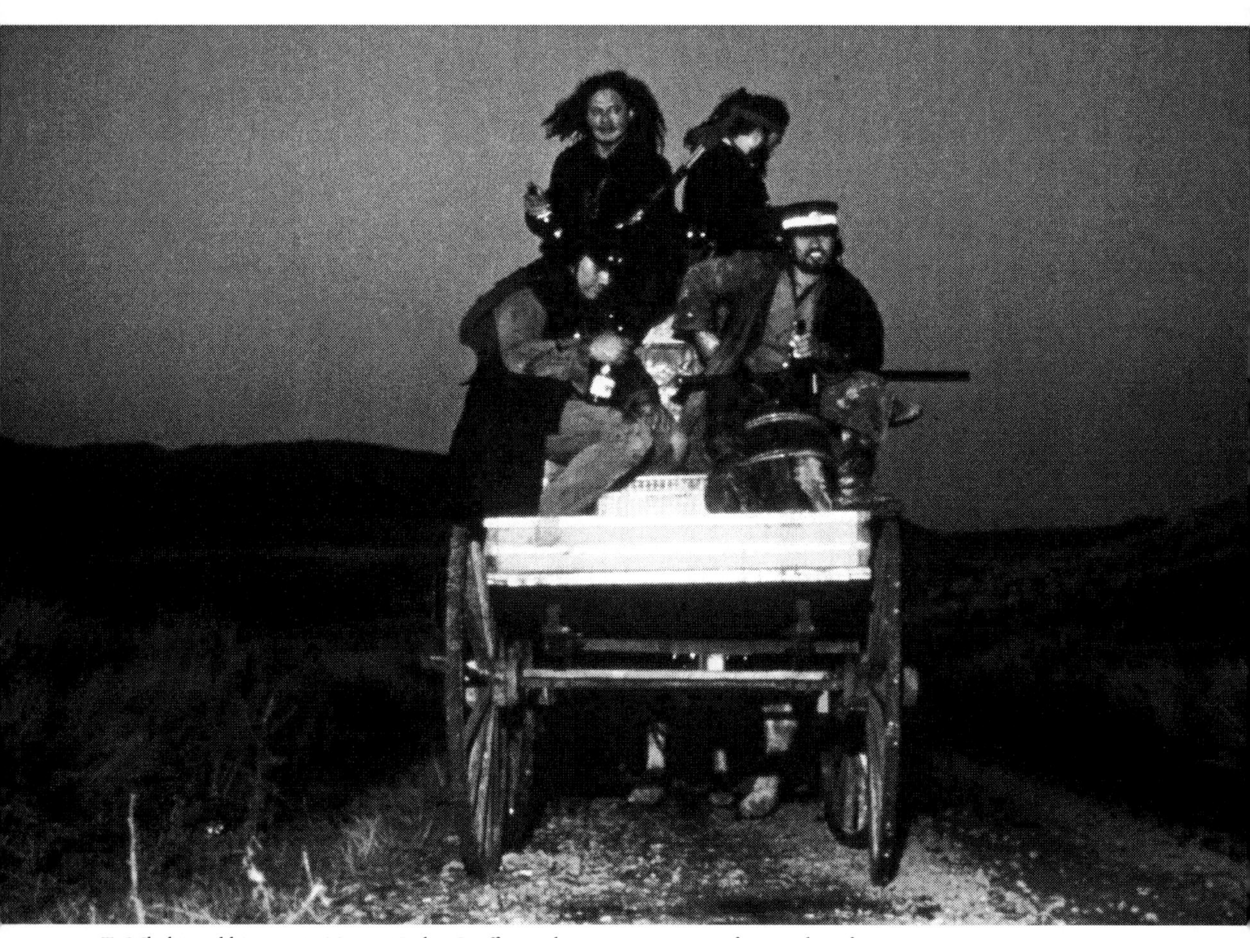

Te Wheke and his men in *Utu*, 1983, dir. Geoff Murphy. Image courtesy of Kino/Photofest.

Setting and genre

A quarter century ago, Brian McDonnell published an article entitled "Images of Aotearoa: Rural and Urban Settings in NZ Films."[2] Until the late 1990s, most New Zealand films had been located in rural or even uninhabited settings, even though the bulk of the population had long since become urban.[3] For that urban population, largely devoid of Māori until well past 1960,[4] the rural setting was a nostalgic reminder of the country's predominant national narrative: a saga of strong pioneers settling a virgin territory. In film, the genre associated with such sagas is the western, one of the more common genres, historically, in New Zealand cinema.

The settling of the country by British colonialists and the nineteenth century land wars parallel the US historical experience, making the New Zealand appropriation of a particularly Hollywood genre seem natural and logical. As Martin Blythe writes,

> The case can be made that during the Twenties and Thirties, an era that New Zealand's cultural historians discuss as the formative years of the national identity, there was a crucial three-way collision between British, Māori and American cultures. This took shape [among other things] around [...] the appeal to British history and tradition as opposed to American mythologies of the frontier. For [...] the film-going public there must have been a certain ambivalence in watching Hollywood films (especially westerns) that better expressed the New Zealand settler experience than did the more class-bound British product of the time.[5]

Film production within Aotearoa New Zealand – whether made by locals for local purposes, or by locals "for the world" (as Rudall Hayward's films proclaimed), or by nonlocals for an offshore market – has generally worked within the conventions of established genres. From the beginning, local audiences have accepted international generic conventions, and local films have incorporated disparate influences inflected by Aotearoa New Zealand's particular mix of cultures and national history. Does the symbolic function of landscape in the national narrative become problematised in New Zealand film when linked to the conventions of globally recognised genres?

The western's ability to comment on contemporary political events through its representation of similar issues displaced into another context, and the moral and social issues generally associated with the genre, make it potentially useful for filmmakers in Aotearoa New Zealand

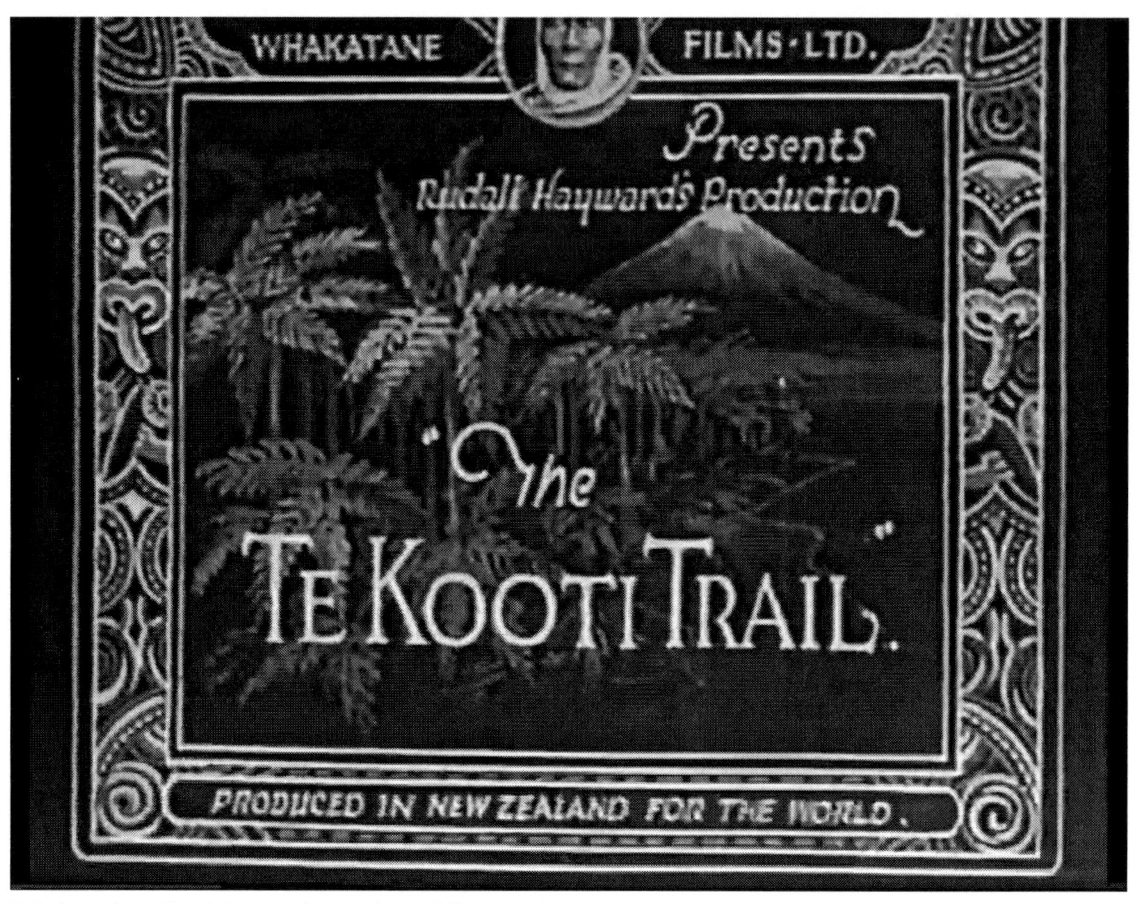

Title frame from *The Te Kooti Trail*, 1927, dir. Rudall Hayward.

inclined towards commenting on national debates.[6] It makes reading commentary off such films a given of academic analysis. Westerns typically deal with control of land and the imposition of one cultural system over another. The ultimate "civilising" of the wilderness or "badlands" often involves a romance between individuals from the different cultures, which fits with Blythe's observation about New Zealand cinema in general: that the relation between the races in Aotearoa New Zealand can be read off the representation of individual mixed race romances. Perhaps the country's cinematic use of imported generic conventions could be read as reflecting the state of the country's sense of national identity, including race relations.

Unlike most New Zealand films, New Zealand westerns often include important scenes involving rivers. The river sometimes provides a place for lovers to escape into a private world or a fugitive to hide; sometimes it's a boundary to be crossed or the vehicle for a journey; sometimes it is a means of purification and healing, but also sometimes a place polluted by death; and sometimes it seems to be there for its aesthetic beauty. What interests me in Rudall Hayward's *The Te Kooti Trail* (1927), Geoff Murphy's *Utu* (1983) and Sam Pillsbury's *Crooked Earth* (2001)[7] is the river's role in presenting the impact of colonialism, specifically, the relation between Māori, ownership of land and the representation of the national narrative in Aotearoa New Zealand's national cinema.

Each of these films appeared at a distinct moment – pre-Second World War, the early 1980s and just past the millennium – in New Zealand film history. For Aotearoa New Zealand, 1940 was important as the centenary of the Treaty of Waitangi, a founding document for the country and the on-again/off-again legal basis for relations between Māori and Pākehā. Rudall Hayward was the most successful Kiwi filmmaker before the Second World War, and his features often dealt with Māori–Pākehā relations. In 1977, Roger Donaldson's *Sleeping Dogs* "kick-started" feature filmmaking in Aotearoa New Zealand once again, beginning a period that established Donaldson and Murphy as the country's best directors. Their departures for Hollywood occurred around the time a decline in quality was associated with tax law changes in the early 1980s.[8] Then, in the early 1990s, three very different sorts of Kiwi directors appeared on the scene in quick succession with domestically and internationally successful films: Jane Campion and *The Piano* (1993), Lee Tamahori and *Once Were Warriors* (1994) and Peter Jackson and *Heavenly Creatures* (1994). These films and directors changed the way people inside and outside Aotearoa New Zealand thought about what Kiwi filmmakers could do. These were all films deeply embedded in Kiwi history and culture, and they were discussed domestically in those terms. Many people thought the key to success had been found.

The commercial success of these films made a government led by the fiscally conservative National Party pay serious attention to the potential "cultural capital" of what at the time could hardly even be called an industry. Although film production and national history have intertwined throughout New Zealand history,[9] it was never the case until the 1990s that the New Zealand government looked upon New Zealand filmmaking as an important source of foreign exchange, that it *could* consider domestic filmmaking that way. Apart from the hope that government funding for filmmaking might be recouped through the commercial success of such films, the government, whether led by either the Labour or National parties, hardly put any direct pressure on film production in terms of its content or personnel. New Zealand cinema's representation of national narratives, in other words, is not generally controlled by the government, but the government has subtly supported films expected to be commercially successful, along with films offering leverage for other sorts of commercial exploitation, especially tourism.

The commercial success of the 1990s, the change in government attitude towards a developing screen industry and the powerhouse of international activity that comes under the brand "Peter Jackson"[10] have changed the relation between New Zealand filmmaking and Aotearoa New Zealand's national history. More options are open to the country's filmmakers, young and old, not just because of technological (and resultant economic) changes. If the 1990s produced a new generation of filmmakers, that generation has been succeeded by yet newer filmmakers, including more women and more Māori; there is little homogeneity among them anymore. Still, in 2001, just before *The Lord of the Rings* altered various landscapes forever, one of those Kiwi directors from that golden period between "kick-start" and "tax shelter" resurfaced with an NZ-made film. Was *Crooked Earth* a throwback or a sign of the future?

While Aotearoa New Zealand's national history presents more of a continuum than does its film history, and one film from a particular historical moment cannot be taken for an accurate reflection of that moment, the temptation is nonetheless irresistible to compare away, and then contemplate the results. This is especially true given the changing level of Māori involvement in the films in question. It is not that Māori have not themselves engaged in exploiting their own exotic qualities for commercial gain in the Western world. The point, for me, is the extent to which Māori can be said to be in control of that exploitation – a point to which I shall return.

Moments in time

In 1993 *The Piano* recreated a moment from nineteenth-century history when Europeans were beginning to build settlements in the bush. In 1994 *Once Were Warriors* opened with a *trompe l'oeil* image of pristine scenery that turns out to be a billboard near an Auckland council estate. The one film engages with the historical moment in which land is changing hands and, consequently, the social fabric of family and community is being built up for one group (European settlers) and undermined for the other (Māori); the other film, set in a slightly ambiguous moment of the twentieth century, ignores the results for those European settlers to focus on consequences for displaced Māori whose own communal fabric was virtually destroyed.

Original commentary on both of these films read them primarily as melodramas and only occasionally mentioned Māori, land and national history. Because they were seen to be unique, especially outside Aotearoa New Zealand, they were even less often situated within the history of national cinema in Aotearoa New Zealand. Both films, though, are dinkum Kiwi in that the integral role of Māori and landscape in the cinema of Aotearoa New Zealand has been a virtual given since the late nineteenth century when films first appeared here.[11]

In *The Piano* and *Once Were Warriors*, the relevant scene in each film that supports the underlying discourse of the relation between Māori and land as part of the mainstream national narrative shows, in the first instance, Stewart, the enterprising colonist, trying to trade guns for land sacred to Māori as a burial ground, with Stewart justifying his actions because Māori "don't do anything" with the land. In the second instance, Jake Heke and his family sit across from Beth Heke's marae in the countryside beyond Auckland, discussing class distinctions between Jake and Beth's family.[12] In Campion's film, the scene references a contemporary historical moment: the moment when difficulties arise between Māori and Pākehā over control and use of the land. In Tamahori's film, the scene references an historical moment prior to that in which the represented event occurs, a vague past history prior to European contact in which – it is generally assumed – Māori were better off. Jake's point, though, is that not all Māori were better off, that in fact some, such as himself, are now better off, their ties to the land and the *marae* broken without regret. However, *Once Were Warriors* rejects Jake's opinion. It concludes with the clear message that Māori would be better off for a return to the land and a reconnection with their *marae* and *tikanga* (traditional Māori practice). This small debate was one reason *Once Were Warriors* was controversial domestically.

It is worth noting that *The Piano* is very much Jane Campion's film. She wrote the script, basing it – among other sources – on research at the National Library of New Zealand into pioneer settlers such as her own family. She had official and unofficial Māori cultural advisors, including Tungia Baker, Temuera Morrison and Waihoroi Shortland. *The Piano*, though, is a Pākehā-produced film. Officially, in fact, it's an Australian film, since its producer, Jan Chapman, is based in Sydney. In contrast, *Once Were Warriors* is based on a novel by a Māori, Alan Duff. Riwia Brown, who wrote the screenplay, is also Māori, as is the director, Lee Tamahori. Technically, however, following the same rule as for *The Piano*, *Once Were Warriors* isn't a Māori production, because its producer, Robin Scholes, is Pākehā. Such technicalities get short shrift in common usage, however, and for most people *Once Were Warriors* is a Māori film just as *The Piano* is a New Zealand film. But Lee Tamahori was only the third Māori to direct a feature film, and *Once Were Warriors* came only 7 years after the first Māori-directed film, Barry Barclay's *Ngati* (1987).[13] While arguments involving essentialism are about as tasty as a dog's breakfast, it is important to recognise that Māori access to the medium of feature filmmaking is a recent phenomenon. While none of the westerns in question was directed by a Māori, Māori involvement in the production process changed over the years. So it's worth considering whether these films reflect different attitudes towards Māori involvement in the process of telling the national narrative, with recognisably different results. This is especially true for *Crooked Earth*, since its creative personnel included some of those same cultural advisors to Jane Campion on *The Piano*.

Crooked Earth, however, was directed by Sam Pillsbury. While Campion, along with Vincent Ward, best represents auteurism among New Zealand directors, Pillsbury, who emigrated as a teenager from the United States, never achieved that artistic status. He played significant roles in the production of Murphy's *Goodbye Pork Pie* (1980) and *The Quiet Earth* (1985), and he directed *The Scarecrow* (1982) and *Starlight Hotel* (1987) in Aotearoa New Zealand, but his most recognisable film title is probably *Free Willy 3* (1997). Pillsbury's return was hailed as a positive sign; expatriate filmmakers returning to this country would contribute their enhanced expertise to an enlarged but still immature national cinema. And on the surface, given the inclusion of figures such as writers Greg McGee and Waihoroi Shortland with actors Temuera Morrison and the highly respected Nancy Brunning, *Crooked Earth* would seem to offer scope for a bipartisan approach. Yet *Crooked Earth* illustrates the homogenising influence of globalisation on the film industry and raises questions about maintaining a locally specific cinema.

Landscape and aesthetic debate

In 1857 the US painter Louis R. Mignot produced *The Sources of the Susquehanna*, a painting of one of the eastern United States' major N/S rivers that represented an ongoing debate within the new republic as to whether its pristine natural resources should be protected for posterity (and for the benefit of tourists) or exploited for commercial purposes without regard to ecological (and aesthetic) consequences. The same painting also came to function within the debate between North and South about economic issues that eventually erupted in the US Civil War.[14] In New Zealand significant paintings of rivers have featured in similar debates, particularly work by Petrus Van Der Velden, who may have shared influences with Mignot, since the American studied in Holland, albeit years before the Dutchman's temporary emigration to Aotearoa New Zealand.

According to David O'Donnell:

Early European images of Aotearoa were landscape paintings in the Romantic style. Romantic conventions appear in a late-nineteenth century painting such as *Otira River* (Petrus Van Der Velden), which, amid strong chiaroscuro, depicts an untamed river as dark, turbulent, and frightening. Strong symbolic connections exist between the conventions of Romantic painting and the anxiety of the Pākehā settler mentality, struggling to "break in" the land and establish "civilisation" in an exotic and sometimes terrifying landscape. As Francis Pound writes, "*Otira River* may connote, in its battle of light with dark, that constant battle, which according to the Christian constitutes the true history of the world, of the Light with the forces of darkness." In Van Der Velden's New Zealand landscapes, colonized spaces symbolize the struggle of nineteenth century colonisation itself, fuelled by Christian imperatives to bring "civilisation" to the far corners of the globe.

The country's earliest films, grounded in the tradition of nineteenth century paintings of Aotearoa, supported this Manichaeistic view of New Zealand's colonisation.[15]

One would therefore expect to see this sort of contrast in Hayward's films, rather than in *Utu* or *Crooked Earth*, given the later films' appearances after postcolonial challenges to colonialist versions of Aotearoa New Zealand's history had entered debates about national identity. While technology is a factor, especially the ability of colour and faster film to capture more precisely the nuances as well as scope of New Zealand scenery, it is *Crooked Earth* that most often invokes the sublime, through its panoramic images of a lone Māori warrior on the mountaintop, silhouetted against the sky.

Although relatively few New Zealand films feature rivers, two of Aotearoa New Zealand's classic book titles are Jane Mander's *The Story of a New Zealand River* (1938) and Mona Anderson's *A River Rules My Life* (1963), neither of which engages with the discourse of Romantic landscape painting. The latter describes life on a sheep station for which the river in question functions as a boundary, controlling the tenants' movement, including their access to people on and off the station. In the former the river is the medium for the characters' journeys into and away from their backblock logging operation and towards their changed lives in a new land that is itself undergoing massive alteration as ancient trees are felled and hauled away. In contrast with the nineteenth century's Romanticised view of picturesque rivers, these twentieth-century texts consider rivers in more practical terms, reinforcing the settlers' view of the land they have colonised and come to identify with. While Mander's novel deals with economic issues almost entirely without regard to the Māori–Pākehā issues inherent in discussions of land usage and *kaitiaki* (guardianship), these three films base their dramatic conflict in Māori–Pākehā relations. Perhaps if *The Story of a New Zealand River* had been filmed in the early 1990s, as nearly happened, that novel's sub theme about what commercial exploitation was doing to native forests might have survived the adaptation process. And there would have been a female Pākehā version of the national narrative at odds with earlier versions produced by Pākehā men, given that it would be Mander's version, and would, had the original intention come to fruition, have been directed by Jane Campion.[16]

Lone rider, swimming woman

When Rudall Hayward made *The Te Kooti Trail*, about a charismatic Māori leader of the nineteenth century who marauded among more vulnerable Māori tribes as well as fought colonialist rule, Te Kooti's exploits were within living memory. In Hayward's film, a small Māori community sympathetic to British forces comes under attack from a group of Te Kooti's men. A lone Māori warrior leaves the community's relative safety in order to bring reinforcements. In a set piece from Hollywood representations of Native American/settler conflict, the attacking forces, pausing briefly as they spread out along a ridge overlooking the settlement, come racing down the hill and spot the warrior rushing away on horseback. Some of them pursue Taranahi, the lone warrior, and a chase scene ensues. To save himself, Taranahi jumps into a river to hide until his pursuers give up the chase. The long shots of men on horseback chasing a lone rider, the pursuit, his subterfuge in sending his horse forward as a decoy while he hides along the riverbank – these could be scenes from a tick sheet for Hollywood westerns.

In Hayward's version of nineteenth-century history, colonialists have had a beneficent effect on Māori and only "bad" Māori attack colonialists and their "good" Māori allies. Between *The Te Kooti Trail* and *Crooked Earth*, a Māori renaissance occurred; along with reclaiming lost land and economic benefits, Māori have developed an analysis of colonialism that specifies social and cultural damages in addition to economic harm. *Crooked Earth* plays on this revisionist history.

A title at the film's beginning tells us that

> In 1840 the Treaty of Waitangi was signed […] The treaty promised Māori ownership and control of their lands, but over the next 130 years, most of their land was taken. In the 1980s, […] the long battle for justice began […] [*sic*].

The story begins with the death of a tribal elder who had worked towards a treaty settlement left to be signed by his successors. His two sons, Kahu Bastion, the younger brother who stayed behind, and Will Bastion, the older brother who has returned from military service overseas, are antagonistic, but Will does not contest Kahu's desire to take up their father's mantle. However, rather than accept the treaty settlement, Kahu wants to reclaim tribal lands, preferably, it would seem, through violent means. Kahu is an egotist who compares himself to Che Guevara and Malcolm X. While he critiques the ongoing effect of colonialism on Māori, he engages in drug deals involving a globalised apparatus for trade and profit, apparently with no concern for the negative effect locally of marijuana's availability. Although Will is at odds with the Pākehā establishment, as represented by the Army he has left, he opposes the drug trade and the military-style violence because of their harm locally.

Crooked Earth also has a lone Māori rider, Api, a young daredevil who distracts the police – including Māori on horseback but led by a Pākehā – by riding away from the hidden marijuana greenhouse they seek. Trapped at a waterfall, first the horse and then the man jump; once again, a river becomes the means of a sympathetic Māori's escape from the bad guys in pursuit. Since the pursuers are all law enforcement officers, they may be read as representing colonialism, in sharp contrast with the politics of *The Te Kooti Trail*.

In between these two films, *Utu* is historically accurate in its depiction of Māori against Māori, but its critique of colonialism rests on a different revisionist view of history. Colonel Elliot, the English commanding officer, is the bad guy, along with Te Wheke, but at least a desire to revenge the murder of his relatives motivates Te Wheke's turn on his former allies whereas Elliot acts out of hubris and racism. Lieutenant Scott, the "colonial," as Elliot calls him, is among the good guys, accepted by Wiremu as being on the "same side," being also a New Zealander. In reality, British troops respected their Māori opponents and were less concerned with winning land from them than were the colonial soldiers.[17]

One of the *kūpapa* (Māori fighting for the British) announces his decision to join Te Wheke to Wiremu while their small party of soldiers pauses by a stream – and Te Wheke's forces attack. The warring sides spoil the water's purity as bodies, including that of the *kūpapa*, fall dead into it, their blood and their staggering about disturbing the stream. Such a scene contrasts sharply with the purifying and healing qualities of rivers as represented in *Bad Blood* (Mike Newell, 1982) and the short *Twilight of the Gods/Te Keremutunga o Nga Atua* (Stewart Main, 1995).

Utu, like *Crooked Earth*, includes the escape by a fleeing character off a cliff into a pool located by another waterfall. Perhaps because Merata Mita was a cultural adviser for *Utu*, the character who jumps is a Māori woman, Kura. When she surfaces and sees her male pursuer hesitating at the cliff's edge, she challenges him to follow her example. The challenge has its sexual connotations, but its most striking feature is Kura's independence and the man's need to push himself to keep up with her daring. Kura is an active narrative agent throughout the film, constantly challenging the men.

Given the preponderance of roles for men in early Kiwi films, the rarity of images of active women individualises each one. In the films under discussion, images of women in association with water contribute to the gendering of identity; some are there to be looked at, while others play active roles in the narrative. Occasionally, an ambiguous association of gender with active and passive roles occurs, as in *The Te Kooti Trail*, when Taranahi woos Monika by playing his flute before carrying her to the *waka* (canoe) where they float down the river. During all this she passively gazes at Taranahi, a gaze that simultaneously expresses her admiration for his manly strength and beauty, and objectifies him for her scopophilic pleasure. In contrast, in *Utu* Kura comes down river from the waterfall and stands to offer her challenge to the man she sees staring back at her from above.

Where *Utu* is progressive in associating Kura and the waterfall with heroic action, including a challenge to armed men, *Crooked Earth* is regressive. It isn't just that it's a man in *Crooked Earth* who goes over the waterfall. Api has been flirting with Will's daughter, Ripeka, and at one point he finds her bathing in a stream. In *Utu*, the river is a place for Māori/Māori death, an occurrence in a realistic setting for its historical context. In *Crooked Earth* the river is associated with sex (and fertility), but within the context of an exploitation scene straight out of the book of "Hollywood" clichés as directed by a Pākehā director with Hollywood experience.

Neither of the two other films, involving a Māori/Māori romance (*The Te Kooti Trail*) and a Māori/Pākehā romance (*Utu*), needs to objectify the Māori female nude in this way. Yet a Louis Steele painting from 1908 entitled *Spoils of the Victor* shows a half-naked Māori woman bound to the palings of a *pa*; the image, as in *Crooked Earth*, is orientalist in nature.[18] In *Crooked Earth* Api controls this situation through his gaze. Although he is a Māori male looking at a Māori female, he might be said to have absorbed that same orientalist gaze embedded in Steele's painting, the gaze of the colonialist looking at a vulnerable and exposed Māori female. Pillsbury exemplifies rather than questions a colonialist gaze through imposing it via the agency of a male Māori character.[19] In a film that purports to be about contemporary struggles between Māori and Pākehā over land rights grievances, and among Māori over how best to accomplish the greatest common good, this scene identifies *Crooked Earth* as an exploitation film rather than a genuine effort at contributing to local cultural debates.

Conclusions

Relative to *The Te Kooti Trail*, *Utu*'s response to contemporary Māori activism marked a positive change in the representation of Pākehā–Māori relations. Can the same be said of *Crooked Earth*?

Utu, like Hayward's films, is set during historical moments of violent colonisation involving military force. Hayward features Māori with personal connections to the history they enacted, but he does not acknowledge them as cultural advisers. *The Te Kooti Trail* is liberally respectful but also paternalistic towards Māori. When Murphy made *Utu*, he accepted Māori as cultural advisers as well as actors. Although *Utu* can still be seen as a Pākehā's telling of the story, it is a sympathetic telling that can countenance the prospect of "a thousand warriors on the streets of Auckland" (a reference to the contemporary upheavals in the wake of the divisive Springbok tour of New Zealand in 1981). By the millennium, it was standard practice to call in Māori cultural advisers, and *Crooked Earth* was no exception. Greg McGee wrote the original script, but Waihoroi Shortland, a former Māori language commissioner, also wrote a version; together they get official credit, but Sam Pillsbury himself played a role in the final version, as did Don Selwyn and Ruth Kaupua. According to Pillsbury, "Frankly I would have been extremely reluctant to delve so deeply into a culture that wasn't mine without a writer ally like Wassie [Shortland]."[20] However, the possibility exists that cultural advisers may find their work co-opted.

Crooked Earth seems like a remarkably direct response to *Utu* 20 years on. In both the films Māori brother kills Māori brother, thereby satisfying both Māori *tikanga* and Pākehā law in *Utu*, as Wiremu makes clear; in *Crooked Earth* we know only that somehow justice has been served. To the extent that the two brothers must resolve their conflict to satisfy the narrative arc, and to the extent that personal attributes underpin that resolution, the film largely avoids dealing with Pākehā responsibility for Māori economic conditions. Jake has lost again: Will's reluctant choice is to return to the land, accept *tikanga* and responsibility, but benefit from his Pākehā training provided by the Army. This time the *kūpapa* survives, as an odd compromise between *Utu*'s *kūpapa* (without turning radical) and Wiremu (while rejecting the Pākehā, or at least their army).

Crooked Earth is not a "bad" film *qua* film. It has the usual advantages of beautiful New Zealand scenery, attractive actors and the lure of Māori culture. It has dramatic conflict and an engaging chase scene involving horses and helicopters. In fact, it is an immensely interesting film, but less as a film *per se* than as an historical document when set in the context of a timeline including *The Te Kooti Trail* and *Utu*. Comparison of *Crooked Earth* with these two earlier westerns reveals cultural changes during the twentieth century to do with representation of Māori and attitudes towards women, which also shows that *Crooked Earth* engages in exploitation and sensationalism.

Representations of land invoke social and political issues associated with New Zealand history. Māori filmmakers have tended to represent landscape differently, as in Merata Mita's *Mauri* (1988), where the connection between the land and a harmonious spirit among people or within an individual is crucial to the narrative's dramatic conflict and structure. For the *tangata whenua* (people of the land), ownership gives way before *kaitiaki*. As a Māori perspective has gained visibility (through Māori protests over land rights and the ensuing media coverage, and through occasional dramatic productions dealing with land rights issues), differences between Māori and Pākehā viewpoints regarding the land have themselves become available as the stuff of narrative conflict.[21]

Films made in contemporary New Zealand by "outsiders" tend to exploit landscape for its scenic potential rather than for the spiritual or cultural benefit of the country and its people. The many Bollywood films shot in New Zealand usually incorporate the landscape as though it were part of a fanciful new topography of India, as in *Dil Hai Tumhaara* (Kundan Shah, 2002). Martin Campbell's *Vertical Limit* (2000) exemplifies the use offshore productions make of New Zealand locations as substitutes for other sites. Although born in Aotearoa New Zealand, Campbell says, "We came to Mount Cook in the Southern Alps in New Zealand simply because it duplicates the Himalayas" (Film New Zealand promotional map). In neither case is there a spiritual quality to this use of the land.

The spiritual, however, does not necessarily exclude the commercial. Since tourism in Aotearoa New Zealand began in the nineteenth century, there have been Māori guides and other commercial operations associated with, for example, the Rotorua area. John O'Shea's *Broken Barrier* (1952) examines both Pākehā exploitation of "exotic" Māori qualities for offshore audiences and Māori self-exploitation by having his Pākehā protagonist, a writer guilty of making up stories of "exotic" Māori customs, consider the way his Māori mate's girlfriend appears first dressed in traditional Māori costume for her work as a guide and then in fashionable European clothes when she goes out with the pair. This self-exploitation makes the writer feel slightly less guilty about his own exploitation, although he foregoes such writing for the future. O'Shea, with his usual cleverness, gets subtle aspects of exploitation out there for debate, particularly differences between self-exploitation and outside exploitation.

In an earlier essay,[22] I explored whether Eva Rickard, who became an icon of Māori activism from her appearance in the opening program of the groundbreaking television series *Tangata Whenua* (1974), was able to achieve her own goals of championing and sustaining Māori culture by appearing in *Mauri* and *Flight of the Albatross* (Werner Meyer, 1996), as opposed to being co-opted by the medium, especially in the later film. To run counter to the purpose of that essay, I can reduce that discussion to the following: Mayer does exploit

Rickard's presence in *Flight of the Albatross*, but Rickard could also be said to have gotten what she wanted. *Mauri* is something different: Rickard plays a character who mirrors her own role in life at that point, and who acts within a narrative world conceived within a Māori spiritual topography of the world. This is something other than exploitation.

To me, *The Te Kooti Trail* and *Utu* represent aspirational qualities of a New Zealand "national identity," while *Crooked Earth* represents a regression in terms of that identity. It speaks under the influence of a "Hollywood" mindset about women and indigenous people that makes it seem a lesser film than the previous two, largely because it exploits women and Māori for sensationalist effect. This is not to say that the earlier films didn't have Hollywood in their sights, at least as an influence in terms of their idea of what a successful film required. But the exploitation of sensationalism belongs more to a commercial "Hollywood" form of filmmaking than to a twentieth-century tradition of New Zealand filmmaking. The addition of an international component (in the form of the Asian drug lord) distracts from the inward focus of the story (on events pertaining to New Zealand's specific colonial history) in the earlier films. At the same time, while the influence of films from Britain and America can be seen in all of these films, the earlier films resist or avoid some generic clichés that *Crooked Earth* embraces. Hayward's films use the western genre in support of a then current colonialist mindset; *Utu* challenges that mindset. *Crooked Earth* seems regressive from the point of view of New Zealand cinema's contribution to the representation of Aotearoa New Zealand's national identity, despite the involvement of senior Māori cultural figures in its production.

At the time of this writing, the newest, most successful film in New Zealand film history looks to be *Boy* (2010), by the newest most successful New Zealand film director, Taika Waititi. Waititi has already made a war film, in the form of his short *Tama Tu* (2004). When he decides to make a western, the humour will surely be back; the cultural advisors very likely will not. Waititi's take on everything seems largely his own, although much like that of his generation with regard to the media. His use of generic conventions as well as his representation of women will surely add another perspective to the relation between New Zealand film and the national narrative. His previous commercial successes assure him the opportunity to exploit that cultural freedom.

Notes

1. This essay began as a conference presentation I prepared for the Australian and New Zealand History and Film conference in 2002. At one point David O'Donnell and I combined this conference presentation with his class lectures on landscape in New Zealand theatre and film. The resulting co-authored essay, however, was never published. My focus was always on rivers and westerns, David's was on beaches and psychodramas, and our joint effort attempted to associate these elements with globalisation. For this current essay I have reverted to my original material, to develop it in terms of how my examples drawn from New Zealand cinema relate to New Zealand's history. I would like to thank David O'Donnell for the pleasure of learning from

his analysis of the relation between landscape and NZ theatre and film, especially for introducing me to the discourse around romanticism and the sublime associated with Petrus Van Der Velden's painting of the Otira.

2. Brian McDonnell, "Images of Aotearoa: Rural and Urban Settings in NZ Films," *Alternative Cinema* (Spring/Summer 1984–85): 5–7.

3. Jonathan Dennis, "A Time Line," in *Film in Aotearoa New Zealand* (2nd ed.), ed. Jonathan Dennis and Jan Bieringa (Wellington: Victoria University Press, 1996), 203–04.

4. Ibid., 224.

5. Martin Blythe, *Naming the Other* (Metuchen, NJ: Scarecrow Press, 1994), 19.

6. The genre's usefulness extends to variations on its themes and structure that may disguise the very presence of the genre itself, as, for example, in *Kingpin* (Mike Walker, 1985); see Ron Mikalsen, "*Kingpin*: Can There Be Only One?" *Illusions* 5 (1987): 11–22.

7. Mixed-up film that it is, Vincent Ward's *The River Queen* (2005) includes all these elements. *Pictures* (Michael Black, 1981), which is not a western, provides examples of the river as a means of transportation as well as a source of aesthetic beauty.

8. Geoff Murphy, "The End of the Beginning," in *Film in Aotearoa New Zealand*, ed. Dennis and Bieringa, 130–49.

9. Most obviously in the origins of the National Film Unit, whose first mission was to produce Second World War propaganda; see Margot Fry, Servant of Many Masters: A History of the National Film Unit of New Zealand, 1941 to 1976, unpub. MA thesis, Victoria University of Wellington, 1995.

10. See Deborah Jones, "'Ring Leader': Peter Jackson as 'Creative Industries' Hero," in *Studying the Event Film*, ed. Harriet Margolis, et al. (Manchester: Manchester University Press, 2008), 93–99.

11. See John O'Shea (dir.), *Centenary of Cinema Trailer* (1996).

12. The *marae*'s second appearance in the film occurs in conjunction with the family's need for a burial ground for a member of its next generation. An essay on the relation between Māori and film could be written on the representation of Māori *tangi* or death more generally.

13. See Barry Barclay, "An Open Letter to John Barnett from Barry Barclay," *OnFilm* (February 2003): 11, 14.

14. Katherine E. Manthorne, with John W. Coffey, *The Landscapes of Louis Rémy Mignot* (Raleigh: North Carolina Museum of Art, 1996), 61–66.

15. David O'Donnell, Lectures, in FILM 237 Cinema of Aotearoa New Zealand (Victoria University of Wellington), 25 July 2000 and 24 July 2001; Francis Pound, *Frames on the Land: Early Landscape Painting in New Zealand* (Auckland: Collins, 1993), 102.

16. See Mary Paul, *Her Side of the Story: Readings of Mander, Mansfield, & Hyde* (Dunedin: Otago University Press, 1999), 79.

17. Nicholas Reid, *A Decade of New Zealand Film* (Dunedin: John McIndoe, 1986), 85.

18. My thanks to David O'Donnell for alerting me to this painting.

19. And that is the difference between this scene and a different one involving these two characters in which nudity and agency are more evenly distributed.

20. "Walking a Crooked Mile," *OnFilm* (August 2001), 19.

21. For example, a 1996 episode of *Cover Story* featuring Temuera Morrison dealt with land rights, apparently referencing the 1995 protests at Whanganui; see also, *The Waimate Conspiracy* (Stefan Harris, 2006).

22. Harriet Margolis, "Indigenous Star: Can *Mana* and Authentic Community Survive International Co-Productions?" *Quarterly Review of Film and Video* 19, no.1 (2002): 15–29.

Chapter 4

Unsettled Historiography: Postcolonial Anxiety and the Burden
of the Past in *Pictures*

Cherie Lacey

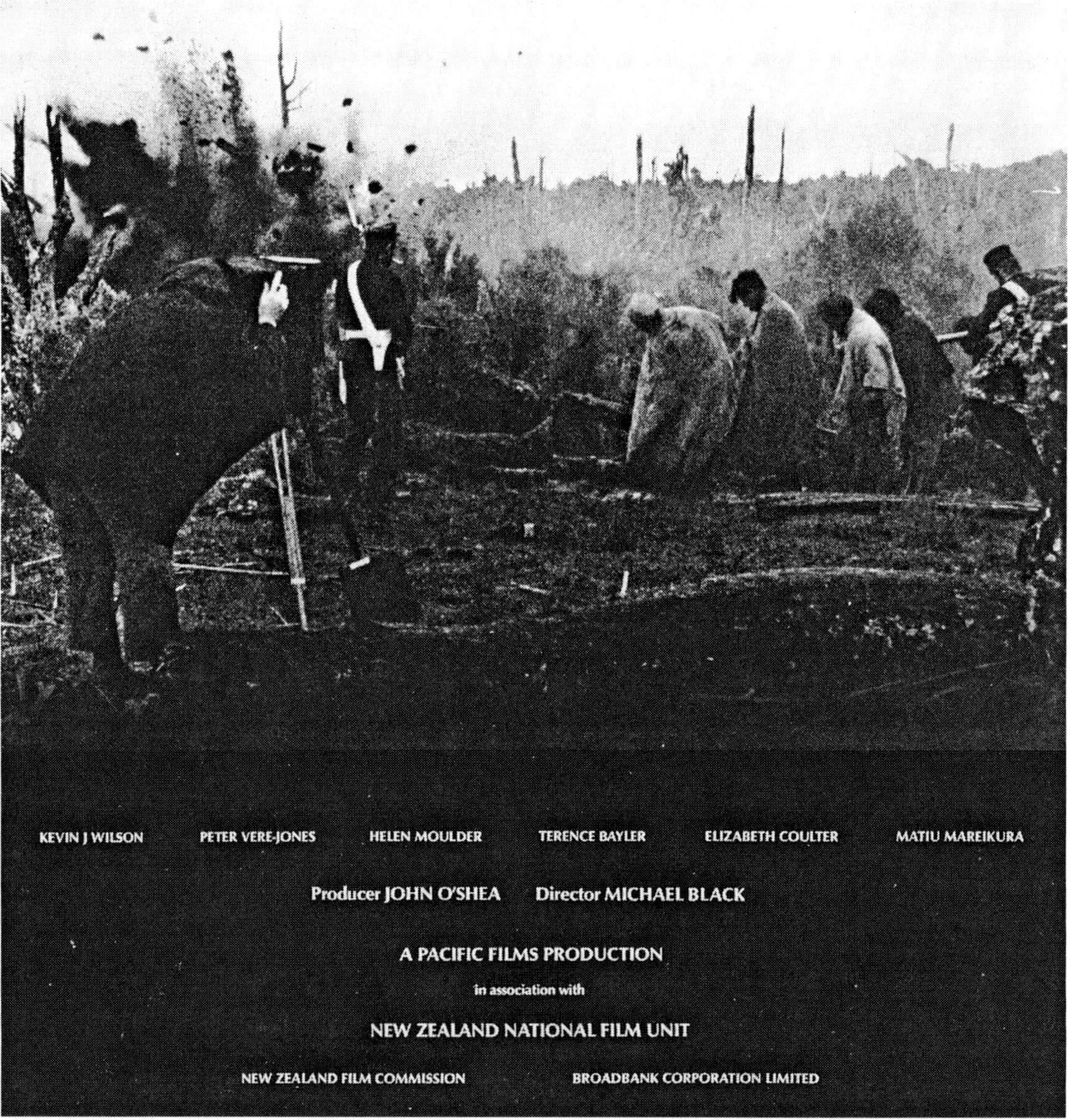

Publicity for *Pictures*, 1981, dir. Michael Black, produced by John O'Shea. Courtesy of the Hocken Archive, Robert Lord Collection, Te Uare Taoka o Hākena.

In one of the final scenes of Michael Black's *Pictures* (1981), Lydia Burton tells her sister-in-law, Helen, that she plans to return to London. She reasons, "life here" – in New Zealand – "is too unsettling." Helen responds by saying "*everything* is unsettling," a comment that both confirms Lydia's complaint and indicates a disturbance that extends far beyond her sister-in-law's personal experience. Indeed, it is a grievance that finds its way into almost "every" aspect of this film, from the filmmakers' experience, to the characters' psychological predicament, and even to the film's critical reception. By all accounts, and whichever way one approaches it, *Pictures* is a thoroughly unsettled, and *unsettling*, film.

Appearing at a particularly anxious time in New Zealand history, the early 1980s, *Pictures* returns to the colonial scene in order to investigate the nature of our present-day conflicts. The film's subject matter is the conflict between the Māori and British colonial forces during the 1870s and 1880s. Based on the real-life biographies of the Burton Brothers, early colonial photographers in Dunedin from the late 1860s, the story depicts the gradual realisation by both brothers of the brutal reality of the colonial project in New Zealand. Walter, the elder and first of the two to emigrate from Britain, accompanies the railway surveyor, John Rochfort, on a trip into the central North Island. On this trip, Walter witnesses and photographs brutal scenes of Māori dispossession and degradation by the colonial forces. Upon his return to Dunedin, as he prepares to show these "shocking" pictures, the authorities warn him against their display, arguing they depict the colony "in a very bad light." He resists displaying his photos, but caves in to depression and alcoholism and, after finally exhibiting the images, commits suicide.

Meanwhile, his brother Alfred arrives in New Zealand with his wife, Lydia. More compliant than Walter, Alfred produces acceptable images of the colony. Beginning with a trip into Central Otago with the Māori guide Ngatai, Alfred takes some picturesque landscape photographs, which gain immediate approval. He soon accompanies Rochfort on another expedition, along the Whanganui River and into the heart of the King Country, where Alfred witnesses the same brutal reality – the deprivation of the Māori at the hands of the colonisers – that so disturbed his brother. Alfred continues to take his acceptable, romantic photographs of the Māori, but is clearly changed by the experience. On his return to Dunedin, he is awarded a gold medal by the local Geographic Society, but his refusal to make an acceptance speech signals his non-compliancy with the colonial project.

Pictures invites the viewer to confront New Zealand's colonial past in an honest and truthful way as possible within the medium of film. At a time when New Zealand in general,

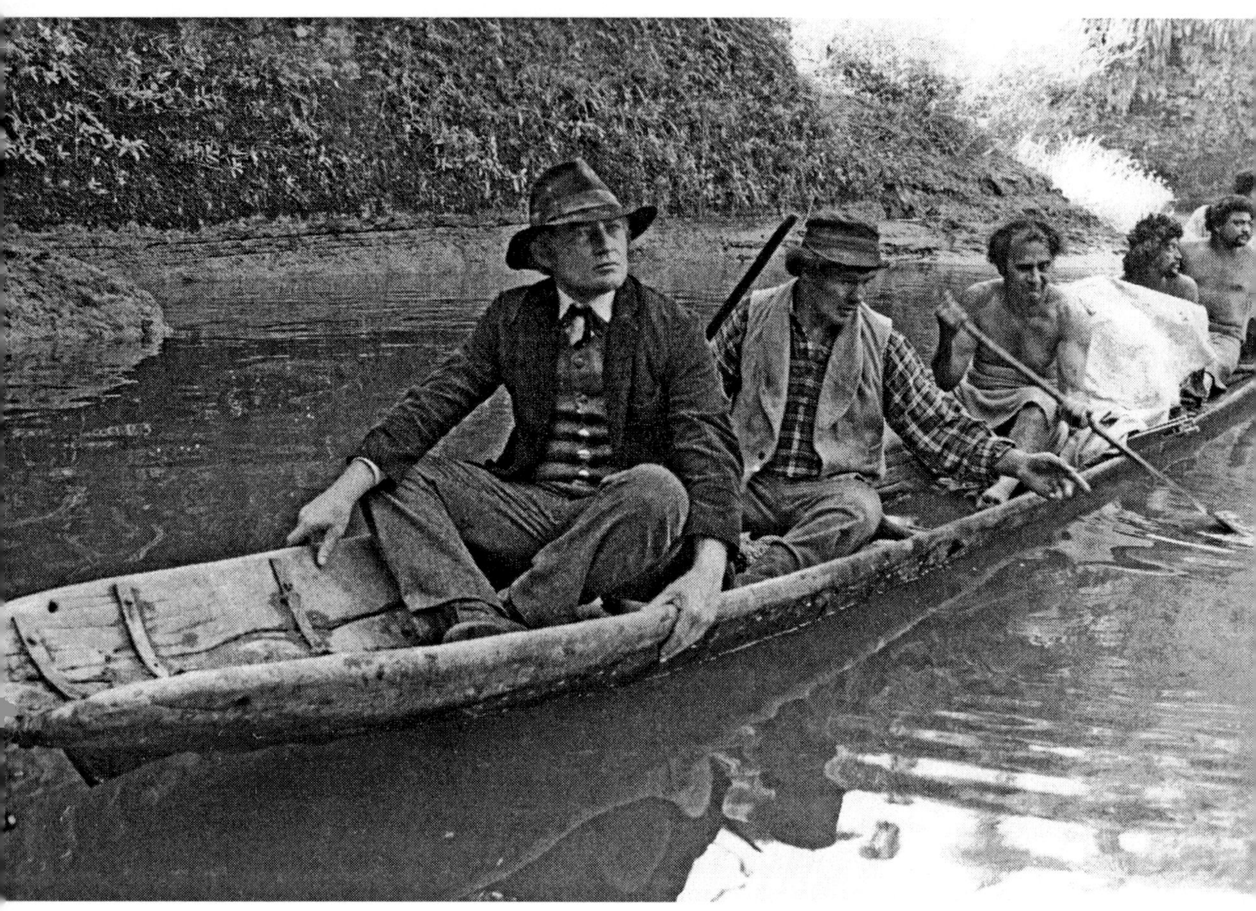

Alfred Burton (Kevin J. Wilson) going upriver in *Pictures*, 1981, dir. Michael Black. Image courtesy of the Hocken Archive, Robert Lord Collection, Te Uare Taoka o Hākena.

and the Pākehā settler in particular, was experiencing an anxious relationship to colonial history, *Pictures* suggests that we merely need to brave images of New Zealand "exactly the way it was" (as is Walter Burton's constant refrain), in order to uncover the seeds of contemporary conflict and, thus unburdened, move on as a nation united. Despite this lofty intention, however, representations of colonialism in the film are extremely restricted and, I will suggest, operate as a strategy of avoidance. They invite the viewer to exchange meaningful confrontation with the trauma of colonial history for a false history of utopic biculturalism, allowing the Pākehā to manage the anxiety of settlement in contemporary Aotearoa New Zealand. In this film, anxiety is not a vague sense of unsettlement about colonial history, but rather an absolute certitude about its continuing influence. Helen's brief comment, a mere *bon mot* within the film's narrative, points us in a direction to discover what, precisely, it is that so unsettles "everything" about this film.

The trouble with history

History, in the postcolonial era, has assumed a dubious importance. The phraseology adopted by many postcolonial theorists to express this relationship to history proves instructive, often betraying a sense of burden, or exigency. Stuart Hall, for example, has said that postcolonialism exists in the "wake" of colonialism, always in the "shadow of history."[1] Vijay Mishra and Bob Hodge open their cornerstone essay, "What was Postcolonialism?" by invoking the language of trauma to describe this relationship. They write: "We wish this were not a matter of return, of repetition, of the twice-told tale. We wish we were not witnessing a past moment by repeating it."[2] Others, such as Homi Bhabha and Iain Chambers, draw on the Freudian concept of the *Unheimlich*, whereby the repressed colonial history returns to unsettle the postcolonial present. This uncanny bond is often related to a kind of haunting, as if, as Jacques Derrida writes, we were always "haunted by something totally other," the other that always returns as "that which has not truly come back."[3]

In most cases, history is figured as the necessary hindrance of our postcolonial present. History returns, it repeats, and comes back to disturb our present, and in so doing, brings with it all kinds of afflictions, such as guilt, melancholy, shame and, of course, anxiety. This is what Michael F. O'Riley has described as the "affective turn" in postcolonialism, "a dimension," he says, "that creates a sense of the imminently important, present, and disruptive."[4] In its anxious form, the return of the past is understood to threaten the perceived unity of the postcolonial subject. As O'Riley says, the experience of anxiety points to the suspended state of the postcolonial subject;[5] poised between past, present and a projected future, the postcolonial self appears anxious, non-unified and continually in negotiation.

Nowhere is this anxiety more apparent than in settler states, such as New Zealand, Australia and Canada. As a settler subject, one is haunted by the spectre of his or her own history as an invader-coloniser, destined to live on in a place as (imaginary) descendants of an imposed colonising sovereignty. It has been argued that, as settlers, people's sense of legitimisation in the new place is premised upon a sort of *forgetting* of the prior occupants.[6] For the early settlers, both history as well as land was conceived as a *tabula rasa*, a utopian space of "historylessness" where the settler-coloniser could start afresh.[7] However, in the postcolonial moment, as history presses in on us, settler subjects might find that the old foundations for their sense of legitimisation are endangered. Attempting to both distance themselves from their colonial past (evidenced in the very term "settler" itself) as well as face up to it with a contemporary liberal conscious, postcolonial settlers thus occupy an ambivalent position. As Alan Lawson has commented, this relationship to history gives rise to an ambiguous identity for settlers, an anxious double bind that cannot help but unsettle them.[8]

Locating anxiety

What this notion of anxiety relies on, however, is an understanding based on one's own experience of it. That is to say, our understanding of anxiety falls back upon how we *feel*. As Jacques-Alain Miller writes, "because it is the good old anxiety, it is known and felt […] it appears, it is felt, one is bothered by it."[9] This, according to Jacques Lacan, is the temptation when working with an affect: "What we can understand is often seen as unequivocal when that thing is an affect – but there is a danger because what we understand is not necessarily what we should believe in, is not necessarily the truth."[10] In our common understanding, anxiety is a kind of fear that knows no object; whereas one can usually pinpoint fear, anxiety appears to us to be utterly objectless.[11] Thus, while the notion of settler anxiety has traditionally relied upon a somewhat vague or metaphorical understanding of the irruption of the past within the present, and how this may unsettle one's national-cultural identity, it might be timely to think further this notion of anxiety itself.[12]

It is precisely this absence of an object in the commonplace understanding of anxiety that Jacques Lacan puts into question. In fact, Lacan aphoristically states that *anxiety is not without an object*.[13] Not only does this statement belie our intuition, it draws our attention to the logic of negation at a discursive level. This relation, of "not being without having," does not mean that we know what object is involved, but that the object is obscure.[14] He argues:

> Anxiety, we have always been taught, is a fear without an object. A chant in which, we could say here, another discourse announces itself, a chant which, however scientific it may be is close to that of a child reassuring himself. For the truth that I am enunciating for you I formulate in the following way: "it is not without an object." Which is not to say that this object is accessible along the same path as all the others.[15]

That is to say, when it comes to anxiety, there *is* an object at stake, even if we cannot quite put our finger on what that object is.

What can we say about this object that anxiety is "not without having"? As Roberto Harari points out, this object is obscure, imprecise and impossible to represent.[16] It is, precisely, the object-cause of our desire: that which motivates our desire but is impossible to reach. This is the object towards which we always strive, in the hope of attaining a sense of full satisfaction, but which, inevitably, is always deferred, temporarily supplemented by a parade of other fleeting objects of desire. In the psychoanalytic tradition, anxiety is the path taken towards this object-cause of desire.[17] Because we cannot confront our desire directly, since desire is always displaced onto other objects, the subject provides us with the most difficult path towards it: that path is anxiety.

Indeed, according to the psychoanalytic tradition, anxiety arises when we are *too close* to the object-cause of our desire. As Samuel Weber points out, this particular object is constituted by its ability to be lost, or ceded. Anxiety thus arises not from the loss of an object, but rather from the loss of this loss.[18] The etymology of the word *anxiety* proves instructive here. Our word *anxiety* comes from the French *angoisse*, which is derived from the Latin, *anxius*, from *angere*, meaning "to choke," indicating a narrowness of breath or sense of suffocation. That is, as the history of the word itself makes clear, anxiety is not a relation to a perceived loss, but rather the overwhelming proximity of the object, as though it is sitting on one's chest, making it difficult to breathe. This is, of course, the physical reaction to anxiety, and indicates not a lack, but rather the *lack* of lack.[19]

Anxiety is therefore a signal, warning us that we are too close to our object, and calls for us to take our proper distance once again. It tells us that we must swap this privileged object for another, a false object, in which we can invest some sense of narcissistic identification. These are the replacement objects I referred to earlier, and they function to reflect back to us a more unified sense of self. In this topos, anxiety signals to us that we may be about to glimpse the unending nature of our desire, and invites us to miscognise the real object-cause of desire for these other, replacement objects. Rather than being a vague state of nervousness, then, anxiety is thus connected to absolute certitude.

New Zealand, the anxious years

That the late 1970s and 1980s were a troubled time in Aotearoa New Zealand has been well documented. It is this period in New Zealand history that is most often described as "anxious," as the country entered its own postcolonial *épistémè*.[20] In particular, race relations between Māori and Pākehā became a key issue for the nation, as did the pedagogical and discursive dominance of traditional European history. At stake was nothing less than the Pākehā construction of the national imaginary. Stuart Murray, for example, points to the disintegration of what Colin James had termed the "prosperity consensus" of New Zealand society from the 1950s to the 1970s.[21] During this period, the nation's deference to Britain remained largely unquestioned, and the country appeared secure in our national-colonial identity. From the early 1970s, however, this sense of security came under pressure as Britain looked increasingly to Europe over its colonies. As Murray writes,

> Britain's growing commitment to greater European union increasingly saw the old ties of the Commonwealth become anachronistic, especially those connected to commerce, and the often uninterrogated relationship with the heritage of British culture began to be eroded and replaced with a less secure apprehension of American cultural forms.[22]

The long-standing Pākehā myth of racial harmony also came under pressure. Māori activism, building in strength over the 1970s, called for a recognition of institutional racism within New Zealand, and challenged the settler myth of the One Nation. Ranginui Walker describes this period as a time of "Māori cultural renaissance,"[23] in which Māori activists mobilised against "the structural relationship of Pākehā dominance and Māori subjection."[24] A number of Māori-driven initiatives sprang up in quick succession, including the formation of the urban Māori group Ngā Tamatoa who, from 1970 until 1979, mobilised against what they saw as historic and contemporary injustices perpetrated by the New Zealand Government; the establishment of Māori-controlled media such as *Te Hokioi* and *MOOHR*; the passing of the Treaty of Waitangi Act in 1975, which established the Waitangi Tribunal; the Māori Land Rights Movement; Bastion Point; the Waitangi Action Committee (WAC); He Taua; and the Māori People's Liberation Movement of Aotearoa.[25]

The Land Rights Movement in general, and the creation of the Waitangi Tribunal in particular, gave rise to a new understanding of New Zealand history. Indeed, as Paul Hamer has argued, "the Tribunal was at the forefront of a nation coming painfully to terms with its past for the first time."[26] Particularly from 1985 on, when the Tribunal was granted retrospective powers, New Zealand's colonial history came well and truly into question. Alan Ward writes:

> When the jurisdiction of the Waitangi Tribunal was extended in 1985 to hear Māori claims concerning actions of the Crown since 1840, the government, rather unwittingly, had charged it with nothing less that a comprehensive review of New Zealand's colonial history. Centrally, this included the great matter about which Māori had been smouldering for generations – that is, the manner in which ownership and control of most lands and waters had been transferred from Māori to settlers.[27]

Within this intellectual environment, a new generation of academic historians, such as Judith Binney and James Belich, came into prominence. Turning their focus to figures and events in New Zealand's colonial past, their brand of revisionist history further interrogated the hegemonic dominance of European interpretations of New Zealand history.[28]

While this is a simple historical gloss of the period, it highlights the radical process of change that New Zealand as a nation underwent at this time. Foundational histories of the Pākehā nation came under scrutiny and revision, as did previously uncontested attitudes and beliefs. The sense of security that came with being Britain's favourite colony eroded, and gave way to attempts to forge a new bicultural identity that was geographically and politically closer to home. Such fundamental changes gave rise to a felt sense of anxiety, dislocation and unsettlement for the Pākehā, as their claim to legitimisation in New Zealand became increasingly strained. As Murray writes, "the crises of the mid 1970s to mid 1980s triggered a full range of fears that lay in New Zealand's status as a settler community, exposing the crucial doubts over the legitimacy and validity of the national project."[29] As the Pākehā nation was confronted with the unfinished business of the colonial past, a crucial question arose: how should the past be narrated?

Anxious historiography

It has been said that settler subjects have a distinct relationship to history, that they see history differently.[30] The ambiguous positioning of the settler subject, identifying as both coloniser and colonised, means that they must deal with unfinished business in certain ways. Alan Lawson has pointed out that, in settler societies like New Zealand, the colonial past remains unfinished at the narrative level. This is evidenced, Lawson says, by the fact that stories about colonial history keep being recirculated, as well as how easily they are "reactivated, recognised and read" by settler society.[31] Such stories function to legitimise the settler presence, as well as delegitimise indigenous prior claims. Due to the reliance upon historical narrative, says Lawson, the settler is, by and large, a narrativising being:

> The settler, it increasingly seems to me, is above all a teller of tales. It is in narrative that settler subjectivity calls itself into being and it is in narratives that it can be located and its symptomatic utterances analysed. The settler [...] is "essentially" a narrating subject.[32]

In order to narrate themselves into being, the settler subject often turns to the period of early settlement or early conflict, as though the kernel of the nation can be found in these early days of settlement. As Julian Thomas says of the Australian situation: "The early period of white settlement has been regarded as a special source of information about Australia" – a key witness, as it were, in the continuing arguments about the country's character and destiny. "The entire man is, so to speak, to be seen in the cradle of the child."[33] Similarly, in the Canadian context, Cynthia Sugars notes the national obsession with identifying Canadian "firsts." For her, these attempts seek a foundational narrative for Canada's white origins, an "ab-originality that is not aboriginal."[34] She goes on to say: "The urge for origins has long been an obsession in Canadian cultural history, perhaps because such origins are a chimera."[35] Lois Parkinson Zamora has identified this "urge" as an "anxiety of origins," an anxiety that, she says, characterises New World cultures, and appeals to the need for legitimisation on the part of the settler.[36]

New Zealand follows this general pattern. For the "last place on earth to be settled by humans" (as we are so often told), New Zealand has produced an over-abundance of books on New Zealand history; national history is, for New Zealanders, a national obsession. The popular claim that "New Zealand has no history" seems to be supplemented by the proliferation of it; as Thomas has put it, "this is a strange cultural problem: more history is demanded by an assertion of the lack of it."[37] "This," he goes on to write, "is not absence but its opposite: a pervasive fascination with history and a strong belief in its importance."[38] And, as Lawson and Sugars have noted of their respective nations, it is very often the early days of European settlement to which we return. In particular, I would like to suggest, two major events (or series of events) occupy a privileged position in the New Zealand national imaginary as foundational events for the Pākehā settler: the signing of the Treaty of Waitangi, and the New Zealand Wars.

Both narratives operate as strategies of legitimisation for the settler, but in very different ways. On the one hand, The Treaty turns on a narrative of belonging, a story of peaceful co-existence that provides a kind of utopic origin for Pākehā. As Avril Bell writes:

The shift to Treaty rhetoric [since the 1980s] has neatly served a number of ends for Pākehā. Firstly, in the face of the retreat of the "mother country" from her colonies and her realignment with Europe in the 1970s, the Treaty offers an *alternative origin* that signals a break with Britain. Pākehā now have a new nationalist origin as one of the two "founding peoples" of Aotearoa New Zealand.[39]

On the other hand, the story of the New Zealand Wars, based on the conflict between Māori and Pākehā, narrates a belonging that is based on the assertion of sovereignty. This history, as Lamb has argued, is characterised by struggle and survival, in which Pākehā asserted themselves as the new governing power in the colony. As the 2005 TVNZ series, *Frontier of Dreams*, put it: "Eventually, New Zealand would be dominated by a new tribe. The world of the Māori would be upturned. But the seed of a new nation would be sewn."

These narratives of legitimisation, however, reveal a certain paradox. While they testify to the obsession with settler origins, producing an abundance of historical material, they also rely on a kind of historylessness. Historylessness, or forgetting, has become a common trope in settler societies, and is another kind of legitimising strategy of the settler subject.[40] The notion of historylessness has been related to the utopian visions of Australia and New Zealand. As new societies, both nations are projected into the future, always imagined as the nation-to-come, something always under construction.[41] As part of this national construction, settler societies are required to leave behind Old World traditions of History and politics, while simultaneously producing new traditional forms.[42] As Stephen Turner has suggested, historylessness, or forgetting, is required in order that the settler occludes the trauma of dislocation from the Old Country and finds a way to belong in the new one.[43]

Thus, we can say that, in the New Zealand context at least, settler historiography oscillates between two opposing points: between remembering and forgetting, history and historylessness. This indicates that, at the foundation of New Zealand's national imaginary, there exists a kind of narrative instability, one that remains unsettled. This is particularly apparent in the postcolonial era. Here, we experience an overproximity of history, a pressing in of the past that is experienced as anxious, and one that threatens the imaginary unity of the settler subject. However much facing up to history is required to legitimate the settler, it is difficult to face the past head on. Postcolonial anxiety, as a response to the immediacy of the past, warns us to retreat into a false history, one that, I believe, is characterised by forgetting. This is a safe, utopic state of historylessness, one that allows the settler to live on in a fantasy of ideal biculturalism under the sign of the Treaty. It is this narrative instability, between history and historylessness, that I believe betrays a particular form of settler postcolonial anxiety, and is presented in its textual form in the film *Pictures*.

New Zealand the way it was

At the time of *Picture's* release, there was almost universal praise by New Zealand critics for the film's "fairness" and "balance" in depicting the country's colonial past. Ivan Butler's review in *Films and Filming* claimed that the film was "obviously designed to show the unacceptable face of colonialism," and that "a balance was fairly evenly maintained."[44] Peter Wells, writing in the *Listener*, said:

> One of the things I liked a lot about this film was its honesty in stating what is involved in a colonising process. On the one hand, for the conquered race, a loss of land, a threat to identity, even life. But for the conquerors, a loss is involved too, as well as a slow and painful process of realisation.[45]

Nick Roddick, from the *Monthly Film Bulletin*, similarly praised the film's even-handedness:

> The reassessment of history is never an easy task, especially a history as clouded with noble self-deception as that of the colonisation of New Zealand. All credit, then, to *Pictures* for tackling the subject, and for bringing to its reassessment a remarkable clarity and a considerable complexity of perspective [...] *Pictures* deserves to be seen, not only for its very real qualities, but for the way in which it faces up to the realities of New Zealand's – and, by extension, Britain's – colonial past.[46]

Consistently placed alongside Geoff Murphy's *Utu* (1983), *Pictures* emerged from the reviews as the more considered, effective and powerful of the two.[47]

During the production of the film, the filmmakers themselves appeared to be highly aware of the similarity, in content at least, to Murphy's *Utu*, and of maintaining what they believed to be a "fair balance" in the portrayal of the past. Director Michael Black, in an interview in *The Otago Daily Times*, said that "*Pictures* should balance *Utu*. It is more serious, thought-provoking, and doesn't rely entirely on action. *Utu* showed the Māori point of view; *Pictures* is more understanding towards the Pākehā."[48] Producer John O'Shea, in an article in the *Auckland Star* pointedly titled "This movie is not *Utu*," wrote, "now that *Utu* has given the public the cowboys and Indians version of the Land Wars, the way has been cleared for *Pictures*."[49] In a letter to his daughter Barbara in 1982, O'Shea reveals his desire for a larger number of Māori to see the film since, he says, it represents New Zealand in a more balanced, conservative way (than *Utu*, one presumes). He tells her:

> While [*Pictures*] is continuing the sell quietly and well abroad, the two main chains here are proving very difficult. Kerridge-Odeon want to start the film in the Berkeley Cinema at Mission Bay, rather than Queen Street. That's a "blue rinse area" – and though we want the affluent middle classes to see the film, the commercial potential is not that good if we can't also bring in a wider swathe of audience. Especially the Māori audience – many of whom would, I feel, like to see their point of view put forward in a rather more restrained and conservative way than is usual. Their attitude is too often left in the hands of vehement activists.[50]

At the time of its release, the advertisements for the film in New Zealand papers proclaimed, "*Pictures*, the way New Zealand was." In fact, much of the publicity surrounding *Pictures'* New Zealand release highlighted the historical authenticity of the film – in particular, the historical fidelity to the details of its mise-en-scène. For example, the filmmakers took pains to point out to reporters that all the props used in the film were antiques on loan from local museums. The cameras used in the film were the very same as those used by the historical Burton Brothers themselves. As O'Shea himself wrote, "It is the aim of Pacific Films to give the film as authentic a look as possible within the limits of time and money."[51]

Seeds of anger

At the same time as the film sets out to portray an honest representation of the colonial past, *Pictures* has clear ties to the time of its making. From its earliest conception, the film was intended to expose the historic origins of the present postcolonial troubles. Indeed, one of the early titles that were suggested was *Seeds of Anger*, although O'Shea passed it off as being too "obvious" and "crass." Nonetheless, the discarded title signals the centrality of contemporary concerns for the film. In a letter to a London reporter, O'Shea clarified the relationship between the film's historic content and the present:

> *Pictures* tries to uncover some of the paths that were taken in New Zealand, and find where the seeds of anger were planted along the way – the pragmatic European intent to drive the country forward, ignoring Māori hesitancy about "progress." Like all period films, *Pictures* is a fiction – it looks at the past with an almost contemporary consciousness, with

a keener awareness of sexism, racism, and incipient political repression than was evident at the time. Maybe we'll get slammed for that – "history" is a bit of a sacred cow.[52]

At the same time that Black and O'Shea were making *Pictures*, O'Shea penned an article for *The Listener*, sparked by some of the film's themes. Although the article was never published, it proves a telling insight into some of the concerns occupying the filmmakers. In it, O'Shea expresses his desire to explore the roots of the "deep dismay that pervades [the] country" during this time. In particular, he writes, it is the Pākehā who experiences a kind of postcolonial anxiety (although he did not use this term), brought on by a lack of strong foundation in New Zealand:

> As eloquent and articulate Māori friends told me of their joys and sorrows, one could not help but be conscious that no Pākehā has found his *turangawaewae*, his place to stand, that place where you have a past, present and a future [...]. It's a lucky Pākehā who knows he has a present and a future in New Zealand. But for all Pākehās [*sic*], the past is paper thin. The brevity of the Pākehā past here can gradually, especially as one grows older, become as oppressive [...].[53]

It can be said, then, that *Pictures* was intended from the beginning to provide Pākehā with a foundational narrative, a kind of textual *tūrangawaewae* upon which to construct a strong identity. By facing up to the past in an "honest and balanced" way, the present-day Pākehā may thus shake themselves free of their colonial ghosts, and move on into the future with a new sense of belonging and surety.

However, the kind of narrative that the film *Pictures* provides displays the same kind of instability identified earlier. On the one hand, it attempts to give us an authentic representation of the past, while simultaneously bringing us back into the viewing present. In moving between a narrative of conflict (of the New Zealand Wars), and a narrative of peaceful co-existence (in the present and projected future), the film betrays the kind of historiographical anxiety we have already described as common to settler societies. History is the support for the settler's desire for legitimisation, which takes form in the fantasy space of the film. However, when the proximity to the colonial scene proves too close, too uncomfortable, the film takes its distance once again by retreating into the present. We are invited to exchange meaningful historical confrontation for something with which we can identify: the present-day liberal attitudes of postcolonial, bicultural Aotearoa New Zealand. That the filmmakers were conscious of this dynamic does not detract from its importance. In fact, in their very conscious (and perhaps confused) attempts both to confront the viewer with the reality of New Zealand colonialism, as well as to reveal history from a contemporary perspective, Black and O'Shea display the same anxious relationship to truth as their characters.

Looking to the film itself nowhere is this relationship more apparent that in the Burton Brothers' photos themselves. Walter's "Māori War Series," upon which the entire narrative pivots, are presented as the real, brutal, uncovered face of European colonialism. Presenting

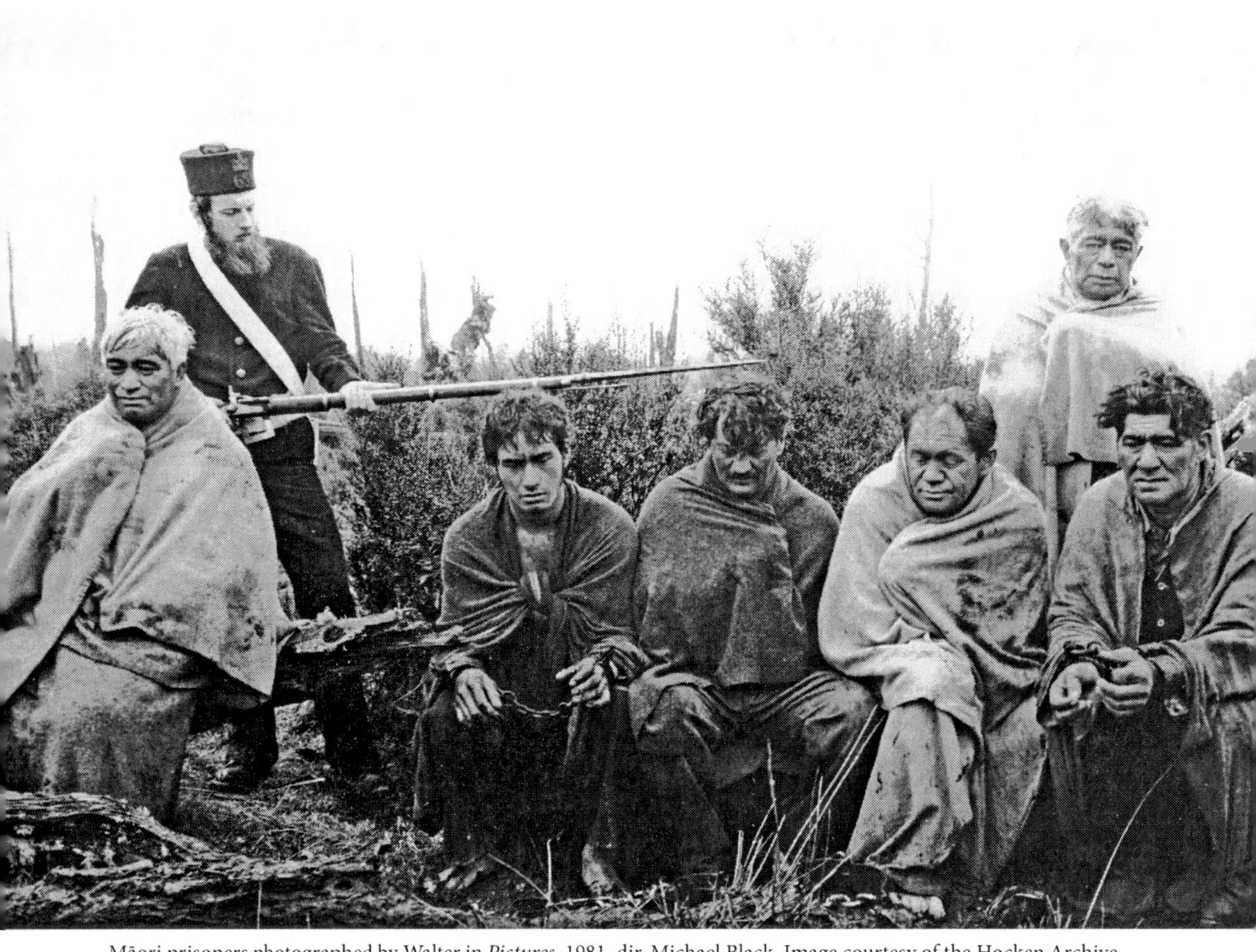

Māori prisoners photographed by Walter in *Pictures*, 1981, dir. Michael Black. Image courtesy of the Hocken Archive, Robert Lord Collection, Te Uare Taoka o Hākena.

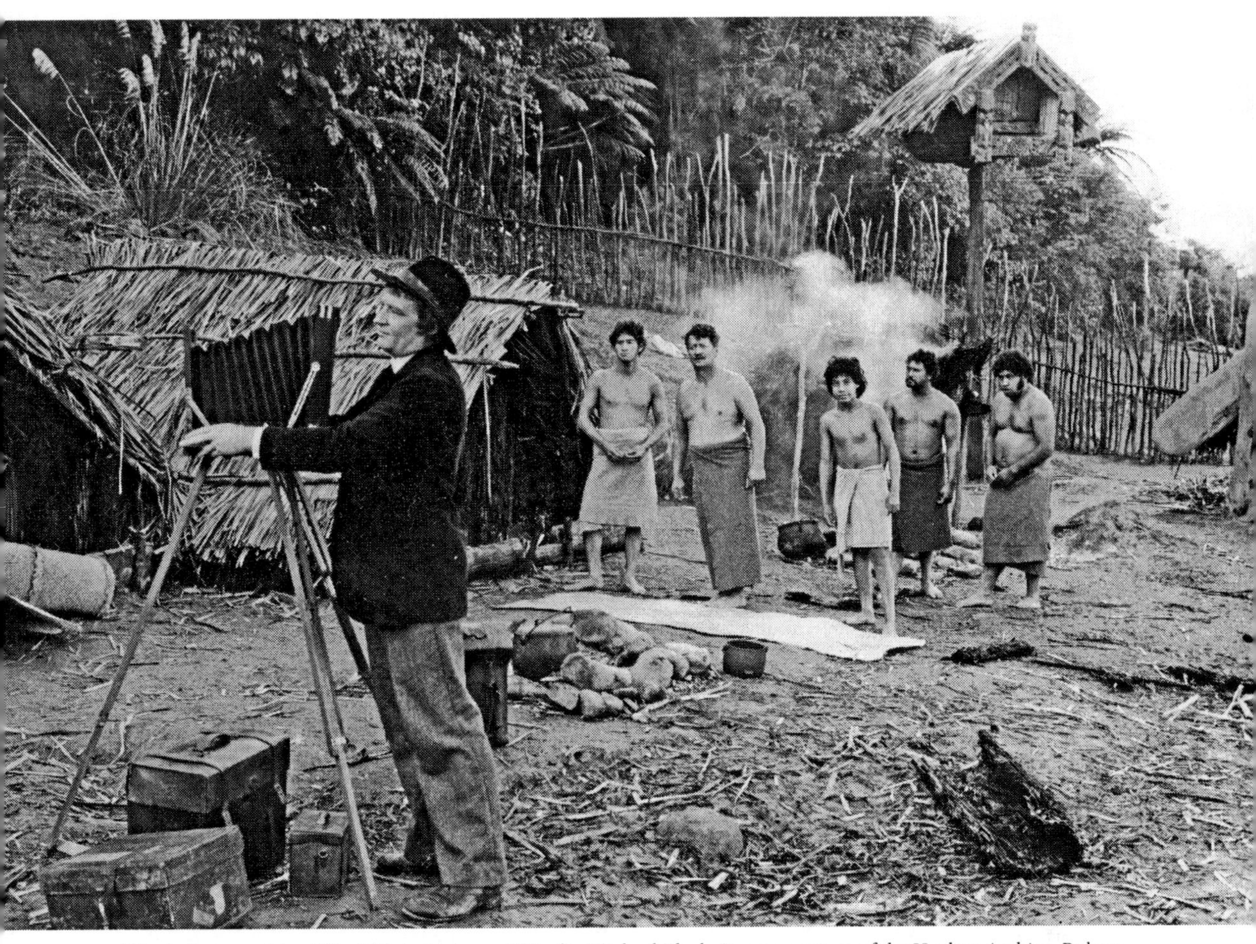

Alfred photographing Māori life in *Pictures*, 1981, dir. Michael Black. Image courtesy of the Hocken Archive, Robert Lord Collection, Te Uare Taoka o Hākena.

them to his peers back in Dunedin, he is told, "I have never seen such disgusting photographs," and that they could not possibly be exhibited since, "they show the colony in a very bad light." These are in contrast to the other genres of photography presented in the film – studio portraiture, the picturesque landscapes and the Romantic "Māori at Home" series – which are clearly marked out as staged, constructed and therefore false.

Due to his "almost contemporary consciousness" (as O'Shea put it) of the suffering of the Māori, not to mention the social documentary genre on display in his photographs, Walter is clearly marked out for audience sympathy. He is joined in this position later by Alfred, who also comes to realise the impact European colonisation has on the Māori. While it is difficult for the viewer to identify with Walter, being somewhat of a pathetic and self-loathing figure, Alfred is a much more valid option for audience identification. Indeed, his psychological movement from ignorance to knowledge is intended to mirror that of the audience's own. This allows viewers to distance themselves from the truly colonial characters in the film, like Rochfort and Lydia, and thereby also to distance themselves from the guilt of colonisation. As Reid Perkins has commented, "clearing the Pākehā of guilt through clearing the Pākehā figures of identification of guilt removes them from the taint of colonialism by shifting them off to one side."[54]

Indeed, what the filmmakers have achieved is a displacement of contemporary, liberal attitudes and beliefs onto real-life historical figures, creating a short circuit between New Zealand in the 1970s and New Zealand in the 1870s. For Perkins, while the director

> [...] has been astute enough to perceive the role practices like photography played in the colonising process, he has failed to recognise that photographers of that era just did not have access to the type of artistic and political consciousness he would like to ascribe to them – and thus lacked anything to wrestle with [...] what Black has done, then, is to graft a liberal and artistic consciousness that's very much part of the 1970s onto the 1870s.[55]

Moreover, while the film goes to great lengths to prove its historical authenticity, using copies of the real-life Burton photos and even re-staging certain photographic scenes, no such "Māori War" photos ever existed. This was first pointed out in Sandra Coney's 1983 review, and later discussed in Perkins' analysis:

> I was fascinated, though, by the revelation of this particular episode in colonial history [...] [However], no such photographs were ever taken, or suppressed. This is a profound sort of lie [...] *Pictures* takes real people, a real piece of history, then builds a lie into it, a lie which is not insignificant or peripheral, but is the moving force for the whole film. By this breathtaking act of artistic dishonesty, director Michael Black and screenwriter and producer John O'Shea have distorted history to Pākehā advantage.[56]

On closer inspection, it becomes clear that, when we actually see Walter's photos on screen, they are merely a mixture of images from Alfred's lauded "Māori at Home" series from 1885.

Moreover, there is very little filmic portrayal of the Wars themselves, confined solely to a few brief moments right at the beginning of the film, showing Walter taking his pictures. Indeed, looking back over the early versions of the screenplays, as well as the correspondences between the director, producer and co-writer Robert Lord, it becomes clear that all references to the Wars were increasingly omitted. In early drafts, for example, the first two scenes of the film go into some detail to portray the Wars, giving dialogue to the soldiers and the Māori prisoners. In fact, the second scene, a "bush montage," was originally described "a series of scenes of ravaged North Island villages and of Māoris [*sic*]."[57] Further, early screenplay drafts include references to real-life historical events that took place during the Wars. For example, as they share a drink at the hotel bar, Rochfort tells Walter of the "Hursthouse" incident:[58]

He was ambushed near Te Kumi. Some half-crazed Maoris pulled him off his horse. Locked him and his assistant in a *whare* for days. No food. No drink. And that was just the beginning. The things they did to them. It makes my blood boil.[59]

By the final cut, and with practically all references to the Wars taken out, the viewer is left to confront the Wars only obliquely, through Walter's "Māori Wars Series," which, as we now know, did not ever exist. The unpleasant parts of colonial history, that with which the film claims to bring us face to face, are thus only ever represented in Walter's photos, a product entirely of the 1980s. Rather than bring the viewer face to face with the colonial past, then, the film takes flight from any uncomfortable history, retreating into the present. This is a history that legitimises the settler by projecting backwards a contemporary liberal attitude, one that provides a site for identification in the present. In this way, history – the traumatic history of the conflict between Māori and Pākehā – takes its "proper" distance once again. Within the fantasy space of the film, the postcolonial anxiety of colonial history is managed, restrained and controlled, giving space for postcolonial settlers to remember to forget their problematic past.

Notes

1. Julie Drew, "Cultural Composition: Stuart Hall on Ethnicity and the Discursive Turn," in *Race, Rhetoric and the Postcolonial*, ed. Gary A. Olson and Lynn Worsham (Albany: SUNY Press, 1999), 230.
2. Vijay Mishra and Bob Hodge, "What Was Postcolonialism?" *New Literary History* 36 (2005): 375.
3. Jacques Derrida, *The Post Card: From Socrates to Freud and Beyond* (Chicago: University of Chicago Press, 1987), 195.
4. Michael F. O'Riley, "Postcolonial Haunting: Anxiety, Affect and the Situated Encounter," *Postcolonial Text* 3, no. 4 (2007): 1.
5. Ibid., 1–2.
6. Stephen Turner, "Settlement as Forgetting," in *Quicksands: Foundational Histories in Australia and Aotearoa New Zealand*, ed. Klaus Neumann, Nicholas Thomas, Hilary Eriksen (Sydney: UNSW

Press, 1999); Cynthia Sugars, "(Dis)Inheriting the Nation: Contemporary Canadian Memoirs and the Anxiety of Origins," in *Moveable Margins: The Shifting Spaces of Canadian Literature*, ed. Chelva Kanaganayakam (Ontario: TSAR, 2005), 177–203; Alan Lawson, "Proximities: From Asymptote to Zeugma," in *Postcolonising the Commonwealth: Studies in Literature and Culture*, ed. Rowland Smith (Waterloo, ON: Wilfred Laurier University Press, 2000), 19–39.

7. Lorenzo Veracini, "Historylessness: Australia as a Settler Colonial Collective," *Postcolonial Studies* 10, no. 3 (2007): 271.

8. Alan Lawson, "The Anxious Proximities of Settler (Post)Colonial Relations," in *Literary Theory: An Anthology*, ed. Julie Rivkin and Michael Ryan (Massachusetts: Blackwell, 1998): 1210–23.

9. Jacques-Alain Miller, "Introduction to Reading Jacques Lacan's Seminar *Anxiety*," *Lacanian Ink* 26 (2005): 10.

10. Jacques Lacan, *Seminar X (1962–1963): Anxiety* (Unpublished): Seminar 2, 3.

11. As Renata Salecl explains:

the usual perception is that we fear something that we see or hear – that is, something that can be discerned as an object or situation. Fear would thus seem to concern what can be articulated. In contrast, we often perceive anxiety as a state of fear that is objectless, meaning we cannot easily say what it is that makes us anxious. Anxiety thus seems to be an uncomfortable affect, more horrible than fear because it is unclear what provokes it (p. 18).

12. My understanding of anxiety here relies upon the psychoanalytic tradition, particularly that associated with Jacques Lacan. While there are other, differing explanations of the anxiety phenomenon, I believe this is most relevant because of the long history between the fields of postcolonialism and psychoanalysis (see the work of Homi Bhabha, Mrinalini Greedharry, Ranjana Khanna, or Kalpana Seshadri-Crooks).

13. Jacques Lacan, *Seminar X (1962–1963): Anxiety* (Unpublished), Seminar 7, 4–5.

14. Ibid., 4–5.

15. Ibid., Seminar 10, 1.

16. Roberto Harari, *Lacan's Seminar on Anxiety: An Introduction* (New York: Other Press, 2001), 33.

17. Lacan calls it the *objet petit a*, or the object small a. I will continue to call this object the "object-cause of desire" in an attempt to allay the confusion surrounding Lacanian terminology.

18. Samuel Weber, *Return to Freud: Jacques Lacan's Dislocation of Psychoanalysis* (Cambridge and New York: Cambridge University Press, 1991), 159.

19. As Charles Shepherdson writes: "while Freud appears to formulate anxiety as a response to separation or loss, Lacan insists that anxiety is not a response to the loss of an object, but rather arises when lack fails to appear" (p. xxxi).

20. Jacob Pollock, "We Don't Want Your Racist Tour: The 1981 Springbok Tour and the Anxiety of Settlement in Aotearoa/New Zealand," *Graduate Journal of Asia-Pacific Studies* 2, no. 1 (2004): 35; Avril Bell, "Bifurcation or Entanglement? Settler Identity and Biculturalism in Aotearoa New Zealand," *Continuum: Journal of Media & Culture Studies* 20, no. 2 (2006): 254; Stuart Murray, "Precarious Adulthood: Communal Anxieties in 1980s Film," in *Contemporary New Zealand Cinema: From New Wave to Blockbuster*, ed. Ian Conrich and Stuart Murray (London and New York: I. B. Tauris, 2008), 169–70; Alistair Fox, "Inwardness, Insularity, and the Man Alone: Postcolonial Anxiety in the New Zealand Novel," *Journal of Postcolonial Writing* 45, no. 3 (2009): 263–67.

21. Murray, "Precarious Adulthood," 169.

22. Ibid., 170.

23. Ranginui Walker, *Ka Whawhai Tonu Mātou: Struggle Without End* (Auckland: Penguin, 2004), 209.

24. Ibid.

25. Ibid., 199–225.

26. Paul Hamer, "A Quarter-century of the Waitangi Tribunal: Responding to the Challenge," in *The Waitangi Tribunal: Te Roopu Whakaman i te Tiriti o Waitangi*, ed. Janine Hayward and Nicola R. Wheen (Wellington: Bridget Williams Books, 2004), 5.

27. Ward, "Foreword," in *The Waitangi Tribunal*, ix.

28. See, for example, James Belich, *The New Zealand Wars and the Victorian Interpretation of Racial Conflict* (Auckland: Auckland University Press, 1986); *"I Shall not Die": Titokowaru's War, New Zealand, 1868–9* (Wellington: Allen & Unwin, 1989); *Making Peoples: A History of the New Zealanders: From Polynesian Settlement to the End of the Nineteenth Century* (Auckland: Penguin, 1996); *Paradise Reforged: A History of the New Zealanders from the 1880s to the Year 2000* (Auckland: Allen Lane, Penguin Press, 2001). Or Judith Binney, *The Legacy of Guilt: A Life of Thomas Kendall* (Auckland: Oxford University Press, 1968); *Mihaia: The Prophet Rua Kenana and his Community at Maungapohatu* (Wellington, Oxford University Press, 1979); *Redemption Songs: A Life of Te Kooti Arikirangi Te Turuki* (Auckland: Auckland University Press and Bridget Williams Books, 1995); *Encircled Lands: Te Urewera, 1820–1921* (Wellington: Bridget Williams Books, 2009).

29. Stuart Murray, "Precarious Adulthood," 171.

30. Julian Thomas, "A History of Beginnings," in *Quicksands: Foundational Histories in Australia and Aotearoa New Zealand*, ed. Klaus Neumann, Nicholas Thomas, Hilary Eriksen (Sydney: UNSW Press, 1999), 115.

31. Lawson, "Proximities," 19.

32. Ibid., 27.

33. Thomas, "A History of Beginnings," 118.

34. Cynthia Sugars, "(Dis)Inheriting the Nation: Contemporary Canadian Memoirs and the Anxiety of Origins," in *Moveable Margins: The Shifting Spaces of Canadian Literature*, ed. Chelva Kanaganayakam (Ontario: TSAR, 2005), 178.

35. Ibid.

36. Lois Parkinson Zamora, *The Usable Past: The Imagination of History in Recent Fiction of the Americas* (Cambridge: Cambridge University Press, 1997), ix.

37. Thomas, "A History of Beginnings," 125.

38. Ibid.

39. Avril Bell, "Bifurcation or Entanglement? Settler Identity and Biculturalism in Aotearoa New Zealand," *Continuum: Journal of Media & Culture Studies* 20, no. 2 (2006): 257.

40. Lorenzo Veracini, "Historylessness: Australia as a Settler Colonial Collective," *Postcolonial Studies* 10, no. 3 (2007): 271.

41. Ibid., 271–72; Thomas, "A History of Beginnings," 124; Jonathon Lamb, "The Idea of Utopia in the European Settlement of New Zealand," in *Quicksands: Foundational Histories in Australia and Aotearoa New Zealand*, ed. Klaus Neumann, Nicholas Thomas, and Hilary Eriksen, 80–81.

42. Veracini, "Historylessness," 272.

43. Stephen Turner, "Settlement as Forgetting," in *Quicksands: Foundational Histories in Australia and Aotearoa New Zealand*, ed. Klaus Neumann, Nicholas Thomas, Hilary Eriksen, 20.

44. Ivan Butler, "Pictures," *Films and Filming* 338 (1982): 34.

45. Peter Wells, "Pictures," *The New Zealand Listener* (18 June 1983): 30.

46. Nick Roddick, "Pictures," *Monthly Film Bulletin* (1982).

47. Both films were made almost simultaneously. *Utu*, however, was released to New Zealand audiences first, in 1983. The director and producer of *Pictures*, in order to avoid direct comparison with *Utu*, and in order to obtain international testimonials, decided to release the film overseas initially (in 1981). This explains why, in their reviews of *Pictures*, which is dated prior to *Utu*, reviewers are able to compare the film directly with *Utu* (even though it appears that it was released after *Pictures*).
48. Philip Wakefield, "Local Interest in Latest New Zealand Film," *Otago Daily Times* (27 May 1983).
49. Kristen Warner, "This Movie Is Not *Utu*," *Auckland Star* (28 May 1983).
50. "Letter to Barbara from O'Shea", 23 May 1982, D1159, MA1180, Box 280.
51. Unpublished, untitled document, no date, from Production Records, "Pictures," folder titled "Burton Brothers." MA1143, D1159, Box 240, Pacific Films Collection, New Zealand Film Archive, Ngā Kaitiaki O Ngā Taonga Whitiāhua.
52. "Letter to Mike from John O'Shea," 30 June 1980, Scrapbooks: "1978–79," "1980–82", D4678, MA1216, Box 7, Folder 1a, John O'Shea Personal Papers Collection, New Zealand Film Archive, Ngā Kaitiaki O Ngā Taonga Whitiāhua.
53. "The Long Bright Land?" unpublished, January 1980. D4678, MA1216, Box 7, Folder 1a, John O'Shea Personal Papers Collection, New Zealand Film Archive, Ngā Kaitiaki O Ngā Taonga Whitiāhua.
54. Reid Perkins, "Imag(in)ing Our Colonial Past: Colonial New Zealand Films from *The Birth of New Zealand* to *The Piano*," *Illusions* 26 (1996): 17.
55. Ibid.
56. Sandra Coney, "Pictures," *Broadsheet* (July/August 1983): 45.
57. "Screenplay." January 1980. Production Records, Scripts: "Pictures," D1159, MA1166, Box 271, Pacific Films Collection, New Zealand Film Archive, Ngā Kaitiaki O Ngā Taonga Whitiāhua.
58. Charles Wilson Hursthouse was a Captain in the New Zealand militia and performed survey work in Taranaki and the King Country. He served in the Taranaki Rifle Volunteers at Waireka and Mahoetaki and in several other engagements, and later was an officer in the Military Settlers Force and Volunteer Militia Scouts (Cowan 175). The incident referred to by Rochfort in the screenplay is based on a real-life account, in which Hursthouse and several others were captured at Te Uira by the prohet Te Mahuki and his Tekau-mā-rua movement. He was later rescued and went on to write several accounts of early settlement in Taranaki. Cowan's account may be found at http://www.nzetc.org/tm/scholarly/Cow01NewZ-fig-Cow01NewZ175a.html. Accessed 27 November 2010.
59. "Screenplay." January 1980. Production Records, Scripts: "Pictures," D1159, MA1166, Box 271, Pacific Films Collection, New Zealand Film Archive, Ngā Kaitiaki O Ngā Taonga Whitiāhua.

Chapter 5

Cross-currents: *River Queen's* National and Trans-national Heritages

Olivia Macassey

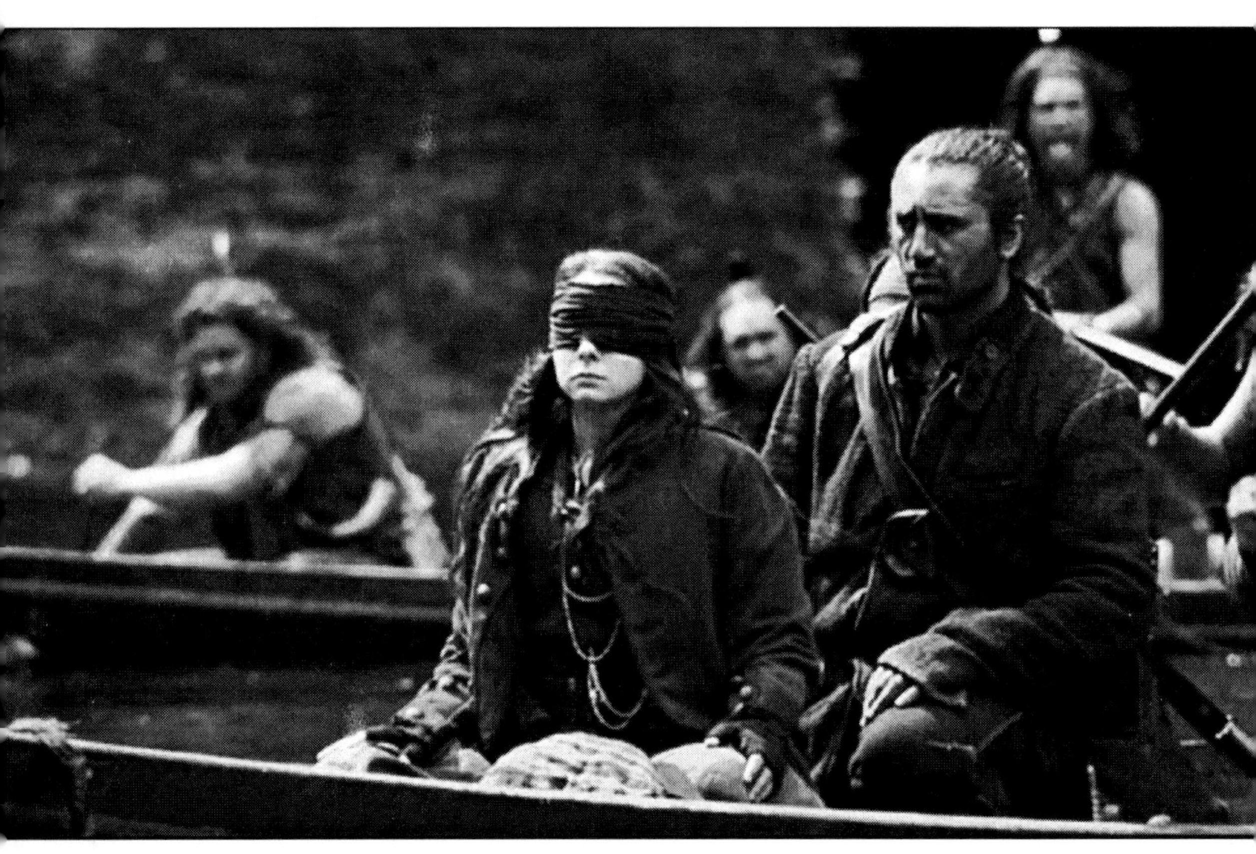

Sarah being taken upriver in *River Queen*, 2005, dir. Vincent Ward.

When I first watched the period drama *River Queen* (Vincent Ward, 2005), one of my first thoughts was: "I wonder if they can fit a piano onto that boat?" That this image suggested itself to me – a piano, lashed to the hull somewhere in front of a pallid Samantha Morton as she travels upriver into the interior – is a function of the way in which this film situates itself in relation to Aotearoa New Zealand cinema, but also a function of its position in relation to an international production trend in period film since the late 1970s. In a curious double moment, the iconography of *River Queen* at once conjures up another cinematic settler, Ada, travelling by *waka* in Jane Campion's *The Piano* (1993), yet it also makes me think of the upriver journey of the titular madman of Werner Herzog's *Fitzcarraldo* (1982). I can read my phantom piano as a signifier of a particular type of European taste and culture which appears regularly in Northern Hemisphere period drama. Still, a piano not only turns up in Aotearoa New Zealand in *The Piano*, but gets thrown out the window in Geoff Murphy's *Utu* (1983). Having a piano onboard is, in a sense, a metaphor for aesthetic and generic insertion in an international market niche.

In this chapter, I will attempt to explore my double take, situating *River Queen* within the wider context of costume drama as an international production trend, and analysing its consequent use of aesthetic and generic elements. Despite its generic inheritance, this film positions itself locally in relation to both the colonial history of Aotearoa New Zealand and to contemporaneous cinematic articulations of New Zealand identity. *River Queen*, I suggest, negotiates the choppy waters of that estuary where the river of the local feeds out into increasingly international waters. In combining an attention to the specificities of local, national history with the signifying practices of a transnational trend in contemporary cinema, the film productively destabilises the conventional claims to authority on which the latter tends to rely.

Period drama as a transnational production trend

River Queen emerged after over two-and-a-half decades of successful Anglophone period film. Successful British films such as *Chariots of Fire* (Hugh Hudson, 1981) and *A Room with a View* (James Ivory, 1985), and on television, Granada's *Brideshead Revisited* (1981) had been followed by an era of increased production of period films, which continued strongly for two decades, seemed to stagnate as the last century turned, and rallied in the new one. The heritage turn in Australia began slightly earlier with a series of "prestige" films supported by the Australian Film Commission and other funding bodies, including *Picnic at Hanging Rock* (Peter Weir, 1975) and *My Brilliant Career* (Gillian Armstrong, 1979). The success of these earlier films helped to identify a niche for period film as a species of specialty film, in the United Kingdom and beyond.[1] Such films have often been read primarily in relation to the national pasts they represent, and the national cinemas they (at least partially) inhabit. Their tendency to Victorian and Edwardian period settings means that they depict eras conceptualised as foundational to our own societies, and hence are readily available to be read as allegorical representations of national pasts.

As allegories for national pasts, contemporary period films are often found wanting. In Britain, for instance, the period film boom coincided with a general heritage revival in the 1980s, a movement often critically associated within Britain with social neo-conservativism and the policies of the Thatcher Government, encapsulated in the National Heritage Act of 1979. Many commentators saw period films as part of an emerging heritage industry which commoditised an elite past for international consumption whilst ignoring the social and political realities obtaining at the time of their production. Prominently, Andrew Higson suggested that in these films, film form and aesthetics themselves facilitate and solicit conservative ideological positions.[2] The emphasis of these criticisms is on the role the films play in constructing national identity and selling it abroad. Similarly, the Australian quality period film cycle, derisively dubbed the "AFC genre" (in allusion to the sponsorship of such films by the Australian Film Commission), came under fire as nostalgic, conservative and reactionary in their imagining of an Australian past.[3]

Both *The Piano* and *Utu*, set in the 1850s and 1860s respectively, index foundational moments in the history of the modern nation state.[4] *The Piano* in particular has drawn criticism for the allegorical implications of the interpersonal relationships between the main character Ada, and her two potential partners, repressed coloniser Alisdair Stewart and the interstitial, almost Pākehā-Māori coloniser George Baines, who lives with the indigenous locals and speaks Te Reo Māori. For example, Anna Neill suggests that *The Piano* articulates a non-British white settler identity: Alisdair demonstrates the same patriarchal, abusive attitudes to Ada and to Māori, and is finally rejected. Alisdair's trajectory refers to "the alienation and ultimately the humiliation of the colonial settler class and at the same time to the triumph of the new settler culture which becomes indigenised by its association with the Māori victims of colonial oppression."[5] With its male suitors polarised between a British colonial soldier (who expires), and a Māori warrior (whom Sarah eventually chooses), *River Queen* too can be read as an allegory for the forging of a modern Aotearoa New Zealand. Sarah's reconciliation with her son, who has a Māori father, and eventual acceptance into a family unit consisting of that son and his uncle Wiremu, can be read as a naturalising of Pākehā settlement. Sarah occupies an interstitial place similar to that of George Baines, and like him, her partial immersion in the Māori community is marked with a tattoo. Ward himself clearly conceptualises his film in allegorical terms: "it captures quite a core experience that feels relevant – who we are and can we find a way between different cultures and groups of people."[6]

However, to examine a film such as *River Queen* solely through the prism of national allegory affords an incomplete view, because to do so is to leave unaccounted its imbrication in the wider context of period film as a transnational production trend. Claire Monk argues that since contemporary period films primarily address international audiences and niche markets, it is productive to read them in these terms rather than as articulations of a specifically national identity and heritage.[7] In her study *Contemporary Costume Film*, Julianne Pidduck deliberately shifts away from such a national focus, arguing that costume films should be seen as "global products addressing international audiences."[8] Pidduck argues that period films draw on foundational English cultural referents, traditions and concerns which are part of a common postcolonial legacy for Anglophone audiences. Pidduck suggests that the international western appeal of period film is contingent on formations of taste, space and subjectivity which are predicated on this legacy.[9] As I will briefly demonstrate below, *River Queen's* deployment of generic period film characteristics signals its reference to just such formations. The facts of international marketing and distribution of contemporary period films and their often transnational production and financing underscore the transnational nature of period film circulation and address.[10] The international legibility and circulation of period film is derived from colonial and neo-colonial circulation of both cultural forms and capital.

Period drama's transnational career over the past three decades has been made possible by specific developments in the way Anglophone cinema is produced and circulated: for example, conglomerate era Hollywood's own increasingly transnational character, the rise of international co-production, and the infrastructural facilitation of specialty or niche production and distribution to target increasingly fragmented audiences.[11] *The Piano*, for Pidduck, is a good example of a film produced in this context because it is a co-production with a relatively low budget and auteur direction, it was strongly marketed by Miramax – the flagship of specialty distribution – and it achieved cross-over success with good box office in several key markets.[12] *River Queen* is also a product of this context: its relatively low budget, international stars and its status as a UK/NZ co-production (produced by Don Reynolds and Chris Autry) are all hallmarks of the trend, as are its debut at the Toronto Film Festival and Ward's auteur stamp.

Lynette Read has suggested that Ward's status as a "New Zealand filmmaker" has been partly facilitated by processes of globalisation which extend the boundaries of New Zealandness.[13] Similarly, one could argue that the Aotearoa New Zealand Government's recently established Film Production Fund, and the availability of personnel who had previously worked on films such as the *Lord of the Rings* trilogy (Peter Jackson, 2001–2003), *Without a Paddle* (Steven Brill, 2004) and *The Last Samurai* (Edward Zwick, 2003) have provided the material pre-conditions for *River Queen's* emergence as a New Zealand film.[14] The Film Production Fund was a finite source, mandated to fund feature films that both included significant local content and were commercially viable to the extent that they could attract some forty percent of matching funding from "external sources."[15] In the case of *River Queen*, an external element was provided by the UK Film Consortium, the Film

Council and Invicta Capital, among others; and by the transnational appeal of Samantha Morton and Kiefer Sutherland as British colonists. The way in which Aotearoa New Zealand is positioned and positions itself in relation to global networks of capital and distribution affects and effects the way *River Queen* operates as a local text.

The demands of genre

If *River Queen's* funding is predicated on its commercial viability in an international context, then it must also be read as a genre film, ensuring its *legibility* in that context by drawing on a repertoire of conventional characteristics and aesthetic properties common to recent period romance films. That *River Queen* follows the literal and metaphorical journey of a central female protagonist, Sarah, and gives narrative weight to the vicissitudes of her interpersonal relationships with potential love interests marks it as generic. A central spirited heroine following her heart is a staple of period romance, particularly from the 1990s onward. Sarah's pivotal role enables the "female narration, agency and expression" that, as Pidduck points out, is central to the genre. Despite their availability for allegorical readings, period films from disparate national contexts share an interest in love and sexuality which are accessible to international niche audiences.[16] This is true of *The Piano*, which, despite being read by some as an allegory for Pākehā identity, was more commonly engaged with *internationally* in terms of female agency and desire.[17] It's also true of other internationally successful period romance films set in colonised spaces (which I term colonial heritage romance) such as *My Brilliant Career, Out of Africa* (Sidney Pollack, 1985) and *A Passage to India* (David Lean, 1984). In these films, a universalised western discourse pits the individual agency and romantic interests of central characters against a repressive society. Since the repressive society in such films is necessarily colonial, the result is that this conflict is by its very structure analogous to colonial power relations between colonised and coloniser.[18] *River Queen* typifies this pattern: the repressive elements of society are crystallised in the imperial societal order crystallised in the figure of Major Baine, and to a lesser extent in that of Sarah's father, a man who seems to be dead set against both Sarah's love and decolonisation itself. (In this sense, he's cast in the same mould as *The Piano's* repressed spoilsport Alisdair Stewart). However, *River Queen* differs from colonial heritage romance *per se* in that the romance plot in the personal sphere is juxtaposed with a prominent action plot in the public sphere – the literal replaces the allegorical as the protagonists are increasingly swept into bloody warfare.

In keeping with its adherence to generic conventions, *River Queen* is also concerned to accurately reference the historical period in which it is set. This concern is apparent in *River Queen's* attention to period detail and recreation in the mise-en-scène. When I saw *River Queen* at the cinema, I picked up a ten-page booklet which details the use of special mud, distressed costumes and authentic period guns, and quotes the director's remark that "it was crucial for a film in this period to look authentic."[19] The film was extensively researched over a period of several years, and draws on a variety of historical sources. These include diaries and newspaper stories of nineteenth-century women who had crossed cultures, such as Anne Evans and Caroline Ngoungou; as well as contemporaneous colonial accounts of warfare between Crown and Māori forces. Such "crucial" detail attests to period drama's need to demonstrate an authoritative discourse of historical accuracy. Period drama's sense of historicity is constructed partly through painstakingly recreated mise-en-scènic detail and its realist cinematographic presentation, which (along with extra-textual elements such as canonical source material, high production values and marketing) connote both quality and authority. The veracity of such accounts of the past is thus reliant on formal conventions.

However, *River Queen's* mise-en-scène moves beyond existing genre convention. For example, the costumes are not always intended to be true to any one time period, and in particular the film's main character, Sarah, seldom wears the kind of costume we usually associate with the genre. Rather, this heroine wears an odd mixture of feminine attire and old army cast-offs, most notably a military style jacket. According to costume designer Barbara Darragh, "[Sarah] has grown up without a mother, so she has her own take on femininity."[20] Sarah also manifests what Ward calls "cross-dressing" – another such example is, he explains, "a naked Māori in a top hat or with a kilt and full-face moko."[21] Sartorial hybridity here is not confined to the Māori characters (as it largely was in *The Piano*). Intriguingly, director Vincent Ward links authenticity not to an aesthetic but to local history, via the ancestry of locally sourced extras as well as an emphasis on consultation with local iwi (Māori tribes). By taking part in this film, Ward feels, the Whanganui extras "were in some sense dealing with a part of who they are and where they "belonged.""[22] Authority is thus derived not from the language of convention but rather from interpersonal connections to place and to cultural memory.

The construction of a sense of time and place in *River Queen* follows the conventions of the genre: for instance, the ample use of the protagonist's voiceover, and the use of captions function to structure the film and anchor it temporally. The close-ups of letters and emphasis on writing, which supplement voiceover narration in the opening and closing sequences, are also typical of period film.[23] The film's impressionistic, blurred montages and slow-motion passages, however, are not, and act to undermine both the illusion of linear time and the integrity of the constructed authentic image, highlighting the (often covert) pastiche at the heart of all period film. *River Queen's* visual artistry, however, does dovetail with period film's cinematic reliance on aesthetically pleasing imagery; for example in its intermittent use of aesthetically motivated shots, such as a mid-close-up of Sarah and Boy asleep, shot through lace. Such shots are prevalent in period film (which shares Ward's preoccupation with European art cinema). Others, such as the long tracking shots straight up the Whanganui River, are generic in that they are extraneous to straightforward diegetic requirements, landscapes which primarily act as touristic spectacles for the film viewer. Andrew Higson has argued that these types of shots, namely exterior wide shots which do not perform the function of establishing location or of showing character point of view, are directly linked to, and solicit, the gaze of the admiring spectator.[24] Certainly, the helpful booklet on *River Queen* which I picked up at the cinema concluded with an illustrated

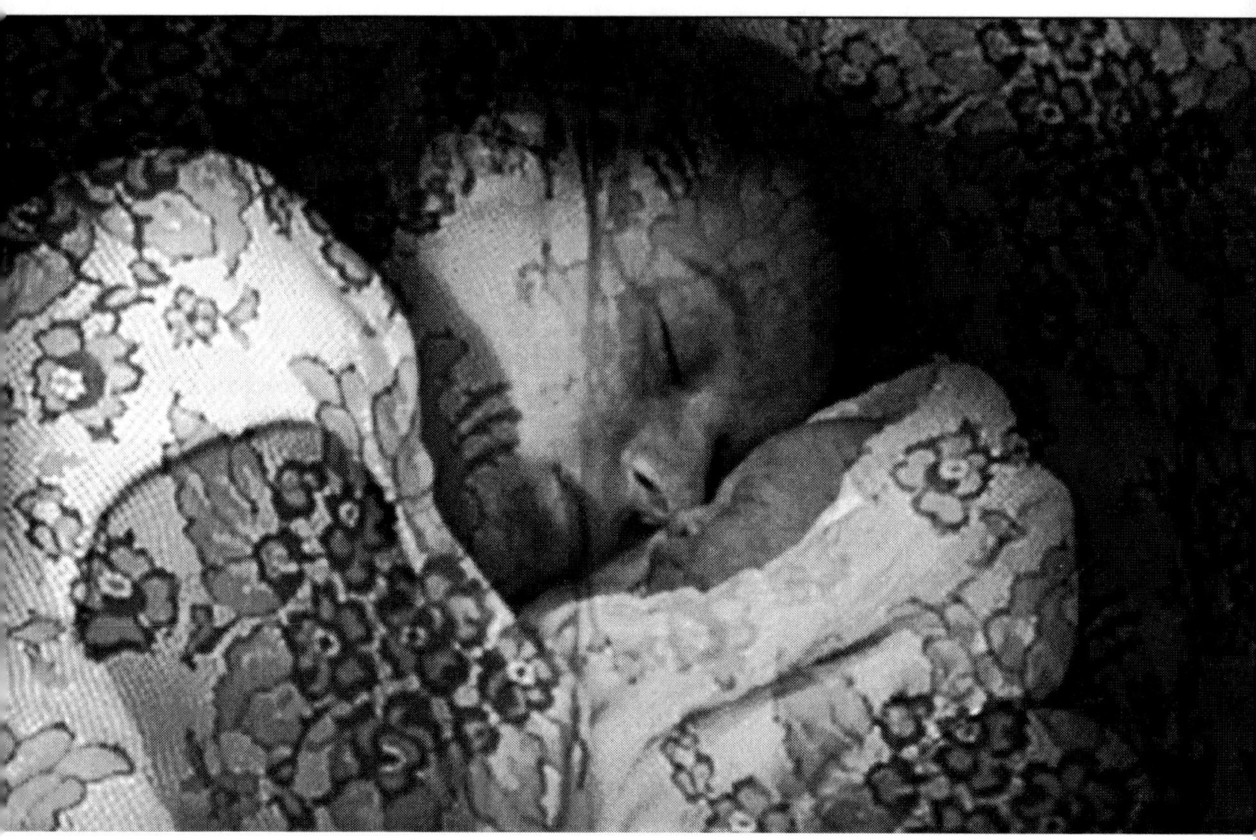

Sarah and Boy asleep, shot through lace, in *River Queen*, 2005, dir. Vincent Ward.

summary of the region's "pleasant climate," accessibility and tourist attractions – including river tours.[25]

River Queen also shares with other period films set in colonised spaces, including *The Piano*, a recourse to a specific filmic language inherited from imperial conditions of representation; a set of tropes, imagery and film grammar which together act as a kind of shorthand for particular themes, and which we might term "imperial grammar."[26] For instance, the film's promotional tagline – "with darkness all around, only the heart can see" – signals its position within the narrative tradition of the dangerous journey into the heart of darkness or interior of the exotic landscape, a theme associated formally with the imperial trope of the white woman in the open boat. Geographically centred around the Whanganui River, the story involves several journeys made by Sarah, the first via steamer and later blindfolded in a *waka*. Journeys upriver are common to narratives of colonial exploration. According to co-writer Toa Fraser, while writing *River Queen*, he and Ward derived inspiration from watching a number of films which include *Apocalypse Now* (Francis Ford Coppola, 1979), *The Mission* (Roland Joffé, 1986) and Werner Herzog films *Fitzcarraldo* (1982) and *Aguirre: The Wrath of God* (1972).[27] All of these films employ the same trope of the white protagonist's journey upriver into the heart of darkness. Strangely, a number were also notoriously fraught with difficulty and disaster during production, a fate which similarly befell *River Queen*.

A further example of how this trope formally inflects *River Queen* is that of the presentation of Te Kai Pō's place in the Whanganui River, one of the film's repeated motifs, recurring as a premonition for Sarah. It is reminiscent in appearance, shot and central framing of the island of the Huron in Bruce Beresford's 1991 film *The Black Robe*. In the latter, the upriver settlement is the subject of premonition for the protagonist Laforgue, a young colonial missionary who, like Sarah, journeys up a river with indigenous people in an open boat. Aesthetic similarities between the two films are further echoed by those of their narratives: while Sarah is a mother, the priest Laforgue is in some sense a Father; both are on a spiritual journey in search of children, whites penetrating the darkness of the interior. Both bring western medical enlightenment, as they minister to the (influenza struck yet warlike) natives. The use of this shorthand as an aesthetic device clearly brings inadvertent baggage onboard the film.

River Queen and Aotearoa New Zealand cinema

At the national level, the eclectic visual style of *River Queen* makes comparisons between it and other Aotearoa New Zealand films almost irresistible, right from the first shots of the opening sequence: a woman in nineteenth-century dress looks out at a West Coast beach. The fact that she is our narrator tempts me to see the film as a sort of unofficial sequel to *The Piano*. More almost-familiar shots follow, one of someone shimmering beneath the surface of water, another of a mysterious rolling thing that could almost be a whale from

Whale Rider (Niki Caro, 2002). A high-angle wide shot of a winding, heavily CGI'd fantasy river, not unlike that of *Lord of the Rings* completes the sequence: a pastiche of Aotearoa New Zealand on film, recognisable from home, from abroad – and from the box office. I'm not alone in this interpretation. Reviewing for the *New Zealand Listener*, Philip Matthews explicitly locates *River Queen* in terms of other local films, saying that "as in a hallucinated history of New Zealand film, the nutty romanticism of *The Piano* blends into the land-wars western *Utu*." Characterising these two comparisons as representational of the European art movie influence, and that of American B-movies, he sees a third influence in the fantasy epic: "these misty mountains and winding rivers," he says "are straight out of *Lord of the Rings*."[28] Similarly, Tim Wong, reviewing the film more favourably in the journal *Landfall*, says that "you could be forgiven for thinking this was another trip down river by the Fellowship."[29] Again, though, these uncanny resemblances may be a function not just of *River Queen*'s reference to other cinematic articulations of Aotearoa New Zealand (or Middle Earth) but also symptomatic of the wider repertoires which such films themselves may index: further afield, Kate Stables in *Sight and Sound* complains of *River Queen*'s "echoes of other movies," which include *The Piano*, but also *The Last of the Mohicans* (Michael Mann, 1992) and *The Searchers* (John Ford, 1956).[30]

River Queen shares more with *The Piano*, in particular, than their nineteenth-century Aotearoa New Zealand bush setting. The similarities and coincidences between the two are marked enough that to read the former as a sequel to the latter is not merely fanciful. Each begins with voiceover narration from its main protagonist, one in an Irish, the other a Scottish accent. In each, the main narrative strand centres around a single mother who must follow her heart on a journey inland. There, she is torn between two possible suitors who embody different allegorical positions: politics are played out through interpersonal relationships. The resolution of each film is briefly interrupted by the near-drowning of its heroine, before each finishes with a scene of heterosexual coupledom with solidly built house and happy family. Most arrestingly, each features digital amputation. Sarah's lover Wiremu suffers the loss of a finger, for reasons that are far less central to *River Queen*'s plot than Ada's mutilation is to that of *The Piano*. Seeking to rescue his nephew Boy, who has been captured by enemy forces, Wiremu is asked for his finger as a substitute for Boy's freedom. He abruptly and angrily chops off his own finger, and (like Ada) appears in shocked slow motion as a horrified Sarah looks on.

Despite having a more eclectic approach to period costume and impressionist cinematographic style, *River Queen* bears a number of aesthetic similarities with *The Piano*. It uses the same deliberate aesthetic contrast between a white woman in a wedding dress and the dark Aotearoa New Zealand bush that appeared in the earlier film. As Ward puts it, "one woman with pale features would stand out."[31] As noted above, both films feature strikingly similar images of the foreshore: *River Queen*'s opening shot would not be out of place during Ada's landfall and beach visits. Moreover, both films use the specific piece of imperial imagery of a "civilised" European picturesquely seated in an open boat – *River Queen*'s seminal image is of Sarah travelling upriver blindfolded, while *The Piano*'s Ada is

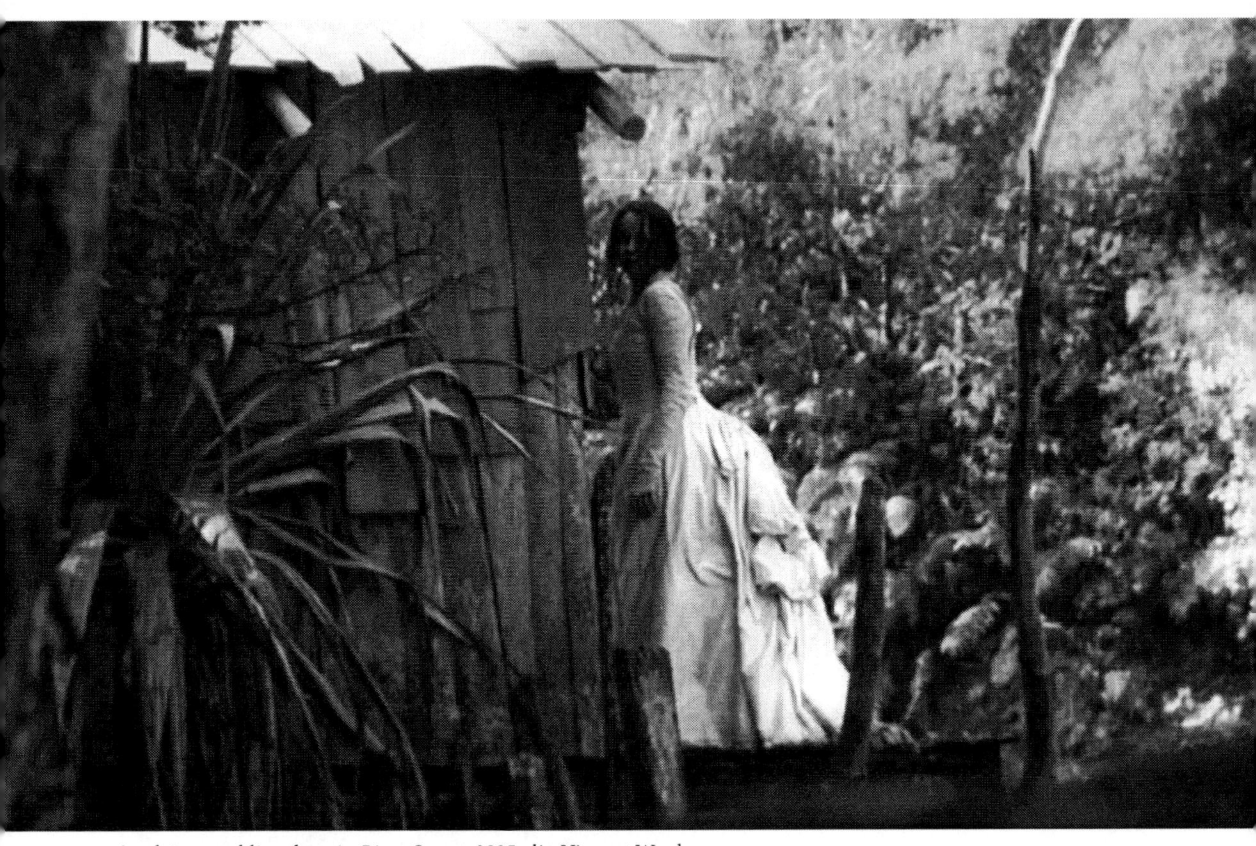

Sarah in a wedding dress in *River Queen*, 2005, dir. Vincent Ward.

first seen handed out of a longboat and later ensconced in a *waka*. In each, this imagery at once encapsulates the period film staple of women's romantic adventure, and the symbolic entry of European convention and culture into the Antipodean natural setting.

In the later film, though, there are several significant changes. Firstly, the process of colonisation is underscored, and made explicit through detailed conflict in *River Queen*, which has a strong historical action-film component and is set in the Whanganui River district during the New Zealand Wars. These wars, which broke out in the 1860s, arose out of issues which were percolating at the time in which *The Piano* is set, an aspect made conspicuous by its absence in the earlier film, as several commentators have noted. As Annie Goldson observes, "[the] active military struggles against colonial occupation that were waging throughout this period are altogether absent from [*The Piano*], although admittedly the film is rather vague about its exact period."[32] The warfare in *River Queen* seems to be loosely based on that between Māori followers of the Pai Mārire movement (led by Rīwha Tītokowaru), and mixed British colonial and kūpapa Māori (who, for a number of reasons, fought alongside Crown forces in the New Zealand Wars). In particular, the central armed conflict in the film references a victory against colonial forces at Te Ngutu o te Manu, translated as The Beak of the Bird.[33]

However, the conflict and characters in the film are not straightforwardly representative of actual historical figures and events, but rather a pastiche of them. While Colonel Baine bears a resemblance to the figure of Gustavus von Tempsky, the character of Te Kai Pō seems to be created by the amalgamation of Rīwha Tītokowaru, who fought at Te Ngutu o te Manu, and the prophet Te Kooti Arikirangi Te Turuki. At one point, we see Te Kai Pō having sex with a young woman before his troops desert him. This scene is in reference to the suggestion, related by James Belich, that Tītokowaru lost his own forces at one point due to a breech caused when he had sexual relations with the wife of another chief.[34] On the other hand, during her peregrinations through the Whanganui River, Sarah was perhaps likely to have run into either Te Kooti, or his various pursuers, coming the other way. The action in *River Queen* begins in 1868; by late 1869, wanted by the colonial forces, Te Kooti was hiding in the area. At one point he occupied a bush camp while the women and children with him were sent to the upper Whanganui, and later pursued by a local chief named Topia and his men.[35]

River Queen explicitly references an aspect of colonial history neglected until recently, albeit in an indirect fashion. (In itself, this reference is not unproblematic, as Annabel Cooper's contribution to the present volume demonstrates.) Belich notes that although Tītokowaru's victory was one of the greatest of Māori over Pākehā, his achievements were "gradually watered down" until he no longer featured in general histories of Aotearoa New Zealand.[36] However, *River Queen* presents its historical referents primarily in terms of an interpersonal conflict between individuals, rather than as a result of systematic colonial policies or even of the actions and decisions taken by powerful historic leaders. This strategy preserves the non-specificity demanded by allegory: Te Kai Pō is thus *the* Māori prophet chief rather than a specific individual. It is telling that in this film, the conditions of belonging are explicitly predicated on active engagement with Māori. Sarah, the interstitial, proto-New Zealander figure chooses a Māori lover, and her kinship bond with him thus further authorises her presence in Aotearoa New Zealand. Her son Boy, the offspring of both indigenous and settler parents, is in the film's logic the true inheritor of the nation. But at an allegorical level *River Queen* is strangely messy. For example, Wiremu's acceptance of digital mutilation could be interpreted as an acceptance of castration in order to secure Boy's future.

There are significant shifts in the use of imagery, too, between *The Piano* and *River Queen*, which signal the latter film's unwillingness to fully embrace genre conventions, in favour of an eclectic attention to the local. The mannered aesthetic of period romance used by the earlier film's cinematography and costuming is destabilised. The painterly, unpopulated landscape, says Wong, is "replaced firmly by the grime and muck of colonisation."[37] While Sarah still looks picturesque in her boat, her muddy military coat acts as a reminder of the colonial violence on which her presence is predicated. And, despite *River Queen's* self-conscious aestheticism, many of the film's spectacular shots evade capture by a touristic gaze. Often, they seem extraneous to the "real" spectacle. For instance, an artistic shot of Te Kai Pō copulating majestically with another chief's wife, framed by rafters as the camera swoops above, briefly interrupts an important action sequence. The film's viewer is thus obliged to supply narrative significance to the shot from his or her own understanding of the historical figure to which it refers. Indeed, Sarah herself seems almost extraneous at times, despite being the visual focus of many of the more aesthetically pleasing shots, as both imagery and narrative refuse to fully privilege her story over that of the wider conflict, or vice versa.

For some commentators, *River Queen's* recurrent intertextual iconography and ambiguous address can only disturb. "The unintentional effect is like one of Guy Maddin's camp pastiches of early films," complains Matthews, "as possibly meaningful images arise and disappear back into the murk, leaving us none the wiser."[38] But pastiche too has its precedents in local costume film. Stewart Main and Peter Wells' own camp film, *Desperate Remedies* (1993), which privileges pastiche, performance and theatricality, and Don Selwyn's Shakespearian adaptation, *Te Tangata Whai Rawa O Weneti* (2002), which fashions its past out of a hybrid local present, both refuse to provide the type of authenticity usually demanded of the genre, and each challenges the authority of dominant historical narrative (from the European metropole) which drives this demand. Straddling the space between the buoyant international period niche and those more experimental craft, *River Queen* doesn't provide a period-piece with a piano, but nor does it entirely reject the idea of doing so. Rather, it offers a re-working of a popular transnational genre through a different and localised view of heritage.

Conclusions

The intersection of *River Queen's* engagement with the specifics of place, and its inherited generic address, seems in some ways unresolved. Ward says of his film, "I think it's easier for a New Zealand audience than any other audience – I've felt that New Zealanders have responded by and large very well to it, *particularly women who are over 25.*"[39] Despite the local focus of this description, Ward is also inadvertently citing the demographic most often associated with period drama spectatorship internationally, a demographic that *River Queen* certainly courts with its strong female protagonist, love story, and promotional focus on images of Samantha Morton as Sarah. In its double address, *River Queen* still raises questions about the ideological function of period cinema's use of aesthetics, and the availability of its interpersonal relationship narratives to readings as glib allegories. *River Queen*'s imbrication in an international western costume film trend – and, I suspect, Ward's visionary directing style, which has a tendency to reproduce and recycle imagery – sometimes cause aesthetics from an imperial grammar to re-inscribe old, imperial tropes in a film that essentially seeks to present a more progressive account of the colonial past. This phenomenon is perhaps unsurprising given the imperial heritage of the very markets which shape the trend. However, *River Queen*'s fluid and localised aesthetic and historical address moves it outside the paradigm of imported authenticity and destabilises the conventional political function of period cinema's museum aesthetic. Like its heroine Sarah, this film is, in a sense, finding its way between different cultural contexts and groups of people. It may have ventured up the creek without a piano, but in doing so, *River Queen* hits some interesting notes.

Notes

1. Graeme Turner, "Art Directing History: The Period Film," in *The Australian Screen*, ed. Albert Moran and Tom O'Regan (Ringwood: Penguin, 1989), 100.
2. Andrew Higson, *English Heritage, English Cinema: Costume Drama Since 1980* (Oxford: Oxford University Press, 2003). See also Cairns Craig, "Rooms Without a View," *Sight and Sound* 1, no. 2 (1991): 10–13; and Tana Wollen, "Over Our Shoulders: Nostalgic Screen Fictions for the 1980s," in *Enterprise and Heritage*, ed. John Corner and Sylvia Harvey (London: Routledge, 1991): 178–93.
3. Susan Dermody and Elizabeth Jacka, *The Screening of Australia: Anatomy of a National Cinema*, vol. 2 (Currency Press: Sydney, 1988), 30–33.
4. Bridget Orr, "Birth of a Nation? From *Utu* to *The Piano*," in *Piano Lessons: Approaches to The Piano*, ed. Felicity Coombs and Suzanne Gemmell (London: John Libbey, 1999), 148–60.
5. Anna Neill, "A Land Without a Past: Dreamtime and Nation in *The Piano*," in *Piano Lessons: Approaches to The Piano*, ed. Felicity Coombs and Suzanne Gemmell (London: John Libbey, 1999), 139.
6. Nick Grant, "Not Drowning, Waving," *Onfilm* 23, no. 1 (December 2005): 24.
7. Claire Monk, "The British Heritage Film Debate Revisited," in *British Historical Cinema*, ed. Claire Monk and Amy Sargeant (London and New York: Routledge, 2002), 188–91.
8. Julianne Pidduck, *Contemporary Costume Film: Space, Place, and the Past* (London: BFI Publishing, 2004), 4.
9. Ibid., 4–12.
10. Ibid.
11. See Yannis Tzioumakis, *American Independent Cinema: An Introduction* (New Brunswick: Rutgers University Press, 2006), 246–66.

12. Pidduck, *Contemporary Costume Film*, 9. See also Madeleine Dobie, "Gender and the Heritage Genre: Popular Feminism Turns to History," in *Jane Austen and Co.: Remaking the Past in Contemporary Culture*, ed. Suzanne R. Pucci and James Thompson (Albany: State University of New York Press, 2003), 247–60.
13. Lynette Read, "National Identity and the Films of Vincent Ward," *Metro Magazine* 148, (Spring 2006): 124–30.
14. Sue May, "River Queen: The Making of the Film on the Whanganui River," [pamphlet] (Wanganui: Whanganui Inc., 2005) provides an indication of crew involvement in previous projects.
15. Jennifer Lawn and Bronwyn Beatty, "Getting to Wellywood: National Branding and the Globalisation of the New Zealand Film Industry," *Postscript: Essays in Film and the Humanities* 24, no. 2 (2004–2005): 124.
16. Pidduck, *Contemporary Costume Film*, 2004.
17. Stephen Crofts, "Foreign Tunes? Gender and Nationality in Four Countries' Reception of *The Piano*," in *Jane Campion's The Piano*, ed. Harriet Margolis (Cambridge, New York, Melbourne: Cambridge University Press, 2000), 135–61.
18. Olivia Macassey, "Torn Stitches of the Heart: Post-imperial Trauma and Colonial Heritage Romance Cinema, 1979–2005." PhD diss., University of Auckland, 2009.
19. May, "River Queen".
20. Ibid. , 8.
21. Grant, "Not Drowning, Waving," 24.
22. May, "River Queen," 5.
23. Pidduck, *Contemporary Costume Film*, 54–57.
24. Higson, *English Heritage, English Cinema*, 38.
25. May, "River Queen," 14–16.
26. Macassey, "Torn Stitches of the Heart," 141–61.
27. Nick Grant, "Backyard Glitz," *Onfilm* 23, no. 1 (December 2005): 28.
28. Philip Matthews, "Watery Grave," *New Zealand Listener* (January 28–February 3 2006).
29. Tim Wong, "Out of the Mist," *Landfall* 211 (April 2006): 176.
30. Kate Stables, "Films: River Queen," *Sight and Sound* 18, no. 4 (2008): 75.
31. Quoted in May, "River Queen," 5.
32. Annie Goldson, "Piano Lessons," in *Film in Aotearoa New Zealand*, ed. Jonathan Dennis and Jan Bieringa (Wellington: Victoria University Press, 1992), 197.
33. See James Belich, *The New Zealand Wars* (Auckland: Penguin, 1988), 235–48.
34. Ibid., 272.
35. Judith Binney, *Redemption Songs: A Life of Te Kooti Arikirangi Te Turuki* (Auckland: Auckland University Press, 1995), 191–97.
36. Belich, *The New Zealand Wars*, 257, 318.
37. Wong, "Out of the Mist," 177.
38. Matthews, "Watery Grave," 2006.
39. Emphasis added. In Nick Grant, "Not Drowning, Waving," 24.

Chapter 6

Tracking Tītokowaru over Text and Screen: Pākehā Narrate the Warrior, 1906-2005

Annabel Cooper

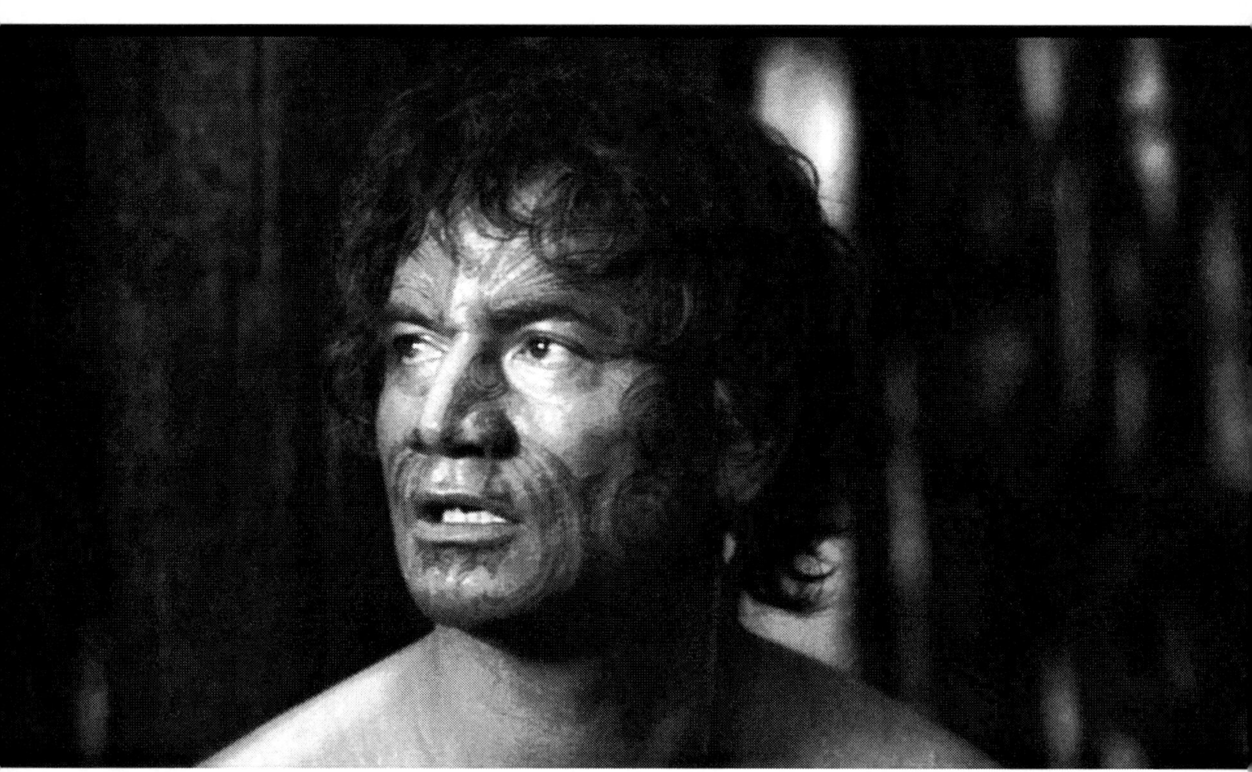

Temuera Morrison as Te Kai Pō in *River Queen*, 2005, dir. Vincent Ward.

A word for you. Cease travelling on the roads. Stop forever the going on the roads, lest you be left there as food for the birds of the air and the beasts of the field, or for me, because I have eaten the European as beef. He was cooked in a pot. The women and children partook of the food. I have begun to eat human flesh. Kua hamama toku koro koro ki te kai i te tangata. My throat is constantly open for the flesh of man. I shall not die. I shall not die. When death itself is dead, I shall be alive.[1]

The origins of this missive, enunciated here by Te Kai Pō, the warrior chief in Vincent Ward's feature film *River Queen*, lie in a letter calculated to strike fear into the hearts of European soldiers and settlers advancing on Taranaki land. Written on 25 June 1868 by the Ngāti Ruanui *rangatira* (chief) Rīwha Tītokowaru, it has been quoted ever since in various forms as Pākehā novelists, filmmakers and historians have returned to construe and reconstrue the meanings of Tītokowaru and Tītokowaru's War.[2] From James Cowan's series of articles, "The White Slave," in 1906 to Ward's feature film a century later, Tītokowaru has signified certain extremes of warrior masculinity in the Pākehā imaginary.

In analysing the texts of Tītokowaru's War in the light of both nation and gender, I draw on the term Susan Jeffords uses in discussing feature films on Vietnam, that they constitute a body of texts which work towards the "remasculinisation" of America. In the spirit of Robert Burgoyne's inquiry into historical feature films in the United States as the site through which dominant national narratives are reinterpreted, I ask whether a somewhat different process of "remasculinisation" can be traced through successive Pākehā re-imaginings of Tītokowaru. Burgoyne argues that contemporary historical films seek "a message from the past [...] that will validate the increasingly hybrid and polycultural reality of American life":

In combining the viewpoints of dominant and nondominant peoples [...] these films also register another more difficult and disturbing theme, which I will call "identity from across." The films I treat in this study insistently return to a certain hard kernel of historical truth – that social identities in the United States have largely been shaped by relations of opposition and antagonism, and that fear and hatred of the other have exerted [...] [a] powerful influence on the moulding of ethnic and racial identity [...]. The stories of nation that these films unfold convey a strong sense of the way white identity, for example, has shaped itself in contrast to its perceptions of black identity, or the way American "civilisation" has defined itself in contrast to conceptions of Indian "savagery"

– an oppositional logic that works against the idea that nationalism can be reconceived and reconfigured to express new forms of social coherence.[3]

Although American and New Zealand historical films do not engage with the same colonial pasts, Burgoyne's argument has remarkable pertinence in a discussion of Pākehā historical and cinematic views "across" to Tītokowaru's War. This chapter therefore analyses not only the trajectory of successive accounts of this war, but also attends specifically to narration across cultures through analysis of the figure of the Pākehā-Māori, a historical intermediary significant in Tītokowaru's story, who in each version anchors the point of view of Pākehā readers or viewers.

Pākehā conceptions of Māori masculinity have circled uneasily around a discourse of savagery in articulating Māori men through the figure of the warrior. Brendan Hokowhitu has argued that Māori men have been persistently cast in terms of physicality,[4] in a lineage in which sporting prowess descended from a warrior ethos. Savagery – especially by contrast with narratives of the North American West – has nevertheless not historically been the dominant discourse in Pākehā New Zealand Wars narratives. This is perhaps surprising given early European observers' fascination with cannibalism.[5] More common are discourses centring on the "worthy opponent," often noble in defeat, with Rewi Maniapoto and Wiremu Tamehana emblematic historical figures; and the flamboyant "rebel," with Hōne Heke Pōkai the best-known figure of this type. Later in the century, the popularisation of resistance figures centred more on the romantic utopianism and the pacifism associated with Rua Kēnana and Te Whiti o Rongomai, respectively. The dominant ideology of racial harmony, prevailing for much of the twentieth century, precluded the dominance of more antagonistic accounts.

Terror or savagery is nevertheless a persistent minor strain in Pākehā accounts of the Wars, and is arguably especially interesting given that it disrupts the prevailing ideology.[6] Pursuing this minor strain of "extremes" of warrior masculinity takes us to an analysis of accounts of Te Kooti Arikirangi and his contemporary, Rīwha Tītokowaru, my subject here. His story has been told in a number of accounts. The first significant one is James Cowan's, which began as a series of racy newspaper articles based on Cowan's extensive interviews with Kimble Bent, a renegade soldier who had lived as a follower of Tītokowaru; they were later revised as *The Adventures of Kimble Bent: A Story of Wild Life in the New Zealand Bush* (1911). In his general history of *The New Zealand Wars* (1922–23), Cowan documented Tītokowaru's War in its own right, rather than as a dimension of Bent's Pākehā-Māori existence. Two novels of the 1960s drew on *The Adventures of Kimble Bent*, as did the television docudrama, *The Killing of Kane* (1971). In the 1980s, by which time more critical perspectives on the New Zealand Wars in general had been produced in written histories and also on screen, James Belich's work brought a new level of attention to Tītokowaru's War, both in his books and later as one focus of the documentary series *The New Zealand Wars* (1998). Belich's work on Tītokowaru's War sparked Maurice Shadbolt's *Monday's Warriors* (1990), a storyline in the television drama *Greenstone* (1999), and *River Queen*.

Some background to the *fabula* of Tītokowaru's War is necessary here. Rīwha Tītokowaru had trained as a Methodist minister, but when war broke out in Northern Taranaki in 1861, he fought in support of the resistant Te Atiawa. He converted to the new Pai Mārire religion founded by the prophet Te Ua Haumēne: later, he too became a prophet of Pai Mārire. At the Battle of Sentry Hill (1864), he received a severe facial wound and lost an eye, and thereafter bore a marked disfiguration. The First Taranaki War was followed by extensive confiscations of land in the region, although it was not immediately seized and settled, and by the infamous "bush-scouring" campaigns which devastated Southern Taranaki, his home, in 1865–66. In 1867–68 he conducted a *hikoi*, or march, around the region, preaching peace in an attempt to pre-empt settlement. The strategy proved unsuccessful and confiscation proceeded. In 1868 Tītokowaru began raiding outlying farms and settlements, and finally turned to war.[7]

Cowan's were not the first accounts of Tītokowaru's War,[8] but they had broader appeal than those which preceded them. Constituting one of New Zealand's first major oral histories and based on interviews with Bent but also with veterans from all sides of the conflict, *The Adventures of Kimble Bent* went on to have a determining influence in providing a rich and extensive source on which all subsequent written and visual texts drew.[9] It also instantiated a specific point of view on Tītokowaru's story: that of a sympathetic Pākehā insider, a cultural intermediary in the process of encountering difference. As Chris Hilliard notes, Cowan saw boundary-crossers like Bent as especially emblematic figures in New Zealand history: "People who crossed the 'frontier' between Maori and Pakeha were an abiding interest [...] he argued that Maori and Pakeha had *become* one people through their interactions with each other."[10] Nevertheless, in Cowan's accounts conflicting ideologies converge. Despite his attentive respect for Māori informants, and his detailed accounts of Māori life both from Bent's and his Māori informants' perspectives, his writing is also frequently marked by a frontier discourse of savagery and primitivism, and by repeated reference to fanaticism. Chapter XVI, "The Cannibals of the Bush," in *The Adventures of Kimble Bent* recounts the victory celebrations after Tītokowaru's first major victory, the battle of Te Ngutu o te Manu:

Yelling like furies, shouting ferocious battle-songs, waving their weapons in the air, the victorious warriors were there with their spoils [...] The next moment [Bent] was surrounded by a howling mob of Hauhaus, grinning, yelling, laughing fiendishly, shaking their weapons in his face, all in sheer hate and contempt of anything with a white skin.[11]

Cowan's immersion in Wild West discourses of savagism is apparent in accounts of warriors squatting on the ground, "their faces smudged with charcoal or with red ochre, the paint of the war-path."[12] Yet even in this chapter, which proceeds with gleeful horror to describe the cooking and eating of one enemy soldier's body, Cowan's description is detailed and precise, situates cannibalism within older Māori traditions and more recent history, and draws as much on his Māori witnesses' distaste for the practice as it does on Bent's vivid fear that he might join the pile of corpses heaped upon the funeral pyre.[13] Cowan also marks the disjuncture between Tītokowaru's assertions in the letter to the colonists declaring his hunger for Europeans (which he has quoted earlier[14]), and his personal refusal to engage in the practice; and indeed Cowan consistently represents Tītokowaru himself as a voice of restraint, in contrast to the excesses of his "warrior band," and emphasises Tītokowaru's dual roles of prophet and military leader.

The discourses apparent in Cowan's narratives – on the one hand, of fascination with savagery and fanaticism circulating especially around the figure of the warrior and the practices of dismembering and eating human flesh, and on the other, narratives of intimate cultural encounter, detailed accounts of battles from the perspectives of both sides, and ethnographic detail of religious ritual and the practices of daily life – anticipate much of the terrain on which subsequent accounts would be played out. Nevertheless, although parts of Cowan's general history of the Wars[15] were adapted in Rudall Hayward's films, creative artists steered clear of Tītokowaru until the mid-twentieth century, when two novels appeared in the context of New Zealand involvement in other non-European wars. Frank Bruno's *Black Noon at Ngutu* (1960) is a bush-fighting yarn of the colonial side of the conflict, written by a veteran of the Korean War. Errol Braithwaite's Vietnam-era *The Evil Day* (1967), the third novel of a trilogy, charts the colonial soldier Hugh Williams' gradual realisation that to contend with extreme violence means adopting it.[16] Braithwaite carefully includes several warm relationships between Māori and Pākehā in the trilogy – taking up one of Cowan's themes – but he renders Tītokowaru as Williams' savage nemesis, a character whose malevolent fanaticism demands an equivalent, violent, response. If *Apocalypse Now* was the United States' adaptation of *Heart of Darkness* in response to Vietnam, *The Evil Day* was Pākehā New Zealand's.

The Killing of Kane

Coming only four years after *The Evil Day*, however, the first screen rendering of Tītokowaru's War is also the first postcolonial analysis of the New Zealand Wars. The little-known television docudrama *The Killing of Kane* (1971), written by Warren Dibble, marks a shift towards a more self-critical Pākehā analysis of the Wars in general, a shift which was undoubtedly fostered by Dibble's marriage to a descendant of Tītokowaru, and by the participation in the production of Taranaki Māori from the Eltham, Stratford and Patea Māori Clubs.[17] The dramatisation frames the events explicitly within the question of the alienation of land, from the opening voice-over quoting another of Tītokowaru's letters – "England was named for your country, New Zealand was made for our country. Away with you […]" – and a scene in which a land deal proceeds.

Like *The Evil Day*, *The Killing of Kane* draws closely on Cowan, but it selects differently, producing an entirely different emphasis. The action encompasses two events in Tītokowaru's War: the attack on the Turuturu Mōkai redoubt early in the campaign, and the killing of the Irish renegade Charles Kane, who deserted to Tītokowaru but later was discovered in a plan to betray him. Despite the bloodiness of the attack on the redoubt and the protracted hunting down of Kane, in *The Killing of Kane* there appears to have been a considerable effort to render Tītokowaru in Māori terms, and to render Māori society as normative, though mediated and interpreted through two European perspectives: those of Kimble Bent, and, surprisingly, the colonial commander Thomas McDonnell. Both characters explain Māori perspectives and practices in some detail. The letter proclaiming Tītokowaru's revival of cannibalism is translated by McDonnell, cutting to Tītokowaru declaiming the words in Māori. McDonnell then turns to explain to his trooper that Tītokowaru "wouldn't eat flesh himself. It would destroy his *mana tapu.*" Napi Waaka as Tītokowaru, in a performance closely based on Cowan's account, is a figure of *mana* and *gravitas*, emphasising the two dimensions of his historical significance most important to Māori: his role as a Pai Mārire prophet,[18] and his role as military leader. He speaks mostly in Māori, not all of which is translated in subtitles. Sequences of some length show him enacting the rituals of selecting warriors for the attack on the redoubt, and declaiming *karakia*, or prayers: both scenes are effectively scripted by Cowan.

The corollary of *The Killing of Kane*'s emphasis on interpretation in Māori terms is its focus on the question of how to be Pākehā in a Māori context, explicitly addressing a generation of Pākehā newly conscious of their uncomfortable status as colonisers ignorant of indigenous culture. Kane, arrogant and unsympathetic, refuses to conduct himself appropriately. Kimble Bent, an assiduous scholar of Māori society, attempts to explain, his shifting pronouns marking his ambiguous identity: "it's the way they do it Kane, everything's shared, even the work"; "when you came over to us […] what did you expect, you'd be made a *rangatira* [chief]?" The querulous Kane blunders arrogantly across Māori *tikanga* (cultural practice), telling Tītokowaru how to plan an attack, and then trying to win favour through a botched attempt to enact the battlefield ritual of *whāngai hau* (cutting out the heart of the first enemy to be killed).

The Killing of Kane anticipated the shifts of the 1970s and early 1980s when, concurrently with the growth of Māori nationalist movements, broader Pākehā critique of the New Zealand Wars moved beyond the academic arena. Histories such as Dick Scott's *Ask That Mountain* (1975), Binney, Chaplin and Wallace's *Mihaia* (1979), and Tony Simpson's *Te Riri Pakeha* (1979) were not the first to take a critical stance on the Wars, but had a broader popular appeal than the histories which had preceded them.[19] The revisionist scrutiny continued on screen, in the controversial television drama series *The Governor* (1977) and two feature films: Michael Black's *Pictures* (1981) and Geoff Murphy's *Utu* (1983).[20]

By the early 1980s, then, a few cultural producers in several media had taken up the story of Tītokowaru. If the existence of these texts marked a sense that there was a compelling cultural narrative in these events, the variation between the accounts suggests that it still lacked a clearly interpretable public meaning. It was, therefore, a sustained engagement with the historiography which brought Tītokowaru into greater prominence.

James Belich: Book, book and documentary

James Belich's revisionist monograph, *The New Zealand Wars and the Victorian Interpretation of Racial Conflict* (1986), gave more prominence to Tītokowaru's War than any earlier history. It was followed by *"I Shall Not Die": Tītokowaru's War, New Zealand 1868–1869* (1989). Seeking to take the history of the Wars to a wider audience, Belich set out in this second book to present Tītokowaru's story in appealing popular terms – scholarship in the guise of a ripping yarn – and in 1998 he scripted and presented a five-part documentary series, *The New Zealand Wars*.[21] More than any other text in recent decades, this series reconfigured the significance of the New Zealand Wars in popular memory,[22] garnering a cumulative audience of two million viewers during its first screening. A writer and presenter of considerable flair, Belich cut a swathe through the historiography and generated a prolific regrowth in the historical literature, fiction and film of the Wars in general, and Tītokowaru in particular.[23] Fronting up assertively to the camera, Belich contended that during the New Zealand Wars a series of Māori leaders produced technical innovations which marked them as, above all, highly intelligent fighters: that Imperial and then colonial armies suffered so many unexpected defeats despite superior numbers and firepower because they were out-thought and out-engineered. While this argument was descended from Cowan's characterisation of Māori as "worthy opponents," Belich effected a form of "remasculinisation," a re-casting of the Wars not as defeat but as triumph, and a reconceptualisation of Māori masculinity through the trope of the warrior by enhancing its association with intellect rather than "savagery." As Jenny Murray has suggested, this might have come at a paradoxical cost: in making the case for Māori strategy as a series of rational adaptations, Belich comes close to recreating these *rangatira* as descendants of the Enlightenment.[24] In this process something of the quality which Cowan conveys, of a world in certain respects incommensurable with the colonial one, is lost.

The case of Tītokowaru, whom Belich regards as the most sophisticated of the Māori generals (he allocated half of Episode Four of the documentary series to Tītokowaru's War[25]), is all the more interesting in that he rendered him not only a remarkable strategist but also a remarkable orator: a man, in short, of ideas – a theme which had its roots in Cowan and was taken up in *The Killing of Kane*, but which Belich used extensively and systematically to forge for the first time a recognisable public identity for Tītokowaru. Belich's use of Tītokowaru's letter announcing his adoption of cannibalism illustrates the character of this "remasculinisation." Fully aware of its eloquence and rhetorical force, he quotes it in full as the startling concluding paragraph of a chapter of *I Shall Not Die*.[26] Nevertheless, he is careful in his interpretation. He too points out that "Tītokowaru never ate human flesh himself."[27] But Belich expands beyond Cowan's hint that the purpose of the letter was to incite fear in the settlers, and situates the letter as part of a far-reaching strategy:

Tītokowaru was no grim bush chieftain, an isolated traditionalist ignorant of European ways. He was a student of Europeans in general, and he knew his particular enemies quite well [...]. He guessed McDonnell would await reinforcements, train them, then use his huge superiority in numbers to reapply the bush-scouring campaigns of 1865–6. The only way to pre-empt the inevitable was to provoke a premature attack, ideally on a place of Tītokowaru's choosing, carefully prepared in advance [...].[28]

In Belich's reading, Tītokowaru's shifting strategies, hitherto difficult for Pākehā to comprehend, are entirely explicable in terms of, and legitimated by, a defence of tribal territory and resources. Tītokowaru conducts a peaceful defence as far as he can; but when it fails he turns to war. Heavily outnumbered, he must make use of public relations (inducing terror in the settler population), provocation (to ensure McDonnell is driven to attack at Te Ngutu before he can gather an even larger army) and deception (inviting him to attack in the wrong place). In brief, Belich argues that Tītokowaru's strategies in successive battles were so sophisticated that it took over a century and an effective revolution in racial politics for Pākehā to recognise their importance: they could not be understood until Pākehā were ready to acknowledge the brilliance of Māori strategy.

In *The New Zealand Wars'* translation from book to television documentary, minor events and historical figures are eliminated, paring the narrative back, so that Belich's forceful script and narrative voice-over deliver a driving campaign and the clash of powerful military men. As a man of peace forced into war by colonial treachery and intransigence, Tītokowaru faces McDonnell and then his formidable replacement Whitmore, the one ambitious and cruel, the other arrogant and charmless. Both receive just but unanticipated desserts as routs at Te Ngutu o te Manu and then Moturoa pile up the casualties; Tītokowaru moves rapidly, and astonishingly, to reclaim most of confiscated Taranaki within the short year of his campaign before its sudden collapse at Tauranga-Ika. To this extent, then, the series produced a sharper, clearer narrative than any previous account. Except for the mystery of its ending, Belich gave to the events of Tītokowaru's War a structure both intelligible and dramatic, producing Tītokowaru as a highly complex, clever and powerful individual.[29]

Belich's work, both written and televisual, continued the critique begun in the 1970s and early 1980s by undertaking a substantial revision of the trope of the warrior. It effects a "remasculinisation" in calling into question prevailing discourses of Māori masculinity, whether of heroic defeat, rebelliousness or savagery, but without explicitly addressing masculinity. Indeed, despite the use of female historical figures in the *New Zealand Wars* documentary, Belich's revival actively deployed *Boys Own* fervour and associations between nationalism and masculinity, evoking what Graham Dawson in *Soldier Heroes* has called the "pleasure-culture of war."[30]

Tītokowaru had found, in effect, a champion, and a new generation of writers and filmmakers took up the banner. Novelist Maurice Shadbolt wrote: "Belich tells a truly terrible, truly epic story. Tītokowaru strides through his pages like a tragic figure from a Greek drama."[31] Shadbolt's own novel *Monday's Warriors* (1990), based in part on Belich's MA, follows Belich's interpretation, and opens Tītokowaru to "being known" through the device of making Bent his confidant and the novel's narrator. Whether or not Belich's interpretations prevailed in subsequent screen versions is one question we might address in an analysis of the television drama series *Greenstone* (1999) and *River Queen* (2005), the two major Wars screen fictions after the *New Zealand Wars* documentary.[32] One effect of Belich's work is plain: it brought Tītokowaru's War to prominence as a subject for screen narratives.

Greenstone

Greenstone, a costume melodrama, drew in an eclectic fashion on colonial history, including interpolating one storyline and two characters from the Tītokowaru *fabula* into events of the Musket Wars and the Treaty era.[33] The chief Rongopai is a pacifist Christian minister based on the character of Tītokowaru. The disaffected priest Father Michael, initially a reverential follower and confidant and then a horror-struck virtual prisoner of Rongopai, much more loosely references Kimble Bent's relationship to Tītokowaru.

Like Tītokowaru, Rongopai travels the region preaching peace and justice, and the return of alienated land, but a series of betrayals follows, including an attack by the land-hungry British and their Māori ally[34] on Rongopai's peaceful village (in reference perhaps to the historical attack on Pōkaikai, whose people had agreed to make peace but were attacked). The treachery triggers Rongopai's turn to war, beginning with a night-time attack on a redoubt and the removal of its commanding officer's heart (in reference to Turuturu Mōkai), in order to provoke a counter-attack. Subsequently, dressed in formal European suit and top hat like Tītokowaru at Te Ngutu o te Manu, Rongopai draws his enemies into a trap. As the attackers approach to find Rongopai's village apparently defended only by a rudimentary line of palisades, warriors pop up to fire from concealed positions outside the fences, routing them in a Te-Ngutu-style victory.

Belich's interpretation is not the only source at work. The intermediary figure Father Michael, receiving guns for Rongopai, speaks the language of *Heart of Darkness*: "A horror has descended upon us. I know not where to turn. Forgive me. Forgive me." "Horror" is the term attached to Rongopai's turn to violence, although the series appears ambivalent about attributing it directly to him. In the attack on the redoubt it is the war-hungry separatist chiefs Ramaka and Wahana and their warriors who are shown slitting the throats of the unwary soldiers, and *Greenstone* only briefly alludes to cannibalism. Rongopai drives an axe into the chest of the dead captain, but we do not see the subsequent removal of the heart. His letter is stripped of both the eloquence and the specificity of the original: "Come to me. I wait. I hunger. Rongopai."[35] At the end of the series Rongopai readily reassumes the mantle of peaceful leadership. The series' confused and opportunistic use of history is apparent here, but also perhaps the enduring difficulty of reconciling two opposing dimensions of Māori masculinity articulated in the Pākehā imaginary and reiterated through the Tītokowaru narratives: fearful violence and heroic leadership.[36]

River Queen

Fictionalised events from Tītokowaru's War provide the backdrop to the cross-cultural romance of Vincent Ward's feature film *River Queen*. Tītokowaru becomes Te Kai Pō; Kātene Tuwhakaruru, a scout for the colonial army who defected to Tītokowaru, becomes the warrior Wiremu; and the character of Hōne draws on Major Kēpa Te Rangihiwinui, military leader of the Whanganui people allied with the colonial troops. Some historical characters are conflated: for example, the sartorial flair of the flamboyant Gustavus Von Tempsky and the ruthlessness of Thomas McDonnell merge in the character of Major Baine. Notably, the film substantially shifts the figure of the Pākehā–Māori intermediary: Sarah O'Brien clearly derives in part from Kimble Bent but is more obviously drawn from events in the lives of two other historical figures: Annie Evans, who was taken to a secret location later in Tītokowaru's life to nurse him through an illness, and Caroline ("Queenie") Perrett, who was captured as a girl and despite "discovery" as an adult remained the rest of her life in Māori society.[37] Consistent with Bruce Babington's characterisation of *River Queen* as "fabulous history,"[38] events do not map precisely on to historical events, although Tītokowaru's letters are quoted, there is a version of the battle of Te Ngutu o te Manu, and a version of the collapse of Tītokowaru's campaign at Tauranga-Ika.[39] More importantly for our purposes, events in Tītokowaru's War are used and departed from in *River Queen* in ways that point to the kinds of meaning Ward was making, and refusing, of the Tītokowaru *fabula*, particularly in the tropes of warrior masculinity and the culture-crossing subjects.

The central concern of *River Queen* is not the war story but the story of characters who cross the cultural divide, whom Ward – like Cowan – regards as emblematic figures in New Zealand history. *River Queen* arose out of his own youthful experience of living in a remote Urewera village:

> I was the only Pākehā there and mostly Māori was spoken. I always wondered if I could transfer my experience into a feature film, the experience of someone who goes into a community thinking they will learn about the community but in fact learning as much about themselves.
>
> My story doesn't tell Queenie's story or Doctor Annie's story directly but they were the lodestones for a story about a woman who went into another community and is changed by the experience. That's a real New Zealand story because New Zealand has been formed not by Māori and Pākehā so much as by the people in between Māori and Pākehā trying to find a way of co-existing.[40]

River Queen too invokes *Heart of Darkness* in its Pākehā intermediary's journey upriver to meet the "mysterious chief Te Kai Pō," which becomes a journey "into the interior." Sarah travels into an unknown wilderness but, more like Bent than Marlow, she finds no heart of darkness: not horror, but home. Having called up the *Heart of Darkness* trope – as well as other colonial screen river journeys like those in *The Mission* (1986) and *Black*

Robe (1991) – *River Queen's* visualisation of ordinary life in the Māori community refuses "horror" and undoes the discourse of "native savagery." As in Cowan's *Kimble Bent*, the intermediary's eyes make available a detailed rendering of life in a Māori community in the midst of the Wars. Alun Bollinger's luminous cinematography and the film's deep, saturated palette portray a tranquil visual harmony between Māori settlements and their spectacular scenic settings. If this visual affinity risks essentialising the Māori presence in the landscape, it also sustains its prior and peaceable occupancy, through imagery of the exteriors and interiors of temporary settlements, and the daily work of travelling, gathering, growing, cooking and eating food, caring for children and sleeping. Unlike Marlowe, Sarah does not return to tell the tale, but willingly remains to reconstitute her family and make a life. Like Bent in *The Killing of Kane*, she learns how to be Pākehā in a Māori setting.

The process of Sarah's acculturation, however, is erased by the gap between the film's timeframes, and offered as a fait accompli when we see her working in the gardens at the end.[41] Indeed, cultural encounter is effectively subsumed under sexual encounter, not only in Sarah's developing relationship with Wiremu, but also through the underlying sexual currents of her encounters with Te Kai Pō. And, as Danny Keenan has pointed out, the other cultural intermediary subject in the film – Wiremu – is strikingly underdeveloped by comparison with Sarah, and in contrast with his namesake, the "Māori-Pākehā" in Geoff Murphy's *Utu*.[42] And if Sarah is Ward's primary interest, he is also, clearly, fascinated by the background story. Indeed, one of the film's problems is that the war story is too big and too complex to remain backdrop. The impetus to tell it in its historical detail overloads the film's narrative clarity, and Temuera Morrison's charismatic performance as Te Kai Pō ensures that the background plot moves insistently forward. *River Queen's* historical narrative follows Belich in several respects: in situating the New Zealand Wars as a central element in New Zealand history, in making Tītokowaru's an emblematic campaign and in exploiting the dramatic potential of surprise reversals and the triumphant underdog outwitting mighty opponents.

The film's central battle sequence draws on recognisable elements of Te Ngutu o te Manu. Tītokowaru's letter to the colonists is read, almost word for word, by Te Kai Pō, who confirms Cowan's and Belich's reading of it as an act of provocation by adding in anachronistic vernacular: "That should raise their temperatures a little." While the enemy approach through the bush, Tītokowaru's trap is suggested as Te Kai Pō sketches out a plan in the earth, predicts the enemy's movements and issues instructions to his warriors. Instead of deceptively fragile palisades, the skipping and singing of bare-breasted women tricks the approaching constabulary; but just as the attackers register that their approach appears to have been unnoticed, they are the target of a lethal ambush from hidden positions outside the *pā*. The elements of provocation, planning, decoy and ambush are those described by Belich in his account of Tītokowaru's first major victory.

River Queen resists characterisation of Tītokowaru as a "savage" warrior. Indeed, the most frightening soldiers belong to the other side, in the chilling ruthlessness of Major

Baine, the menacing impassivity of Hōne, and the grim butchery of an unnamed, heavily-set warrior who, in a scene based on an event prior to Te Ngutu o te Manu, kills Wiremu's crippled son.[43] Despite a rousing *haka* before the first battle, and the onslaught of bullets which devastate the unsuspecting attackers, the male leads Wiremu (Cliff Curtis) and Te Kai Pō (Temuera Morrison) extend the range of representations of Māori masculinity. Wiremu's gentleness, fatherliness and protectiveness do so most markedly. Te Kai Pō is both far-seeing leader and prophet, dreaming prescient dreams which Sarah, who brings a Celtic mysticism to the narrative, shares. In this respect, *River Queen* returns to the centrality of the supernatural in the Māori world that Cowan described. To the watching Pākehā-Māori, Te Kai Pō remains enigmatic: like Bent, Sarah speculates about his strategies and cannot entirely explain his reasoning. The casting of Temuera Morrison in this role – Ward never considered anyone else[44] – associates the character with strikingly disparate modes of Māori masculinity, as Morrison is well known for two previous roles, the violent, hard-drinking Jake in *Once Were Warriors* (1994), latter-day warrior when the warrior ethos had outlived all purpose; and charismatic Dr Ropata in the popular medical soap *Shortland Street* (1992–).

Te Kai Pō is the dominant figure of the warrior in *River Queen*. He is first seen on horseback high on a ridge, authorising a terrifying rain of fire on the colonial river settlement. A close-up reveals a handsome face adorned with a striking *moko*, only an apparently blind eye referencing the untattooed, disfigured face of the historical Tītokowaru. His fearful power is enhanced by a long shot from far below, and by Sarah's awed voiceover asking "Why was he looking at me?" The question anticipates the sexual tension which will carry through to their later encounters. If this frisson is somewhat peripheral to the plot, it is perhaps best explicable in terms of the film's rendering of Te Kai Pō's *mana* as sexual authority. In a series of shots, for example, he occupies centre frame, the cluster of unnamed Māori women who flank him endorsing his chiefly masculinity. Although Sarah sits apart as a visual equal, shares his prophetic dream and is not absorbed into the subservient conjugal entourage, she appears to recognise an authority which has as much to do with physicality as with rank. Indeed, one wonders if the shift from a male to a female intermediary was driven in part by Sarah's value in enhancing Te Kai Pō's sexual *mana*.

The unhistorical decoy – the bare-breasted women noted above – offered invitingly to the gaze of viewers as much as to the approaching soldiers, endorses this dimension of Ward's departure from historical sources in his portrayal of warrior masculinity in the character of Te Kai Pō. The film makes use of Kimble Bent's story about the mysterious end of Tītokowaru's campaign. The usually accepted explanation in Pākehā historiography, deriving from Kimble Bent, is that Tītokowaru was discovered in an affair with the wife of an allied chief, which resulted in the dissolution of alliances, the loss of his *mana tapu* and the abandonment of Tauranga-Ika on the eve of battle. Augmented perhaps by Belich's one cryptic comment about Tītokowaru's active sexual life,[45] the story is deployed beyond its origins at Tauranga-Ika and is reworked into scenes at both of the film's major battles which depart in significant ways from the historical accounts of Tītokowaru's military leadership.

In the sequence based on the battle at Te Ngutu o te Manu, Ward does not draw on Cowan's Māori veterans and Kimble Bent, who described Tītokowaru's direction of the battle, his European dress and the fearful sound of his voice. Cowan's Tītokowaru strides up and down in the *pā* at Te Ngutu clad in full European suit and hat, shouting commands:

All this time within the stockade in the bullet-swept clearing the war-chief Tītokowaru remained walking up and down, taiaha in hand, reciting prayers to his Māori gods and shouting to his soldiers. "*Patua, kainga!*" he cried; "kill them, eat them!" And again and again he shouted in his far-carrying voice, "*Whakawhiria, whakawhiria!*" bidding the warriors encircle their foes.[46]

With him was the priestess Tangamoko, the woman who had that morning garbed the young warrior Tutangē with the sacred war-mat.[47]

River Queen plays this scene quite differently. Where in Cowan's account the *voice* of Tītokowaru so compellingly commanded his troops and terrified his enemies, *River Queen* reallocates the controlling voice to Sarah's son Boy, who calls out misleading commands in English to the attacking troops.[48] *River Queen* displaces the chief's power away from the voice as the means of military control, to the penis. From scenes of battle we cut to a slow-motion close-up of Te Kai Pō's face inside a *whare* (see illustration on p. 136 above), panning back to reveal him naked above an un-named woman whose face we do not see. Sexual mastery of the woman beneath him signifies military dominance of the enemy, as facial expressions indicating imminent orgasm cut to the slaughter of enemy soldiers. The scene is paralleled by a similar sequence during the preparations for the next battle; but here, following the events of Tauranga-Ika, it occurs before the battle and is discovered, leading to the disruption of a major alliance and to retreat. While there is some indication of Belich's accounts of carefully scripted battles, then, Ward's Te Kai Pō is cast less as a sophisticated strategist and more as a sexual mystic heaving his way ecstatically to victory.

River Queen refuses the simple association of the warrior trope with savagery, and extends the range of interpretations of the warrior, especially through the character of Wiremu. James Belich's enterprise had been to "remasculinise" Tītokowaru as both intelligible and intelligent, to define him primarily as a prodigious strategist who exercised precise control of the battles he fought, with the one exception of the only partially explained retreat from Tauranga-Ika. Adopting, to some extent, Belich's thoughtful warrior, Ward nevertheless retreats from Belich's insistence on the rational, and restores a kind of cultural incommensurability through the trope of prophecy.[49] Yet remasculinisation in *River Queen* is effected through unreconstructed sexual mysticism, which accords Te Kai Pō *mana* in proportion to the Māori women's subordination, and the transposing of battlefield violence to sexual conquest. If the savagery and the fascination with cannibalism have diminished, the physicality has come back in, in an equally disturbing and a specifically gendered fashion.

Conclusion

Tītokowaru's star as a subject of screen and fictional narrative rose after Belich's intervention in the historiography. Along with renewed attention to Te Kooti Arikirangi in Judith Binney's major biography (1995), this marked a shift of Pākehā focus to some of the more problematic Wars narratives, and away from the apparently more containable narratives popular through much of the twentieth century. Belich concluded Episode Four of *The New Zealand Wars* with the striking assertion that Pākehā had wilfully forgotten Tītokowaru, thus paying him "the ultimate compliment" of acknowledging the threat he posed to Pākehā settlement in the late 1860s. There is justification in this claim. But the earlier archaeology of Tītokowaru narratives, from Cowan's fertile but contradictory texts through Braithwaite's narrative of horror to *The Killing of Kane*, marks a continuity of Pākehā fascination with a figure who summons both the warrior as savage cannibal and the warrior as far-seeing military leader and prophet of his people.

The persistence of the Pākehā-Māori point of view in these narratives – the ambivalent cultural intermediary – must also be understood as a key element. What does it signify? Fascination with the more troubling dimensions of cultural difference, certainly, especially the tropes of savagery and cannibalism. Yet these are figures who assimilate into Māori society in taking on a Pākehā-Māori identity. Atypical historically, and to this extent a vehicle for a fantasised rather than an actual account of colonisation, they nevertheless provide a surprising if ambivalent counter-weight to the discourses of Otherness.

Notes

1. Te Kai Pō, Vincent Ward, *River Queen* (New Zealand: Silverscreen Films, 2005). The Māori text is translated in the following sentence. Tītokowaru's letter of 25 June 1868 is held in the Rīwha Tītokowaru Collection, Alexander Turnbull Library, Wellington, MS-Papers-3006-01 and MS-Papers-3006-02.
2. The New Zealand Wars first erupted in the decade following the signing of the Treaty of Waitangi, which established annexation by Britain in 1840, in conflicts from the north of the South Island to the north of the North Island. The most sustained period of the conflict was 1861–72, when a series of interrelated wars broke out across the entire centre of the North Island, in Taranaki, Waikato and the East Coast. Tītokowaru's War of 1868–69 was one of the later conflicts of the 1860s but Tītokowaru himself had fought in Taranaki earlier in the decade also. The final, brief conflict occurred in 1916, when government forces invaded Rua Kēnana's settlement at Maungapōhatu in the Urewera.
3. Robert Burgoyne, *Film Nation: Hollywood Looks at U.S. History* (Minneapolis: University of Minnesota Press, 1997).
4. Brendan Hokowhitu, "Tackling Māori Masculinity: A Colonial Genealogy of Savagery and Sport," *The Contemporary Pacific* 16, no. 2 (2004).
5. Gananath Obeyesekere, *Cannibal Talk: The Man-Eating Myth and Human Sacrifice in the South Seas* (Berkeley: University of California Press, 2004).

6. Note that it continues to persist: see Danny Keenan, ed. *Terror in Our Midst? Searching for Terror in Aotearoa/New Zealand* (Wellington: Huia, 2008).

7. James Cowan, *The Adventures of Kimble Bent: A Story of Wild Life in the New Zealand Bush* (London: Whitcombe and Tombs, 1911; reprint, Capper Press, 1975). James Cowan, *The New Zealand Wars: A History of the Maori Campaign and the Pioneering Period*, 2 vols. (Wellington: P. O. Hasselberg, Government Printers, 1922–3; reprint, 1983). James Belich, *"I Shall Not Die": Tītokowaru's War, New Zealand, 1868–9* (Wellington: Allen & Unwin/Port Nicholson Press, 1989).

8. Cowan was preceded by, for example, Thomas W Gudgeon, *Reminiscences of the War in New Zealand* (London: Sampson Low, Marston, Searle and Rivington, 1879). George S Whitmore, *The Last Maori War in New Zealand under the Self-Reliant Policy* (London: Sampson Low, Marston & Company, 1902).

9. For an account of Cowan's significance for "New Zealand Wars epics" more broadly, see Bruce Babington, *A History of the New Zealand Fiction Feature Film* (Manchester: Manchester University Press, 2007), 154–60.

10. Chris Hilliard, *The Bookmen's Dominion: Cultural Life in New Zealand 1920–1950* (Auckland: Auckland University Press, 2006).

11. Cowan, *The Adventures of Kimble Bent*, 180–81.

12. Ibid., 182.

13. Ibid., 180–94.

14. Cowan translates as follows:

Cease travelling on the roads, cease entirely travelling on the roads that lead to Mangamanga (Camp Waihi), lest ye be left upon the roads as food for the birds of the air and for the beasts of the field, or for me. Because I have eaten the white man; he was cooked like a piece of beef in the pot. I have begun to eat human flesh, and my throat is continually open for the flesh of man. Kua hamama tonu toku korokoro ki te kai i te tangata. I shall not die, I shall not die. When death itself shall be dead, I shall be alive (Ka mate ano te mate, ka ora ano ahau).–From TITOKO. (Ibid., 118)

15. Cowan, *The New Zealand Wars*.

16. Frank Bruno, *Black Noon at Ngutu* (London: Robert Hale, 1960); Errol Braithwaite, *The Evil Day* (London & Auckland: Collins, 1967).

17. Chris Thompson, dir., *The Killing of Kane*. (New Zealand, 1971).

18. Pai Mārire, founded by Te Ua Haumēne, was one of a number of Māori adaptations of Christianity. Meaning "good and peaceful," it rapidly came nevertheless to signify terror for settlers, and its followers more commonly referred to as Hauhaus. Tītokowaru was one of its prophets.

19. Earlier mid-century works included Keith Sinclair, *The Origins of the Maori Wars*, 2nd ed. (Wellington: New Zealand University Press, 1961); Ian Wards, *The Shadow of the Land: A Study of British Policy and Racial Conflict in New Zealand 1832–1852* (Wellington: Historical Publications Branch, Department of Internal Affairs, 1968).

20. Although the character of Te Wheke in *Utu* and the story surrounding him was probably based mostly on Te Kooti and in part on Kereopa te Rau, there are elements of the Tītokowaru narrative here too. There is, for example, a "turn": the main character Te Wheke initially fights with the colonial forces, but on arriving with the troops in his own "friendly" territory to find that his village is the site of a massacre by colonial troops, he swears *utu*, or revenge. The "bush-scouring" strategy in Southern Taranaki and the attack on the undefended village of Pōkaikai, and their probable impact on Tītokowaru's strategy, are likely historical sources.

21. James Belich, *The New Zealand Wars and the Interpretation of Racial Conflict* (Auckland: Auckland University Press; Oxford: Oxford University Press, 1986); James Belich, *"I Shall Not Die": Tītokowaru's War, New Zealand, 1868–9*; Tainui Stephens, dir., "The New Zealand Wars," (New Zealand, 1998).

22. As I argue elsewhere, in "Bicultural Identities, Masculinity and Historical Amnesia: Televisual Memories of the New Zealand Wars," Special Issue on "Memory and Identity," *European Journal of Cultural Studies* (2011) 14: 3, forthcoming.

23. Belich's predilection for Tītokowaru was apparent early on: his MA was written on Tītokowaru's War.

24. Jenny Murray, "Review: The New Zealand Wars," *Historical News* 56 (1988): 14.

25. Episode Four, "The Taranaki Prophets."

26. Belich, *"I Shall Not Die": Tītokowaru's War, New Zealand, 1868–9*, 57.

27. Ibid., 56.

28. Ibid., 56–7.

29. Stephens, "The New Zealand Wars."

30. See also Cooper, "Bicultural Identities, Masculinity and Historical Amnesia."

31. Shadbolt in publisher's blurb, Belich, *I Shall Not Die*.

32. Another was the documentary *Von Tempsky's Ghost* which, as Titokowaru is not its focus, I will not discuss here. It is worth noting, however, that Tītokowaru's words, taken from his speeches and particularly his oration over the body of Von Tempsky, open and close the documentary. A further feature film project was mooted for some time although it was finally dropped: Lee Tamahori was reported to be working on a screenplay entitled *I Shall Not Die*, written by Ian Mune.

33. Trumpeted before its screening as an impending blockbuster, *Greenstone* was the first major attempt at a local television historical drama since the controversy surrounding *The Governor*. *Greenstone's* promise, however, quickly evaporated. Set in the Treaty era but interpolating events of the New Zealand Wars two to three decades later, saddled with some improbable casting, and burdened with excessive costuming, the series' attempts to hook an international market for the exotic failed, and instead ensured that a large part of its New Zealand audience found it laughably improbable. It was cut in production from twelve to seven episodes, and was quickly abandoned by viewers.

34. In line with *Greenstone's* mix-and-match approach to history, the attacking chief Te Manahau is based primarily on Hongi Hika, a figure central to the Musket Wars in the North in the early decades of the nineteenth century.

35. Chris Bailey, "Greenstone" (New Zealand, 1999). Episode 6.

36. For a more extended discussion of Māori masculinity and leadership, see Brendan Hokowhitu, "The Death of Koro Paka: 'Traditional' Māori Patriarchy," *The Contemporary Pacific* 20, no. 1 (2008).

37. The credits situate *River Queen's* relation to historical sources by naming three figures (Tītokowaru, Caroline Perrett and Anne Evans), "without whose stories this one would not have happened." Earlier drafts of the script used the names of historical figures, including Tītokowaru, although the names had been changed by the final version so that the historical referencing was less direct (Russell Campbell, seminar for Department of Film and Media, University of Otago, 2008).

38. Bruce Babington, "What Streams May Come: Navigating Vincent Ward's River Queen," *Illusions* 39 (2007): 9.

39. Ward has said that he kept a "little library" of historical texts on set. Undoubtedly the retreat from direct reference to historical individuals was effected in part to avoid the consequent demands of accuracy and verisimilitude, especially in a context where the descendants of historical figures might make objections to the representation of their ancestors.

40. "Vincent's Obsession," *Weekend Herald* (21 January 2006), 3.
41. As Danny Keenan has pointed out, a great deal more attention is paid to Sarah as an intermediary than to the other culture-crossing character, Wiremu; yet Wiremu's position raises questions that are at least as interesting. Danny Keenan, "Finding Wiremu: Centre and Substance in River Queen," http://www.newzealandwars.co.nz/gallery.html.
42. Ibid.
43. Cowan and Belich both record this incident, in which a few people were discovered in a clearing as the colonial and Māori allied forces approached Te Ngutu o to Manu, hoping that their approach was unnoticed. Katene's crippled child was among them, and was killed.
44. "Interview: Vincent Ward. Interview by Clint Morris," http://www.webwombat.com.au. Accessed 10 September 2008.
45. "He made strong friendships with both men and women, and may have been very active sexually with the latter." Belich, *I Shall Not Die*, 6.
46. Cowan, *New Zealand Wars*, 209.
47. Cowan, *The Adventures of Kimble Bent*, 171.
48. This too has a historical basis, but it derives from another battle.
49. This interest of Ward's is even more apparent in the later *Rain of Children* where the Māori world has elements inexplicable and unavailable to Pākehā.

Chapter 7

Rites of Passage in Post-Second World War New Zealand Cinema: Migrating the Masculine in *Journey for Three* (1950)

Simon Sigley

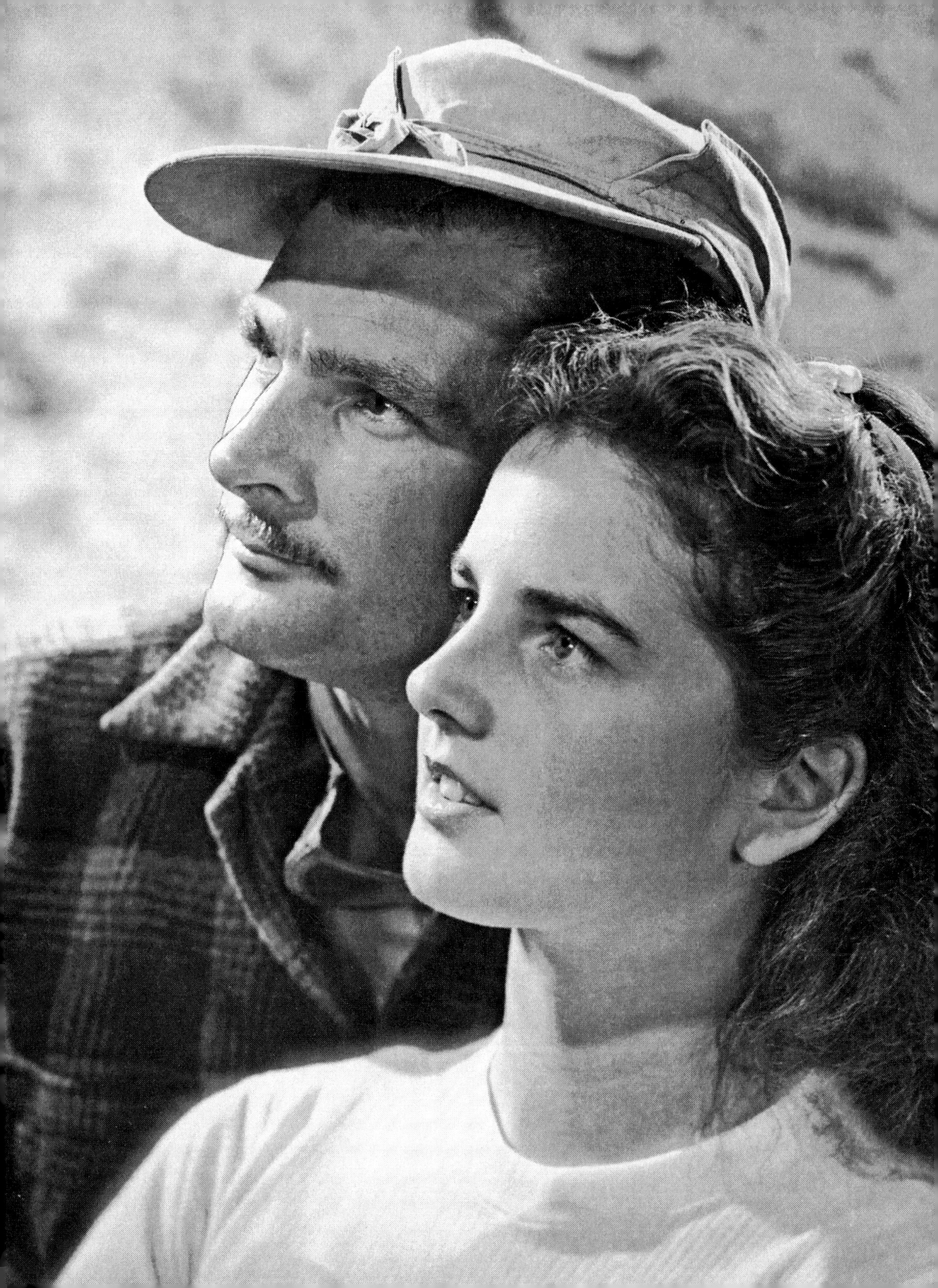

"Colonisation is not just an early morning fog that dissipates mid-morning as the bright sun of national identity comes out."[1]

Introduction

In July 1947, the Labour Government resurrected the assisted passage scheme, allowing selected ex-service British personnel to migrate to New Zealand at no cost and non-service people to come by paying only ten pounds.[2] With that decision came an intensive state effort, across a variety of British media, to encourage emigration. The most high-profile "advertisement" used to persuade young Britons to leave the "grey" United Kingdom (UK) for a brighter future half way around the world was *Journey for Three* (1950), a sponsored docudrama commissioned by the Labour Department and made by the National Film Unit (NFU). At a time when the cinematic production of feature-length narrative fictions was nonexistent in New Zealand, this enterprising film's representational strategy sought to weave together the sponsor's objectives, a fictional narrative structure and dramatic spectacle. Themes deployed in the film include masculinity, mateship, landscape, femininity and "the crimson thread of kinship," which ostensibly united Albion's disparate diasporic children.[3]

Being made for British audiences, the film is very revealing in terms of New Zealand colonial attitudes towards its "mother country" in 1949. It is no less revealing in terms of attitudes to gender (New Zealand was certainly "a man's country" at this time) and to Māori. At the same time, the film is a sophisticated cultural artefact and not a simple piece of propaganda. It is one of the most ambitious narrative films made in the country up to this time, displaying a certain knowledge of international film culture – of Italian neo-realism and the Griersonian documentary movement – as well as of Hollywood. For such a film to gain admission to British cinemas (to be included within the required quota for British Empire films), it had to partly disguise its basic function as an advertisement for immigration to New Zealand. It did so by adopting narrative, fictional form, and by presenting a seemingly

Stuart Pilkington and Margaret McNulty in a studio photo for *Journey for Three*, 1950, dir. Michael Forlong, New Zealand National Film Unit. Image courtesy of Archives New Zealand/Te Rua Mahara o te Kāwanatanga, Wellington Office [AAPG W3939 box 2.

frank, realistic picture of the challenges of immigration. What makes the film particularly fascinating is the way its supposed realism is soaked in ideological attitudes – perhaps unconsciously – concerning New Zealand's identity (as frontier and outdoor playground) and the gender roles appropriate to the pioneer task of breaking in the country and nation-building.

Journey for Three tells the stories of three migrants, two women and one man, as they arrive in New Zealand and adapt to the different social, physical and cultural environments they encounter. The neo-realist texture of the film is established in several ways: the actors are non-professional and embody aspects of their own recent migration to New Zealand[4] (enacting others thought to be typical); shooting is largely on location and the geography of place features strongly; there is a belief that ordinary people matter enormously; and the use of a "naturalistic" aesthetic completes the Italian neo-realist influence.[5] In other respects, however, the film emulates the classical Hollywood style of filmmaking at work in, for example, *Casablanca* (1942) – "hommage" is paid to it in one camera set-up – whilst also exhibiting the influence of German alpine cinema; Arnold Fanck's *The White Hell of Pitz Palu* (1929), among others, had impressed discerning New Zealanders in the early 1930s[6] and the NFU style of shooting striking mountain scenery, seen also in Brian Brake's *Prelude to Aspiring* (1949), shows a clear affiliation to that visual style. *Journey for Three* also has generic debts to the British documentary tradition's practice of ennobling manual labour through a narrative that concentrates on the difficulties the male migrant has in the Public Works Hydro Construction Camp at Lake Pūkaki in the South Island. By contrast, the women's adaptation to their new urban surroundings in Wellington and Christchurch is represented as being considerably less problematic, a difference explored later on in this essay.

The genesis of *Journey for Three*

In the aftermath of World War Two, several Commonwealth countries, such as Canada, Australia and New Zealand, saw that natural population growth was insufficient to meet the employment demands of new secondary and tertiary industries. A clear and growing shortage of skilled industrial labour encouraged policy makers to accelerate immigration. In response, the New Zealand government set up the Dominion Population Committee in December 1945. The tone of its report back to Parliament in September 1946 was measured. In line with government preference, which recognised the need to rehabilitate New Zealand servicemen, it favoured natural population growth, which the family benefit allowance sought to stimulate, over rapid immigration. The Prime Minister, Peter Fraser, had already rebuked young married New Zealand men and women for letting the country down by not fulfilling their procreative duties: "A country was not worth carrying on if its people were so steeped in selfishness that they sacrificed the future of humanity for their own evanescent pleasure."[7]

The committee, however, also recognised that increasing the nation's population through immigration was necessary. Migrants were to be selected with regards to occupation (industrial rather than agricultural), age (under 35), health (TB free), and bonded to work in designated industries and locations for two years after arrival.[8] Furthermore, with an eye on assimilation, the housing shortage and "the crimson thread of kinship," it was implied that only single British immigrants of European race and colour apply in the first instance. Under the direction of the highly regarded H. L. Bockett, Secretary for Labour and Director of Employment, the Immigration Branch of the Department of Labour and Employment sought to design the most efficient advertising campaign – a campaign that would compete against the vast attractions of both Australia and Canada. The initial documentary idea was for a short film "showing every aspect and step from the time a ship arrives at a New Zealand port down to the worker actually engaging in his new employment and actually living in his new accommodation."[9]

Bockett discussed the proposed film with Stanhope Andrews, the producer at the NFU, in May 1948, and sent him a treatment in mid-July outlining the general orientation of the sponsored documentary, by which time two important changes had occurred: the 15-minute short documentary had expanded to approximately 30, and "It is suggested that an added human interest could be achieved by using the theme of a young man or woman" making his or her way to New Zealand.[10] The "pure" and rather pedestrian sounding initial documentary concept was showing the first signs of being inflected by narrative strategies more typically associated with cinematic fictions.

The person responsible for this new direction was Michael Forlong, a talented young director Andrews had dispatched to discuss the project with Bockett. Along with several other NFU staffers, Forlong was very keen to start making feature films and clearly impressed Bockett during their meeting.

Stan Andrews, knowing how keen I was to make a feature film, took the precaution before despatching me to a meeting with the Department concerned of giving me a stern lecture to the effect that in no way was it to be any sort of feature film. I don't quite know how it happened but somehow I left the meeting with instructions to make a story film to encourage Brits to immigrate to New Zealand![11]

While the resulting treatment Bockett sent to Andrews presented the free and assisted immigration scheme to New Zealand in a positive light, it did not shy away from some of the real difficulties that British migrants could reasonably expect to encounter: local prejudice against "Pommies" existed; accommodation was scarce; the nightlife and other organised urban entertainments were neither sophisticated nor numerous; culture shock was anticipated as city-bred migrants found themselves in small-town New Zealand; the working environment was smaller and less formal; and they would be expected to perform a wider range of functions within their occupational category rather than specialising in one particular aspect of it.

A pioneering masculine narrative

Although the film features the stories of three emblematic migrants, two of whom are single young women – a demographic the New Zealand government had identified as particularly desirable in terms of filling certain employment categories – the *combined* screen time of the women's migration experiences is significantly shorter than that of the man's.[12] The film runs to about 44 minutes and can be broken down into the following sections:

- Opening credits and life on board the boat with each of the three principals introduced along with their reasons for leaving the United Kingdom; 6′0″.
- Arrival in Wellington: Cassie's story; 3′40″.
- Arrival in Christchurch: Margaret's story; 4′35″.
- Arrival at Lake Pūkaki hydro camp: Harry's story; 7′15″.
- The three friends together at the Hermitage in Mt Cook; 5′0″.
- Harry's participation in mountain rescue of injured workmate; 15′0″.
- Conclusion with heterosexual couple formation; 2′0″.

Clearly, the masculine storyline situated in the "great outdoors" forms the core of the film. Harry's experiences are dramatised in both narrative and cinematic terms, and his journey becomes an exemplary rite of passage from the "effeminate" urban wen of London to the ruggedly masculine New Zealand frontier.[13] His passage is exemplary in several respects. It constructs New Zealand as essentially a man's country; positions the nation as rural rather than urban;[14] perpetuates the powerful myth of the pioneer; and participates in the pursuit of place that Pākehā have practised since large-scale settlement began in the mid-nineteenth century.

Journey for Three can be situated as another instance of what Peter Gibbons has elsewhere described as cultural colonisation, which is effected through different cultural practices and technologies, such as writing, printing and the visual arts, including, perhaps most powerfully, filmmaking.[15] As a cultural artefact, *Journey for Three* participates in making settlement by Europeans in lands occupied by non-Europeans an ineluctably historical process with various consequences, especially the marginalisation of prior Māori occupation and the inscription of locally born Pākehā as legitimate inhabitant/inheritor of a new world that incorporates "indigenous" and "exotic" elements, both material and symbolic.

The process of cultural colonisation enables secondary migrants to feel as at home in their composite environment as the primary were ostensibly in theirs before contact with the European world. "Indigenisation entails knowing about the local world,"[16] says Gibbons, which means that in order to feel "settled" in it, Pākehā acquire some superficial knowledge of the land (the names of flora, fauna and place, for example) and various cultural motifs and practices that Māori possess. The admixture of Māori knowledge into the cultural toolkit of the coloniser adumbrates the European settlement process by cloaking it in the longer presence of Māori in these islands.

Like many early migrants to New Zealand, Harry (Stuart Pilkington) is clearly unsettled upon arrival in the new land; in this instance, the homosocial environment of a work camp at Lake Pūkaki where a dam is being built to raise water levels by 30 feet.[17] After first imagining New Zealand as a luxuriant wilderness area where he would be "Out in the open, like [in] the stories" he had consumed back in England, with "Roaring mountain torrents, vast forests [and a] tent under tall trees," Harry is existentially distraught when the ride to the work camp reveals "bare tussock-covered country with hardly a tree and lots of dust." This keen sense of dismay amplifies the very first words he utters upon sighting the coastline of New Zealand from the ship: "Not much to look at, is it?" Of course, it *is* much to look at as they are steaming past a vista that highlights Mt Taranaki/Egmont.[18] Narratively, this establishes Harry as the kind of character that a New Zealand audience would regard as a "whingeing Pom," the twentieth-century descendant of the nineteenth's "new chum." The former vociferated their displeasure with aspects of life in New Zealand, thereby shaking the native-born Pākehā New Zealander's somewhat fragile sense of achievement (or complacency), while the latter lived comfortably on money sent regularly from "home," in which case they had no need to engage in physical labour, usually a source of male pride, and were thus outside the hegemonic masculine order.[19]

The social and built environments Harry encounters upon alighting from the bus compound his deception with the landscape. "I wondered if I had ended up in an army camp. There were rows and rows of huts, all exactly alike. I couldn't believe I had come halfway around the world for this." His deepening gloom is accentuated while seeking bedding and a mattress. "It was a Saturday afternoon. I found a group of men listening to a horse race on the radio. It's a favourite pastime up here, and they weren't very cooperative." While this scene links narratively to an earlier scene of Margaret at the race rack in Riccarton, it also suggests, extra-diegetically, that the workingman's leisure time is sacrosanct; it was surely a plus for any worker contemplating migration to learn that Capital did not dictate unconditionally.

By way of striking contrast with Harry's woes, the women's arrival and integration proceeds happily, although the narrative is structured to show that they, too, encounter settlement difficulties. However, these are minor, fleeting irritations, quickly offset by the many positives that living in New Zealand enables. Cassie (Elizabeth Armstrong), for instance, meets a vindictive fellow worker at the woollen mill in Petone who accuses her of taking employment away from New Zealanders. Cassie's rebuke curtly points out that she was encouraged to come and work here, that she has not taken the woman's job, and that "Your mother and father was a Pommie before I was. Get on with your job and leave me to mine." It is also made clear that Cassie's other work colleagues are "very friendly and nice." Margaret's moment of trial occurs when she is "ticked off for not making a bed properly" by a sharp-tongued Sister in front of a patient.

In both cases, however, the unpleasantness is momentary and amply counterbalanced. More broadly, the filmic feminine is structured around notions of docility, conviviality and malleability. This ideological configuration allows the women in *Journey for Three* to adapt more easily; it would not matter where in the British world they were, the film implies, they would "fit in."[20] Cassie's story of settlement in Wellington, the capital of New Zealand, focuses on the recreational activities that allow her to meet New Zealand girls through such sports and activities as netball and tramping. She is careful, however, not to practise the latter as frequently as other girls, who tramp on a weekly basis, for fear of seeing her legs become, as her voiceover remarks, "too muscly." This concern with becoming less feminine through contact with New Zealanders suggests, albeit somewhat obliquely for the moment, the notion that New Zealand is a land made for the muscular qualities of strength and action.[21] These presumed masculine "virtues" are necessary in the face of the many arduous challenges that attend the process of colonisation and settlement – the physical acquisition of land from its former occupants by conquest, threat of force or tortuous legal channels, and its transformation from incorrigible wilderness into harmonious pastoral paradise by dint of considerable investment of capital and labour.

Visually, Cassie's story is marked by shots of New Zealand girls in rapid and energetic motion, be it on the netball court or in the bush. By contrast, when we see her with other women who have come out on the same assisted scheme as she, the scenes are set indoors, suggestive of a domestic and "feminine" interior, thereby figuring England as "soft" and given over to the material comforts that weaken the masculine, which is set against the New Zealand "hard," symbolically conceived as a remedial space to preserve former imperial and contemporary commonwealth virility. One might read this as an antipodean antidote to the perception produced by the Boer War of national decline. As Jock Phillips notes, "There was a fear [in England] that the urban life was producing a physical deterioration in British manhood, which would serve the country ill in the Social Darwinist struggle with other races."[22] As we will see, Harry, too, will be discursively and visually constructed as belonging to a "feminine" England, which is unfavourably contrasted with imagery of the rough bluntness of a "masculine" New Zealand.

Cassie's time in the narrative limelight is brief, and Margaret (Margaret McNulty) fares only marginally better. As the nascent love interest of the male migrant, Margaret appears more frequently throughout the film, notably at the end when she and Harry walk comfortably as a couple into the future through a sunlight sylvan glade adjacent to her hospital. Harry's injured colleague lies inside recovering from the mountain ordeal that acts as the narrative trigger for Harry's transformation from "whingeing Pommie" to "real hard-case New Zealander" – the *sine qua non* of successful settlement via "mateship," induction into the pioneering masculine and the "team." It is clear at the end of the film that she will quit urban Christchurch and her nursing profession for the "wilds" of the work camp, and in readying Margaret for her future role as female support for the "male way of life," she is constructed as being predisposed to maternity and nurturing.

Her letter to Cassie describing her new life begins: "I like my work very much. It's all interesting but I like it best when I'm on duty in the children's ward." Her voiceover pauses significantly at this point as a series of three shots presents the tender scene of Margaret feeding a very young child. The opening shot is visually complex and semantically rich.

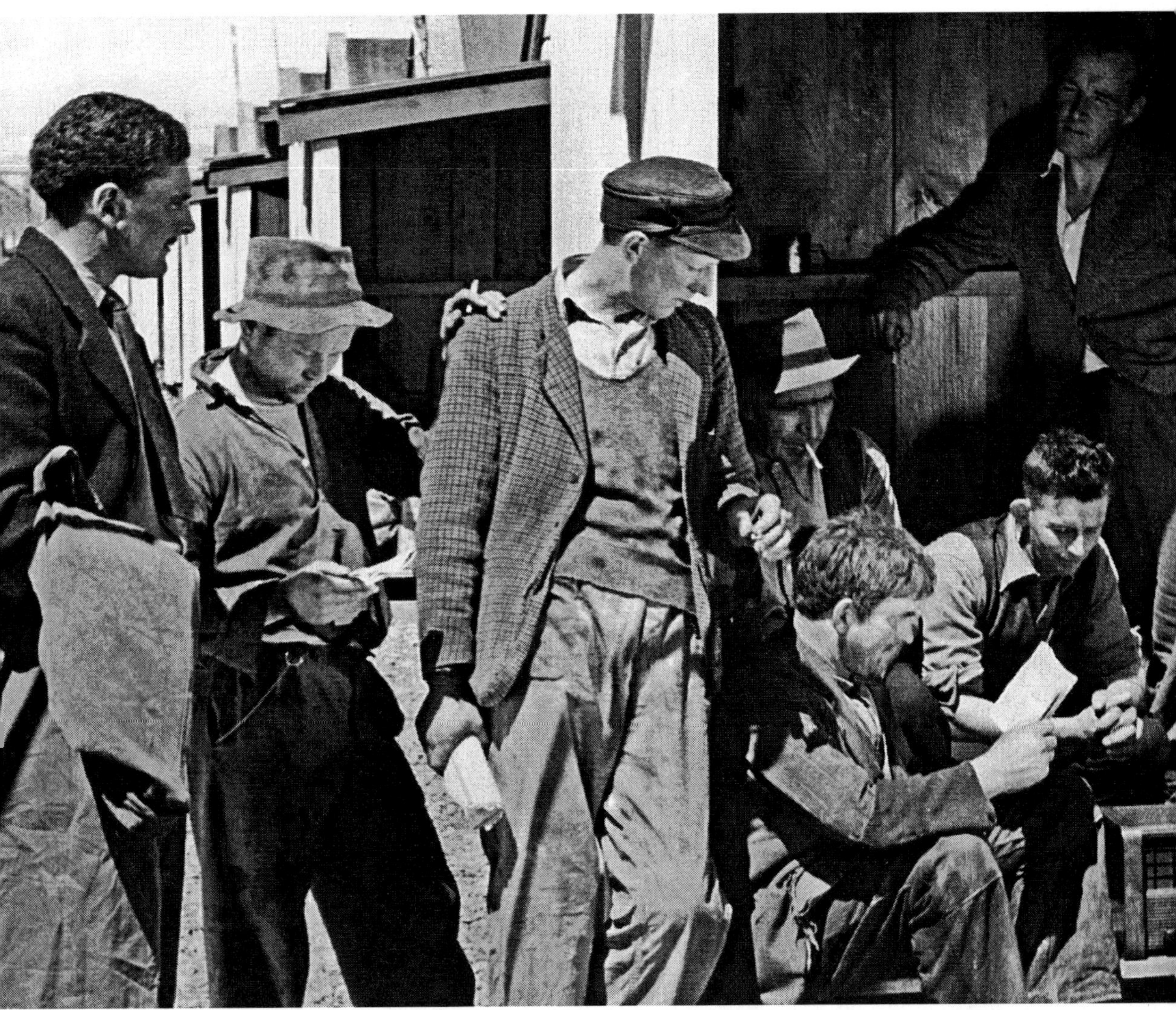

Harry's arrival at the work camp intrudes on a masculine ritual: listening to horse races on the radio, in *Journey for Three*, 1950, dir. Michael Forlong, New Zealand National Film Unit. Image courtesy of Archives New Zealand/Te Rua Mahara o te Kāwanatanga, Wellington Office [AAPG W3939 box 2].

It quickly cross-dissolves from Cassie and her boyfriend in a Wellington coffee bar into the image of a large wall-hung picture of three children on a primitive seesaw (a plank of sawn and dressed timber laid across a section of tree trunk, suggestive of one of the primary extractive industries of the early colonial period). The combined weight of the boy and girl in the foreground has lifted the other, younger child high above them, suggestive of the procreative duty (and pleasure) that heterosexual romance should encompass. (Cassie and her boyfriend are included in this heterosexual union via the linkage the cross-dissolve establishes.) The camera briefly frames this image before tilting down to reveal Margaret, a hospital bed and the child she is tending in a loose medium shot. The combined effect of mise-en-scène and camera movement has succinctly described the procreative duty of heterosexual couple formation the narrative has in store for Harry and her.

The other major role she has in the pioneering masculine narrative of *Journey for Three* is that of moral guardian.[23] Margaret reminds Harry of his duty during their (chaste) weekend together at the Hermitage, a state-owned ski resort in the Aoraki Mt Cook National Park. On the mountains, Harry announces that he is leaving his job at the work camp. Margaret's reasoned response not only expresses her disappointment but also reminds Harry of the warning she had earlier given him on the voyage out about his unrealistic expectations of the "boy's own" adventurous life he imagined awaited him in New Zealand. She also asks him if he had not promised to remain for two years in the job he was offered as part of the assisted immigration scheme. If a man is only as good as his word, then Harry's decision to leave without fulfilling his promise reveals him as less than dependable, less than honourable, less than honest.

The implicit reproof in Margaret's question stings him into a defensive posture: "But I didn't know it was going to be like this; I'm not going to stay." When she asks him to reconsider his decision, he ripostes, in a tone that combines defiance and anger; what can it mean to her whether he stays or goes? Thus confronted, with eyes cast down and softened voice, she demurely begins, "It means a lot to me, Harry." Then, raising her gaze to confront his and speaking more forcefully, she continues, "It means a lot to me that you set out to do what you said you'd do." Harry, upbraided, lets his head fall down, chastened to the core at this evidence of dereliction from the masculine code of honourable conduct.

Māori presence and Pākehā indigenisation

The process of cultural colonisation noted earlier finds further expression in the way in which the absence/presence of Māori is textually and visually constructed.[24] During the women's urban settlement stories, there are no Māori on screen; nor does their voiceover mention them. When Māori do make a screen appearance, their eruption into the film's diegesis is sudden, dramatic and clichéd.

When Harry arrives in the homosocial environment of the camp at Lake Pūkaki, he describes how the masculine culture of this new "frontier" is both unpleasant and unsettling

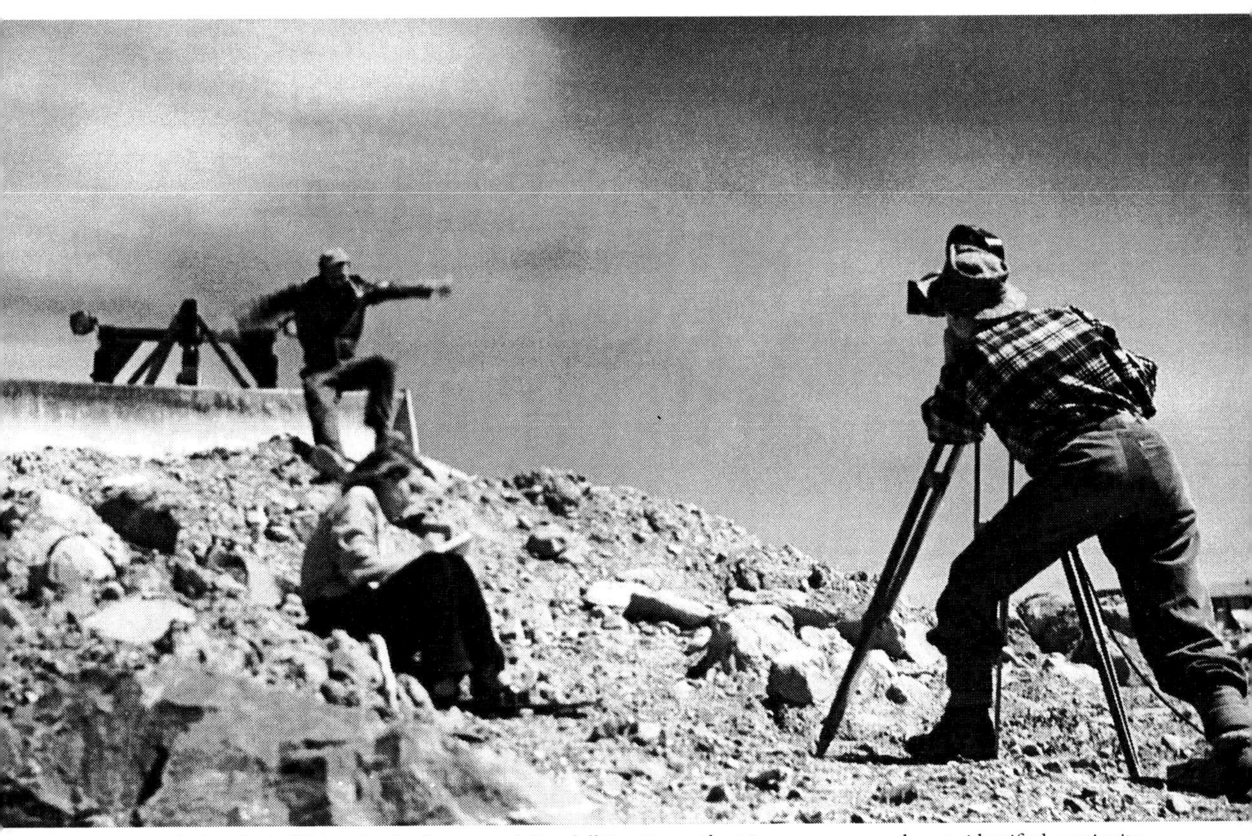

Harry fleeing the bulldozer. In the foreground, Randall Beattie on the 16 mm camera and an unidentified continuity girl, in *Journey for Three*, 1950, dir. Michael Forlong, New Zealand National Film Unit. Image courtesy of Archives New Zealand/Te Rua Mahara o te Kāwanatanga, Wellington Office [AAPG W3939 box 2].

– the men argue with their superiors, thus upsetting his concept of proper hierarchical order; versatility and improvisation in the "back country" are necessary, thus disturbing the specialised urban work culture he brings with him; and the men have a strange sense of humour, thus destabilising his notion of interpersonal dynamics. Upon this last observation, a bulldozer driver greets him with a hazing ritual that ridicules and humiliates him. He is pursued by the 'dozer driver in a sequence that effectively constructs and conveys, through a rapidly edited series of shots and an under cranked camera, a formidable threatening presence of man/machine. The sequence clearly identifies the intimidating 'dozer driver as Māori.

Although it is not the intention of this section to pursue the varied psychological consequences (for Māori and Pākehā) that attend the traumatic experiences of colonisation, it is tempting to speculate that this partially comic, partially threatening sequence expresses obliquely, and in a symbolically condensed form, some of that history – indeed, that it is a synecdoche for aspects of colonisation. Furthermore, it is also possible to read the 'dozer sequence as an instance of the complex process of European indigenisation – the becoming native to this land through the adoption and display of Māori cultural motifs and practices. This also speaks to the ambivalent admiration that Pākehā have of Māori.

In the 'dozer sequence, as the new visitor and potential settler, Harry is "welcomed" onto the land with an abridged and transformed *pōwhiri* – the traditional Māori welcome ceremony – the purpose of which is to lift the *tapu* (alterity) of the *manuhiri* (visitors), which, once removed, will allow them to become one with the *tangata whenua* (home people). The *pōwhiri* process is a gradual and ritualised one leading to the formation of a new community – a successful blend of two peoples.[25] A full *pōwhiri* traditionally comprises ten stages, but the one most germane to the film sequence and theme of implicit Pākehā indigenisation is the *wero* (challenge).

The fittest and fastest warrior of the *tangata whenua* carried out the *wero* in order to determine the peaceful or belligerent intentions of the visitors. Bob, the Māori 'dozer driver, clearly challenges Pākehā Harry in a ritualised way upon his arrival – the film tells us he has similarly "welcomed" at least half the camp's newcomers – and laughs at the fearful reaction he provokes. When he descends from his machine, his stance is assertive (legs apart, hands on hips) and, viewed from behind, with the distant mountains echoing his virile stance, his position dominates Harry, who, in the background, visually constrained between Māori, machine, lake and mountains, picks himself up and, angrily, dusts himself off. As director/demiurge of this moment, native-born Forlong, implicitly, if not explicitly, is clearly on Māori Bob's side in this encounter. The hazing/*wero* of English Harry serves then several purposes: it introduces him to the rude rigours of "frontier" life; offers the possibility of joining this new community; and marks Pākehā Forlong as indigenous through having incorporated the *wero* into his cultural toolkit. He is no longer *manuhiri* but *tangata whenua*, with English Harry as an avatar of an earlier colonial moment carried into the present.[26]

The last shot of this sequence then cross-dissolves into the second of the film's Māori "moments," a clichéd pendant to the similarly clichéd first representation of Māori masculinity as potentially lethal. Inside the YMCA hut, where the men relax from the rigours of nation-building in the wilderness, Bob is now pictured in the foreground playing an upright piano while another Māori male leans over its top in a tight two-shot that seems to have been inspired by a similar set-up in *Casablanca* (1942), where Humphrey Bogart's character, Rick, exhorts his piano-playing friend, Sam (a black man) to play "You Must Remember This"; Forlong's audience almost certainly would.

The song that Bob begins to play is the diegetically apt (a group of disparate men bound together by circumstance and lacking the company of women) wartime favourite, "Lili Marleen" (1938) – a nostalgically sensuous love song. Thus, of the two scenes in which Māori masculinity is bodied forth, the first constructs it as violent while the second softens it via the expedient performance of a romantic tune – beloved by soldiers on opposite sides during World War Two. If we remember that primary and secondary migrants to New Zealand fought each other in bloody battles over land in the nineteenth century, the song may then take its haunting place as a *sotto voce* invocation of the fraught and complex processes involved in the continual *pōwhiri* of encounter between *tangata whenua* and *manuhiri*. In the film's diegesis, the imagined new masculine community at Lake Pūkaki is impressively idealistic in its ideological work of eventually blending several differences (Māori/Pākehā, New Zealander/British, Māori/English). Had "Lili Marleen" been sung, the first four lines of the second verse would have sounded apposite: Our two shadows/Looked like one,/That we held each other so fondly/Someone would think we were one.[27]

Moreover, as a synecdoche of colonisation, the 'dozer/*wero* sequence may be read as a displacement strategy, representing the imaginary and fantastic dissolution of deep enmities through sharing a common adversary. While Māori had good historical reason to challenge the English, the local born New Zealander with a nationalist cultural agenda also had good grounds to assert the particularities of place in the shaping of nascent national identity, and, like other insular peoples, to be suspicious of the difference (and potential danger) that came from distant shores. For both, English Harry, with his metropolitan manners and occupational sophistication, was a potentially "bad import" who had to be made over to preserve the "essence" of New Zealand culture, which was

> in the land, in the blackened earth [...] not in the city, the place only of unreality in Nationalist discourse, the place of the woman, the foreigner, the internationalist, the cosmopolitan, the fashionable, the aesthete, the homosexual and the Jew.[28]

Francis Pound's polemic points to a complex web of negative discursive presumptions that seek to explain why "real hard-case New Zealanders" would, if only in their imaginations (and sometimes in the weekend), flee the city, and why national identity was resolutely rural and excessively masculine in so many textual and visual inventions of New Zealand from the 1930s to the 1970s.

The influence of *Casablanca* tentatively reveals some of *Journey for Three*'s cinematic indebtedness to Hollywood narrative and visual form. In a sequence that immediately

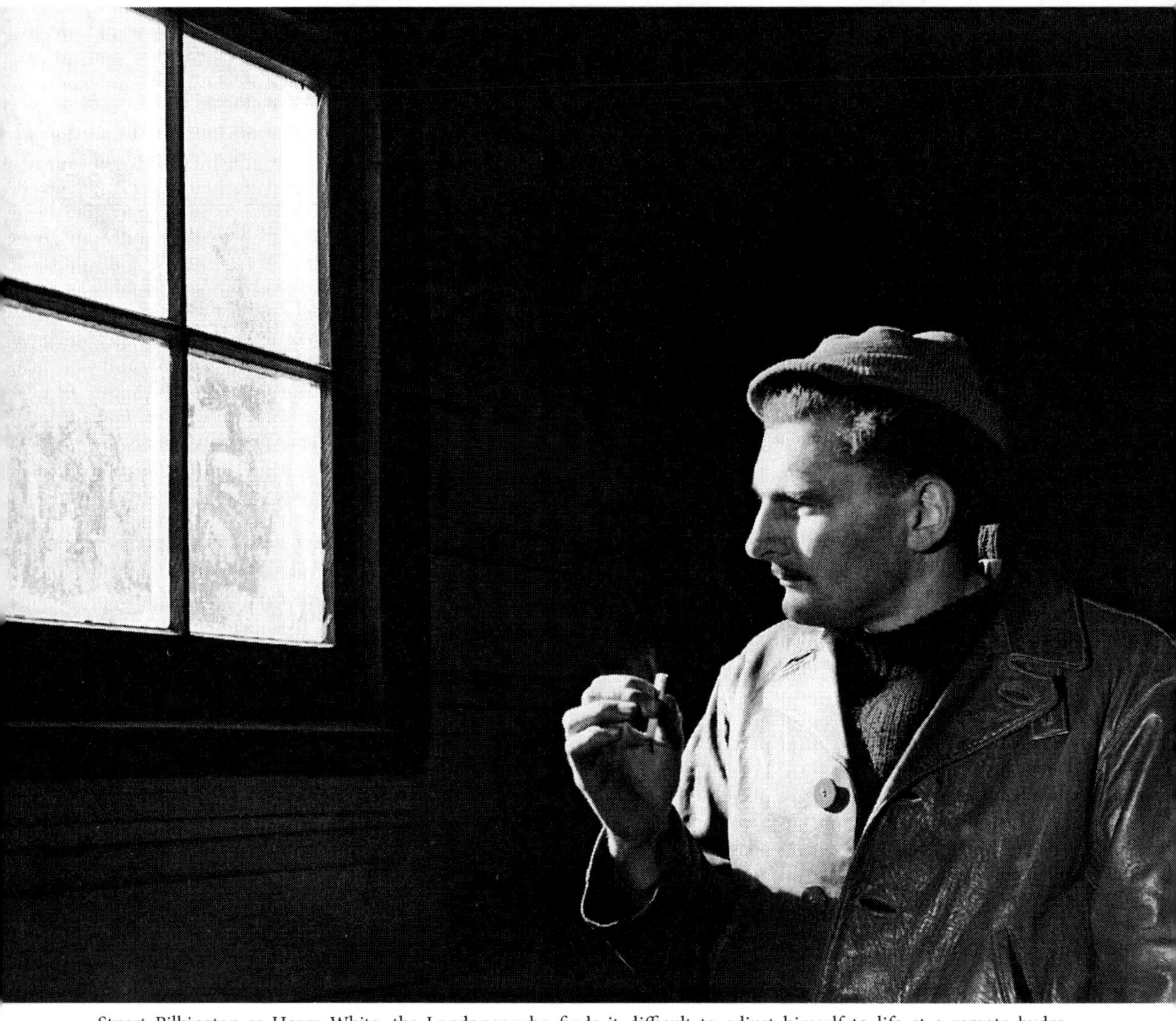

Stuart Pilkington as Harry White, the Londoner who finds it difficult to adjust himself to life at a remote hydro construction works camp, in *Journey for Three*, 1950, dir. Michael Forlong, New Zealand National Film Unit. Image courtesy of Archives New Zealand/Te Rua Mahara o te Kāwanatanga, Wellington Office [AAPG W3939 box 2].

precedes Harry's decision to leave, Forlong powerfully establishes Harry's estrangement from the hegemonic masculinity of the camp with considerable filmic style. After the three friends have caught up with one another during the long Labour Day weekend spent skiing at the Hermitage, Harry is alone again. The sequence begins with a close-up of Margaret in a framed photo on a shelf in Harry's hut. The camera tilts and pans from her to Harry, lying on his bed, pensive. He gets up and goes outside. A slightly high-angle camera set-up places him in a medium shot and the camera tracks back as Harry walks in darkness past several huts. The angle adds an ominous visual "weight" to his existential oppression and the soundtrack contains three distinct sonic textures during his "long night of the soul." The first uses the plaintive notes of a solo harmonica playing the opening bars of "Blue Smoke," a song written in 1940 by Ruru Karaitiana on the troopship *Aquitania*, as it sailed off the coast of Africa, which adds yet another layer to the film's voyaging theme.[29] The succeeding sound contains the raucous jazz rapture of a Dizzy Gillespie-like trumpet peel; and the third consists of human voices, men enjoying one another's company. This surprisingly adept 50-second sequence shot (there are no cuts as the camera remains resolutely with Harry) constructs its emotionally provocative and powerful texture through an adroit juxtaposition of aural and visual elements, with sound being used to articulate and amplify the protagonist's inner confusion and alienation.

"A man alone don't stand a chance"[30]

Withdrawing into himself, Harry's "rebellion" against the social and cultural values he encounters does not lead to any form of action capable of producing a positive outcome. Suffocated by the hegemonic masculine culture and unwilling to have his life ordered by its priorities, he decides to leave. His masculinity is clearly at odds with the natural and social environments he is sent to – his work history is urban and specialised, and his interests do not include the "great outdoors." He is thus, in a sense, made "effeminate" in the eyes of the dominant masculinity of the work camp – even his war experiences as a stretcher-bearer situate him at some remove from the warrior ideal of masculine combative endeavour.[31]

Harry's socialisation is cosmopolitan English and the repressive cultural milieu that encouraged New Zealand men "to look for a form of homosocial bonding that replicated the male only social milieu of colonial times" is unknown to him.[32] He becomes an alienated male in the local "man alone" tradition, but for different reasons – an unwillingness to adapt to very changed circumstances – and the ribbing he receives isolates him. The crude camaraderie and common culture of the men he meets are not inclusive enough to admit "soft" Harry, who derives no adequate sense of purpose or identity from the masculine value system of the society he migrates to. Unlike his colleagues, who value the rigours of "roughing it" in the "back country" – a central experience to the male in the colonies – he does not fear domesticity, as the archetypal man alone did. Instead, he seems to yearn for its "softening" influence and the creature comforts it provides.

In 1949, one in three adult New Zealand males had seen service overseas (often forging strong bonds of friendship); thus, memories of war experiences were still fresh and the Returned Services Association was a force in the land.[33] The martial attributes and skills of soldiering, which ultimately prove useful during the rescue of a fellow worker injured during a mountain climbing excursion, facilitate Harry's inclusion into the masculine group from which he has felt ostracised; he is able to properly secure the injured man's badly broken leg. In proving his courage on the mountains – an activity he has not formerly essayed – Harry discovers that in New Zealand, where interpersonal dynamics are grounded in physicality rather than speech, it is physical prowess that will earn him the approval of his peers. He is rewarded with group inclusion after demonstrating his mettle, and celebrated as having the attributes of "a real hard-case New Zealander." There is an internal feeling of belonging and identity proper to Harry, and an external welcome and identity afforded by his newfound "mates," who now respect him as a man and a team player.

In the rear of the truck that drives them from the mountain, the rescue party relaxes after the rigours of their alpine ascent and descent. The other men question Harry about his reasons for coming to New Zealand and compare the attractions of his home country with those available in his new one. Harry's new appreciation of place is now grounded in lived experience rather than imagination – a poor companion and no substitute for the real thing, the film seems to say, thus affirming that the bookish and the intellectual have no real grip on understanding in the new world – and pragmatic with regards to advantages and disadvantages, rather than idealistic. New Zealand, however, is still positioned as a symbolically powerful space for the English cultural imaginary. Its semi-utopian function is on display as Harry enumerates the many and varied leisure activities that only the wealthy can access and enjoy in England, whether these be the gentler pursuits of golf, tennis and skiing, or the more "manly" stalking of deer and shooting of pig. The film situates the "real" New Zealand as a frontier space where any male can hunt game and find his masculine identity and pride affirmed. New Zealand, the film repeatedly asserts, is a demotic not an aristocratic land of adventure, where "You can do as you like," as Harry points out to his new "mates."

Ideologically, New Zealand's place is affirmed as a land of opportunity in which the virile sons and nubile daughters of the British Empire/Commonwealth may multiply, grow strong and prosper, and thus preserve the race's future. Another of the ideological aims of the film is temporal linkage: to connect past pioneering endeavour with present purpose; to show continuity and fidelity to the myth of an always-open "frontier" society, as well as progress and, inevitably, change. Colonisation, therefore, presents itself as a perennial cultural practice involving the settlement and indigenisation of the initially unsettled and exotic in an extended *pōwhiri* whose function is to found a new community.

In the film, Harry meets a man who had migrated from the United Kingdom 30 years earlier when "times were tougher," but he has "done alright" and now owns his own farm. This time frame places him as a young man at the conclusion of the First World War; he may even have come out on the ex-servicemen's assisted passage scheme when it was introduced in 1919 (as Johnson had in John Mulgan's seminal novel, *Man Alone*). He is a man who has made a prosperous new life after a murderous European debacle and assures Harry (another survivor of another grim war) that "the opportunities are still here." They were, but not in the rural sector, which this man represents; the government sought to encourage import substitution by developing local manufacturing industries. The myth, however, of New Zealand as essentially outdoor, masculine and rural imposes itself on the film's diegesis and the sponsor's objective for the film, which was to encourage industrial workers to migrate. The "great outdoors" ideological orientation maintains the country, former outpost of empire, as a powerfully symbolic repository of traditions that venerate the muscular virtues of the pioneer. "His" ability to endure physical hardship made him strong in times of war (on the battlefield) and peace (most powerfully on the rugby field). Bonds of indefectibly masculine mateship would reinforce the "crimson thread of kinship" that ran through British veins.

But not, however, for Stuart Pilkington, the actor who played Harry White. In reality, he turned out to be a "bad import," marrying Elizabeth Armstrong (Cassie McLeod in the film) and returning to the United Kingdom with her.[34] The rigours of existence in New Zealand proved no match for the "soft" charms and comforting allure of England – a personal and collective territory that better reflected his emotional and professional needs. Like Dorothy in Oz, for Pilkington there is "no place like home."

Reception in the United Kingdom and New Zealand

Released in March 1950 at the Odeon in Leicester Square (London) with Noel Coward's *The Astonished Heart*, *Journey for Three* received a positive reaction from the British press, who responded favourably to the comparatively realistic representation of the existential and physical challenges that migration to New Zealand could provoke:

> What is pleasant about this unpretentious little essay in self-advertisement – apart from its glimpses of magnificent snow-covered mountains – is that it states its argument with no apparent exaggeration. A New Zealander's life, it says in effect, may seem tough when judged by the standards of big industrial towns with their teashops and cinemas, but at least it is a wonderfully open-air life, providing almost everyone with the out-of-doors opportunities which only the British rich can enjoy.[35]

The more apparently egalitarian access to such outdoor leisure pursuits as hunting, tramping, horse-riding, skiing and tennis was a marked feature of the film's construction of New Zealand as a latter day "South Seas Paradise," bountiful provider of pleasures that "Better Britons" living here neither idly dreamed of, nor eyed enviously, but experienced in the flesh.

Michael Forlong was no doubt excited by the praise that came his way via another comment in the British press that again noted the film's "honesty":

> Although this 38-minute semi-documentary could be labelled "propaganda," it is propaganda of a refreshingly different type [...]. Thanks to some unusual ideas by the producer and by Michael Forlong, the director, there is no attempt to whitewash conditions in the Dominion – indeed some may be deterred by the uncompromising manner in which the film is made.[36]

After its auspicious West End opening with Coward's film, the film was partnered with that great British boy's own adventure story, *Treasure Island* (1950), for general release throughout the United Kingdom, which ensured a long run; it was still being screened in 1951.[37] Such success surely vindicated the decision to inflect the "straight" documentary originally commissioned with Hollywood-inspired narrative techniques, and Forlong was quick to remind his sponsor, H. L. Bockett, of this in a letter he sent to him from England following the release of the film. The "honesty" of the film and the fact that there had been little attempt "to gild the lily" were tactfully attributed to Bockett himself: "Your policy in this was, I am sure, a very wise one and has done much more good than if we had just tried to sing our praises."[38]

In this honest willingness to recognise that life in New Zealand could be difficult for British migrants, yet still find space to vaunt the nation as a modern progressive playground, it is possible to hear the distant echo of John Grierson's nationwide radio talk, given during his month-long visit to New Zealand in 1940. Grierson had come to advise the government on documentary production and left a strong impression. His radiophonic invocation concluded thus:

> So when you send us your films never send merely the scenic ones. Put in something about the real things you do. Do not be ashamed to describe your problems. Remember we are pretty imperfect ourselves, and if you always appear in the spit and polish of perfection we know very quickly that you are either inhuman or you are liars. Above all your country must send us films about people, so that we can see their faces and remember that New Zealand is not just a couple of spots on a distant map but a real place with a flash of the future in its eyes and a beat in its heart.[39]

Forlong's letter to Bockett concluded with the hope that *Journey for Three* might now receive distribution in New Zealand. Given its success in London this became more likely – external praise tended to make local cultural productions more significant for domestic audiences. Bockett's response indicated that a deal with Robert Kerridge, the owner of a nationwide theatre circuit, was probable.[40] The film was eventually paired with Alberto Cavalcanti's *For Them That Trespass* (1949), "a very much better film" than *A Run for Your Money*, described as "just a small British comedy which is not likely to prove particularly sensational at the box office."[41]

Reviews of the film in Wellington were generally positive, with the landscape, acting and film score receiving special mention.[42] While the script was deemed "fairly adequate," the film was seen to mark an important step forward in terms of local production, which indeed it was.[43] Ten years separated *Journey for Three* from the last locally made feature-length film, *Rewi's Last Stand* (1940), a sound version of Rudall Hayward's 1925 silent original of the same name. The *Dominion's* reviewer noted that it was "stretching credulity" to believe that the many "pleasures of outdoor life in New Zealand […] are the common experience of migrants to this country," but remarked that the film's emphasis was on the possibility "that such diversions are within the reach of all – if they work to that end."[44] As if in echo to the British press, "honesty" was the principal element praised by the film reviewer of the much-read national weekly magazine, the *New Zealand Listener*. While pointing out the absence of any single scene depicting the "suburban wilderness," the film still tried "to give a true picture of this country and its people." The "honest intent" of the film kept "breaking through," and some dialogue "had the authentic New Zealand ring."[45] The review ended with an admonition that reveals the realist aesthetic temper of the time: to stick to the basics, eschew art and remain true to the palpability of the real. "If this [review] sounds too much like a report on inexperience, let us remember that the Film Unit staff has a creditable record in the field of pure documentary. I hope they don't forget it themselves."[46]

They would not be allowed to. The election of the first National Government in November 1949 (after 14 years of Labour administrations) ushered in a period of intense scrutiny about state spending, and the NFU was about to be pruned. Reorientation of the Unit's scope and functions brought Forlong's second docudrama project (on the life of one of the most illustrious scientists of all time, the New Zealander Ernest Rutherford) to a close and contributed to the eventual departure overseas of several core filmmakers, including Forlong.[47] The successful experiment in making feature-length films that imaginatively projected the nation to domestic and international audiences encountered a dissuasive economic rationality; if there was no money in it, the new government made clear, there was no point in proceeding. Although individual members of the NFU had extended their abilities and might have been expected to play an important part in developing a domestic film industry, their departure overseas further depleted already scarce technical and artistic competencies.[48] The cinematic journey was a fugitive one and the Hollywood-like epilogue of *Journey for Three*, with Margaret and Harry walking towards their future (the number three may imply a child), would receive no stately benediction.[49] Although the next local feature-length film, the independently made *Broken Barrier*, screened in 1952, it was the only such venture in the 1950s and a further 12 years separated that film from *Runaway*. As the incoming National Government proceeded to restructure the NFU, it was ruefully noted that "It cannot be said that New Zealand is a lucky country with its ventures into creative fields."[50]

Notes

1. Peter Gibbons, "Cultural Colonization and National Identity," *New Zealand Journal of History* 36, no. 1 (2002): 15.
2. Megan Hutchings, *Long Journey for Sevenpence: Assisted Immigration to New Zealand from the United Kingdom, 1947–1975* (Wellington: Victoria University Press in association with Historical Branch, Department of Internal Affairs, 1999), 49.
3. "The crimson thread of kinship" epigram belongs to Sir Henry Parkes, Premier of New South Wales, who reportedly pronounced it at the 1890 Federation Conference in Melbourne, to which New Zealand was invited.
4. Margaret McNulty, one of the three principal characters, arrived in New Zealand in early 1948; shooting for the film began in late 1948.
5. Roberto Rossellini's *Rome, Open City* (1945) screened in Wellington in 1948 and Michael Forlong, a member of the Wellington Film Society, would most certainly have seen it.
6. Simon Sigley, *Film Culture: Its Development in New Zealand, 1920s–1970s* (Unpublished PhD thesis, University of Auckland, 2004), 102.
7. Hutchings, *Long Journey for Sevenpence*, 37–38.
8. Migrants who paid their own passages or airfares in full substantially outnumbered those in the assisted scheme, and reflected a broader age range.
9. Memorandum for the Hon. Minister of Immigration, 22 October 1947. Archives New Zealand, L1 Box 139, 22/2/14 Part 1.
10. Memorandum for the Producer, NFU, 14 July 1948. Archives New Zealand, L1 Box 139, 22/2/14 Part 1.
11. Michael Forlong, *Departure Lounge: An Autobiography* (Unpublished manuscript, 1991), 28.
12. The film has several running times. The one I am working on is the British release version held in Archives New Zealand, which has catalogued the film with three running times of 50, 42 and 39 minutes. The last is described as "British Release Version." However, my copy of the film is 44′20″ long, so some inaccuracy exists.
13. For J. O. C. Phillips, "fears lay deep in English culture that city life was effeminate and that the advances of leisuretime and material comforts was making men soft." *A Man's Country?: The Image of the Pakeha Male, a History* (Auckland: Penguin Books, 1996), 87.
14. Yet for over 100 years New Zealand has been one of the most heavily urbanised societies in the world.
15. Peter Gibbons, "Cultural Colonization and National Identity," *New Zealand Journal of History*, 36, no. 1 (2002): 5–17. Other notable NFU productions from the period in this vein include *Meet New Zealand* (1949), *The Valley Settlers* (1952), *Bushman* (1952) and *Pumicelands* (1954).
16. Gibbons, "Cultural Colonization," 8.
17. The pent-up post-war demand for an increasing array of electrical appliances and utilities and the burgeoning secondary manufacturing industries all required increased electrical capacity, and the government responded with large-scale infrastructural developments to build a modern nation.
18. I thank my colleague Brian McDonnell for pointing this feature out to me.
19. Jock Phillips has already noted that the "colonial respect for hard work left a literary record in the frequent expressions of contempt for the remittance man, the 'new chum' who enjoyed a life of ease on the basis of cheques sent from home." *A Man's Country?*, 16.
20. Except of course when they did not, which happened. A group of trained psychiatric nurses expressed dissatisfaction with the limited duties expected of them; other nurse trainees expressed

alarm at the amount of domestic work hospitals wanted them to do. Hutchings, *Long Journey for Sevenpence*, 45–49.

21. There are many other texts in addition to Phillips's seminal book that discuss the myth of New Zealand national identity and the masculine. See, for example, Ian Carter and Nick Perry, "Rembrandt in Gumboots: Rural Imagery in New Zealand Television Advertisements," in *Te Whenua Te Iwi: The Land and the People*, ed. Jock Phillips (Wellington: Allen & Unwin/Port Nicholson Press in association with the Stout Research Centre, 1987), 61–72; Kai Jensen, *Whole Men: The Masculine Tradition in New Zealand Literature* (Auckland: Auckland University Press, 1996); Robin Law, Hugh Campbell and John Dolan, eds, *Masculinities in Aotearoa/New Zealand* (Palmerston North: Dunmore Press, 1999); Alistair Fox, *The Ship of Dreams: Masculinity in Contemporary New Zealand Fiction* (Dunedin: Otago University Press, 2008); and Francis Pound, *The Invention of New Zealand: Art and National Identity, 1930–1970* (Auckland: Auckland University Press, 2009).

22. Phillips, *A Man's Country?* 142.

23. A role familiar to women raised in New Zealand's particular variety of Puritanism; see Lawrence Jones, *Picking Up the Traces: The Making of a New Zealand Literary Culture 1932–1945* (Wellington: Victoria University Press, 2003), 236–38.

24. Uncertainty surrounds the arrival of the Polynesian ancestors of Māori in New Zealand, with scholars questioning the time and circumstances of first arrival, previously thought to have occurred between 950 and 1130 AD.

25. Information on this practice was obtained from www.Māori.org.nz/tikanga. Accessed 12 March 2010.

26. One of the NFU's most talented directors, Forlong's first encounter with film production occurred when he worked on the government's centennial celebration film, *One Hundred Crowded Years* (1940), as scriptwriter and assistant director. His career with the NFU spanned the years 1944–52, after which he enjoyed a successful film career overseas in Norway and the United Kingdom.

27. Written as a poem by Hans Leip in 1915.

28. Pound, *The Invention of New Zealand*, 37.

29. "Blue Smoke" was a popular record in New Zealand in 1948, topping the hit parade for six weeks and selling in excess of 20,000 copies within the year. The song seeks to encapsulate the sentiment felt by Māori women as they said farewell to their men – now soldiers bound for war – from small town trains stations. www.nzhistory.net.nz/media/photo/blue-smoke. Accessed 13 March 2010).

30. A phrase inspired by John Mulgan's seminal novel, *Man Alone* (1939), in which the main protagonist, an Englishman named Johnson, at the end of his journeys across various frontiers (psychological, social, political, geographical) – including an extended stay in New Zealand after the First World War – ruefully observes to himself that "A man spends too much time alone."

31. Once he has been accepted, the men share war experiences and we learn that Harry's stretcher-bearing duties were with the paratroops in various "hotspots" in Normandy; this knowledge elicits expressions of respect from the other men who "Wouldn't have liked that caper."

32. Fox, *The Ship of Dreams*, 24.

33. Phillips, *A Man's Country?* 264.

34. Douglas Lilburn mentions this in a radio programme devoted to the music of *Journey for Three*. Douglas Lilburn, MS-Papers-2483-133, Alexander Turnbull Library.

35. "A Film from New Zealand", *Manchester Guardian* (6 March 1950). Archives New Zealand, L1 Box 139 22/2/14 Part 1.

36. "*Journey for Three* – Scots Girl in New Zealand Film", *The Scotsman* (6 March 1950). Archives New Zealand, L1 Box 139 22/2/14 Part 1.

37. Interview. Michael Forlong, New Zealand Film Archive, A0328. See also the report to the Cabinet Sub-Committee on Publicity, Part IV. "Notes on Distribution", p. 15, 1952, Archives New Zealand, TO 1 18/1.

38. Letter. Michael Forlong to H. L. Bockett, 18 March 1950. Archives New Zealand, L1 Box 139 22/2/14 Part 1.

39. Reprinted as "No More Scenery, Please! What's Wrong with New Zealand Films?" *New Zealand Listener* (10 May 1940, 12).

40. Letter. H. L. Bockett to Michael Forlong, 31 March 1950. Archives New Zealand, L1 Box 139 22/2/14 Part 1.

41. Letter. Robert Kerridge to Geoffrey Scott, 12 July 1950. Archives New Zealand, AAPG W3435 11 3/3/5. Scott became Manager of the NFU in 1950 following Stanhope Andrews' sudden resignation.

42. The musical talents of New Zealand's most prominent composer, Douglas Lilburn, were given cinematic expression when he scored the film, which was played by the recently established New Zealand Symphony Orchestra. Lilburn had previously been commissioned to write the music for two shorter NFU documentaries, *Backblock Medical Service* and *Rhythm and Movement* (both 1948), and he also scored *The First Two Years at School* (1950). The incoming National government, however, which won the November 1949 election, sought to make the NFU cost effective and decided that commissioning original orchestral music from local composers was unnecessary when royalties for recorded music were less expensive.

43. *The Evening Post* (29 August 1950), 7.

44. "*Journey for Three* Embodies Vitality of Life in N.Z.," *The Dominion* (29 August 1950), 12.

45. "Journey Towards What?" *N.Z. Listener* (1 September 1950), 18.

46. Ibid.

47. Forlong, *Departure Lounge*, 51.

48. Key personnel, such as Bob Allen (sound), and Randall Beattie (camera), found work in the United Kingdom.

49. The reputation of New Zealand cinema as one of mostly first time directors is here confirmed; once they have proven their talent, local filmmakers often experience the frustrations of trying to make a second feature-length film and leave.

50. A. R. Dunlop, "Must the Film Unit Have Its Head Chopped Off?" *The Southland Daily News* (Saturday 8 July 1950), 8.

Chapter 8

Cinema and the Interpretation of 1950s New Zealand History:
John O'Shea and Roger Mirams, *Broken Barrier* (1952)

Barbara Brookes

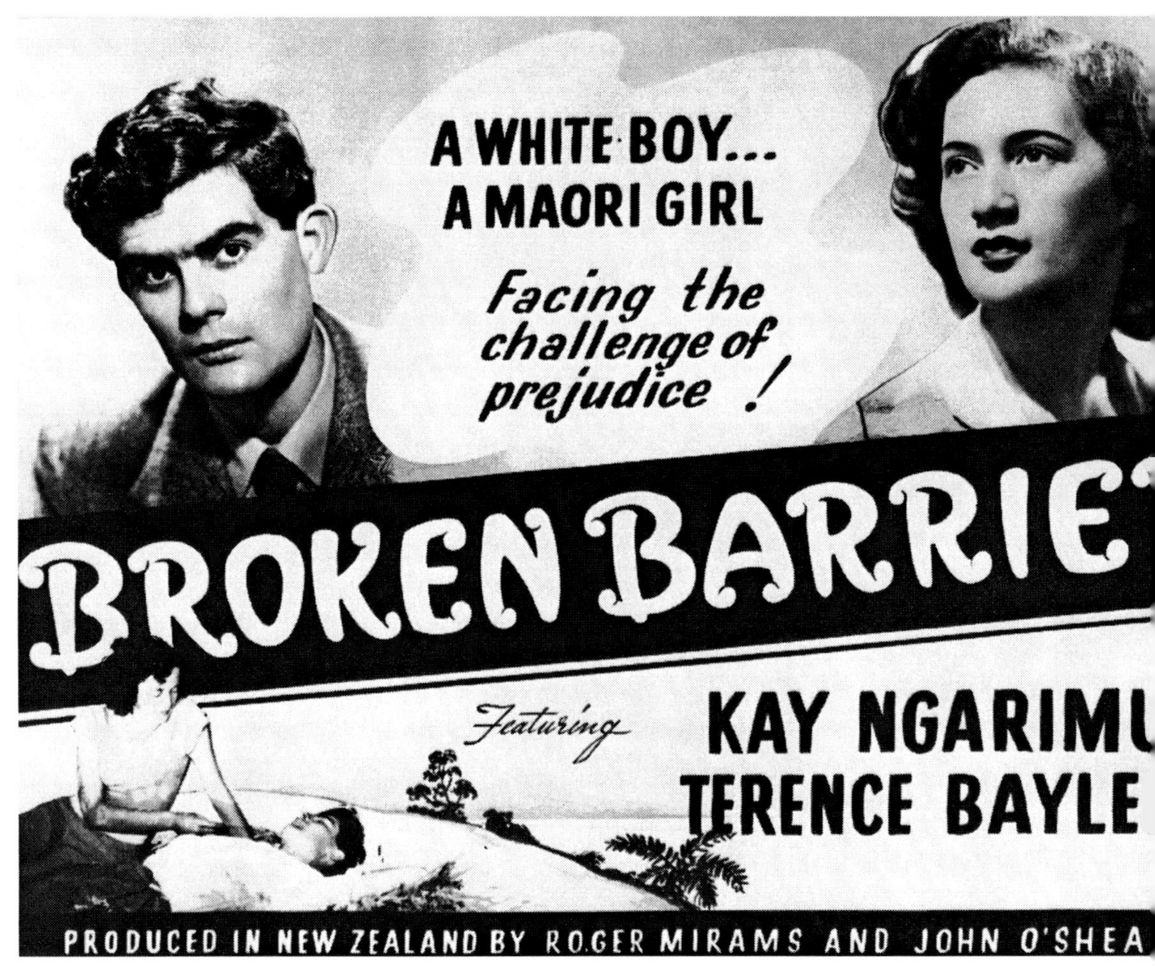

Publicity for *Broken Barrier*, 1952, dir. John O'Shea, courtesy of Pacific Films Collection, New Zealand Film Archive Ngā Kaitiaki O Ngā Taonga Whitiāhua.

Broken Barrier is a film that "made" history in two senses. First, John O'Shea launched his feature filmmaking career, scripting and directing the only feature film made by New Zealanders between 1940 and 1964. Second, in focusing on the story of a relationship between a Pākehā man and a Māori woman, Broken Barrier has come to stand for a "courageous" interpretation of 1950s New Zealand by exploring "mixed" marriage.[2] I want to suggest that although the film was made in New Zealand, it was very much influenced by the tide of American cinema and theatre current at the time. Hollywood helped provide the interpretative frameworks through which the filmmakers made sense of and depicted their own society.

Tracing the history of Broken Barrier reinforces arguments about the influence of American culture in New Zealand while at the same time it emphasises a particular history of race relations.[3] My aim is to use the film to help understand the porous nature of cultural production in the early 1950s and to locate a significant development in New Zealand cinema history within it. Broken Barrier was in part an outgrowth of a genre of "social problem" filmmaking dominating Hollywood in the late 1940s.[4] Such narrative films integrated "a larger social conflict into the individual conflict between its characters."[5] In the late 1940s, racial questions preoccupied the makers of social problem films in Hollywood. The problems of race relations facing New Zealanders, however, were different from those on the agenda in the United States, where intermarriage was a much more vexed question. The theme of intermarriage chosen by O'Shea and Mirams to highlight tensions in Māori–Pākehā relations, therefore, owed more to a genre than to a pressing social issue.

New Zealand historians have paid little attention to feature film beyond noting that New Zealanders were avid film-goers; the field is often left to those in Film and Media Studies.[6] This division makes sense in that film, like literature, requires a mode of analysis different to that usually employed by historians. Those interested in New Zealand's cultural history, however, are likely to be rewarded by a more thorough engagement with what New Zealanders saw on screen. Wayne Brittenden's The Celluloid Circus: The Heyday of the New Zealand Picture Theatre is an enticing introduction into the film business in New Zealand, conveying in lively prose and numerous images the country's enthusiasm for film between 1925 and 1970.[7] Miles Fairburn has picked up on Gordon Miram's 1945 observation that "there are three words written on New Zealand's heart – ANZAC, HOLLYWOOD, and HOME," using it to make a case for New Zealand's cultural exceptionalism lying in the way the country drew its identity from a pastiche of other cultures.[8] Geoff Lealand's A Foreign Egg in our Nest? has examined the influence of American popular culture in New

Zealand.[9] Simon Sigley's PhD thesis and prize-winning 2008 article in the *New Zealand Journal of History* indicate the way film raises issues of "high" and "low" culture, censorship and politics.[10] I want to take up Sigley's point that "films were not merely rarefied aesthetic objects but points of entry into a society or culture at a particular moment in history."[11] Using *Broken Barrier* as the point of entry, I aim to explore facets of New Zealand society in the early 1950s, from the local consumption of Hollywood film fare to the interracial theme, and the difficulty of producing New Zealand feature film. *Broken Barrier* provided a local response to the possibilities that cinema offered for visualising of racial difference. How the film was received suggests that the plot device was less effective than the local settings.

In his 1945 book *Speaking Candidly*, Gordon Mirams noted that there was "one theatre seat to every six persons" for a New Zealand population of just over one and half million. While American patronage of the movies may have been higher, New Zealand was better provided with cinemas. In the United States there was one movie theatre for every 8700 persons, while in New Zealand there was one for every 3000.[12] New Zealand and Australia were reputed to be second behind Great Britain as the biggest market for Hollywood films. Actors Bob Hope and Greer Garson were household names during the Second World War due to their prominence on New Zealand screens.[13] Further, as the numbers of American servicemen within New Zealand swelled during the War, so too did the popularity of Hollywood.

In the most comprehensive discussion contextualising *Broken Barrier*, Laurence Simmons writes that the film "belongs to and was partially inspired by, or was a response to, a long tradition of representation of the Maori in New Zealand film."[14] Simmons regards the exploration of the theme of intermarriage as unusual and courageous.[15] Martin Blythe's *Naming the Other* begins with an awareness of the influence of Hollywood in New Zealand, but in his discussion of *Broken Barrier* he is concerned primarily with the film's role in promoting the myth of integration in New Zealand.[16] Both authors have illuminated the relationship between the film and the domestic context, helping to build a genealogy for New Zealand cinema. But if we widen the lens away from our own national history of filmmaking, we can find that there were other important, transnational, influences at work in the genesis of *Broken Barrier*.

Film scholars engaged in the project of developing an understanding of national cinema have been eager to ask what makes a New Zealand work distinctive. My aim, in contrast, is to ask how we might understand *Broken Barrier* if we see it as part of an international genre of "social problem" theatre and filmmaking, one with which its originators were deeply engaged. Through *Broken Barrier* we can see how these concerns become localised and how New Zealand material is made to speak to the international concerns of the genre. I also want to "follow the money" and see what that tells us about this film.[17] In this way I suggest we can usefully remap the context of *Broken Barrier* and hence remake the history of New Zealand cinema. In effect, we can appreciate how a national story was refracted through the lens of Hollywood film, foregrounding a particular social issue preoccupying those in the United States.

The genesis of *Broken Barrier*

Roger Mirams and John O'Shea together produced *Broken Barrier*. Mirams produced his first film, "When the Gangsters came to Christchurch," at the age of 13 in 1931 and created his first production company at the age of 20, in 1938.[18] O'Shea trained as an historian. Both served in the Second World War in the Italian campaign, Mirams as a war correspondent and cameraman. Their wartime experience heightened their appreciation of the politics of race within New Zealand society. In observing the racial politics of other cultures, Mirams and O'Shea became aware of New Zealand's unique colonial history.[19]

The ex-servicemen were eager to follow developments in European cinema on their return to New Zealand. O'Shea wrote "If ever people want to know about the war in Europe, I can think of no better way to acquaint them with it than seeing *The Conformist* by Bertolucci or Rossellini's *Germany, Year Zero*."[20] Both Mirams and O'Shea were passionately interested in feature films, most of which were made outside New Zealand.

At the time of *Broken Barrier*'s release, John O'Shea was asked his purpose in making the film, and he replied, first "entertainment" and second, "to show the reactions to a marriage between a Maori and a Pakeha in a country which prides itself on its lack of prejudice."[21] Entertainment, then, was a driving force: Mirams and O'Shea wanted to make a film that, by having good box office sales, would repay their investment. In particular, if they could sell the film abroad, they could make enough to go on being feature filmmakers. The second purpose, to examine intermarriage between Māori and Pākehā, was tied closely to the first.

John O'Shea was closely attuned to successful cinema entertainment through his role, in the late 1940s, as editor of the *Monthly Film Bulletin* of the Wellington Film Society. Resurrected in December 1945 after its earlier demise discussed by Sigley, members of the Society eagerly awaited French, Italian, Polish, Australian, Dutch and American feature films and documentaries.[22] On 1 December 1949, O'Shea advised readers in the "What's Coming" column to watch out for "Three films combating anti-Negro prejudice" that they had been "favourably received": *Pinky, Home of the Brave* and *Lost Boundaries*.[23] In the words of one New Zealand newspaper, 1950 was "something of a vintage year for film fare" with "Hollywood's sudden absorption with the formerly untouchable Negro problem."[24] Mirams and O'Shea would have noted the success of all these films (*Pinky* was the second top-grossing American film of 1949).[25]

As young men (both in their early 30s) avidly interested in film, Mirams and O'Shea likely read whatever was available on the medium, including the British Film Institute's *Monthly Film Bulletin*. In November 1949, the *Bulletin* noted that "The *Crossfire-Gentleman's Agreement* (films about anti-semitism) cycle has now passed, and the Negro problem occupies 'advanced' filmmakers in Hollywood."[26] *Variety*, that "must-read" for all interested in the entertainment world, commented in the same month that "Films' leading star for 1949 was not a personality, but subject matter, and "one – racial prejudice – that until very recently was tabu [*sic*]." The Hollywood "Negro-Tolerance Pix" had achieved a $20,000,000 box office payoff.[27] These films, wrote Ralph Ellison in 1949, despite their "absurdities," were "all worth seeing" for creating emotional involvement. That they succeeded on this level, he noted, "is testimony to the deep centres of American emotion that they touch."[28]

Mirams and O'Shea admired Italian film and the neorealism that promoted "on-location shooting, the use of non-professional actors, and improvisation of script."[29] European neorealists turned their back on the artifice of the studio and sought real locations and real people.[30] New Zealand had no big studio for aspiring filmmakers to reject.[31] The place with the most resources, the government-created National Film Unit, employed Mirams after the war. It was the one place where a cameraman could make a living. Mirams had wanted to make a film on Māori for "some time," and he had shot footage of "Maori celebrations thinking it might end up with a 20-minute documentary on the Maori."[32]

In late 1947, Mirams left the National Film Unit and formed the independent Pacific Film Unit with a former NFU colleague, Alun Falconer. They became freelance New Zealand representatives for Fox-Movietone News, which was based in Australia. The company lent them new equipment and let them use it for any work they undertook.[33] Mirams and Falconer approached the Rehabilitation Department for a loan of £1500 "to float a small public company" but were refused. No government work came their way because of the monopoly exercised by the National Film Unit. The tabloid newspaper *Truth* publicised Mirams's plight (Falconer went to China), seeing it as an indication of the lengths to which "the State will go to preserve its monopolies." The paper also accused the government of reneging on its promise "to smooth the track from service life to business street."[34] The aspiring filmmakers found it difficult to cobble together a living; but a successful feature film could prove the road to success.

An important external impetus to the making of *Broken Barrier* came via Gordon Mirams, author of *Speaking Candidly*, the Dominion film censor, and Roger's brother, who had worked with the film division of the information section of UNESCO in Paris after the Second World War. At UNESCO, fellow workers expressed enthusiasm for a film about New Zealand race relations, and Gordon Mirams urged his filmmaking brother to consider this topic.[35] Gordon Mirams was also aware of the criticism made by the foremost British documentary maker, John Grierson, that New Zealand film was full of images of the land, sheep and butter, and "of Maoris who staged shows for rich tourists" but never of the daily life of the people.[36] When, sometime in the first half of 1950, Roger Mirams met up with John O'Shea, they discussed the possibility of a film over lunch. "The following day," according to Mirams, "O'Shea had written the first draft of the story."[37]

As O'Shea worked on his draft, New Zealand critics and audiences continued to grapple with American films that dealt directly with the question of race. On 3 March 1950, the New Zealand *The Listener*'s film critic "Jno" (disliked by John O'Shea for his lack of attention to the visual qualities of films)[38] reviewed *Pinky*, "Darryl Zanuck's latest social problem picture." The reviewer described it as "a film of good intentions." It was

an advance on *Gentleman's Agreement* – it has a far more explosive theme [...]. In a sense, too, it is an improvement on *Home of the Brave* [...] since it provides a simpler and more comprehensible statement of the Negro problem.

Yet, according to the critic, the film achieved "only an indifferent measure of success." The review concluded,

> I was disappointed by the timidity of the studio in the so artfully contrived happy ending. In other words, I'm still waiting for a film on race prejudice that pulls no punches, but no doubt it will come if we are patient enough.[39]

Home of the Brave, the film that "launched Hollywood's cycle of problem pictures in the late 1940s,"[40] was received in New Zealand as "a terse, modern allegory" and "recommended as good adult entertainment."[41] The film adapted a successful Broadway play by Arthur Laurents by substituting what was then called a "Negro" character for the Jewish protagonist. A young "Negro" private, Peter Moss, breaks down and in doing so indicates the way that racism had wounded him. Made independently by Stanley Kramer, the film "was shot on a shoe string budget and without big name stars." Donald Bogle has noted how *Home of the Brave* "caught the movie industry and the critics off guard. It was a commercial and critical success, proving that audiences then were ready for a new type of black film and black character."[42] *Lost Boundaries*, another of the Hollywood cycle that was well received in New Zealand, was made by Louis de Rochemont, who was determined "to prove that true life stories and location shooting were ultimately more realistic than sound stage work."[43] "Based loosely on a true story," the film is a story of a young couple, "both with negro blood," who settle in a New Hampshire town and pass as whites until their true identity is revealed after twenty years. *New York Times* critic Bosley Crowther wrote of *Lost Boundaries* that the "statement of the anguish and ironies of racial taboo is clear, eloquent and moving."[44] The success of all these films suggested that the race "problem" film made popular entertainment, the first of O'Shea's stated reasons for making *Broken Barrier*.[45] The second reason he gave was to shake New Zealand's complacency about being a country without racial prejudice.

Post-war race relations in New Zealand

Of course, the social context in America was very different to that of New Zealand. There was no legal segregation between Māori and Pākehā, and there had never been any anti-miscegenation laws. Such differences made for a distinctive history of racial contact. In New Zealand, rates of intermarriage were comparatively high.[46] Māori, unlike Australian Aboriginal people, were citizens. Whereas three Australian jurisdictions legally regulated Aboriginal marriages between 1901 and 1911, no such barriers stood in the way of Māori–Pākehā relationships.[47] Nor were depictions of cross-cultural relationships formally policed in any way in New Zealand. There was no equivalent to the American Production Code which prohibited images of racial miscegenation on screen from the 1920s until 1954.[48] Various American states prohibited marriage between African Americans, Asians and Native Americans. Idaho, the latest to retain such a prohibition, did not repeal its ban on Native American–White Marriages until 1959.[49] In contrast, if there was any national objection to "race mixing" in New Zealand, it was to marriages between Māori and Chinese – which prominent Māori and Pākehā saw as leading to a "degradation of the race" in the late 1920s.[50] Such anti-Chinese sentiment was common elsewhere.

The Second World War and the post-war period saw increased rates of Māori urbanisation – Māori and Pākehā had to confront new expectations of each other, sometimes at a distance, and sometimes in intimate relationships. The tremendous bravery of the Māori battalion in the Second World War reinforced the view that Māori and Pākehā were New Zealanders together, but Māori people were sometimes made unwelcome in places in their own country.[51] In the same year that *Broken Barrier* was released, *Te Ao Hou* was launched by the Department of Māori Affairs as a magazine for the Māori people to keep them informed of events in communities and the work of relevant government departments, an important initiative as the pace of Māori urbanisation quickened. In 1952 a series of talks on Māori–Pākehā relations were broadcast on radio.[52] In local North Island theatres, the drama club of Ardmore Teachers' College was touring with a production of *Deep are the Roots*, the successful Broadway play about American racial prejudice written by Arnaud D'Usseau and James Gow that featured miscegenation as a key dramatic element.[53]

New Zealand cinemas were dominated by tales from abroad, by British and American films in particular. Māori, or Pākehā New Zealanders for that matter, were absent from the feature films on screen. Cinema as entertainment came from outside the country.[54] The National Film Unit sought to overcome this deficiency through locally made film, usually documentaries which showed New Zealanders to themselves, beginning with the *Weekly Review* in 1941. In 1951, Michael Furlong made *Aroha*, a film that uses fiction to promote integration and persuade Māori to abandon *tohunga* (traditional healers) and to use modern medicine.[55] Aroha lives in a Māori Girls' hostel, enjoys herself at university and is sought after by Pākehā boys. Her hostel friends accuse her of becoming a "white Māori." Aroha goes against the wishes of her elders in insisting her father be taken to hospital, where he recovers from his life-threatening illness. An advocate of modernity in this sense, she also upholds tradition by eventually choosing to marry a Māori man from her community. "We have so much that is good of the Pākehā world," she concludes, "and so much that is good of our own." Another notable example of the Film Unit's work is the health education film, *Tuberculosis and the Maori People of the Wairoa District* – made in cooperation with the Ngāti Kahungungu people – released in the same year as *Broken Barrier*.[56]

The National film Unit clearly had no difficulty working with Māori communities and was keen to use film for educational purposes. But Mirams and O'Shea were critical of both the monopoly and the propaganda purposes of the National Film Unit. Mirams claimed a film on race relations "was too controversial" for the government unit.[57] "Why is it," O'Shea asked in 1952, "that a film about the Maoris, other than sweet sugar and spice and tourist come-ons, has never been made before?" He blamed the government, "the dead hand that was laid on even the slightest criticisms of New Zealand life, the fear of saying anything other than 'Look – ain't we wonderful.'"[58]

One intent of Miram's and O'Shea's film was, according to Mirams, to educate Pākehā, especially those "in the South Island" who "might not have the same knowledge of the race-relationship problems which existed between Maori and pakeha [*sic*] in the north."[59] That the device for the discussion of the problem became intermarriage was, I suggest, due to Hollywood. The impact of American film on the climate of opinion should not be underestimated.

Pinky and *Broken Barrier*

Pinky, a Twentieth Century-Fox Film, was a great success in New Zealand. The *Evening Star* described it as "a sincere and compelling film, brilliantly acted."[60] Jeanne Crain plays Pinky, a Southern black woman so named because of her light-skinned complexion, who goes North to be trained as a nurse. (In fact the actress was white, in order not to contravene the American Production Code's rules against depicting miscegenation on screen). Her washerwoman grandmother has scrimped and saved to support her. Pinky passes as white, falls in love with a white doctor named Tom who does not know her origins, and then flees home when he suggests marriage. Back home, she nurses the white plantation owner, Miss Em, to repay a debt for her grandmother. Miss Em counsels her to always be herself. *Pinky* is a film about women's independence as well as race, for she refuses to take Tom's offer to go away, forget her past and begin a new life with him and instead seeks to make good the challenge made to her by Miss Em, who wills Pinky her plantation, by using the building to run a nursery school and a clinic for her own people. This is the "happy ending" (ironically the rejection of romance) which the *Listener* reviewer saw as a failure.[61]

Broken Barrier is also about a young woman sent away to predominantly white society to become a nurse and her mother worries how "living and working in a city has changed her." In the case of *Broken Barrier*, however, a young Pākehā man, also named Tom (played by Terence Bayler), finds Rawi (Kay Ngarimu), not in the city but in Mahia, on the East Coast of the North Island, where he is employed for a time on the family farm. They meet on her ground, where he is the outsider. Rawi's mother, noticing the attraction between the two, sees that Tom is tested on the *marae* at a Māori gathering. Tom enjoys the easy hospitality of the family and openness of relations between the sexes which seems more informal than in Pākehā society but decides that "falling for a native girl is much too complicated." Rawi goes back to Wellington hospital and eventually Tom follows her. He takes Rawi to meet his snobbish, well-heeled family, who clearly disapprove of her. Rawi supposes that Tom's father thinks that marrying "a Maori girl would bring bad blood into the family." The film then cuts to a scene of Rawi sorting blood samples in the hospital, a scene reminiscent of one in *Lost Boundaries*.

Tom, in fact, is not what he seems. He is a journalist, seeking stories about Māori society for an American magazine – perhaps a reference to the 1948 film *Gentleman's Agreement*, in which Gregory Peck masquerades as a Jew in order to write articles about anti-semitism.

Tom hopes "to soak up enough native colour for a dozen articles."[62] Rawi leaves Tom when she finds he has been writing articles about "Savage Maori and Cannibalism" and goes home, realising that her own people need her nursing help. Tom takes a job in the forestry service and becomes friends with Johnny (Bill Merito), a Māori workmate: "this time it's the white man learning from the brown."[63] Such interracial friendship, causing white characters to become more tolerant, was a frequent motif in social problem films.[64] Learning about Tom's relationship with Rawi, Johnny advises Tom that "the light and the dark can always be together."[65] After an unlikely event involving Johnny sacrificing his life to save Tom in a forest fire, Tom seeks Rawi out, all is forgiven and it seems they will marry and begin a life together in Mahia.

Pinky and *Broken Barrier* tell different stories about very different societies. They are both concerned, however, with romance across race and its implications and they both engage in denial. *Pinky*'s parents remain unmentioned in the film apart from the fact that her mother is dead. Rawi's father, Alec (George Ormond), is acknowledged to be half European "but all Maori when it comes to hospitality." It is her Māori mother Kiri (Mira Hape), however, who is given voice in the film. Both Pinky and Rawi themselves come from mixed parentage – yet the idea that they themselves might enter such relationships is made the central problem of both films.

The "epidermal system of the film text" is at play in *Broken Barrier* as it was in *Pinky*.[66] In casting for *Broken Barrier*, Mirams and O'Shea had hoped to find a blonde Pākehā male for the lead role to contrast with Kay Ngarimu, whose "very fine features," according to Mirams, made her an obvious choice for the film. When Mirams met up with Terence Bayler, he told him he was unsuitable because of his dark features and dark hair. Bayler immediately offered to peroxide his hair, he was so keen to get the part. This endeared him to Mirams and, in the end, Mirams and O'Shea decided to make Tom of Irish extraction to explain Bayler's colouring.[67] Transgressive romance is used in both *Pinky* and *Broken Barrier* as a "vehicle for social critique."[68] As she realises she is falling for Tom, Rawi thinks how when she was young "I never had any worries about colour." She continues, "The law in this country says our colour doesn't bar us from anything – we can become whatever we like – but there is nothing in the rules about falling in love."[69] In *Broken Barrier*, Rawi and Tom's relationship is said to "help overcome the barrier of race prejudice that time has placed between them."[70]

In the case of *Pinky*, her romance would lead to her becoming someone else: in her boyfriend's words, "there'll be no Pinky Johnson after we're married. You'll be Mrs Thomas Adams for the rest of your life." Pinky replies, "Tom, you can change your name, but I wonder if you can really change what you are, inside." In the end, she rejects Tom and accepts her grandmother and Miss Em's advice – to be true to who you are. Romance would have remade Pinky into a white woman, a choice she rejects to embrace the fact that, as she says, "I'm a Negro […]. I don't want to be anything else."

Broken Barrier suggests that Tom, in fact, will become "Māori" and be easily accepted into Rawi's community. Love makes him re-evaluate his life – he will give up writing articles about "primitive peoples" – an occupation which he comes to find distasteful – and instead, like generations before him in New Zealand, Tom will marry into a Māori family. Rawi, too, re-evaluates her goals. She leaves the city – home of Pākehā values – and returns to Mahia to assist her own community. The phrase "the future lies with them" is also said in Māori. The film ends with the text on screen of the sentence from the United Nations Declaration of Human Rights, Paris, 1948: "There shall be no discrimination on the grounds of race or colour."

The reception of *Broken Barrier*

Pinky, a Twentieth Century-Fox Film, had high production values, stars in the leading roles, and dialogue.[71] *Broken Barrier* was made in Mahia and other North Island locations, used local people, and, because of cost and a lack of technology, had voice-over commentary rather than spoken dialogue. It was made on a shoestring budget (financed by Mirams and O'Shea themselves, with some help from Edith and Richard Campion), relied on Kiwi ingenuity, and, apart from the leading actors, used willing local people to take part. Mirams claimed that "local subject and settings" were "essential for [the] success of the film":

The time is long past when local audiences would accept any film simply because it has been locally made. That is a very good thing, but it means that any films which are made here now must measure up to the imported products in technical standard and entertainment value [...] filmmaking is an expensive and speculative business.[72]

Mirams was clearly pleading for financial support for the making of films, but there was no response, apart from the socialist *People's Voice*, which promised that "Under a People's Government the production of full-length films would be a regular feature in New Zealand."[73]

The financial success of the film depended greatly on overseas success, "for that is where the profits must come from."[74] The makers avoided use of the word "pakeha" in the film since they were aware it would not be understood overseas.[75] Although Mirams and O'Shea had wanted to undermine the "grass-skirt-cum-Rotorua conception"[76] of Māori so often exported, in filming they could not resist displaying thermal wonders and Māori uniqueness. The pamphlet promoting the film by Grand National Pictures in London highlighted "The strange Maori arts, folk-lore and war chants ('hakas'), the background to a modern, absorbing love story. One of the world's greatest scenic attractions – the uncanny thermal regions of Rotorua, with their boiling mud-pools and gushing geysers."[77] One report of the trade showing in London that preceded the New Zealand launch was dispiriting. The film was labelled a "Racial problem drama" with appeal "to unsophisticated audiences. Rather slow-moving and unexciting romantic drama."[78] No note of this reached the New Zealand public, who were told that the film had been received well in England "as an authentic picture of New Zealand life." Copies were said to be on their way to Paris and New York.[79]

Broken Barrier, advertised as "New Zealand's First World Standard Film," had its "Gala World Premier" at the Regent Theatre in Wellington on Thursday 10 July. The premier, replete with floodlights, bunting, flowers, marching girls, the Port Nicholson silver band and dignitaries filmed on arrival, had, *The Dominion* noted, all the features of first film nights "in America's movieland capital."[80] The fashions worn by the wives of the mayor, the governor general and the producers were described in the women's page of the newspaper.[81] The *Dominion* concluded "There are faults in *Broken Barrier* but there are many virtues. Certainly it may be said that here is a processed product other than food which really deserves that ubiquitous commendation, 'Well made New Zealand.'"[82]

Conscious of their debt to the local community, Mirams and O'Shea ensured that the next gala opening was held the following Monday at Gisborne's Regent Theatre. Coloured lights, palms, flowers and foliage decorated the theatre. The gala mood was heightened by the Gisborne Highland Pipe Band, two teams of marching girls and a flashlight photographer. "Murmurs of recognition, amusement and surprise, were heard during many of the locally-shot scenes," which were judged to be "convincingly natural." The local reviewer found the "thought dialogue" soundtrack, although unusual, effective for getting inside the heads of the characters. If this was "the first 'child' of Pacific Films," then with "'brothers and sisters' there would be a very fine family indeed for the New Zealand feature film industry."[83]

Responding to the advertisements for "New Zealand's First World Standard Feature Film," "More than twelve thousand viewers saw *Broken Barrier* in the first week of its release." It became Kerridge's box office leader of the month[84] and did particularly well on the East Coast and in Hawke's Bay, where the patrons knew the locality and the extras; hence, it had particular appeal to Māori audiences in that area. In Ōpōtiki, the manager of the Regent theatre painted a lavish display for the theatre including Māori carving, a meeting house and bush scenes. The local Whakatōhea Māori Youth Club sent "two Maori maidens in full costume each night" to hand out give-away photos of the stars.[85] At the Auckland premier, a friend wrote to John O'Shea, "It wd.[sic] have delighted you the way the Maoris picked up every point with glee. The comments around me showed that you have hit reality hard, and that the film is absolutely, genuinely, 'of this land.'"[86]

Mirams and O'Shea covered every possible publicity angle promoting the film. To attract the readers of the *Dairy Exporter*, they highlighted the "many farming sequences" in the film.[87] In the *Returned Servicemen's Association Review* they stressed that Kay Ngarimu was the sister of the winner of the Victoria Cross, and that the film was produced by two ex-servicemen.[88] They were interviewed on radio by the popular personality Aunt Daisy, broadcaster Elsie Lloyd, and made a publicity programme with a Miss McMillan.[89] In a speech to the Wairoa Rotary club, they emphasised that they set out to make an entertaining film about life in New Zealand which showed "the way people think about each other not about such usual ingredients as bashings and shooting-ups." To that audience, they concluded, "Really, of course, the most remarkable thing about life here in New Zealand is the harmony that exists between the two races."[90]

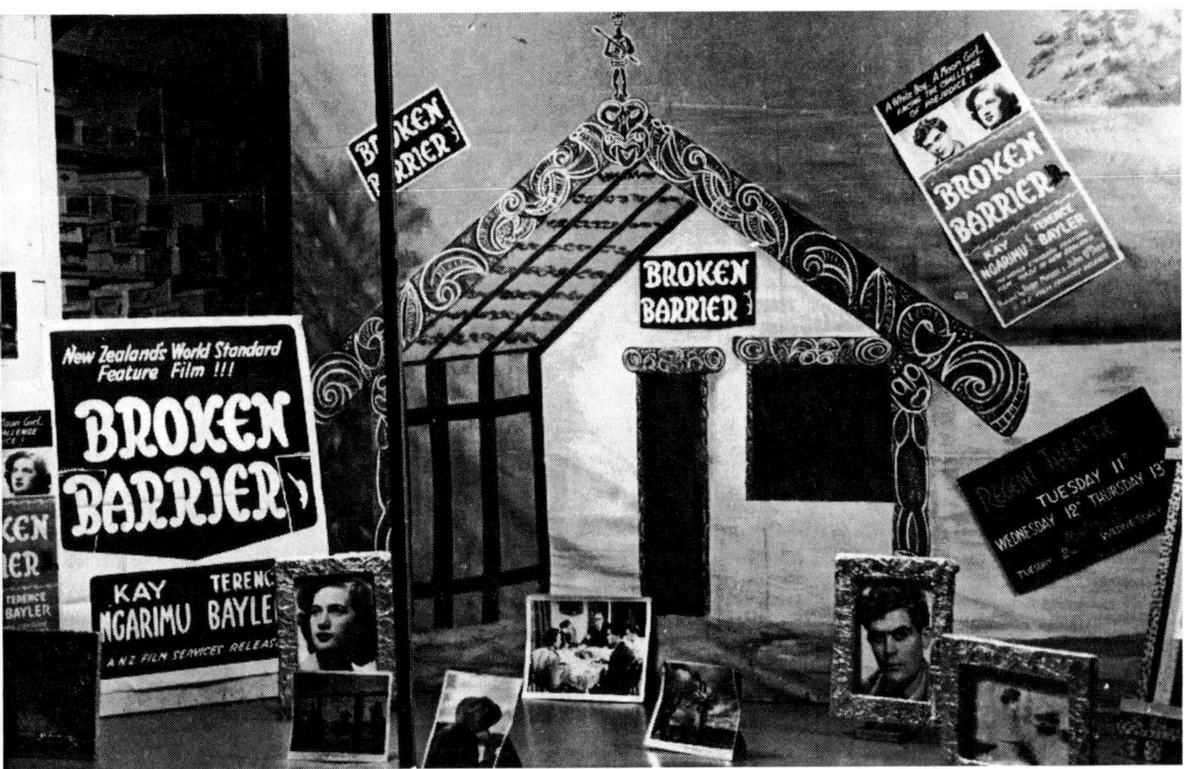

Broken Barrier Farmers Trading Co. window display, Ōpōtiki, 1952, courtesy of Pacific Films Collection, New Zealand Film Archive Ngā Kaitiaki O Ngā Taonga Whitiāhua.

There was no doubt that the local audiences enjoyed seeing New Zealand on screen. One farming family who had never been to the cinema made a special effort to go to *Broken Barrier* at the Meteor theatre in Palmerston North "because it was a New Zealand film."[91] The Christchurch *Star* hailed the film as a "remarkable achievement" which provided "a warm and ironic commentary" on the couple's situation.[92] Many reviewers praised the honesty and unpretentiousness of the film:

> A Maori timber worker's reaction to a bush fire – "What's all the panic about, eh?" – spoken as only a Maori timber worker could speak it; a group drinking beer outside a country dance hall […]. Real characters, situations and scenes filmed as they occur only in New Zealand – they are the down-to-earth material from which the Dominion's first fiction motion picture was made.[93]

Reviewers in Wellington's *Dominion* and Auckland's *Herald* found the absence of direct dialogue a deficit. The film's pictorial qualities were said to outweigh a "number of handicaps which the film has in comparison with the imported product."[94] The most telling criticism, however, was made by Margaret Dunningham, a Dunedin-based art historian, in *Landfall*. Recognising the producer's hopes that the film was made with an eye to the overseas market, she noted that "The offence of *Broken Barrier*" was the same as those articles about "exotic savages" that the hero Tom was writing for American papers. It suggested that intermarriage was a national problem when, in fact, Dunningham stated "we have sufficient examples amongst us to know it can be carried off successfully."[95] In *Here & Now*, critic H.W. Gretton wrote that "Unfortunately, overseas audiences will now see [Māori] through the eyes of that incredible journalist, Rawi's boy-friend, and say afterwards; 'the New Zealanders are educating their natives, even marrying them – the pretty ones. How enlightened New Zealanders must be!'" This he felt to be "rotten propaganda":

> Tomorrow morning, when your tram ticket is punched by the same Maori clippie you meet every day, and you don't turn up your European nose at her, then you have the authority of the film for feeling enlightened, and much superior to Rawi's in-laws.[96]

Despite doing little to address the everyday problems of prejudice that existed in New Zealand, the box office success of *Broken Barrier*, according to Gretton, showed how "really hungry" New Zealanders were for films about their own country. He urged Mirams and O'Shea to produce another film about New Zealand showing a community "where brown and white work together daily without any question of a colour bar."[97] In fact, in late 1952 they were considering following it up with a "slightly more elaborate film" about James Brydone, the man responsible for first shipping frozen meat from New Zealand and hence initiating a major export revolution.[98] It was unlikely, Mirams said, "that they would attempt another on race relations."[99]

Mirams and O'Shea had hoped that *Broken Barrier* might be picked up internationally. A visit from American film producer Spyros Skouras raised hopes. Skouras judged the film to be a "good feature effort" and cabled his London representatives to seek possibilities of screenings in other parts of the world.[100] Kerridge-Odean did well with the film, "but on tough terms" that made it difficult for Mirams and O'Shea to recoup their investment.[101] There was no financial return from London. By January 1953, the two men had "only got a little over half" of their own money back, which meant, O'Shea wrote to Bayler, that they had "spent many spare moments feeding the wolves at our respective doors a little bone to see them quiet until we are in the clear." He thought they would have recovered their production costs by the end of 1953.[102] No further feature films eventuated that decade. Mirams moved to Melbourne in 1957 and achieved success in 1960 with action adventure series in which children were heroes, eventually teaming up with Paramount.[103] O'Shea remained in New Zealand and became central later to the creation of New Zealand-made film.[104] Because O'Shea remained in the country, his association with the film has overshadowed what was a joint effort.

Which barriers were broken?

The title and subject of *Broken Barrier* suggests that the barrier that was broken was between the races and this is the way it helped shape historical memory.[105] It has been taken by some to represent things "as they were" rather than fiction. But there were a number of barriers Mirams and O'Shea aimed to break. One was to make a New Zealand feature film which did well at the box office and might make an impression on the international scene. The popularity of *Pinky* and the rest of the cycle of racial "problem" films indicated that audiences were ready for such fare. The interest from UNESCO was another international impetus. Thus the "barrier" of interracial romance portrayed within the film was a device to seek an audience. I do not mean to suggest that Mirams and O'Shea were cynical in the making of their film; rather, encouraged by the success of the American films which raised the issue of racial prejudice, they looked afresh at New Zealand and decided that such a New Zealand story might be timely. Using the big screen to explore issues of racial tension was a departure from the good news stories of the National Film Unit. In a way, the film succeeded in spite of its romantic theme which many of its critics found to be contrived. As H.W. Gretton wrote, "the only time we feel sorry for Rawi is at the end, when she looks like marrying her fool pakeha."[106] It was hard to find anything admirable in the character of Tom. What audiences particularly enjoyed was seeing New Zealand in a feature film, but even then the film was found wanting in light of the usual Hollywood fare.

In 1955, *Broken Barrier* was reissued. Two Wellingtonians, Noel Hilliard, a writer, and Kiriwai Mete went to see the film at the Paramount and decided to write to O'Shea with their criticisms. "We have," they wrote, "had to face and resolve the problem of a 'mixed' marriage and have some understanding of the issues involved." The letter, which John O'Shea took to heart, pointed out that the film was not about conflict between the couple on the grounds of race but a misunderstanding over Tom's intentions when his publisher's letter is discovered. "The fact is that once the two went overboard for each other the issue of prejudice was stone dead and of no dramatic significance thereafter." It was really Rawi, Hilliard and Mete contended, that the film should have followed since she had to look at things from a new angle. Instead, she accepted Tom back "as if nothing had happened." "The real weakness," they continued, was that O'Shea "chose characters far from typical." They liked the way discrimination was depicted in "the snubs on the street and at the boy's parents' home" but felt that their inclusion contributed nothing "to solving the problems they posed." And although there was dialogue about "Maoris being used as tourist attractions," "the makers of the film were themselves not indifferent towards the sales value of Maori picturesqueness on the overseas market." The couple concluded:

> The film seems intended to sell New Zealand racial "tolerance" abroad like butter and frozen meat. We think it is a false picture of race relations here as they really are. In our view the film uses phony methods to get a phony message across.[107]

In suggesting that O'Shea would have done better to follow Rawi's story, Hilliard and Mete were perhaps pointing to a particular feature of race relations in New Zealand where Māori women may have lost social status in their own community by marrying Pākehā men.[108] In his study of mixed marriage, John Harre found that amongst his informants who had married before the Second World War, Māori parents were likely to object.[109]

A film which traced Rawi's family's reaction to the knowledge that the young man they had befriended had abused their hospitality would have told a very different story about New Zealand race relations. How would audiences have reacted to the questions put by elders to one young Māori woman: "Who is this Pakeha you are going to marry? He is nothing. He has no ancestors, nor a canoe. He owns no land. He has no roots, no background. Who is this Pakeha?"[110] Rawi's perspective, and that of her family, is lost in the course of the film. Russell Campbell has outlined how quickly the narrative comes to centre on Tom rather than on any of the Māori characters.[111] No indication is given as to why Rawi might have changed her mind about her unworthy suitor. Martin Blythe suggests that the narrative drive is towards integration, "where the racism of the Pakeha and the simple life of the Maori have passed away through intermarriage."[112]

The film flared, then died and was lost. When a release print was laboriously restored in the 1980s, the film was seen in a new light and hailed as "remarkable achievement in conscious raising in New Zealand."[113] Māori activism of the 1970s led to it being seen in a new and political light. Since then, it has been recuperated as a significant development in New Zealand national cinema which, indeed, it was. Its significance, however, lies not so much in the subject matter of intermarriage but rather in the fact that is was a feature film that put New Zealanders – Māori and Pākehā – and their country in the centre of the frame. The first barrier broken by the film was that of the monopoly on visual representations of

New Zealand exercised by the National Film Unit. Mirams and O'Shea succeeded in their attempt to tell a new story about New Zealand that complicated the usual story of harmonious race relations. They could not, however, resist the comforting vision of integration through intermarriage. The second barrier was making a successful feature film. Although it took the makers a long time to recoup their investment, the film initially drew large audiences and reaped substantial rewards for Kerridge-Odeon.[114]

My remapping of the making of *Broken Barrier* suggests the importance of being cognizant of its historical context as part of an international wave of filmmaking dealing with race issues. Although not made in Hollywood, *Broken Barrier* was an offspring of the Hollywood race cycle, and informed by UNESCO interest in race relations. The theme of miscegenation that made *Pinky* such a daring success in America was much more ambiguous in New Zealand. In the words of one Māori commentator, Tom "went native. Anyone can go native."[115] Since the time of first settlement, Māori had incorporated newcomers into their communities, so there was little that was novel in that theme. Much more important than the love story, perhaps, were the scenes that revealed aspects of everyday life. One observer of a "mixed" film audience noted:

When on approaching the back door of the pleasant farmhouse the family had to shoo the ducks and fowls off the porch the Europeans in the audience laughed. When the white boy drank from the bottle after a Maori boy had had a drink the Maoris laughed; and when the third man, a Maori, received the bottle from the white boy and passed his hand over the neck before drinking, the Maoris in the audience roared.[116]

Such moments of everyday intimacy, and how they played out, struck chords of recognition and, as the observer noted, they might be very different for Māori and Pākehā.

Breaking the barrier of race meant different things in New Zealand than it did in Hollywood. The interpretative frameworks of one culture were not easily transposed onto another. In the history of New Zealand race relations, there was no "cinematic color [*sic*] line" on the screen and rarely in the stalls.[117] Māori and Pākehā viewed the film together; it was in no way socially or politically inflammatory. At the time of the film's release, the directors wrote "in making a love story [the filmmakers] have been prepared to tackle their subject properly and haven't fought shy, as have some American films, of the fact of intermarriage between the races."[118] They were, I suggest, referring to *Pinky*, a film banned in some Southern towns because of an interracial kiss and, if run, shown to segregated audiences. If *Pinky* was a woman's film where intermarriage was rejected because it meant rejecting Pinky's identity as a "Negro," *Broken Barrier* might be seen as a man's film where the dishonourable white hero was inexplicably fortunate enough to both get his Māori "girl" and be accepted by a Māori community.

Notes

1. My thanks to the organisers of the 2008 Australasian Film and History Conference for inviting me to give an address which prompted this piece. Thanks to all the participants in that conference who responded to the address and, in particular, to Russell Campbell. I am also indebted to anonymous readers and to my colleague, Tony Ballantyne, for his invaluable close reading. A version of this paper was first published in the *New Zealand Journal of History* 44, no. 2 (2010).

2. Laurence Simmons, "Casting Aside Old Nets: John O'Shea's First Fight Against Racism," *Illusions* 33 (2002): 16; Laurence Simmons, "*Broken Barrier:* Mimesis and Mimicry," *Landfall* 185 (1993): 131–36.

3. Miles Fairburn, "Is There a Good Case for New Zealand Exceptionalism?" in *Disputed Histories: Imagining New Zealand's Pasts*, ed. Tony Ballantyne and Brian Moloughney (Dunedin: Otago University Press, 2006), 143–67.

4. Russell Campbell, "The Ideology of the Social Consciousness Movie: Three Films of Darryl F. Zanuck," *Quarterly Review of Film Studies* 3, no. 1 (1978): 49–71. My thanks to Russell Campbell for this reference.

5. "The Hollywood Social Problem Film," http://www.lib.berkeley.edu/MRC/socialproblemfilms.html.

6. *Illusions* has been a key outlet for the discussion of film in New Zealand. Collections such as Geoff Mayer and Keith Beattie's *The Cinema of Australia and New Zealand* (London: Wallflower Press, 2007) pay attention to particular New Zealand films. James Belich in *Paradise Reforged: A History of the New Zealanders from the 1880s to the Year 2000* (Auckland: Allen Lane, 2001) devotes about two pages to film. Michael King in *The Penguin History of New Zealand* (Auckland: Penguin Books, 2004) barely mentions the medium. Philippa Mein Smith, *A Concise History of New Zealand* (Cambridge: Cambridge University Press, 2005) has a brief discussion of New Zealand-made film. Redmer Yska in *All Shook Up: The Flash Bodgie and the Rise of the New Zealand Teenager in the Fifties* (Auckland: Penguin Books, 1993) devotes a chapter to film. David Lascelles, acknowledged by all who write on the history of film in New Zealand as an authority, wrote *80 turbulent years: The Paramount Theatre Wellington 1917–1997* (Wellington: Millwood Press, 1997). Geoffrey D. Churchman, ed. *Celluloid Dreams: A Century of Film in New Zealand* (Wellington: Transpress New Zealand, 1997) provides a useful overview.

7. Wayne Brittenden, *The Celluloid Circus: The Heyday of the New Zealand Picture Theatre* (Auckland: Godwit, 2008).

8. Gordon Mirams, *Speaking Candidly: Films and People in New Zealand* (Hamilton: Paul's, 1945), 125; Fairburn, "Is There a Good Case for New Zealand Exceptionalism?," 146.

9. Geoff Lealand, *A Foreign Egg in Our Nest? American Popular Culture in New Zealand* (Wellington: Victoria University Press, 1988).

10. Simon Sigley, "How the Road to Life (1931) Became the Road to Ruin: The Case of the Wellington Film Society in 1933," *New Zealand Journal of History* 42, no. 2 (2008): 196–215.

11. Simon Sigley, "Film Culture: Its Development in New Zealand, 1929–1972" PhD diss., Auckland University, 2003, 10.

12. Mirams, *Speaking Candidly*, 6.

13. Ibid., 15, 23.

14. Simmons, "Casting Aside Old Nets," 16; Simmons, "*Broken Barrier*," 131–36. Russell Campbell discusses *Broken Barrier* in "In order that they may become civilized: Pakeha ideology in *Rewi's Last Stand, Broken Barrier* and *Utu*," *Illusions* 1 (1986): 4–15.

15. Simmons, "Casting Aside Old Nets," 14.

16. Martin Blythe, *Naming the Other: Images of the Maori in New Zealand Film and Television* (Metuchen, NJ: Scarecrow Press, 1994), 158–66.

17. Kathleen McHugh, "Historicizing Media Feminism in its Transnational Contexts" (Plenary Address at the Film and History Association of Australia and New Zealand Conference, December 2008, University of Otago).

18. Mark Juddery, Tributes – 2004, 'Roger Mirams, 1918–2004, http://www.markjuddery.com/html/tributes/2004_roger_mirams.html.

19. Roger Mirams, interview with Elsie Lloyd, 2ZB, Wellington. DCDR76-track 5, Radio New Zealand Sound Archives: Ngā Taonga Kōrero.

20. John O'Shea, *Don't Let It Get You* (Wellington: Victoria University Press, 1999), 95, 98.

21. *Te Ao Hou* 1 (1952): 37.

22. Date courtesy of Simon Sigley. Personal communication.

23. *Monthly Film Bulletin*, Wellington Film Society Inc., 1 December 1949, 3.

24. *Otago Daily Times* (29 December 1950), 6.

25. *Pinky* was only outdone by *Jolson Sings Again* at the box office for the year. *Variety* 30 (1949): 1.

26. *Monthly Film Bulletin*, British Film Institute, 191, 16, 30 November 1949, 193.

27. "20,000,000 Boxoffice Payoff for H'wood Negro-Tolerance Pix," *Variety* (30 November 1949), 1.

28. Ralph Ellison, *Shadow and Act* (London: Secker and Warburg, 1967), 280. Reprinted from *The Reporter*, 6 December 1949.

29. David A. Cook, *A History of Narrative Cinema*, 2nd ed. (New York: W.W. Norton & Company, 1990), 455.

30. Noa Steimatsky, "Neorealism's Transitional Spaces: From Cinema to History" (Plenary Address at the Film and History Association of Australia and New Zealand Conference, December 2008, University of Otago).

31. John O'Shea, interview with Miss McMillan, Publicity programme for Pacific Films, D Series sa-d-00568, Radio New Zealand Sound Archives: Ngā Taonga Kōrero.

32. "New Zealand-Made Films," *Otago Daily Times* (12 August 1952), 6. "Racial Relations Is the Theme of N.Z. Picture," *Evening Star* (16 August 1952), 3.

33. Roger Mirams, Oral History with Jane Paul, 0544B, The New Zealand Film Archive Ngā Kaitiaki O Ngā Taonga Whitiāhua [Hereafter NZFA].

34. *New Zealand Truth* (5 October 1949), 7.

35. *The Weekly News* (9 July 1952), 20.

36. Mirams, *Speaking Candidly*, 204.

37. "Racial Relations Is the Theme of N.Z. Picture," *Evening Star* (16 April 1952), 3.

38. John O'Shea, "Saraband for Blind Critics," *Design Review*, 2, no. 6 (1950), http://www.nzetc.org/tm/scholarly/tei-Arc02_06DesR-t1-body-d7.html

39. *New Zealand Listener* (3 March 1950), 16–17.

40. Donald Bogle, *Blacks in American Films & Television: An Illustrated Encyclopedia* (Simon and Schuster), http://www.tcm.com/this month/article.jsp?cid=133215.

41. *Evening Star* (26 August 1950), 12.

42. Bogle, *Blacks in American Films & Television.*

43. http://www.seacoastnh.com/louis/lostfilm.html; In the *Evening Star* (6 May 1950), 12 *Lost Boundaries* was described as "very successful," while the *Otago Daily Times* (29 December 1950) summed up 1950 as a year of "Film Fare of Genuine Merit," noting *Lost Boundaries* along with *Pinky* and *Home of the Brave.*

44. Thomas Schatz, *Boom & Bust: The American Cinema in the 1940s (History of the American Cinema)* (Berkeley and Los Angeles: University of California Press, 1997), 385.

45. Russell Campbell has written on three of these "social problem" films, *The Grapes of Wrath*, *Gentleman's Agreement*, and *Pinky*, in "The Ideology of the Social Consciousness Movie: Three Films of Darryl F. Zanuck."

46. Angela Wanhalla discusses the difficulty of tracing intermarriage statistically because of shifting census categories. Her analysis suggests that from 1886 to 1896, the total mixed-decent population represented 0.7–0.8 per cent of the non-Māori population but that in 1886, mixed-descent persons comprised 5.3 per cent of the Māori population. Wanhalla, *In/visible Sight: The Mixed-Descent Families of Southern New Zealand* (Wellington: Bridget Williams Books, 2009), chap 3. See also Paul Callister, "Ethnicity Measures, Intermarriage and Social Policy," http://www.msd.govt.nz/about-msd-and-our-work/publications-resources/journals-and-magazines/social-policy-journal/spj23/ethnicity-measures-intermarriage-and-social-policy-pages109-140.html; and John Harre, *Maori and Pakeha: A Study of Mixed Marriages in New Zealand* (London: Pall Mall Press, 1966). In contrast, in the United States currently, "marriage across racial lines is a rare event." Roland G. Fryer, "Guess Who's Been Coming to Dinner? Trends in Interracial Marriage over the 20th Century," *Journal of Economic Perspectives* 21, no. 2 (2007): 71–90.

47. Tim Rowse, "Regulation of Aboriginal Marriage," unpublished paper, courtesy of the author.

48. For an extended discussion of the Production Code Administration, see Susan Courtney, *Hollywood Fantasies of Miscegenation: Spectacular Narratives of Gender and Race, 1903–1967* (Princeton, NJ: Princeton University Press, 2005). Chapter 4 discusses *Pinky*. See also "Race and Ethnicity: THE PRODUCTION CODE AND "MISCEGENATION,'" in *Film Encyclopedia*, http://www.filmreference.com/encyclopedia/Independent-Film-Road-Movies/Race-and-Ethnicity-THE-PRODUCTION-CODE-AND-MISCEGENATION.html.

49. http://en.wikipedia.org/wiki/Anti-miscegenation_laws#cite_note-2.

50. Barbara Brookes, "Gender, Work and Fears of a 'Hybrid Race' in 1920s New Zealand," *Gender and History* 19, no. 3 (2007): 201–18.

51. Simmons, "Casting Aside Old Nets," 12 reproduces a photograph of the separate toilet for Maori at the Rawene Public Library from the 1950s. He also discussed the denial of accommodation and service to Maori in hotels and hotel lounge bars, drawing on Angela Ballara, *Proud to be White? A Survey of Pakeha Prejudice in New Zealand* (Auckland: Heinemann, 1986), 100. Mira Szazsy recalled being denied accommodation "because of the colour of my skin" but also the way being Dalmatian also led to discrimination in Senka Božic-Vrbančic, "After all, I am partly Māori, partly Dalmatian, but first of all I am a New Zealander." *Ethnography*, 6, no. 4 (2005): 537.

52. Bruce Mason, "Notes," *Landfall* 6, no. 4 (1952): 259–60.

53. *The Herald* (2 August 1952), 12.

54. Merata Mita, "The Soul and the Image," in *Film in Aotearoa New Zealand*, ed. Jonathan Dennis and Jan Bieringa (Wellington: Victoria University Press, 1992), 44.

55. Michael Furlong, *Aroha* (National film Unit, 1951). For a discussion of this film, see Blythe, *Naming the Other*, 98–99.

56. Barbara Brookes, "Health Education Film and the Maori: *Tuberculosis and the Maori People of the Wairoa District (1952),*" *Health and History* 8, no. 2 (2006): 45–68.

57. "Broken Barriers Features a N.Z. Problem," unknown publication, May 1952, D1159, Series 31, Pacific Films Collection, NZFA.

58. John O'Shea to George ?, 28 June 1952, D4678, Box 60, Folder 1, John O'Shea Personal Papers Collection, NZFA.

59. *Otago Daily Times* (12 August 1952), 6.

60. *Evening Star* (6 May 1950), 12.

61. *New Zealand Listener* (3 March 1950), 16–17.
62. Transcript of recorded voice track of *Broken Barrier*, undated, Folder 1, John O'Shea Personal Papers Collection, NZFA, 2.
63. Transcript of recorded voice track of *Broken Barrier*, 9.
64. John Nickel discusses this theme with reference to *Home of the Brave* and the Universal Pictures film, *Bright Victory* (1951), in "Disabling African American Men: Liberalism and Race Message Films," *Cinema Journal* 44, no. 1 (2004): 27.
65. Transcript of recorded voice track of *Broken Barrier*, 10.
66. The phrase was one used by Jane Mills, "First Nation Cinema: Hollywood's Indigenous 'Other'" (paper presented at Film History Association of Australia and New Zealand Conference, Dunedin, New Zealand, November 2008). See also, Courtney, *Hollywood Fantasies*.
67. Roger Mirams, DCDR76 – Track 5 "Roger Mirams Producer of Broken Barriers," Radio New Zealand Sound Archives Nga Taonga Korero.
68. Thomas E. Wartenburg, *Unlikely Couples: Movie Romance as Social Criticism* (Boulder: Westview Press, 1999), 3.
69. Transcript of recorded voice track of *Broken Barrier*, 3.
70. Ibid., 13.
71. *Pinky* was produced by Darryl Zanuck for Twentieth Century-Fox and directed by Elia Kazan. For a discussion of the political climate of the film, see Michael Rogin, "'Democracy and Burnt Cork': The End of Blackface, the Beginning of Civil Rights," *Representations* 46 (1994): 15–17.
72. *Otago Daily Times* (12 August 1952), 6.
73. *People's Voice* (27 August 1952), 4.
74. Unsourced newspaper clipping, "Birth of Two Stars," D11159, NZFA.
75. John O'Shea, sa-d-00558-02-pm D Series – Broken Barriers Film, Radio New Zealand Sound Archives Ngā Taonga Kōrero.
76. "Broken Barriers Features a N.Z. Problem," unknown publication, May 1952, D1159, Series 31, Pacific Films Collection, NZFA.
77. Pamphlet, "*Broken Barrier*: A Pacific Films Production," Grand National Pictures Ltd., undated. D1159, Series 31, Pacific Films Collection, NZFA.
78. Unsourced report, D1159, Series 31, NZFA, Wellington.
79. *The Weekly News* (9 July 1952), 20.
80. *Dominion* (11 July 1952), 5, 8.
81. Ibid., 5.
82. Ibid., 8.
83. *Gisborne Herald* (15 July 1952), Clippings, NZFA.
84. Kerridge Odeon House Journal, *Filmwise*, no. 2. D1159, Series 31, NZFA.
85. N. Martin to R.A. Usmar, New Zealand Film Services, 2 December 1952. D1159, Series 31, NZFA.
86. Letter from John, Auckland University College, 3 August 1952, D1159, Series 31, NZFA.
87. Typescript for *Dairy Exporter*, "*Broken Barrier* New Zealand film has Many Farming Sequences," D4678, Box 60, Folder 1, NZFA.
88. "Member of Famous Ngarimu Family Stars in *Broken Barrier*," typescript for *Returned Servicemen's Review*, D4678, Box 60, Folder 1, NZFA.
89. Notes on *Broken Barrier for Aunt Daisy*, D4678, Box 60, Folder 1, NZFA. Elsie Lloyd and Miss McMillan interviews DCDR76 – Track 5 D Series "Roger Mirams Producer of Film *Broken Barriers* [sic]," Radio New Zealand Sound Archives, Ngā Taonga Kōrero.

90. Typecript, "Mahia Peninsula and Many Wairoa People Featured in BB," Address of Mirams and O'Shea to Wairoa Rotary Club. D4678, Box 60, Folder 1, NZFA.
91. Unsourced Newspaper Clipping, D1159, Series 31, Pacific Films Collection, NZFA.
92. Ibid.
93. Ibid.
94. *The Herald* (2 August 1952), 12. The *Dominion* reviewer wrote:

> the film itself may not please everyone. It has broken with certain latter-day conceptions of cinema, principally in leaving its voices behind the camera and relying on flash back or 'thought' dialogue. Some of the parts are not well taken vocally – there is an over-tone of self-consciousness about them (11 July 1952, p. 8).

95. Margaret M. Dunningham, "Broken Barrier," *Landfall* (1952): 326–27.
96. "The Film and the Barrier," *Here & Now* (September 1952), 29–30.
97. Ibid., 30.
98. *Otago Daily Times* (17 November 1952), 6.
99. *Evening Star* (16 August 1952), 3.
100. *Otago Daily Times* (18 November 1952), 8.
101. Brittenden, *The Celluloid Circus*, 129.
102. John O'Shea to Terence Bayler, 30 January 1953, D4678, Box 60, Folder 2, NZFA.
103. Juddery, "Roger Mirams, 1918–2004."
104. In 1992, John O'Shea was awarded the New Zealand Film Commission's first Lifetime Achievement Award. http://www.nzonscreen.com/person/john-oshea/biography.
105. The shaping of visual memory was discussed by Paul Clark, Plenary Address at the Film and History Association of Australia and New Zealand Conference, Dunedin, New Zealand, December 2008.
106. "The Film and the Barrier," *Here & Now* (September 1952), 30.
107. N.H. Hilliard to John O'Shea, 26 October 1955. D4678, Box 2–3, Folder 1, John O'Shea Personal Papers Collection, NZFA.
108. Harre, *Maori & Pakeha*, 77.
109. Ibid., 81.
110. Ibid., 115.
111. Campbell, "In Order That They May Become Civilized," 10.
112. Blythe, *Naming the Other*, 163.
113. http://www.filmarchive.org.nz/feature-project/pages/Broken-Barrier.php.
114. Brittenden, *The Celluloid Circus*, 129.
115. "*Broken Barriers,*" *Here & Now* (June 1953), 29.
116. Ibid.
117. Whitney Strub, "Black and White and Banned all Over: Race, Censorship and Obscenity in Postwar Memphis," *Journal of Social History*, 40, no. 3 (2007): 685. Angela Ballara has suggested that cinema audiences were sometimes segregated in the 1950s and earlier, based on some personal recollections. She cites Athol Congalton's observation from his social survey of Hawera, however, that one of the joint Maori-Pakeha gatherings in the community was "the Friday night film session." *Proud To Be White*, 99–100.
118. "'Broken Barrier', N. Z. Feature Film, Tackles Topic Question," typescript for *Zealandia* (Undated), D4678, Box 60, Folder 1, John O'Shea Personal Papers Collection, NZFA.

Chapter 9

Re-representing Indigeneity: Approaches to History in Some Recent New Zealand and Australian Films

Janet Wilson

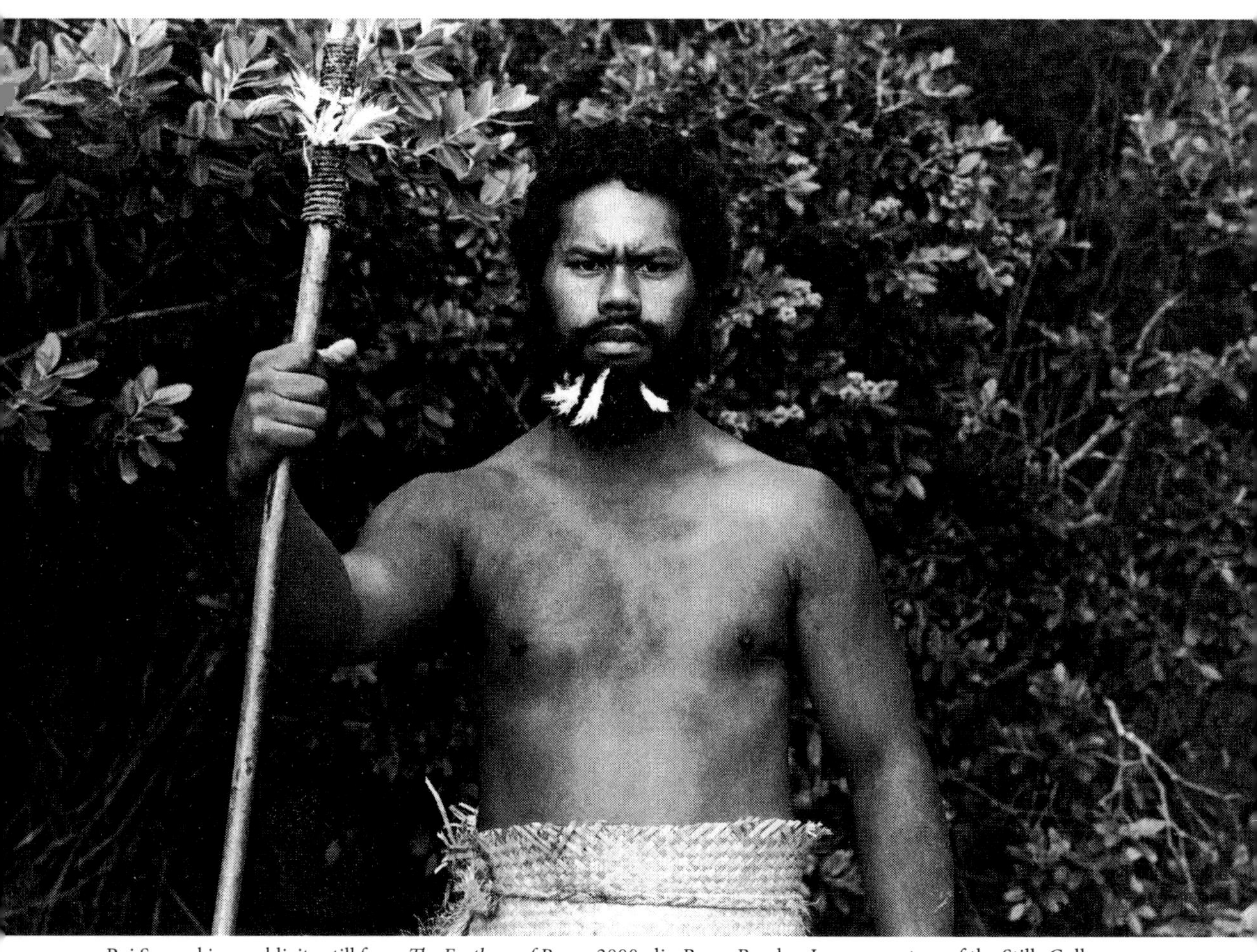

Rei Samuel in a publicity still from *The Feathers of Peace*, 2000, dir. Barry Barclay. Image courtesy of the Stills Collection, New Zealand Film Archive Ngā Kaitiaki O Ngā Taonga Whitiāhua.

Changing images of indigeneity in Australasian cinema

The local reception of New Zealand and Australian films about the Māori and the Aborigine has for long been haunted by critiques of visual representations of the Indigene as Other. In both countries in the last 30 years, identity politics have moved to occupy more of the middle ground between the races, as colonial injustices have begun to be redressed, and as reconciliation has become a public project with the land arbitrations of the Waitangi Tribunal in New Zealand since 1984 and the landmark *Mabo* Decision in Australia in 1992.[1] Increasing political awareness and self-empowerment of first peoples and white settler anxieties about the right to speak for and represent the indigene in visual terms have contributed to debates about authorship, ownership and cultural appropriation.[2] During this period cinema has contributed to the mediation of historical memory, especially in Australia,[3] and the reshaping of the national imaginary. Yet in reassessing the colonial past and reconstructing white settler–indigenous relations, cinema as a social medium has previously been hampered in its effectiveness by the limited frameworks available for representing indigeneity and the need to create a wide appeal through drawing on Hollywood models. White directors who attempted to re-narrate and re-represent hegemonic colonial history have been accused of being caught up in the very imperialist ideologies that they purport to critique, resulting in a form of neo-colonialism, or visual imperialism.[4] The tensions between cinema's populist mandate for entertainment, and its role in constructing and reflecting the socio-political discourses of a society, including critical interrogation of public and civic culture[5] (such as how recent history should be represented), reverberate uneasily in the case of indigenous representation and stories.

To approach the representation of history in films about the Indigene, especially in relation to the discourses of "truth" and "authenticity," as well as to the moral and cultural issues concerning the politics of survival, I group the six films to be discussed here into three categories: (i) *Cultural contact*: Australian films, *The Chant of Jimmie Blacksmith* (1978) and *Rabbit Proof Fence* (2002), by white directors Fred Schepisi and Philip Noyce, respectively, based on real events that occurred during colonisation and which stress exploitation, racial inequality, injustice, and represent the Indigene as divided between two worlds, moving between them; (ii) *Cultural recuperation*: New Zealand films about the recuperation of Maoritanga and the mythical and legendary past. Both *Once Were Warriors* (1994), directed by Māori director Lee Tamahori, and *Whale Rider* (2002), a collaboration between white director Niki Caro and a local tribe, stress the need to reclaim the indigenous heritage in order to acquire greater autonomy in the present; and (iii) *Cultural difference: Ten Canoes* (2006), a collaboration between Rolf de Heer and aboriginal director Peter Djigirr, and *The Feathers of Peace* (2000), a collaborative documentary feature by Māori filmmaker Barry Barclay, reconstruct, respectively, from fragments of the past a prior world of tribal autonomy and its devastation under a colonising invasion in order to reshape perceptions of the present. These narratives of cultural recovery are associated with indigenous filmmaking and its revaluing and re-representing of the pre-European contact past.

Collins and Davis's "post-*Mabo* social imaginary," grounded in memory and associated with historical trauma, by which they "backtrack" over debates about Australian identity, is a paradigm in which recent developments can be located.[6] Following the global politics of first peoples' self-determination during the 1990s, indigenous filmmakers of the second wave have continued to transform indigenous representation from colonial constructions of alterity. Warwick Thornton's award-winning film, *Samson and Delilah* (2009), for example, involves a degree of personal testimony and bearing witness, as does *The Feathers of Peace*. Indigenous filmmakers, according to E. Ann Kaplan, provide a visual structure within which the protagonists "often silently endured traumatic experiences can be 'spoken' or imaged"; viewers who are witnesses can acknowledge responsibility for loss and begin a process of mourning.[7] The past, both mythic and historical, is revalued for the messages it conveys to the present in *Ten Canoes*; the film's tropes of memory and mediation have influenced many Aboriginal audiences, while spin-off projects have been a form of cultural renewal for the Yolngu tribe.[8] In the same way, the "living history" of *The Feathers of Peace* documentary was aimed at the descendants of the Moriori.[9] These aspects of their reception exemplify Barry Barclay's belief, as outlined in his concept of Fourth Cinema, that indigenous visual images should be returned to their owners.[10] Nevertheless, the representation of history in films about indigenous peoples continues to be contested by both white settlers and indigenous peoples on the grounds of lack of authenticity, misrepresentation through distortion or under-development, or cultural contamination. The flaws of such filmmaking can be summarised as sentimentalism, universalism, triumphalism and a limited critique of European cinematic practices, values and ideologies.

Re-narrativising colonisation and white settler guilt: *The Chant of Jimmie Blacksmith* and *Rabbit Proof Fence*

These two feature films made by white Australian directors, 25 years apart, are imaginative reconstructions of historical events, which draw on written biographical testimony, fictional accounts and documentary evidence; they challenge colonial constructions of the Aborigine as either villain or victim by casting their protagonists as resistant to colonisation and capable of extraordinary feats and achievements. The directors target the international marketplace in ways that conform to Hollywood norms, but the moral purpose is to confront white Australia with its negligence and misconduct in the handling of race relations.

Fred Schepisi's feature film about the axe murders committed by a half-caste Aborigine, Jimmie Governor, the subsequent manhunt, his capture and death, was based on a screen adaptation of the 1972 novel by Thomas Keneally, *The Chant of Jimmie Blacksmith*.[11] In his recreation of racial conflict in an inglorious episode of Australian history, Schepisi, like Keneally, aimed to raise the conscience of the nation about its negative race relations and to challenge the verdict of history by presenting the half-black man's confused state of mind. In attempting to create a hero out of Jimmie Blacksmith, who rebelled against the injustices meted out by the white farmers he worked for by murdering their women, Schepisi hoped to expose the hollow indifference of Australian nationalism to racial discrimination. Both novel and film set out to reframe the hegemonic white settler narrative of national unity and progress by drawing attention to its underlying suppressed history.[12] But while the novel launches its critique through authorial irony, the film exposes the cultural gap too nakedly to cast any such new perspective onto the story. Historical referents – the Boer War (in which Dowie Stead, fiancé of one of the murdered women, and his associates on the manhunt for Jimmie, plan to enlist), the issue of Australianness as Federation looms[13] and the contemporary newspaper reports of the manhunt for Jimmie and his half brother Mort (which Jimmie reads), reinforce the victim image of a man who has violated the legal and social codes of the social system which had symbolically imprisoned him.

As critic Kevin M. Brown has shown, a "racial" register, due to an "uncritical habitation and racialisation of already given structures," limits Schepisi's production.[14] The film is based on the "Manichean delirium" which Frantz Fanon saw as characteristic of colonialism, and identifies Aborigine/settler cultures as "fixed, mutually impermeable expressions of racial and national identity."[15] Jimmy's psychological conflict, stemming from his desire to be a white man in a black man's world, is imaged in a mise-en-scène which draws on romantic and realist traditions of filmmaking. The pre-credit sequence suggests the irreconcilability of the half-caste's worlds: the boy's initiation ceremony is celebrated in terms of a romanticised, ahistorical, timeless, native world, close to nature; while the sharp outlines and square lines of the house of Reverend Mr Neville, who adopts Jimmie and engenders his love of white society, are suggestive of order and rationality, but also of borders, control and constraint. The conspicuously positioned window offers a view to the outer world, but the direction of the gaze will be reversed in the final scenes as audiences view the gaoler's eye gazing in through the Judas hole at Jimmie awaiting his doom in the cell. The film's rigid binarism also appears in the white settler evangelical farming communities, with straight fencelines demarcating boundaries as images of the enlightenment values of order and stability and reason, and the contrasting close-up, blurred, grainy images of aboriginal rural society, either in confused clusters at drinking parties or in domestic disarray, suggestive of disorder, mystery, irrationality and kinship.[16]

Verdicts on *The Chant of Jimmie Blacksmith* include that it was somewhat patronising in its exotic framings and imagings of the aborigine, either in a unitary way as timeless and untameable or as a "berserk boon hacking to death white ladies."[17] In reinforcing these entrenched stereotypes, the film reflected the generally inadequate representation of

Aborigines in the 1970s and 1980s as well as Schepisi's lack of consultation with Aborigine groups.[18] However, it was the first film to treat seriously the issue of race relations by framing them in specific social, political and historical contexts, appropriating to this end the techniques, stylisation and aesthetics of the AFC genre (the "new wave" films of the 1970s and 1980s funded by the Australian Film Commission, usually period dramas like *Picnic at Hanging Rock* or *My Brilliant Career*); this is generally concerned with the myth of innocent settlement.[19]

Rabbit Proof Fence, an adaptation of Doris Pilkington-Garimara's biography of her aboriginal mother, Molly Craig, who as a child escaped from confinement in Moore River Native Settlement in the early 1930s by walking across the Australian desert to return to her mother, was a cinematic response to the Report about the Stolen Generation, *Bringing them Home*, published in 1997.[20] Pilkington's story about half-caste children taken from their mothers in order to be assimilated into white society – a practice of abduction and resettlement which continued from the 1930s to the 1950s – resonated sharply for Australians at a time of national sensitivities after the Report was issued, and the reception of Noyce's film was caught up in the debates that the Report catalysed.[21]

In adapting Molly Craig's story, Noyce played on a number of generic conventions and production formulae for international movies. He foregrounded the emotional drama of separation, loss and reunion, introduced familiar cinematic genres such as the "outback" movie, and the "aboriginal problem" film,[22] and motifs such as the chase, the tracker and the lost child, and he used Hollywood promotional techniques.[23] Like Schepisi, he breaks the fictional illusion in the film's conclusion by using documentary techniques to reaffirm historical, biographical facts. The dark print and voiceover at the end of *Chant of Jimmie Blacksmith* announce that Jimmie was hanged in January, 1901.[24] *Rabbit Proof Fence* ends with footage of Mollie Craig, now aged 85, with her sister Daisy Kadibill, 79, telling of her recapture and return journey a second time, and then the loss of her own children in the same way. Noyce also deliberately included other details about colonial racial policies in order to fan the public controversy over the Stolen Generation. Notably, in a sequence not in the original narrative and of little relevance to the story, the historical figure, A. O. Neville, notorious Chief Protector of Aborigines in Western Australia (played by Kenneth Branagh), outlines the eugenics programme for breeding out colour. As Therese Davis and Felicity Collins note, the scene functions "to show the political, legal and administrative context for the girls' situation, fulfilling the film's aim of communicating the findings of *Bringing Them Home* including the racist, genocidal thinking that underpinned policies of Aboriginal child removal."[25]

Noyce also follows Schepisi in using a binary expressionist aesthetic in representing the settler–indigenous relationship, rather than developing the cinematic potential of postcolonial critique, embodied in images of desire, transgression and Otherness. The three children who are rounded up by the patrol officers in Southwestern Australia are shown in white captivity through images of confinement, constraint and control – barred windows, padlocked doors – suggestive of a Eurocentric civilisation marked by enlightenment ideals.

The sharp outlines of the mission station building in West Perth, austere white garments of the nuns, and polished, gleaming surfaces of Neville's office contrast to the images of nature and the mystique of connectedness and hope which dominate the indigenous scenes. These reflect Molly's navigational skills, by which she follows her spiritual and literal path to her mother across the desert, as emblematised by the overhanging hawk, and which culminate in the atmospherics of the final moments, where the girls look as though they might be recognised, and where hand-held cameras and coloured filters increase the pathos. Nevertheless, in reprising the colonial settlement theme of enclosure, constraint and imprisonment through the trope of the straight line in the form of two extended barrier rabbit-proof fences,[26] Noyce overturns its colonial associations with white control as found in *The Chant of Jimmie Blacksmith* and earlier colonial adventure films like *Simba* (1955).[27] The longest continuous fence in the world becomes the navigational touchstone whereby Molly finds her way home to Jigalong.

Both films, like other reconstructions of colonisation, represent their protagonists as hybrid figures, able to move between two worlds but trapped by their inability to reconcile their contrasting ways of life. These transitions across social and racial boundaries provide crucial points of reference for white audiences. Noyce, in fact, aimed for a wide international appeal, and used universalising techniques such as a casting strategy which emphasised the white side of the half-caste girls, not the Aborigine side, so that more people would identify this as the dilemma of an abducted child rather than merely a story of racial discrimination.[28]

Despite its international success, *Rabbit Proof Fence*, in dramatising in fictional form the injustices perpetrated against generations of Aboriginal half-caste children, became a target in the "history wars" that followed the *Bringing Them Home* report, in which neo-conservative politicians accused historians and left-liberals of distorting the past to serve left-wing agendas. Noyce was accused of exploiting an indigenous story, of taking licence with historical fact, of misrepresentation, cultural contamination and inauthenticity.[29] This was, no doubt, an inevitable consequence of producing a film that played so directly to the nation's complex sense of collective guilt about the past,[30] that claimed to represent historical truth by fictional means, and that attempted to reinterpret indigenous stories by intervening into contemporary debates. As Houston Wood points out, *Rabbit Proof Fence*, unlike the real life story on which it is based, "reaffirms the white settler tendency to frame how indigenous lives are understood."[31]

Recovering indigenous identity through legend and myth: *Once Were Warriors* and *Whale Rider*

Debates over indigenous representation and renarrativisations of history marked the reception of Australian films about colonisation. In the two most successful feature films about the Māori in New Zealand, *Once Were Warriors* and *Whale Rider*, colonialism is dehistoricised and depoliticised. These films have also been criticised for misrepresenting history, but by contrast to the reception of the Australian films, critiques have focused on their neglect of the colonial past and its present-day legacies such as demands for land reparation and assertion of Māori sovereignty,[32] the universalising of their themes, and the overriding of specific *iwi* and *hapu* affiliations by homogenising Māori as a single ethnic category.[33]

Once Were Warriors invokes the glories of traditional warriorhood (through the word "Once" in the title), in contrast to present-day degradation.[34] The tragedy that besets the Heke family forces Beth Heke to reconnect with the rest of her *whanau*, who reside in a rural setting beyond the Hekes' inner city suburban home. In *Whale Rider*,[35] the grandfather Koro's teaching about earlier cultural practices, ceremonies and mythologies helps shore up community identity in the present. Colonialism, however, is only implied as a possible cause of the tribe's present-day problems such as youthful apathy, lack of direction and urban drift, presented as the background to the "intergenerational dispute" between the protagonist Paikea and her grandfather. Instead, reconnecting to the genealogical myth of discovery and leadership, that of the tribal ancestor Kahutia-te Rangi (known as Paikea), who escaped death by riding a whale to shore when his canoe sank, and in developing her intuitive responses to whales (beached, they become metonymic of the tribe's distress), Paikea – so-named after her ancestor – links the present to the mythical past.

Like *The Chant of Jimmie Blacksmith* and *Rabbit Proof Fence*, which can be read as versions of the "aboriginal problem" film, both features focus on the problems of contemporary Māori due to detribalisation and urbanisation. Earlier Māori-directed films – *Mauri* by Merata Mita (1988) and *Ngati* by Barry Barclay (1987) – had dealt with the everyday life of tiny rural communities to which city life is contrasted, including relationships between Māori and Pākehā who live among them. *Once Were Warriors* also constructs a dialectic between urban and rural environments, but its mise-en-scène of an indigenised urban culture is the source of its visual power and, in striking contrast to *Whale Rider* and all other films about the Māori, it critiques romanticised images of New Zealand landscape. Both films demonstrate renewal of Māori tribal values in order to adapt to the modern day and both meet the demands of urbanisation through newly empowered female protagonists – Beth Heke in *Once Were Warriors* and Paikea in *Whale Rider*.

The extraordinary commercial success of *Once Were Warriors*, the most high-profile film ever made in New Zealand,[36] is partly due to the fact that it broke the mould of earlier filmmaking. Its urban location, life-style, vivid stylisation of youth culture and choreographed scenes of violence contrast dramatically to the *marae* style of Barry Barclay's earlier movies *Ngati* and *Te Rua* (1992), with their pastoral settings and themes. Iconic colonial images of New Zealand are also demolished and reconstructed beginning with the billboard hoax in the pre-credit sequence, of a landscape imaged as a pastoral paradise which turns out to be an advertisement for EnZpower. The Hekes are denizens of an urban underclass, their household is next to the Auckland southern motorway, and the surrounding urban landscape is bleak and desolate, full of empty car wrecks and graffiti. Tamahori's extensive stylisation includes

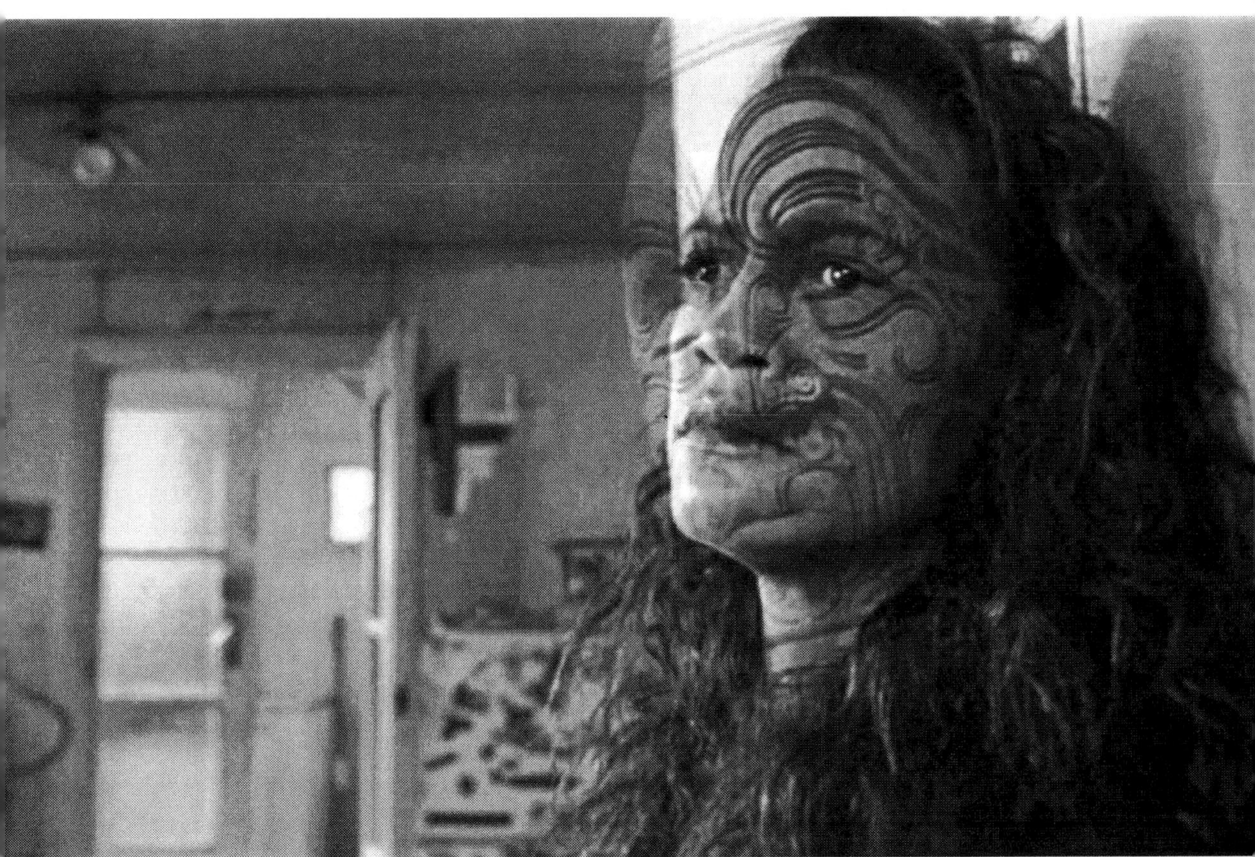

The past superimposing itself on the present in *Once Were Warriors*, 1994, dir. Lee Tamahori.

an "urban ethnic chic," an indigenous aesthetics, notable in the complex tattoo designs worn by the male characters, and especially by Māori motorbike gang (Toa Aotearoa) members, representative of a newly urbanised form of warriorhood; a local/indigenous version of hip hop and rap, which the younger children play, adapted from American youth culture; and elaborately choreographed scenes of violence in the domestic sphere and the pub where Jake Heke ("the muss") rules by his fists.[37] This urban aesthetic, which corresponds to resurgent Māori culture in the 1990s, reinforces the film's social realism and explains its influence in New Zealand, where it encouraged incidents of domestic violence to be re-examined.[38]

The debasement of the warrior ideal from its pre-European flowering is represented by Jake Heke, who lives by violence and ignores the needs of his family. When Grace, Jake and Beth's daughter, commits suicide after being raped, Beth turns to the values associated with pre-contact Māori ascendancy, symbolised by the *marae*. Her transition from a troubled domestic life with Jake to a more independent, self-determining woman is marked by her decision to take Grace's body "home" for the *tangi*. In the film this moment is imaged by the dissolve of her face into an image of an earlier Māori woman with *moko* and tattoo markings, then becoming the carved figurehead on top of the *wharenui* (meeting house).

In *Whale Rider* the problems concerning the tribe or extended family's survival are emphasised by the voice-over at the beginning, when one of the newly born twins dies. The film's focus on anxieties raised by the malfunction of the communal unit in the present day, and the need to resolve internal issues without reference to the wider Pākehā community, is similar to *Once Were Warriors*. In *Whale Rider*, however, the reason for the present-day crisis is never given explicitly other than suggesting a loss of momentum on the part of Koro, the grandfather and current leader.[39] Renewal occurs through reconnection with the ancestral past, and revival of the myth of origin, concerning the tribe's ancestor, Paikea, whose carved wooden image is visible on the top of the central pole of the meeting house. The heroine Paikea confirms her destiny in her plunge into ocean depths to recover the sacred whalebone tooth thrown overboard by her grandfather in a leadership test. In the film's climax, she rides a whale in imitation of her ancestor, so proving her ability to lead the tribe and overturning the Māori protocol that denies women a place on the *marae* and traditionally excluded them from any leadership role. Nevertheless, this imaging of cultural revival by conflating the idea of an "authentic" indigeneity with the timeless and universal, here represented by the rhetoric of "the natural"[40] and of naturalness, shows parallels with the romanticised aboriginal representations of *The Chant of Jimmie Blacksmith* and *Rabbit Proof Fence*.

In both *Once Were Warriors* and *Whale Rider*, the universalising of narrative elements, particularly the utopian community endings, delimits any ethnographic specificity or materialist critique of colonialism. Critics of *Once Were Warriors* see it as being about family dysfunction in general without demonstrating any specific indigenous problem that would make it a Māori film. Houston Wood, in fact, sees it as about the dangers of alcohol rather than the loss of past warriorhood.[41] Nikki Caro's collaboration with the local tribe, Te Kohini or Ngāti Porou, from in and round the village of Whangaroa in the East Coast of the North

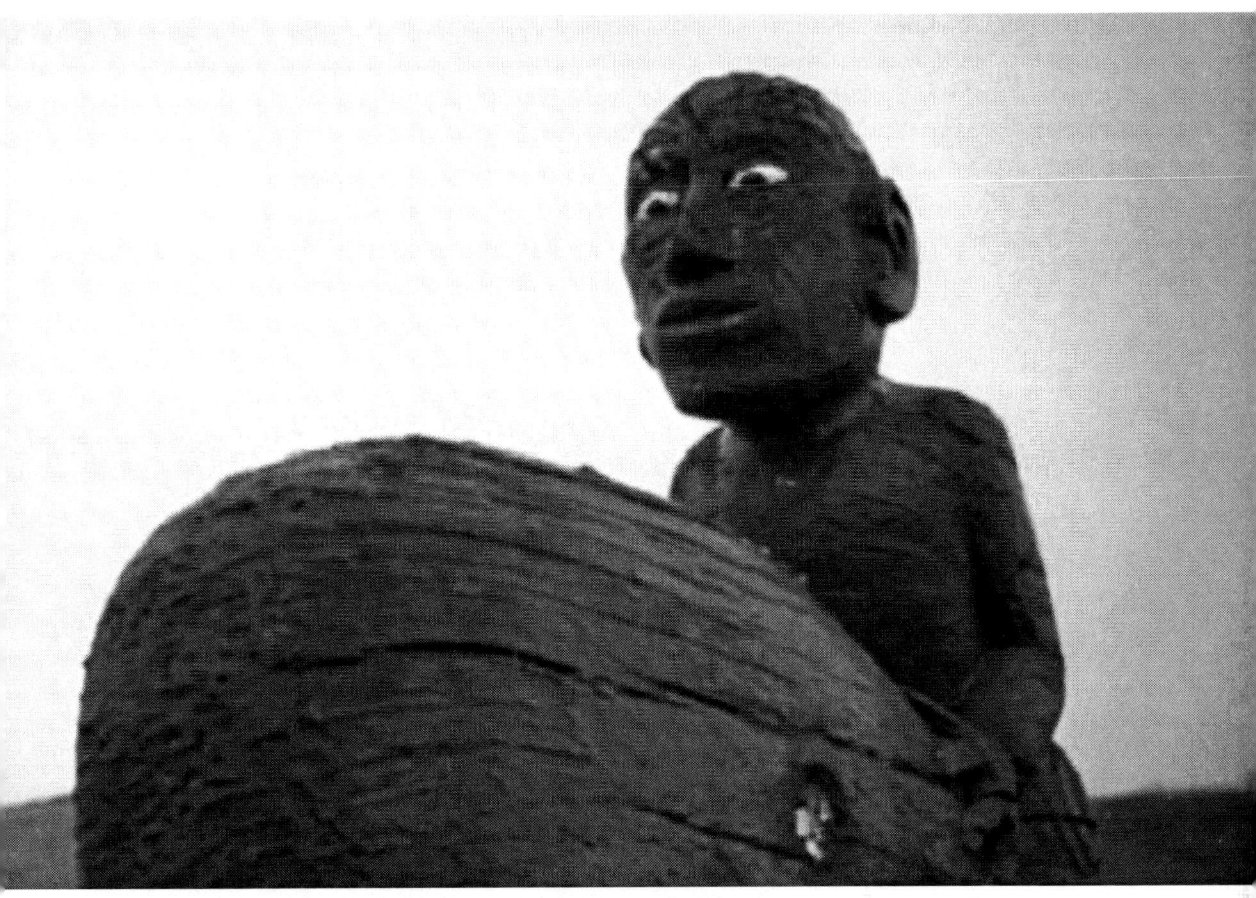

Carved image of Paikea, the whale rider, in *Whale Rider*, 2002, dir. Niki Caro.

Island, does not extend to the narrative of *Whale Rider*, which implies that the Māori are a single, homogeneous people, while the specific Māori genealogical story, which is true of only one or two tribes, is introduced as though it is generally relevant.[42] *Whale Rider* has been seen as making a statement about life on a philosophical and spiritual level rather than as being ethnographically or culturally specific;[43] and Māori critics denounce its concessions to Hollywood, as for example, in the triumphalist conclusion which visualises communal togetherness as the abandoned *waka* is rebuilt, then sets out to sea with all the cast on board, symbolising resolution of the problematic need for renewal.[44]

Understanding cultural difference: Colonial and pre-colonial pasts in *The Feathers of Peace* and *Ten Canoes*

The Feathers of Peace is a documentary which foregrounds justice and the telling of history, while *Ten Canoes* features stories, both contemporary and legendary, and stresses storytelling as process. These different cinematic genres and meta-discourses invite a linked discussion. Both films draw on written accounts, histories, photographs and the techniques of documentary filmmaking to reconstruct a more "authentic" indigeneity than the earlier films, one based on past images and historical facts.[45]

The Feathers of Peace addresses the near genocide of the peaceful Moriori of the Chatham Islands off the coast of the South Island, following invasions by two Māori tribes in 1835. Barry Barclay, a committed activist and a director of the landmark *Tangata Whenua* television series in 1974, and of the award-winning *Ngati*, focuses on the retrieval of the "suppressed past," a "story that's been buried," in order to lay claim to a larger idea of justice.[46] *The Feathers of Peace* was intended for the descendants of the Moriori tribe, but it also explores the complexities of Māori tribal identity. More broadly, it is an oppositional discourse to *Once Were Warriors*, of which the hypermasculined imagery and unremitting violence, in Barclay's words, encouraged a whole generation of Māori to accept the film "as part of their culture," but without speaking out about "whether it's accurate or the effect it might have."[47]

Barclay stresses the concept of peace, as symbolised by the feathers of the Albatross which the Moriori chief wears, and the Moriori policy of non-resistance which led to their widespread slaughter by the Māori. The interviews also offer a "sense of justice or truth-to-history" which was denied the Moriori by the law courts in mainland New Zealand, which adjudicated on Māori claims, awarding them 97.3 per cent of the Islands' territories and the Moriori 2.7 per cent.[48] As Stephen Turner and Stuart Murray point out, the visual image of unjust occupation and widescale slaughter, reinforced by the Māori collusion with colonial legal decision-making, has significant parallels with the European colonisation of New

Ten Canoes (2006), directed by Rolf de Heer, Peter Djigirr. Image courtesy of Palm Pictures/Photofest.

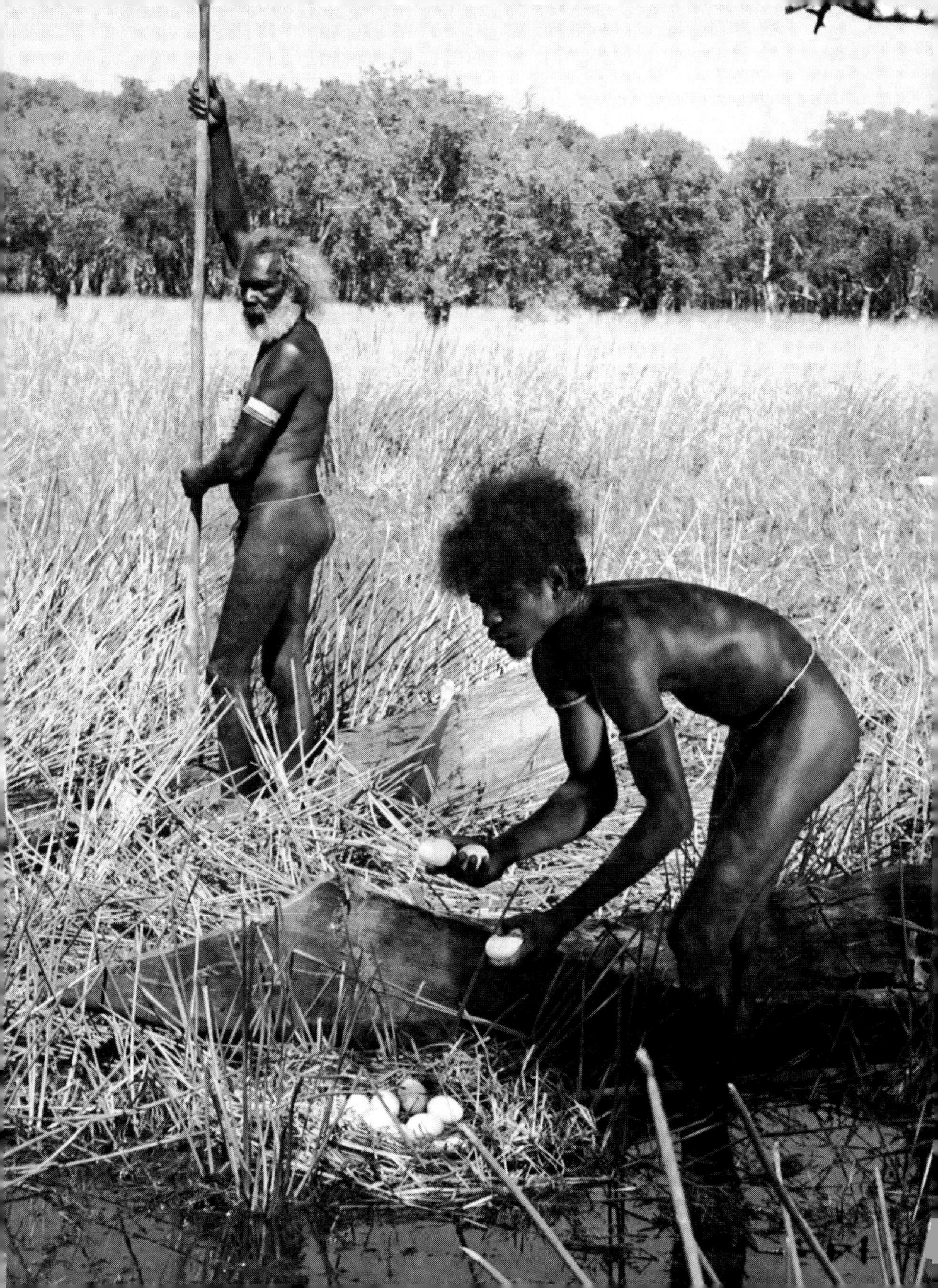

Zealand in which the Māori themselves believed they were unjustly displaced and unfairly treated.[49] Barclay's documentary methods consisted of simulated interviews with historical figures to an off-screen camera; he drew on documentation that had been preserved during the colonial period, including written records of what people actually said. *The Feathers of Peace* has never been widely released, however, for like other documentary features that draw on empirical facts and historical evidence, it has limited appeal to mainstream audiences.

Ten Canoes, the first feature film to be made in an Aboriginal language, also aimed to reconstruct historical authenticity by a return to the colonial and pre-European past. The film represents the world of a particular tribe, the Yolgnu in the village of Ramingining, from eastern Arnhem Land, as it was before European civilisation arrived. It images the tribe's transformative relationship to its roots independent of the white settler order and represents a collective "we" which challenges the cultural erasure that occurred under colonisation. The film draws selectively for its story on images of the Yolgnu people in the form of photographs taken by the anthropologist Donald Thomson in the 1930s, and tribal activities which Thomson recorded ethnographically of the goose egg hunt and the making of bark canoes.

Ten Canoes is a layered cinematic narrativisation at two different levels of an earlier cultural story which belongs to the dreamtime and is retold as a local tribal story. The past is represented as two time frames: an ancient mythical era before time was measured and the pre-colonial past of 1000 years ago (named "Thomson Times" because the images are reconstructed from the Donald Thomson photos). The use of an external narrator, as in the opening ancestral creation myth – a voice-over by David Gulpilil, Australia's best-known Aborigine actor – heightens consciousness of the storytelling process. The aesthetics of representing different historical periods in *Ten Canoes*, in which the recent past is shot in black and white and the mythical past is shot in colour with a mobile camera, is comparable to Barclay's methods in *The Feathers of Peace*, in which black and white is used for the historical scenes while the framing scenes in the present are shot in colour.

Ten Canoes originated in David Gulpilil's request to de Heer that he make a film about his people, the Yolgnu, and the collaboration that was developed with this tribe is crucial to the film's meaning as a cultural artefact. The making of the film, based on the photographs, encouraged the actors (only those tribal members who could claim kinship with the figures in the photographs) to recover discontinued practices such as bark-canoe building and hunting for geese and goose eggs. As Louise Hamby points out, this gave it a complex truth status as local indigenous audiences, seeing the film, began to experience the "Donald Thomson" days because the photos were being used as if this was a "real" past time (although it is a story).[50] Similarly, Barclay comments that in *The Feathers of Peace* the actors were conscious that they were "directly depicting things their own forebears said and did or could have done."[51] In both films, then, the relationship between actors and viewers constructs the visual medium as one which brings the past into the present. In this attempt at syncretic cultural transformation or reconstruction, they illustrate James Clifford's theory of "articulated identity" – namely, that culture consists of disparate parts which can be unhooked and recombined (like an articulated lorry).[52] Although Aboriginal activists like Marcia Langton have spoken out against self-representation in filmmaking because it essentialises Aboriginal people,[53] postcolonial theorist Gayatri Spivak's theory of strategic essentialising – that is, of cultivating discourses of community, tradition and ethnicity as a political strategy, and in order to confront political and historical oppression – can be applied to this selective method of cultural recovery.[54] Barclay seems to recognise this in his comment about the Moriori "that people who are traumatised can struggle to retain their essence is an inspiring thing."[55]

Documentary evidence of how the Yolgnu and the Moriori once lived enables their story to be told, and both actors and audiences to reconstruct the tribal past. As community collaborations, they confirm the importance of the communal, the organising principle in Barclay's filmmaking, in establishing the rights of historical representation.[56] In *Ten Canoes* the representation of indigeneity at all levels is controlled by the Yolgnu community and, not surprisingly, the film's success and the images of the Yolgnu have enhanced their community traditions and restored to them cultural knowledge which was in danger of being lost.

Conclusion: Cinema and the recovery of indigenous culture

In reviewing the typology of these six films, it is notable that there is a development towards the greater self-determination of the indigenous collaborations and community endeavours of the last three. Cultural differences also exist between New Zealand and Australian cinema. In the former, notably in the two Māori films, the present moment is foregrounded on the screen, whereas in the latter representations of pre-contact and colonial history is part of a larger cultural reconstruction; this is also true of the documentary *The Feathers of Peace*. The cinematic medium has made a significant contribution to postcolonial revisionings of history in both countries, both affecting and being affected by political debates on how history should be represented and on competing claims about ownership of the past. *The Chant of Jimmie Blacksmith* and *Rabbit Proof Fence*, as interventions in colonial history and ideology, which also appeal to white settler guilt, have attracted debate over issues of authenticity, fiction and truth-telling. Barclay's *The Feathers of Peace*, concerned with the question of justice and ethnic erasure, implies in its critique of colonialism a further intervention into debates concerning contemporary Māori identity.[57] *Once Were Warriors* and *Whale Rider* stress the need for a new autonomy of the *iwi* or *whānau*, and are located in the present day, which is seen as problematic or unfulfilling. As such, they contrast to more historically inflected films like *Ngati* and *Mauri*, which are set in the late 1940s and the early 1950s, respectively, and to *Ten Canoes* and *The Feathers of Peace*, in which the idea of community dominates the cinematic performance as different people tell their story, or the film tells a collective story which reinforces the idea of community.

Second wave indigenous filmmaking and the cross-cultural collaborations of films like *Whale Rider*, *Ten Canoes* and *The Feathers of Peace* have enabled indigenous peoples to redevelop their cultural identity by drawing selectively from the available material of their collective past. Clifford's "Indigenous articulations" reaches beyond the European world-view in its argument that cultures can be reconfigured through acknowledging the ruptures of colonisation and recovery of remnants of past histories. In *Ten Canoes*, a fragmented, interrupted sense of time is partly restored because parallel (and thematically connected) stories are told in each time frame, and this narrative structure implies some continuity between historic and mythic pasts, that memory turns into dreaming. Culture and epistemological differences are foregrounded, as, for example, in the narrator's comment that "my story" is "not the same as your one" (i.e. that of the western spectator). As Therese Davis says, this is a new form of cultural memory.[58] In *The Feathers of Peace* the different voices become a substitute court of justice, and the film is a form of reparation for historical misrepresentation.[59] What is true of the Aborigines – that after colonisation they can only access the pre-European past in a fragmented way because there is little collective memory of that past – is equally true of the Moriori, who lack a living memory after near-genocide by the Māori, and who, until recently, were widely believed to be extinct.[60] In presenting cultural difference, *Ten Canoes* and *The Feathers of Peace* confirm that the camera is an "imaginative witness." It relays the pre-European past to the present, and by rediscovering and reinventing indigenous peoples, enables them to take up a more independent position in the national narrative.

Notes

1. On 3 June 1992, the Australian High Court determined that the doctrine of *terra nullius*, which denied the native land claim, was untenable: the land was not empty at the moment of settlement, and in certain places native title was not extinguished.
2. See Therese Davis, "Remembering Our Ancestors: Cross-cultural Collaboration and the Mediation of Aboriginal Culture and History in *Ten Canoes* (Rolf de Heer, 2006)," *Studies in Australasian Cinema* 1, no 1 (2007): 5–14, esp. 6.
3. See Felicity Collins and Therese Davis, *Australian Cinema after Mabo* (Cambridge: Cambridge University Press, 2004), 7.
4. Sacha Clelland-Stokes, *Representing Aboriginality: A Post-colonial Analysis of the Key Trends of Representing Aboriginality in South African, Australia and Aotearoa/ New Zealand Film* (Hojbjerg: Intervention Press: 2007), 89, citing Alan McKee, "Films vs Real Life: Communicating Aboriginality in Cinema and Television," *UTS Review* 3, no. 1 (1997): 160–82, esp. 161.
5. Clelland-Stokes, *Representing Aboriginality*, 3, citing Tom O'Regan, *Australian National Cinema* (London: Routledge, 1996), 21.
6. Collins and Davis, *Australian Cinema after Mabo*, 9.
7. E. Ann Kaplan, *Trauma Culture: The Politics of Terror and Loss in Media and Literature* (New Brunswick, NJ: Rutgers University Press, 2005), 135.
8. Davis, "Remembering Our Ancestors," 12.
9. "*Feathers of Peace*: Lynette Read Interviews Barry Barclay," *Illusions* 31 (2000/2001): 2–6, esp. 4.
10. Barry Barclay, "Celebrating Fourth Cinema," *Illusions* 35 (2003): 7–11; Stuart Murray, *Images of Dignity: Barry Barclay and Fourth Cinema* (Wellington: Huia Publishers, 2008), 17–18.

11. Thomas Keneally, *The Chant of Jimmie Blacksmith* (Sydney: Angus and Robertson: 1972).
12. Terry Sturm, "Thomas Keneally and Australian Racism: *The Chant of Jimmie Blacksmith*," *Southerly* 33 (1973): 261–74.
13. See Keneally, *The Chant of Jimmie Blacksmith*, 16–17: "The only true Australians are [...] the aborigines"; also 128–29, 152.
14. "Re-presenting the 'Obvious': An Analysis of the Film *The Chant of Jimmie Blacksmith*," in *Prejudice in the Public Arena: Racism*, ed. Andrew Markus and Radha Rasmussen. Centre for Migrant and Intercultural Studies (Melbourne: Monash University, 1987), 61–71, esp. 63, 70.
15. Frantz Fanon, *Black Skin, White Mask* (London: Pluto, 1986), 1; Paul Gilroy, *There Ain't no Black in the Union Jack* (London: Hutchinson, 1987), 6.
16. Janet Wilson, "Reconsidering Fred Schepisi's *The Chant of Jimmie Blacksmith* (1978): The Screen Adaptation of Thomas Keneally's Novel (1972)," *Studies in Australasian Cinema* 1, no. 2 (2007): 191–207, esp. 194.
17. Clelland-Stokes, *Representing Aboriginality*, 99; citing Colin Johnson, "Chauvel and the Centring of the Aboriginal Male in Australian Film," *Continuum: The Australian Journal of Media and Culture* 1, no. 1 (1987): n.p. Internet: http://wwwmc.
18. Graeme Turner, "Breaking the Frame: The Representation of Aborigines in Australian Film," in *Aboriginal Culture Today*, ed. Anna Rutherford. Special issue of *Kunapipi* 10, nos. 1, 2 (1988): 135–45, esp. 138–39; citing Catriona Moore and Stephen Muecke, "Racism and the Representation of Aborigines in Film," *Australian Journal of Cultural Studies* 2, no. 1 (1984): 35–63, esp. 42.
19. The term "Australian Film Commission genre" was coined by Susan Dermody and Elizabeth Jacka, *The Screening of Australia*. Volume 2. *The Anatomy of a National Cinema* (Sydney: Currency Press, 1988), 32–34; see Tom O'Regan, *Australian National Cinema* (London and New York: Routledge, 1996), 196–97.
20. Doris Pilkington, *Rabbit-Proof Fence* (New York: Miramax Books/Hyperion, 2002 [1996]).
21. See Collins and Davis, *Australian Cinema after Mabo*, 5–6, 135–36, on the anti-Stolen Generation campaign and the history wars; Mark McKenna, "Metaphors of Light and Darkness: The Politics of 'Black Armband' History," *Melbourne Journal of Politics: The Reconciliation Issue* 25 (1998): 67–84.
22. Adi Wimmer, *Australian Film: Cultures, Identities, Texts* (Wissenschaftlicher Verlag Trier, 2007), 17–22; Clelland-Stokes, *Representing Aboriginality*, 94–97.
23. Collins and Davis, *Australian Cinema after Mabo*, 137.
24. He was hanged in Darlinghurst Gaol, 18 January 1901; see G.P. Walsh, "Governor, Jimmy (1875–1901)," *Australian Dictionary of Biography*, Online edition. http://www.adb.online.anu.edu.au/biogs/A090063b.htm. Accessed 1 June 2010.
25. Collins and Davis, *Australian Cinema after Mabo*, 139.
26. Houston Wood, *Native Features: Indigenous Films from Around the World* (New York and London: Continuum, 2008), 10. They are 1139 and 724 miles each.
27. See Richard Dyer, "White," in *Film and Theory: An Anthology*, ed. Robert Stam and Toby Miller (Oxford: Blackwell, 2000), 733–51, esp. 738.
28. Wood, *Native Features*, 11.
29. Collins and Davis, *Australian Cinema after Mabo*, 135–37.
30. On moralising liberals see Richard Mulgan, "Citizenship and Legitimacy in Post-colonial Australia," in *Citizenship and Indigenous Australians: Changing Conceptions and Possibilities*, ed. Nicholas Peterson and Will Sanders (Cambridge: Cambridge University Press, 1998), 179–95, esp. 185.

31. Wood, *Native Features*, 12. See also Clelland-Stokes, *Representing Aboriginality*, 97.

32. See, e.g., Leonie Pihama, "Repositioning Maori Representation: Contextualising *Once Were Warriors*," in *Film in Aotearoa New Zealand*, ed. Jonathan Dennis and Jan Bieringa, 2nd ed. (Wellington: Victoria University Press, 1996), 191–92; Davinia Thornley, "White, Brown or 'Coffee'?: Revisioning Race in Tamahori's *Once Were Warriors*," *Film Criticism* 25, no. 3 (Spring 2001): 22–36; Chris Prentice, "Riding the Whale? Postcolonialism and Globalization in *Whale Rider*," in *Global Fissures: Postcolonial Fusions*, ed. Clara A. B. Joseph and Janet Wilson, Cross Cultures 85 (Amsterdam and New York: Rodopi, 2006), 247–68, esp. 258; Barry Barclay in a letter to *Whale Rider*'s producer, "An Open Letter to John Barnett by Barry Barclay," *Onfilm* 20, no. 2 (2003): 11–14 (cited by Murray, *Images of Dignity*, 4–5).

33. Pascale da Souza, "*Maoritanga* in *Whale Rider* and *Once Were Warriors*: a problematic rebirth through female leaders," *Studies in Australasian Cinema* 1, no. 1 (2007): 15–27.

34. The film is an adaptation of Alan Duff's novel, *Once Were Warriors* (Auckland: Tandem Press, 1990). See Kirsten Moana Thompson, "*Once Were Warriors*: New Zealand's First Indigenous Blockbuster," *Movie Bockbusters*, ed. Julian Streeper (London: Routledge, 2003), 230–41, esp. 235.

35. The film is adapted from Witi Ihimaera's novella, *The Whale Rider* (Auckland: Heinemann: 1987).

36. Ibid., 171.

37. Michelle Keown, "'He Iwi Kotahi Tatou'?: Nationalism and Cultural Identity in Maori Film," in *Contemporary New Zealand Cinema: From New Wave to Blockbuster*, ed. Ian Conrich and Stuart Murray (London and New York: I. B. Tauris, 2008), 197–210, esp. 205–06.

38. Thomson, "*Once Were Warriors*," 238; Clelland-Stokes, *Representing Aboriginality*, 172, citing N. Grant, "New Zealand Movie Milestones," *On Film* (November 1997): 9–10.

39. Prentice, "Postcolonialism and Globalization in *Whale Rider*," 258.

40. Ibid., 259–60.

41. Wood, *Native Features*, 163.

42. Ibid., 14–15.

43. Stan Jones, "Siting *Whale Rider*: A Survey of its Reception in a European Context," *British Review of New Zealand Studies* 14 (2003/2004): 61–83, esp. 72.

44. Wood, *Native Features*, 16–17.

45. Barry Barclay drew on Michael King's *Moriori: A People Rediscovered* (Auckland: Viking, 1989) and was influenced by the quasi-newsreel style of Peter Watkins's *Culloden* (1964). For De Heer's use of the Donald Thomson ethnographic collections held in the Museum Victoria in Melbourne, see Louise Hamby, "Thomson Times and *Ten Canoes* (de Heer and Djigirr, 2006)," *Studies in Australasian Cinema* 1, no. 2 (2007): 127–46.

46. Read, "*The Feathers of Peace*," 3.

47. Ibid., 5.

48. Stephen Turner, "Cinema of Justice: *The Feathers of Peace*," *Illusions* 33 (2002): 9–11, esp. 10.

49. Ibid., 9–10; Murray, *Images of Dignity*, 81.

50. Hamby, "Thomson Times and *Ten Canoes*," 128.

51. Read, "*The Feathers of Peace*," 5.

52. James Clifford, "Indigenous Articulations," *Contemporary Pacific* 13, no. 2 (Fall 2001): 468–89.

53. Marcia Langton, *Well, I Heard It on the Radio and I Saw It on the Television: An Essay for the Australian Film Commission on the Politics and Aesthetics of Filmmaking by and about Aboriginal People and Things* (Sydney: Australian Film Commission, 1983); cited by Davis, "Remembering Our Ancestors," 6.

54. Gayatri C. Spivak, *Outside in the Teaching Machine* (London: Routledge, 1993).

55. Read, "*The Feathers of Peace*," 6.

56. Barclay, "Celebrating Fourth Cinema," 11; Murray, *Images of Dignity*, 3.

57. Ibid., 15.

58. Davis, "Remembering Our Ancestors," 12.

59. Turner, "Cinema of Justice," 11.

60. Sunny Singh, "Writing Against History: Seizing Subjecthood for the Aborigine Narrative," in *New Zealand and Australia. Narrative, History and Representation*, ed. Sue Ryan Fazilleau, Studies in New Zealand Culture 10 (Nottingham: Kakapo Books, 2008), 111–33.

"The Donations of History": *Mauri* and the Transfigured "Māori Gaze": Towards a Bi-national Cinema in Aotearoa

Bruce Harding

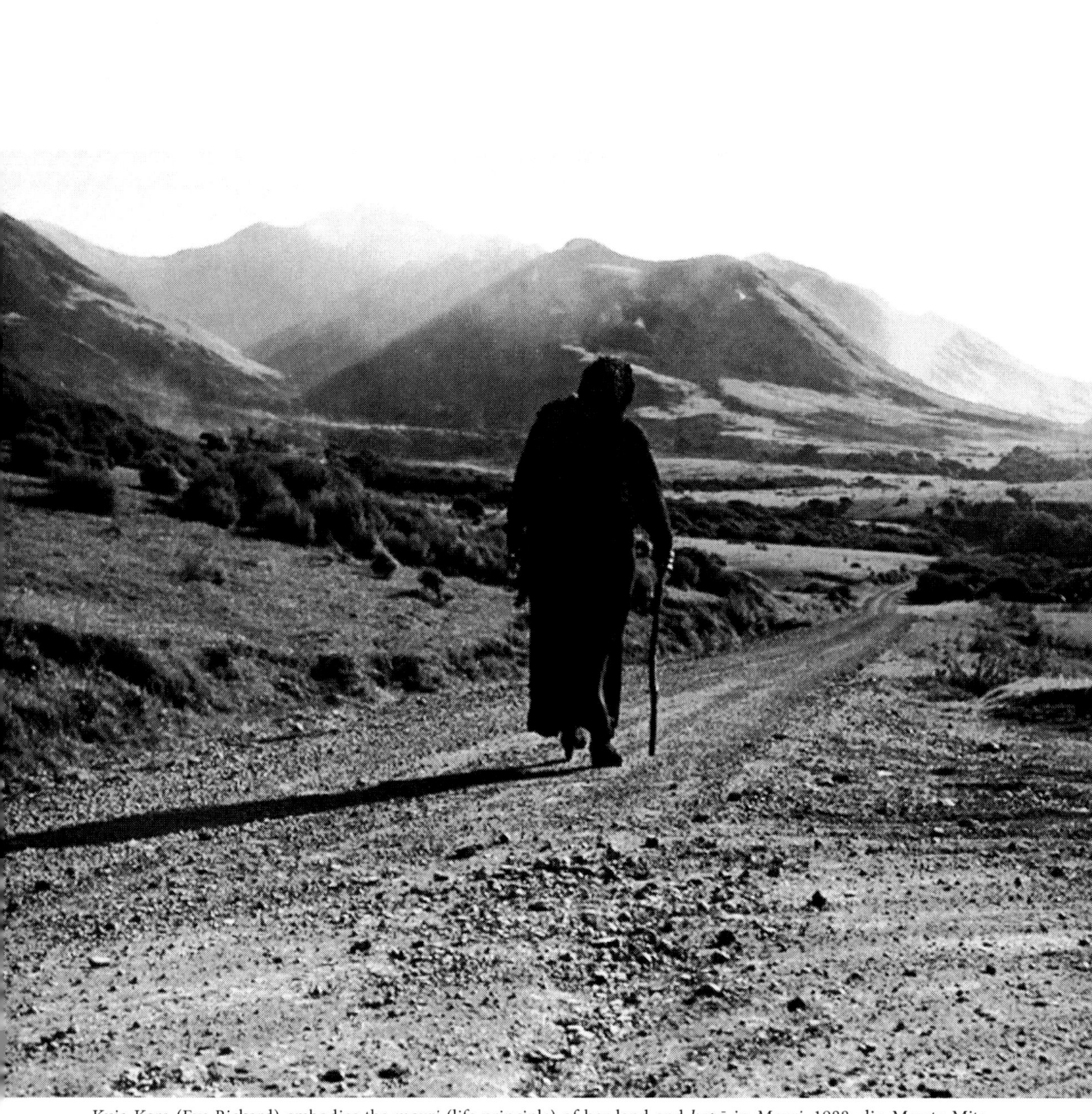

Kuia Kara (Eva Rickard) embodies the *mauri* (life principle) of her land and *hapū* in *Mauri*, 1988, dir. Merata Mita. Photograph by Victoria Ginn.

The audience sees [...] resurrections taking place, a past life lives again, wisdom is shared and something from the heart and spirit responds to that short but inspiring on-screen journey from darkness to light.

(Merata Mita)[1]

Celebrating *Hapū* values and *Iwitanga*

Merata Mita's film *Mauri* (1988) might be regarded as *the* distinctive work, the defining text, of a postcolonising New Zealand cinema which interrogates the damaging legacies of the colonial era and, in its decolonising thrust, suggests viable possibilities for social renewal based on the Treaty of Waitangi (1840), which established a space for white migrants to exist in pre-colonial New Zealand. Mita's film explores Māoritanga values within a small rural *hapū* community in the Bay of Plenty during the 1950s when many rural Māori were relocating away from their *tūrangawaewae* (land-based world) to urban areas for employment. This major internal migration created stress in "race relations" and stressed (if not weakened) the fabric of the *mauri* (or distinctive life-essence) of many Māori *hapū* (or sub-tribal kin units). The plot is centred on a venerable Māori matriarch and guardian of her clan's spiritual values, Kara, as she lovingly nourishes the *mana whenua* values within her Te Mata realm, aided by her ageing friend Hemi (Sonny Waru). The corrosive impact of Pākehā (white) cash-values regarding the status of land – which has a huge ontological value to Māori – is explored in the film and becomes one of its deepest underlying codes of signification. One of Kara's favourite nephews (Willie Rapana) dies in a gang turf war in a town and, upon her deathbed, the old *kuia* finds out that another supposed kinsman has escaped a life of petty urban crime and committed the appalling act of appropriating the name, identity and *taonga* (treasured belongings) of Kara's relative, Rewi Rapana. *Mauri* impressively tracks the agonising path to redemption of this urban outcast, Paki Hemapō (Anzac Wallace), as he struggles to repair the damage which his selfish – and un-Māori action – has done to the *mauri* of Kara's *hapū*. The film has three linked movements: the guardianship of Kara (which she passes broadly to her mokopuna, Awatea); the ethnic inter marriage between a Pākehā farmer (Steve Semmens) and Māori woman (Ramiri) which also reclaims the *mana* of stolen land; and the belated redemption of the criminal Paki (who could not honourably marry Ramiri as he had violated the *tapu* of her dead relative and infringed the *mauri* of Ramiri's tribal group). These intense personal

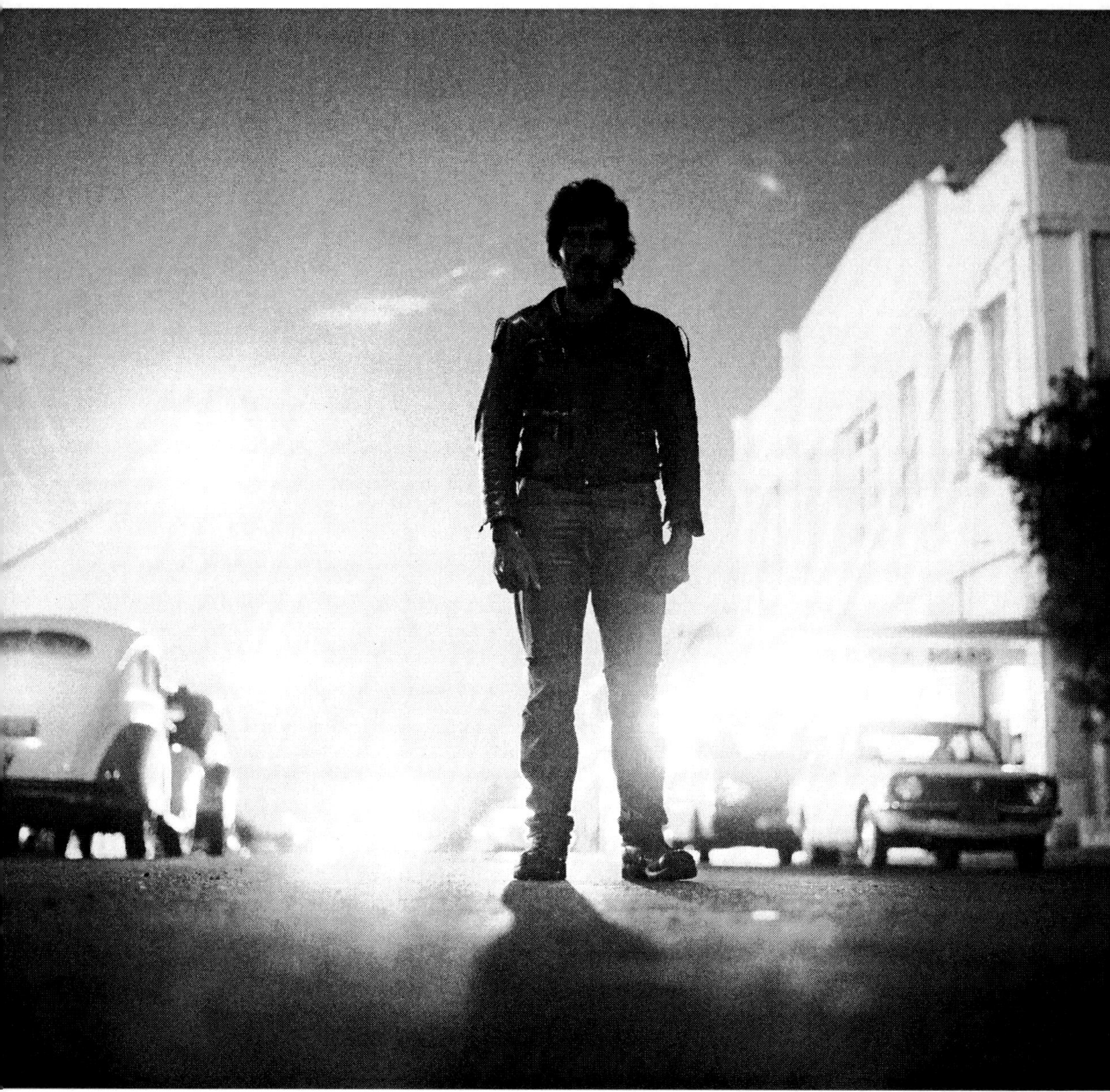

Ōpōtiki stand-off: Herb (Bernard Rua) asserts his leadership of Willy's gang, in *Mauri*, 1988, dir. Merata Mita. Photograph by Victoria Ginn.

bonds are interlinked to demonstrate to a non-Māori audience how the sustaining concept of *mauri ora* works as a vivifying and renewing principle of individual and collective identity within Māoridom. As the first feature film created by a Māori woman director and true *wahine toa*, Merata Mita, *Mauri* takes up where John O'Shea and Rudall Hayward's honourable, but limited, exercises in filmic biculturalism (*Broken Barrier* (1952) and *To Love a Maori* (1972)) were forced to cease. In *Mauri*, Mita fashioned a challenging but cautiously hopeful artefact of "Fourth Cinema": a work which limns the outlines of bi nationalism via the cinematic exploration of strained relationships among and between descendants of the key partners (Māori and Pākehā New Zealanders) who signed Te Tiriti o Waitangi. *Mauri* is expressive of its emergence in the troubled and yet also energised decade of the 1980s, which began, for Māori, mired in the angry racist politics of Muldoonism and concluded with a re-mandated Waitangi Tribunal under the Lange Government. Mita's film uses the medium of personal drama to underscore, at the national level, the continuing potency and relevance of that originating Treaty paradigm and of Kaupapa Māori in ordering positive social relations in Aotearoa/New Zealand.

Mauri acts as a diachronic marker of an evolving ethnic sensibility in Aotearoa New Zealand as it taps into the narrative *langue* of that culture and enacts ideological shifts in the representation of inter-personal and intimate relations between Māori and Pākehā individuals which act as conceptual shorthand for changing social values as *Mauri*, being something of a nationalist film, revisits and refurbishes John O'Shea's *Broken Barrier* as a potent cross-cultural (or educultural)[2] text. Mita's work upholds Davidson Loehr's statement that "A simple definition of 'colonisation' is that it takes people's stories away, and assigns them supportive roles in stories that empower others at their expense."[3] It is in this precise framing of "voice" and agency that Mita's extraordinary film works its "cinema magic" by summoning Māori *wairua* (spirituality) in exploring what Nadine Gordimer once called "a nationalism of the heart that has been brought about by suffering."[4]

John O'Shea's *Broken Barrier* was a path-breaking film about a strained inter-ethnic relationship in a racist Pākehā monoculture and is the *uber*-text behind Merata Mita's *Mauri*, a filmic case study of micro-politics and *mana motuhake* (power of self-determination) in the East Cape locality of Te Mata, which makes a statement about relations between the Treaty partners devolving from the politics of contrast and strained reciprocity in the era of emerging *iwi* Treaty settlements with the Crown[5] and which implies the need for a loose kind of hybrid micro-federalism in New Zealand's state arrangements. While a kind of ethnographic study of a community honouring its past during the 1950s, *Mauri* also points to a future anchored in ancient values, in keeping with the Māori concept of the past always travelling into futurity. Ranginui Walker once delimited the "structural relation" between *tangata whenua* and the white power culture which Mita has so powerfully dramatised: that "social, economic and political subjugation to the tyranny of majority rule" means that "the coloniser decides and the colonised responds within the stultifying and suffocating parameters set."[6] We see micro-resistance to such framing in Kara's opening use of Māori *kawa* (protocol) in the hospital (when she uses the shell to cut the umbilical chord and removes the placenta: "The afterbirth is part of us – it has to go back to the land," she informs the awestruck Pākehā doctor). In the wider context of such enforced subordination, one is reminded of the words of a Jewish psychoanalyst in Arthur Miller's *The Incident at Vichy* (1965) who confronts the self-blaming Austrian prince for the racist oppression he has practised: "It's not your guilt I want, it's your responsibility," the Jew responds, and Miller elegantly points the lesson which is so apposite to Mita's project: to relinquish denial and take to heart the donations of history to one's character and the character of one's people, is the most painful but rewarding job a people can undertake.[7]

Broken Barrier and *Mauri* enact plots set broadly in the 1950s, but the understandings of social relations which underpin each are vastly different in modality and tone, signifying an evolution and a toughening of stances in historicised attitudes. *Mauri* dramatises a clear need for an inter-cultural *rapprochement* in which denial is faced and Miller's "donations of history" are factored into the path towards greater social equilibrium between Māori and Pākehā. What will be unlocked through a reading of *Mauri* as social text is the role which it has played in what Nicolas Tredell has called a "cinema of the mind"[8] and as a marker (*rahui*) text which has limned onscreen the glacially slow pace of conceptual change regarding "race conflict" and a halting crawl towards better relationships in Aotearoa (figured in individual histories which mirror macro-social realities). Professor John Macmillan Brown prophesied in 1927 that when mankind attains to a universal federation, "it may be predicted that New Zealand will be one of the foremost champions of freedom and peace for all men."[9] Mita's *Mauri* deconstructs such sunny and triumphalistic Pākehā optimism by demonstrating very profoundly how New Zealand (Brown's "Britain of the South")[10] needs to set its own federative house in order before embarking on such grandiose visions.

Beyond official (white) biculturalism

While the enlightened filmmaker O'Shea constructed a challenging film text for New Zealand in the McCarthy era of repression and Anglo-dominant assumptions about Britannic superiority, 36 years later the indigenous cineaste Mita provided, in *Mauri*, a contrasting romance replete with "echoic" counter-stereotyping of her Pākehā characters as figures of a buffoonishly racist white minstrelsy. This is comprehensible when even O'Shea's earnestly liberal homily on New Zealand's colour bar essentialised Māori as a noble people (*bon sauvages*) willing to sacrifice themselves for the superior "white man." However, in the socially stressed and officially "bicultural" 1980s, Mita frontally challenged any nostalgia for *L'empire* and for what one analyst calls "an older Britain that may still subsist [and] which preserves like an afterlife"[11] the values and stresses of Belich's "pan-British" or "Britonnic" culture.[12]

The 1950s is the time-setting of this film and was an era sharply characterised by Germaine Greer as one of "fantasy whiteness"[13] (vaunted ethnic purity), when the "whitefellas" on both sides of the Tasman resolutely refused to recognise any "Aboriginality" inhering in the indigenes or within the land itself. Greer asserted that Australasia "will be truly self-governing and independent only when it has recognised its inherent and ineradicable Aboriginality."[14] In her own very singular way, Merata Mita has captured that essential insight in *Mauri*, which is "postcolonial" to the extent that its narrative recalls Susan Najita's discussion of Oceanic texts which allow Pacific (here, Polynesian) peoples "to negotiate their paths towards sovereignty and chart their postcolonial futures" by "allowing themselves and their readers [or viewers] to imagine new futures by exorcising the past."[15] And while *Mauri* re-invests some hope in a barrier-breaching inter-ethnic marriage between local Māori girl, Ramiri (Susan D. Ramiri Paul), and a young Pākehā farmer, Steve Semmons (James Heyward), Mita's Māori characters are far more rounded and humanised in this tale of a nascent localised anti-colonial sub-nationalism. However, in the world *Mauri* constructs, the Pākehā will need to adopt Gordimer's insight that whites who want to fit into the new Aotearoa "must learn a number of hard things" like regarding themselves as immigrants to a radically new country, but "to whose life he [*sic*] has committed himself," and forswearing "the old impulses to leadership" and domination.[16] In this quite radical sense *Mauri* is a revisionist film text, with a *wahine* somewhat reluctantly romancing a Pākehā male, in which Mita, the first female Māori film director, tracks a clear social evolution in which Māori *tikanga* (normative tribal lore/law) can, and should, reasonably co-exist with dominant Pākehā arrangements in a confluent bi-national manner that was simply inconceivable and infeasible in the world of *Broken Barrier*.

Central to Mita's aesthetic (and thus to the *mythos* of *Mauri*) is her claim that Māoridom is "a community under pressure"[17] – a primarily ideological-cultural pressure, as her people reacted to the camera's representation.[18] Mita's 1992 essay "The Soul and the Image" is a profound meditation on the appropriationist quality of much early Euro-footage, with its melodramatic and romantic plot elements enacting serious "cultural and spiritual debasement."[19] The other, more potent and shattering, source of pressure was adaptive shock at the wider social-political onslaught of Pākehā migrants. These clear-sighted assessments of a troubled cultural politics (needing *muruhara*, or redress of grievance and forgiveness) underscore Mita's resolute determination to counter-colonise the Western gaze and to construct challenging work which undercuts the reification of noble savage stereotyping that was definably operative even in such an "enlightened" film as *Broken Barrier*, which, Mita noted, is anchored in a Pākehā frame "and is naïve and romantic."[20]

The Afrikaner academic David Novitz once observed that "The history of European settlement in New Zealand can properly be understood as a lengthy struggle between the indigenous and the imported."[21] This is the point to observe that Mita's work, as naturalised "film anthropology," refreshingly avoids fetishistic and voyeuristic looking at "the Other" (in Mulveyan terms of scopophilic visual pleasure) and, instead, presents Māori culture as *sui generis*, subject to its own internal codes and occasionally mystificatory systems of signification, in places firmly resistant to the Pākehā Gaze and its corrosive stereotypes. It is this non-apologetic internal exploration of a community tied together by *whakapapa* relationships which I am dubbing the transfigured Māori Gaze. This gaze is a clear inversion of the Pākehā "outsider" one, and that probably accounts for the satiric "white minstrelsy" as stereotypes of Māori are deconstructed and replaced by comically inverse ones of Pākehā (most outrageously in the land-hungry and deranged father of Steve Semmons). Such parodic figurations heighten both the reality and normality of Māori as *tangata whenua* (a previously caricatured and unduly romanticised *ethne*) and decolonise simplistic Pākehā tropes while furthering the postcolonising model of citizenship which is the film's primary concern.

Mita herself (b. 1942 of Ngāti Pikiao and Ngāi Te Rangi) received a traditional Māori upbringing in Maketū (a Bay of Plenty town on the Waihi Estuary), and her own experience informs her work as director, producer and screenplay writer for *Mauri*. As James Ritchie, defining "biculturalism," has noted, Pākehā culture "is dominant by power, history and majority. Māori culture is dominant by a longer history, by legacy and by its strength of survival and the passionate commitment of its people."[22] This reads as a *de facto* summation of the "textual unconscious" of *Mauri*, a critical film in exploring the contested discourse[23] of intermarriage in 1950s Aotearoa. This troubling subject had earlier been explored in David Ausubel's *The Fern and the Tiki* (1960) and the remarkable "relationship films" of John O'Shea, all of which essentially naturalised Pākehā presence while accepting Māori *integritas* as the first occupants of Aotearoa and attempting to validate cross-ethnic liaisons. *Mauri* problematises and troubles the ethnic categories on both sides of the Treaty partnership "fence" as it also explores the fracturing and survival of a closed, context-bound sub-community called Te Mata, which operates on the necessarily restrictive, land-based codes (*tikanga*) of Māoridom. *Mauri* accepts that the irredentist sub-nationalism of the Māori sovereignty movement (*imperium in imperio*) will need to merge with the dominant Euro-culture at some level, and in its fusion shall transform the full New Zealand polity. This nascent recognition seems to underlie Mita's dramatisation of the inter-ethnic relationship between Steve Semmons and Ramiri, which functions metonymically in refurbishing the founding national parable of inclusion.

Mauri insists on bridging the two primary cultures of Aotearoa (white and brown) without diluting the indigenous one into patronising gestures of assimilation or vacuous biculturalism, and Mita's genius has been to frontally acknowledge past historical grievances and insist that macro-scale social progress can only be effected by a focus on the quality of relationships between Māori and Pākehā at the micro (local) level. It is here that the concept of "mauri" needs fleshing out; and it is vital to acknowledge that, like so many indigenous tropes, it cannot be reduced to a translatable singular meaning. Williams parsed its several connotations, principally "Life principle, [or] thymos of man"[24] and Johansen limned the broad overarching meaning of relational inter-connectedness that Mita's film intends when explaining that

The whole cosmos of the Maori unfolds itself as a gigantic "kin," in which heaven and earth are first parents of all beings and things, such as the sea, the sand on the beach, the wood, the birds, and man.[25]

Romancing the reconstructed Pākehā

Merata Mita had doughty Pākehā allies and even married one herself (Geoff Murphy), which may be why the unsung hero of this film is a Pākehā farmer (Steve Semmons), who tells his racist father that local Maori are "my friends; I grew up with them," after which Semmens Senior feigns a heart attack, having screamed in rage at the news that his son plans to marry Ramiri. In a way this odd scene spoofs a very serious thematic: where Patrick Evans writes confusingly about the unconscious desire of the Pākehā cultural nationalists to "become Maori,"[26] the real social pressure was for apparently beleaguered Maori to become brown-skinned Pākehā, which was for many not an inviting assimilationist proposition even when genteelly outlined by the bureaucrat Jack Hunn in 1962. Sir Tipene O'Regan addressed this issue of political discourse after the Don Brash "Orewa Speech," or one-nation political fiasco (27 January 2004), when the Leader of the National Party attacked biculturalism and a drift towards racial separatism in New Zealand. O'Regan gave serious thought to ways in which Western ideas have insinuated themselves under the carapace of indigenous Māori culture and progressively colonised it. O'Regan observed that "the carapace remains Maori but the essential body within it is an amalgam of global ideas and language, almost entirely Western."[27] Mita is conducting an audit for meaningful resistance which strongly asserts the resilience of Māori culture to withstand, and adapt to, Westocentric pressures, and *Mauri* pre-emptively critiques "Ngati [Tribe] Redneckery" views like Brash's politicised statement: "We cannot allow the loose threads of nineteenth-century law and custom to unravel our attempts at nation-building in the twenty-first century" (Brash).[28] *Mauri* is unquestionably a revisionist cinema text which sharply interrogates New Zealand's myths of harmonious "race relations." Set in the reactionary 1950s,[29] *Mauri* is also that rare entity: a jurisprudential work in cinematic form which enacts a complex, historicised vision of the complex cultural and legal issues which underpin all sincere attempts to build a culture of genuine social equity. *Mauri*, furthermore, has delivered an art-rich "erotics" of place and time onto the silver screen.[30]

The migration of tradition and "The Māori Gaze"

Ranginui Walker has followed the work of Joan Metge and others in noting that a post-Second World War urban migration further depleted the stock of mana Māori that was encapsulated in "rural tribal enclaves" and exposed the web of tradition to "the full assimilationist ethos of metropolitan society."[31] It is the consequences of this urban drift away from rurally "grounded" *mana whenua* (land-based regional authority) that *Mauri* explores. The trope of the *mauri* is shown as a cohesive life principle in Mita's potent and profound work of cinema art, as the film's *mythos* encompasses birth, a male existential crisis, issues of identity, the appropriation of another's *wairua*, ageing, death and the transition from a terrestrial *tūrangawaewae* to *Hawaiki* (the spirit world). Mita may be deemed what

David Maybury-Lewis has termed an "ethnic entrepreneur,"[32] and the avatar of resistance for enclaved and marginalised First People in *Mauri* is the *kuia* Kara (played with superb calm and power by the principled activist and land protestor Eva Rickard).

Mauri was released in 1988, at a time when South Africa was mired in a violent state of emergency, Mandela was still incarcerated, Thatcher and Reagan were refusing to support economic sanctions against that monstrous apartheid *regime*, and New Zealand was timidly plying a tepid "official biculturalism" while structural neo-liberal microeconomic reforms were tearing the heart out of much Māori employment. The one sign of hope emerged in 1987 in an appeal case of nationwide constitutional significance which re-defined the Treaty of Waitangi within a postcolonial frame. Intriguingly, this reframing underpins the conceptual structure of resistance in *Mauri*. The late Lord Cooke of Thorndon (as President of the NZ Court of Appeal) had enunciated a truly empowering reversal of the infamous, positivist and triumphalistic *Wi Parata* judgement (*Wi Parata v Bishop of Wellington* (1877) 3NZ Jur (NS) SC 72) in the heart-stopping "Lands Case" in the NZ Court of Appeal (*NZ Maori Council v Attorney-General* (1987) 1 NZLR 641). The *Wi Parata case*, coming after the C19 Land Wars, denied the Treaty any legal or juridical significance in the settler colony, whereas the latter case insisted that it is a *de jure* state contract which founded the modern "New Zealand" nation in 1840. *Mauri* arrived, as the product of a former member of Nga Tamatoa, to address a real world in which the pernicious twins of bureaucratic legality and expediency were still in the ascendant, but its plotline frontally addressed these as the film advances the cause of mental-intellectual decolonisation from what Charles Fay once called the "informal empire."[33] Robin Winks once pithily noted that New Zealand was originally "annexed, settled and turned into the market garden of the empire" but went on to act as a state agent of "what may be called ricochet imperialism."[34] Winks deployed this term to describe New Zealand's protectorate in Western Samoa (1920–62), but one can insist usefully on a metaphoric reading in which the colonial Pākehā state exerted ongoing paternalistic control over its Māori citizens as *de facto* wards needing shepherding to attain citizenship. *Mauri* is a film text which illustrates the resilience of colonised mindsets (Fanon and Cesaire)[35] and dramatises the fact (so resonant in New Zealand) that "Perhaps the final irony of informal empire was that precisely because it was informal, it was the most tenacious of all."[36] Mita keeps her focus steadily on the micro-dynamics of resistance to localised sub-imperial pressures, such that her symbol of hope in *Mauri* is actually an enlightened Pākehā farmer's son who starts to decolonise his own assumptions of superiority (shown vividly when early in the film he interrupted a *tohi* ceremony and wimpily pleaded to the unhappy *tangata whenua*, "I didn't mean to offend. Sorry."). Later he told Wiremu Rapana he would "do anything" for Ramiri; and, when challenged as to what that would really mean (in the context of his father's cruel appropriation of the Rapana farmland as a form of micro-*raupatu*, or land confiscation after conquest), Steve declared that he will give "everything" to her.

What Duncan Petrie has called the film's "complex contemplation of colonial oppression"[37] is no identikit PC modelling of human relationships distorted by the pressures of the imperialist project. On the contrary, Mita's Māori males can be disloyal, and some of them act with stupefying folly (not all of which is traceable to colonialist oppression and conditioning), as seen in the angry and treacherous Herb (Bernard Rua), the appalling actions of jailbird Paki Selwyn Hemapō (Anzac Wallace) and the naïvely ambitious "Young Cop" (Temuera Morrison). In Mita's cinematic account of New Zealand life lived under the duress of informal (local Pākehā control) and formal (state-centric) "empire," it is a fundamental lack of *rangatiratanga* (agency) in a range of social contexts which drives much rage, anger and confusion within the indigenous community. Kara observes that "The Pākehā can be a lousy beggar"; and Rickard should know, after her *kuia*'s tribal land was taken by the Crown during the Second World War for an airstrip for the war effort but was never returned and became the Raglan Golf Course. Mita analogises that appallingly arrogant act of Crown/State hegemony in the *faux* consultation about the Māori youth offenders' rehabilitation centre at Te Mata, a *fait accompli* which mocks the principle of active partnership and a fiduciary relationship as implied in the Treaty of Waitangi and which Lord Cooke had declared in 1987 (when *Mauri* was being filmed) to be a cardinal principle of the Crown's obligations to Māori in te Tiriti.[38] Te Mata may be a realm of sheep, gorse and ragwort, but its inhabitants could at least experience some agency (*rangatiratanga*) there due to its isolation – that is, until the Justice Department planned a rehabilitation centre for lawless urban Māori youth there without the courtesy of any proper *iwi* consultation. A mono-legal regime was never contemplated under the Treaty,[39] and the 1987 Lands Case expressly established the legal principle that the New Zealand constitution is duadic, protecting the indigenism of Ngā Tāngata Whenua Māori as partners in a postcolonising society, "with a right to parity of status."[40] Certainly, shared cultural power was on Merata Mita's agenda that year: while on the *Mauri* shoot, she noted of Kiwi films that "So far we've seen a total domination of a kind of white, male, middle-class look at New Zealand. The big screen hasn't been shared with us."[41] Mita was already a key change-agent and cultural *kaitiaki* (guardian figure) in assuming the right of Māori self-representation.

In *Mauri*, Mita is implicitly espousing a model of indigenous bi nationalism, seeking self-determining autonomy for Māori and the evolution of a mature postcolonial social contract.[42] *Mauri* demonstrates the fissures opening up between rural and urbanised Māori, as we see embodied in the fatal conflict between Herb and Willy Rapana for leadership of their urban gang, both men making the unhappy transition as *tūtūā* (landless ones) from rural *tūrangawaewae* to an alienating Pākehā polity, shown when Willy is executed outside an urban pub in a clear gangland set-up.[43] The film splendidly demonstrates what is lost, in terms of grounding, when the *iwi*-based hunter-gatherer or farm-based lifestyle is exchanged for the Pākehā "Big Smoke"; and Mita's text sharply exposes the cynical administrative view of the Treaty as a mere aboriginal consent document, dramatised in the abrupt and horrendous visit by Pākehā Justice Department officials and their Māori compradors who, pressed for time, run through a line of *kuia* and shamefully violate *marae kawa* (protocol). Behind this abysmal misbehaviour lay the operant "deep structure" which allowed arrogant, misinformed (or cynical) Pākehā to deploy clientelism in their treatment of New Zealand's First People. And, it fuelled Mita's clear understanding of Māori disempowerment from her historical location in the angry and divisive 1980s, with an indigeneity discourse not seeking secession but, rather, "about forging a new social contract" for the twin Treaty partners so as to learn the art of "living together differently."[44]

For its part, *Mauri* is an impressive part of a strategy of collective remembering, resistance and resilience, and this is accomplished through a thorough-going reversal of the Pākehā Gaze. Mita's filmmaking praxis of a transfigured Māori Gaze also enacts a scopophilic *exposé* of Pākehā folly in the over-the-top but dangerous actions of Mr Semmens Senior (Geoff Murphy) in his madcap persecution of Awatea and in his rage and racist hate speech and behaviour, in sneakily stealing tribal land from the Rapanas under a false pretext. Yet Mr Semmens' deranged offensiveness suggests the power of the *mauri* of the land and allows space for his son to overcome Evans' "long forgetting" about Māori dispossession. That said, Mita's praxis with respect to Semmens Senior displaces a standard Occidental voyeurism and Orientalising of Māori, subjecting one Pākehā man (a standard cinematic icon of systemic neo-colonialism) to the indignity of being watched in an active, controlling and irreverent sense by Mita's camera. When he later pointed a gun at Paki, yelling "I'll kill you all" before dying of heart failure, Kara invites us to read this seizure as a judgement for his abuse of Māori *wairua*. Humour is a potent way to deconstruct power dynamics, and Mita has ebulliently satirised white paranoia, yet a serious underlying thematic intention emerges from such mania: the suggestion that Mr Semmens is *pōrangi* (out of his mind) due to offending the *mauri* of the land (which he improperly stole from the Rapana *whānau* in collusion with a local district council).

Constitutional power-sharing and a decolonising vision are what *Mauri* envisons, out of the troubled 1980s context which gave birth to the film; but this humane vision is executed through the profoundly emotive and seductive potency of art to spur the imagination and, ultimately, to challenge mainstream thinking about the need for Aotearoa to end the prevalent internal neutering of indigeneity. Mita's vision in *Mauri* clearly looks to the renewal of the wisdom of "the old people" that Macmillan Brown had prematurely declared as lost amidst "the twilight of the gods" of Polynesia,[45] and towards fostering equality and healing, and even reconfiguring the nation to become a New Aotearoa. Ranginui Walker reminds us that New Zealand was for well over a century after the Waitangi charter "a homogenous repressive society ruled by the white male patriarchy" and that the historical process of colonisation experienced by Māori "involved cultural invasion by missionaries, exploitation of resources by privateers, conquistadors and traders, and political domination by colonial administrations."[46] Where Macmillan Brown arrogantly asserted that the arrival of Europeans "into the Pacific" was liberatory, with missionaries who "flashed light upon the chaotic absurdities of the *tapu* system," and that "rum and a new religion broke the chains that shackled the Polynesian soul,"[47] Mita would disagree with his Pākehā triumphalism. Her film is situated in a Māori world that was diminished after the impact of the Tohunga Suppression Act 1907, one in which Pākehā greed has infected deracinated urban Māori and in which the mores of the "ancient order" have been significantly eroded.

Where Patrick Evans writes of imbecilic, arrogant Pākehā *littérateurs* dreaming of "Becoming Maori," Mita's steady focus is on what John Rangihau called the more difficult process of "Being Maori"[48] in a complacent and aggressive monoculture, as she refurbishes, via cinematic narrative, the era of "the old people," but when *tohunga* are often unavailable. So Paki has to ritually cleanse himself and perform his own rehabilitative act of *utu* for the violation of *tapu* in the film's deeply moving finale.[49] Furthermore, Mita accepts a metaphysical world in which Māori are fully capable of what Michel Foucault termed "subjectification" (constituting themselves as subjects and objects of their *own* knowledge) and also possess the agency – despite what Belich called the huge human tsunami of Pākehā settlers after 1860[50] – to reconstitute themselves as agents by deploying "subjugated knowledge."

In *Mauri* the *tangata whenua* emphatically do not want to "become Pākehā" and assimilate into a state of further abjectness. Rather, Mita's core characters resist objectification by the coloniser, and when Ramiri marries Steve Semmens, the film's emancipatory politics envisions a bicultural fusion and, through Steve's generosity to the Rapana *hapū*, the return of stolen Māori land. Steve clearly accedes to this recognition of indigenous alterity when he tells the departing Paki, "One day that boy's going to have to know who his father is." Similarly, Mita's healing art allows space for Pākehā to undergo conceptual change: while Steve's grim, testy Pākehā gaze interrupted the afterbirth ceremony and he was abused by Ramiri for that at the film's opening, he is later shown to be highly protective of Awatea, and as finally redeeming himself by several positive acts of commitment to his Māori neighbours and, ultimately, kin by marriage. All this is simply to assert that *Mauri* strenuously avoids ethical (and ethnic) essentialism, reminding us of Keri Hulme's statement that "Like or loathe the fact, the Mauri of New Zealand is now part-pakeha."[51] Semmens Senior has no place for such a generous vision, calling Ramiri a "spook," stating that the Māori "hate us" and calling Awatea a "tar-baby," later threatening to shoot her and deriding the prospect of miscegenation (decrying the production of "dirty black grandchildren"). This is much more typical of a racist rhetoric used by land-obsessed Pākehā until relatively recent times, and sadly expresses the settler "political unconscious." Not surprisingly, *Mauri* tracks a movement towards an autochthonous "Maori Sublime,"[52] an in-house Māori conversation, yet one intended to be shared with receptive members of the dominant culture (i.e. within the national framework), and one that unproblematically celebrates a Māori epistemology, world-view and ontological system (*Kaupapa Māori*) in a work of what Barry Barclay called emergent "Fourth Cinema."[53]

Mita has produced a postcolonising cinema art which provides, in Iris Murdoch's words, "a sustained *experienced* mental synthesis," a cultural ecology brought to life via a visual discourse which resists the incursions of Western structuralism and "demythologisation, the removal of the transcendent."[54] As Murdoch explains, this kind of work of art allows us to see the world as a "limited whole":

The ability to see (or feel) depends on keeping close to the reality of the world, accepting the facts and following the stream of life. This is described as "mystical." Within the "limits" of our "finite nature" we are able to feel or intuit the world as a whole, though not as a totally comprehended whole.[55]

This is precisely what Kara does by keeping in touch with her *atua* and the tribal *kawa* of her *tipuna* and also by inducting Awatea into the subtleties of a Māori metaphysic (*taha wairua*), the convincing and very moving demonstration of which ends the film. Mita has worked hard to recuperate what Barry Barclay has termed "the dignity of sovereignty,"[56] and she has written eloquently about "the struggle to regain a positive self-concept, to restore self-respect, and to salvage what may be left of a fragmented and exploited culture"[57] in which indigenous "spirituality [is] continuously under attack,"[58] which was clearly her project in making *Mauri*. As Mita once wrote, the Māori filmmaker "carries the burden of having to correct the past and will therefore be concerned with demystifying and decolonising the screen." In that context, Mita described *Mauri* as "a probing enquiry into concepts of culture" and a relentless and uncompromising "parable about the schizophrenic existence of so many Māori in Pākehā society."[59] In this delimited and negative (or non-expansive) sense, Mita proffers what Graeme Turner called a "National Fiction,"[60] with an edge lacking in Barclay's *Ngati* (1987), which, by comparison, seems in its under-texture, elysian, bucolic and even evangelical in its celebration of an East Cape indigenous community.

Mauri is much more explicitly a counter-colonising film than the beautiful but "subfusc" *Ngati*.[61] Mita insists on the distinctiveness of the *tangata whenua* rather than seeing them, in deficit terms, as an embattled minority in their own land. *Mauri* explores the appalling violation of the *mana* and *mauri* of a Māori man (Rewi Rapana) by a fellow Māori (Paki Selwyn Hemapō) who has gone wildly astray in the city into petty crime (foreshadowing Duff's *One Night Out Stealing* (1992)) and later violating the *mea tapu* of his own people. Fleeing a botched bank burglary, where he acted as the gang's lookout, Paki (Anzac Wallace) hot-wired an escape vehicle and drove south from Auckland, collecting Rewi Rapana as a hitch-hiker on the drive south-west of Hamilton. Exhausted and stressed, Paki fell asleep at the wheel, the car veered off the road and crashed, killing Rapana. Panicking, Paki removed Rapana's wallet, medal, bone carving and coat, hauled him into the driver's seat and pushed the vehicle further down the slope, whence it plunged down onto the rocks of a tideline, exploding and incinerating Rapana. Worse than these appalling depredations, to escape the tentacles of the Pākehā law, Paki assumed (appropriated) Rewi's identity and seriously violated both his *mana* and personal *mauri*. This extremely unconscionable violation of *tapu* understandably causes Paki much psychic and spiritual pain and leads him into living a double-life, fooling Willy Rapana [Willie Rapana], Ramiri (whom he cannot marry), Hemi and Kara, and the wider *hapū* community.

It is only as Kara is clearly approaching her end that Paki summons the courage to inform the already suspicious *kuia* of his dire *hara* (shortcoming/"sin") against her *hapū* after he has heard the local doctor (Joanna E. Paiana Paul) discussing the seriousness of Kara's pneumonia. He enters Kara's *whare* (dwelling) and confesses to his past as an 11-year-old urban runaway-rebel who had to steal food and clothes. Paki tells Kara that Rewi had explained the feud with the Semmens family and how the Rapanas were forced to leave the district 20 years earlier. Paki says, "Slowly the shadow of the dead man overtook me until my world was too dark to live in. My name is Paki Selwyn Hemapō of Ngāti Wero." Placing Rewi's bone carving in Kara's hands, the *kuia* acts as a *matakite* (family seer) to him and soberly declares:

> You must remain a fugitive until you have put right the wrong you did to my nephew, Rewi. He's gone; nothing will bring him back. Go to where he is and take his medallion and his *taonga*. You ask for forgiveness [...]. The Pākehā don't understand our tapu. The aura of death is heavy upon you.

They *hongi* (touch noses) as Kara sings a *waiata tangi* (a song of mourning/funereal plaint). Steve Semmens then acts as a decoy to the police (who are spying on Kara's *whare*) so Paki can escape to fulfil his ritual obligation/oblation for breaching *ritenga* (an ordinance of *tapu*) at the crash site, which happens to be beside the shoreline, which was the perfect locale for a *tohunga* (sacred man) to release a person from the restriction of the law of *tapu*, according to Edward Shortland.

After a *matakite* declared the offence and the identity of the avenging spirit/*atua* (both of which, of course, Paki knew), Shortland asserted that traditionally the family *tohunga* used "charms" to discover the path of the spirit ("the road by which the spirit came on earth"[62]). He thus proceeds:

> Going to the river or sea-side, he [the *tohunga*] dips his head beneath the surface of the water, while the relatives most interested in the cure remain seated on the shore to witness his success. Perhaps he does not succeed the first time; so he dips his head in the water a second time. If not then successful, the third time is probably enough; and, raising his head, he assures the anxious spectators that he has seen the path, and that the spirit came from below upwards through a flax bush, or the stem of toetoe, as the case may be [...].[63]

Shortland insisted that the *matakite* and *tohunga* must both be members of the same *hapū* (sub-tribal group) and that the spirits of the dead/*atua* (who dwell beneath the earth in Te Reinga) have the power to return to earth as objects or people and "are believed to be constantly watching over the living" for infractions of sacred *tapu*.[64] This is why Paki must take Rewi's *taonga* (which holds Rewi's sacred *mauri*) to the death-site and appeal, ritualistically in *te reo* (Māori language), for the propitiation of his crimes against Rewi Rapana's *mauri* and *hapū*. Paki has to be his own *tohunga*, suggesting that the outward face of tradition has changed under the pressures of colonisation and local circumstances, but *not* the fundamental practices and active ethics required to restore *hapū* equilibrium (*utu*) and Paki's *mana* into a state of balance. As Jean Smith has asserted, *mana* in Māori culture "was a fluid quality, supernaturally given and taken," and the presence of the attributes of *mana* ("courage, success, repute, hospitality and leadership") was variable and "seen as an

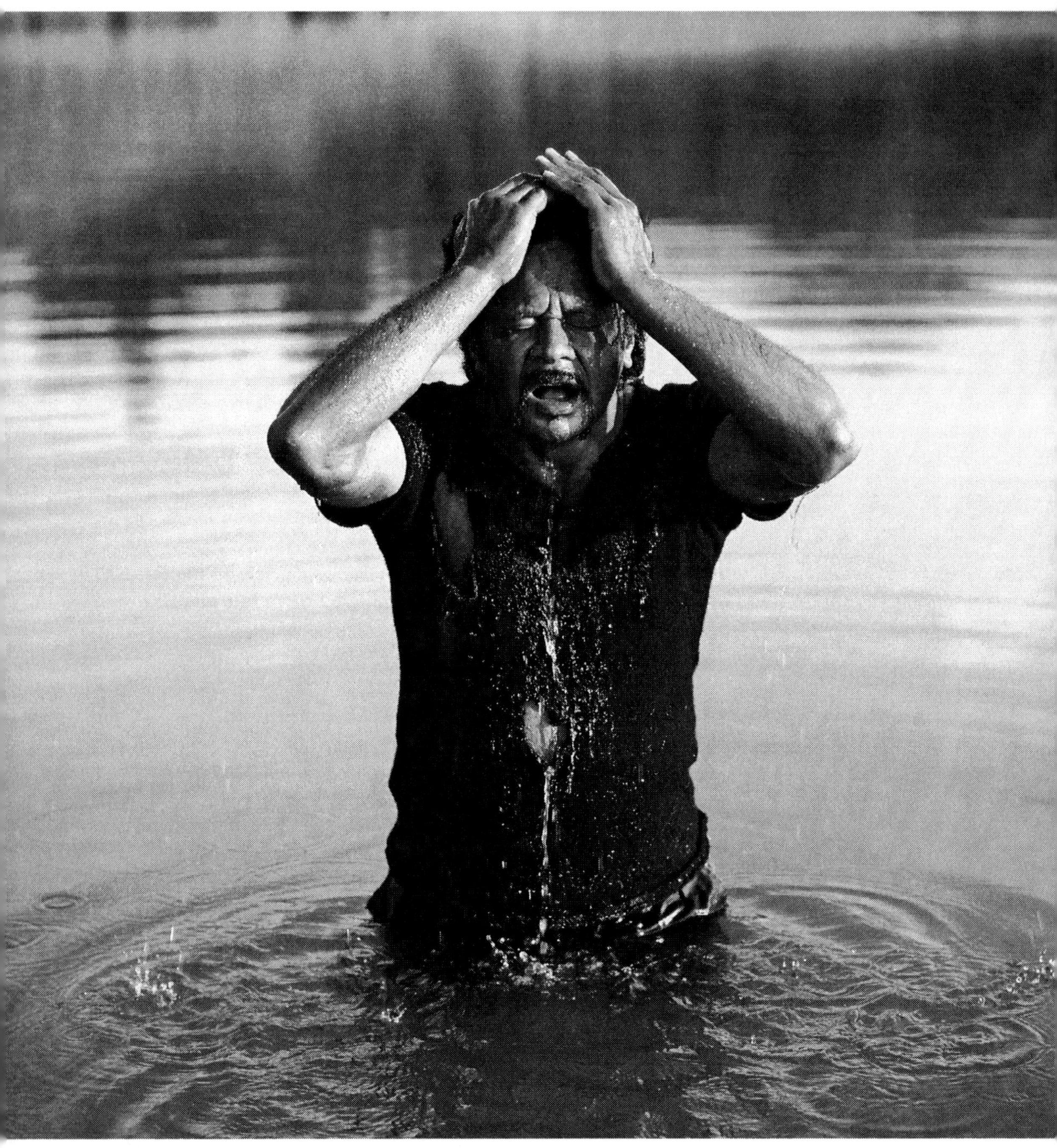

Paki (Anzac Wallace) ritually cleanses himself and frees his *mauri* from his *hara* (transgression), in *Mauri*, 1988, dir. Merata Mita. Photograph by Victoria Ginn.

index of a man's standing with his ancestral *atua*."[65] Thus Paki has imperilled Rewi Rapana's status and "virtue" and, by violating *tapu*, Paki has certainly compromised his own *mana* and the protection of the gods, enduring shame and *whakamomore* (despair) until he enacts the rituals of forgiveness and contrition which Kara insisted he must perform. Paki admits to Ramiri, when she tells him he was the father of her child, "I've broken more than Māori laws"; and on the run from the police, Paki has a vision of a horde of *wero*-chanting warriors on the seashore challenging him to act honourably after he has damaged the *mauri* of the Rapana kin group.

The succeeding and stunning montage must be studied carefully for its associative logic and acutely visual communication of the concept of *mauri* as it cross-cuts from sunrise to an image of Paki signing a chant at the place of Rewi's death, to an image of Kara's mountain in dawnlight, to Hemi chanting beside Kara's bed; to Paki again, ritually seeking absolution for *hara* and crying aloud; to a beautifully framed shot of Awatea looking in the window of her granny's *whare*; to Paki offering Rewi his stolen *taonga*; and then to Kara easefully breathing her last and Awatea running up her mountain. (The visual design here is a *tour de force* and surely owes much to Ralph Hotere, the film's production designer). In the final moments, we see the old (Don Selwyn) and young cop (Temuera Morrison) moving in on Paki on the rock shelf as he *tangis*, and the next cut reveals Awatea running (blended with a vision of keening *kuia*, or senior women), then we see the old cop embrace Paki and *hongi* with him, giving the Pākehā handcuffs, a symbolic trope of Pākehā oppression from Parihaka onwards. Paki surrenders his hands to the cuffs and holds them up, almost in a parodic gesture expressive of Black Power. The film then cuts abruptly back to its central focus on Kara and her *hapū* as we see a heron (*kōtuku*: harbinger of death) soaring in a clear blue sky (to the sound of wind alone), and the film grants us a Kara's eye view from her spirit as it swoops over her *tūrangawaewae* (core place of being). Next, the image of Awatea running up Kara's mount blends with one of Kara's view ascending up and over her mountain as Awatea reaches its summit and, in a heart-breaking gesture, waves a cloth expansively to farewell her beloved grandmother on her way to Te Reinga and, ultimately, on to Hawaiki. In the final freeze frame images of the film, an affecting close-up of a tear-stricken Awatea is splendidly intercut with Kara's high circling view (as heron), gradually pulling away to the north – an image redolent with compressed cultural-spiritual meaning.

Such deep filmic alchemy is rare in the brief canon of New Zealand cinema. It assuredly points to the centrality of the values of the *wharepuni* (meeting house), where Steve and Ramiri are married and where Kara will soon be farewelled. As Sir Tipene O'Regan has asserted, for Māori the *wharepuni* "was and remains the symbol of collective unity, ancestry and tribal memory" as it constitutes a living "tabernacle."[66] It is this intensely political understanding which *Mauri* validates and celebrates in its exploration of the multiple stresses produced by colonisation even as it proffers a pathway for all New Zealanders to join in a united future built on a sturdy, health-giving recognition of cultural difference (without indulging in the scare-mantra about a "politics of division and different kinds of identity"),[67] but with shared aspirations built upon mutual respect and understanding. The "deep structure" of *Mauri* recalls Nadine Gordimer's insightful statement – which resonates, albeit differently, with both Māori and Pākehā – that

> home is not necessarily where you belong ethnogenetically, but rather the place you were born to, the faces you first saw around you, and the elements of the situation among your fellow men in which you found yourself and with which you have been struggling, politically, personally or artistically, all your life.[68]

Thus Steve Semmons' union with Ramiri heals the Millerian "donation of history" (i.e. his father's violent form of *raupatu*) and acts as a positive, rehabilitative expression of *utu* for the Rapana kin group.

Mauri is a genuine *tino rangatiratanga* text (celebrating tribal, land-based power and authority) in the same sense as Hulme's *the bone people* (1984): it is a work which insists on the continued reality of cultural and spiritual differences – and *rangatira* rights – but which also acts as a prophetic, educative, bridging "hope-text" pointing the way to national maturation for the New Zealand polity. In Gordimer's words, the "rethinking, remaking needed" should generate concepts that will "penetrate the cataract of preconceptions grown over our vision."[69] She added a hope which seems to animate *Mauri* as well, when describing "the artist as prophet of the resolution of divided cultures"[70] – the prospect that if white culture will remake itself, indigenist culture will accept this as kindred work by people who have "struck down into liens with an indigenous culture."[71] As O'Regan has asserted, there is an urgent moral imperative abroad "to re-shape New Zealand's political culture so that people are actually dealing with the questions and not with the slogans."[72] It is not at all far-fetched to assert that in *Mauri*, by fusing the lessons of the past with cautious hope for the uncharted postcolonial future, Merata Mita has shown a viable pathway out of that all-too-prevalent New Zealand labyrinth of prejudice and unreason.

Notes

1. Merata Mita, "The Soul and the Image," in *Film in Aotearoa New Zealand*, ed. Jonathan Dennis and Jan Bieringa (Wellington: Victoria University Press, 1992), 51.
2. I owe the locution "educultural" to Professor Angus Hakairo Macfarlane, University of Canterbury.
3. Loehr; cited by Chris Hedges, *American Fascists: The Christian Right and the War on America* (2007; reprint London: Vintage Books, 2008), 11.
4. Nadine Gordimer, "Where Do Whites Fit In? (1959)," in *The Essential Gesture: Writing, Politics and Places*, ed. Stephen Clingman (New York: Alfred A. Knopf, 1988), 33.
5. See Donna Awatere, *Maori Sovereignty* (1982; reprint Auckland: Broadsheet Magazine, 1984).
6. Ranginui Walker, "KORERO: Graveyard or Seedbed," *New Zealand Listener* (8 April 1989): 31.
7. Cited by Arthur Miller, "Uneasy about the Germans: After the Wall" (1990); reprint in *Echoes Down the Corridor: Collected Essays 1944–2000*, ed. Steven R. Centola (2000; reprint New York: Penguin Books, 2001), 229.

8. Nicolas Tredell, ed., *Cinemas of the Mind: A Critical History of Film Theory* (Duxford, Cambridge: Icon Books, 2002), 9.

9. John Macmillan Brown, *Peoples & Problems of the Pacific* (London: T. Fisher Unwin, 1927), Vol. 1, 176.

10. Ibid., 175.

11. Peter Craven, "Introduction," "Made in England: Australia's British Inheritance" (David Malouf), *Quarterly Essay* (Melbourne: Black Inc., 2003), Issue 12, vi.

12. James Belich, *Paradise Reforged: A History of the New Zealanders From the 1880s to the Year 2000* (Honolulu: University of Hawai'i Press, 2001), 338.

13. Germaine Greer, *Whitefella Jump Up: The Shortest Way to Nationhood* (*Quarterly Essay* 2003; reprint London: Profile Books, 2004), 90. I am indebted to Andrew Dean for drawing this essay to my attention.

14. Ibid., 119.

15. Susan Y. Najita, *Decolonizing Cultures in the Pacific: Reading History and Trauma in Contemporary Fiction* (New York and London: Routledge, 2006; reprint 2008); blurb statement.

16. Gordimer, *The Essential Gesture*, 34.

17. Mita, "The Soul and the Image," 49.

18. Ibid., 36.

19. Ibid., 41, 42.

20. Ibid., 44.

21. David Novitz, "On Culture and Cultural Identity," in *Culture and Identity in New Zealand* (Wellington: GP Books, 1989), 277.

22. James Ritchie, *Becoming Bicultural* (Wellington: Huia Publishers/Daphne Brasell Associates Press, 1992), 6.

23. "Discourse" as understood in a Foucaultian manner as "language or image with its socio-cultural roots exposed and its socio-cultural effects revealed." Myra Macdonald, *Exploring Media Discourse* (Oxford: Arnold, 2003), 10.

24. H. W. Williams, *A Dictionary of the Maori Language*, 7th ed. (Wellington: Government Printer, 1985), 197.

25. J. Prytz Johansen, *The Maori and His Religion in Its Non-Ritualistic Aspects: With a Danish Summary* (Copenhagen: Ejnar Munksgaard, 1954), 9.

26. Patrick Evans, *The Long Forgetting: Post-colonial Literary Culture in New Zealand* (Christchurch: Canterbury University Press, 2007), 156–57. This is code for achieving indigeneity (p. 156) and its cruder manifestations were wickedly mocked by Janet Frame in her novel *A State of Siege* (Christchurch: The Pegasus Press, 1966).

27. Sir Tipene O'Regan "The Weka, the Snare and Discourse in the New Zealand Village" (2 December 2004). Inaugural "Out of the Square" Lecture (University of Canterbury/Christchurch City Council).

28. Don Brash (Leader of HM Opposition and National Party), "Nationhood" (27 January 2004); "Brash's blueprint," *Dominion Post* (28 January 2004). Speech at www.national.org.nz/ wcontent.asp?PageID=100019353 (30 January 2004) or www.national.org.nz/speech_article. aspx?ArticleID=1614.

29. The timeframe is subtly established by a famous framed photograph of Queen Elizabeth II taken after her Coronation in 1953, which at one point is glimpsed hanging on the wall of the Te Mata Police Station. One also hung in Sir Winston Churchill's study at Chartwell (Kent).

30. Susan Sontag, "Against Interpretation" (1964), in Sontag, *Against Interpretation* (London: Vintage, 1994), 3–14.

31. R. J. Walker, "Maori Identity," in *Culture and Identity in New Zealand*, ed. David Novitz and Bill Willmott (Wellington: GP Books, 1989), 49.

32. David Maybury-Lewis, *Indigenous Peoples, Ethnic Groups, and the State* (Boston & London: Allyn and Bacon, 1997), 121.

33. Robin W. Winks cited Fay's 1934 book *Imperial Economy and Its Place in the Formation of Economic Doctrine, 1600–1932* in "On Decolonization and Informal Empire," *The American Historical Review* 81, no. 3 (June 1976): 544

34. Ibid., 546. Winks noted that the more common term was "colonial subimperialism."

35. Aime Cesaire, *Discourse on Colonialism* (New York: Monthly Review Press, 1972), and Franz Fanon, *The Wretched of the Earth* (1965; reprint Harmondsworth: Penguin Books, 1967).

36. Winks, "On Decolonization," 556.

37. Duncan Petrie, *Shot in New Zealand: The Art and Craft of the Kiwi Cinematographer* (Auckland: Random House NZ, 2007), 133.

38. See Philip A. Joseph, *Constitutional and Administrative Law in New Zealand* (Sydney: The Law Book Co., 1993), 71–72; and J. G. A. Pocock, "Burke and the Ancient Constitution," *Historical Journal* 3 (1960): 125–43.

39. E. T. Durie, "Will the Settlers Settle? Cultural Conciliation and Law," *Otago Law Review* 8 (1996): 449ff.

40. Roger Maaka and Augie Fleras, *The Politics of Indigeneity: Challenging the State in Canada and Aotearoa* (Dunedin: University of Otago, 2005), 71. This alludes to pan-Māori or multi-tribal configurations, which used a common "Māori" front as a sensible (if ahistoric) strategic essentialism to counter the dominant state discourses so as to access some power and resources.

41. Merata Mita; *New Zealand Cinema: The Past Decade* (front-person Alison Parr): *Kaleidoscope* (TVNZ, 1987).

42. See Maaka and Fleras, *The Politics of Indigeneity*.

43. The film suggests that Herb has used the issue of Willy supporting a Māori woman intermarrying with a rich Pākehā (whose unhinged father stole Rapana land) as a grievance worthy of unseating Willy.

44. Maaka and Fleras, *The Politics of Indigeneity*, 103.

45. Macmillan Brown, *Peoples & Problems of the Pacific*, Vol. II (London: T. Fisher Unwin, 1927), 61.

46. Ranginui Walker; cited by Paul Spoonley, *Mata Toa: The Life and Times of Ranginui Walker* (Auckland: Penguin Group, 2009), 176.

47. See Brown, *People & Problems*, 73–78.

48. See John Rangihau, "Being Maori," in *Te Ao Hurihuri, The World Moves On: Aspects of Maoritanga*, ed. Michael King (Auckland: Hicks Smith/Methuen, 1977).

49. See Allan Hanson and Louise Hanson, *Counterpoint in Maori Culture* (London and Boston: Routledge and Kegan Paul, 1983), 142–46 on redressing abuses and violations in traditional Maori cultural practice.

50. See James Belich, *Replenishing the Earth: The Settler Revolution and the Rise of the Anglo World, 1783–1939* (Oxford: Oxford University Press, 2009).

51. Keri Hulme, Personal Letter to Harding, 24 March 1987.

52. I mean to adopt Jonathan Lamb's concept of "aestheticised and rhetoricised history" in opposition to the rationalist Enlightenment project, as defined in "A Sublime Moment Off Poverty Bay, 9 October 1769," in *Dirty Silence: Aspects of Language and Literature in New Zealand*, ed. Graham McGregor and Mark Williams (Auckland: Oxford University Press, 1991), 97–115.

53. See Barry Barclay, "Celebrating Fourth Cinema," *Illusions* 35 (2003): 7–11. Possibly the concept was inspired by the idea of a "Fourth World" (see David Stea and Ben Wisner, *Antipode: A Radical Journal of Geography* 16, no. 2 (1984)).
54. Iris Murdoch, *Metaphysics as a Guide to Morals* (London: Vintage/Random House, 1992), 3.
55. Ibid., 79.
56. Barry Barclay, "Amongst Landscapes," in *Film in Aotearoa New Zealand*, ed. Dennis and Bieringa, 122.
57. Mita, "The Soul and the Image," 46.
58. Ibid., 51.
59. Ibid., 49.
60. Graeme Turner, *National Fictions: Literature, Film and the Construction of Australian Narrative* (Sydney: Allen & Unwin, 1986).
61. See Stuart Murray's analysis of *Ngati* in Chapter 3 "Communities and Reciprocity: Ngati and The Neglected Miracle," in Murray, *Images of Dignity: Barry Barclay and Fourth Cinema* (Wellington: Huia Publishers, 2008), 53–66.
62. Edward Shortland, *Traditions and Superstitions of the New Zealanders* (London: Longman, Brown, 1854); Ch. VI, 126.
63. Ibid., 126–27.
64. Ibid., Ch. IV, 81.
65. Jean Smith, "Self and Experience in Maori Culture," in *Indigenous Psychology and the Anthropology of the Self*, ed. Paul Helas and Andrew Lock (London: Academic Press, 1981), 146.
66. Sir Tipene O'Regan, "Waitangi Day Address 2004": Onuku Marae [Akaroa]. Typescript, 2.[Held in Ngai Tahu Research Centre archive, University of Canterbury.]
67. Ibid., 4.
68. Gordimer, "Where Do Whites Fit In? (1959)," 34.
69. Nadine Gordimer, "Relevance and Commitment (1979)," in *The Essential Gesture: Writing, Politics and Places*, ed. Stephen Clingman (New York: Alfred A. Knopf, 1988), 139.
70. Ibid., 143.
71. Ibid., 142.
72. O'Regan, "Waitangi Day Address 2004," 9.

Chapter 11

History, Hybridity and Indeterminate Space: The Parker-Hulme Murder, *Heavenly Creatures* and New Zealand Cinema

Alison L. McKee

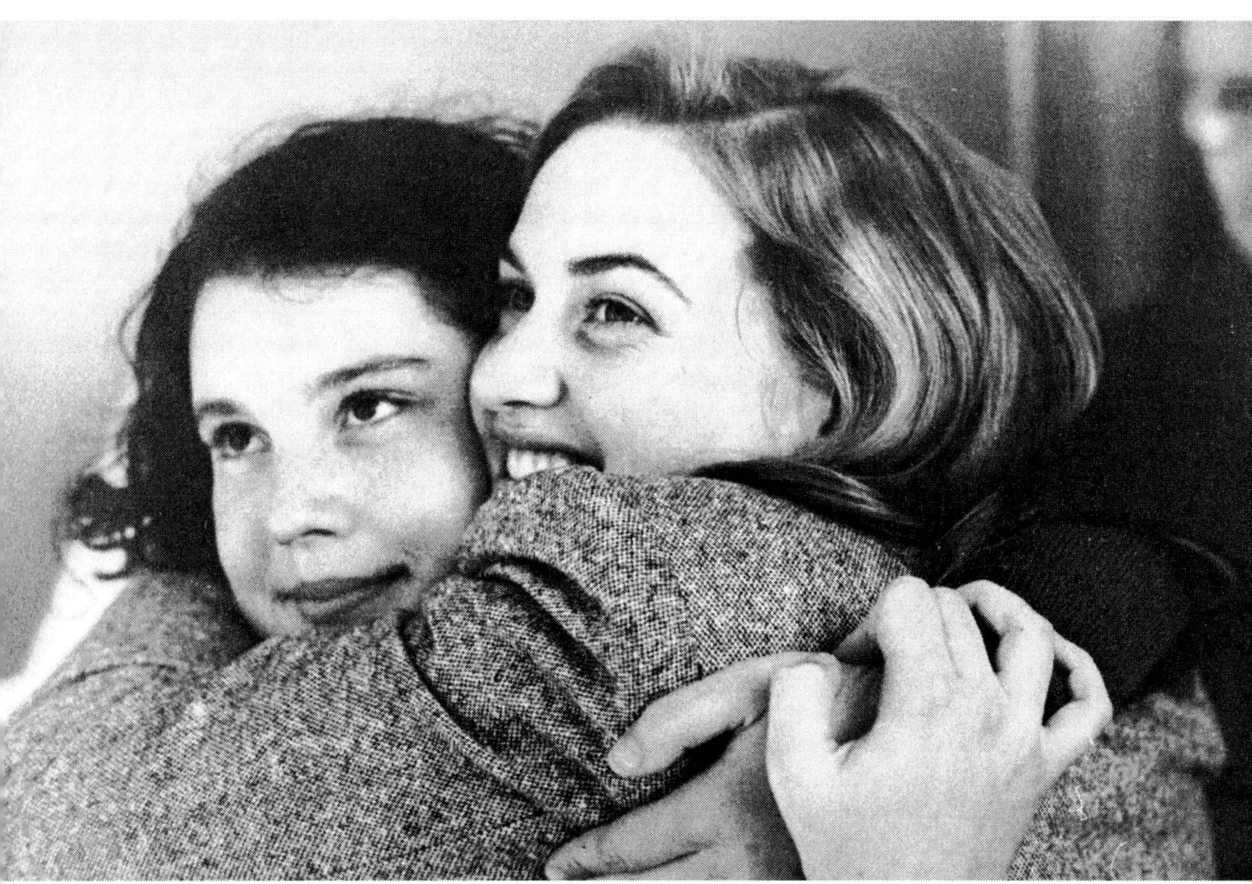

Melanie Lynskey as Pauline Parker and Kate Winslet as Juliet Hulme in *Heavenly Creatures*, 1994, dir. Peter Jackson. Image courtesy of the Stills Collection, New Zealand Film Archive Ngā Kaitiaki O Ngā Taonga Whitiāhua.

In what ways do history, memory and fantasy collide in the production and reception of objects of visual culture? What happens when those images point beyond the imaginative borders of a fictionalised, fantasised space to an actual historical event or series of events? What do these hybrid spaces of history, memory and fantasy have to tell us about the ontologies of popular culture produced and received at the borders of those crossing zones?

Inspired by recent work in the disciplines of visual culture and performance studies as well as the changing geographies and concepts of national cinemas within an increasingly globalised era, I would like to map these questions across the terrain of the 1954 Parker-Hulme murder case in New Zealand and Peter Jackson's 1994 film *Heavenly Creatures* inspired by it. My desire is to invoke these questions as both points of departure and as plot-points, in both a geographical and a narrative sense. Ultimately, this mapping must take place across the larger, curiously imbricated terrain of film, theatre, journalism, novels, and even scholarly discourse itself, as the Parker-Hulme murder has inspired multiple works in different arenas in the past 50-plus years since it occurred. Each work has recast the murder and its related events across actual and imagined epistemologies of space and desire that shift according to the historical vicissitudes of the (co)cultures that produced them.

Until now, however, none has undertaken a historical meta-analysis of the case and its myriad representations as a form of performative historiography. My discussion here consists of a consideration of the Peter Jackson film *Heavenly Creatures* specifically as the locus of two different kinds of historical moments. Less a close textual analysis of the film than a consideration of the way it documents and reimagines events surrounding the notorious Parker-Hulme murder in 1954 Christchurch, I am intrigued by the way it also functions as a pivotal moment in Peter Jackson's own career during a key transitional period in the evolution of the New Zealand film industry. *Heavenly Creatures* engages questions of personal, professional and national identity at multiple levels, and those levels intersect in the crossings of traditional borders among genres, nations, and self and other. The cinematic space of *Heavenly Creatures* visualises issues of hybridity in narrative as well as in the actual construction of images, as a detailed discussion of its emblematic opening sequence will demonstrate. The result is that the film and its images occupy an ontologically indeterminate narrative space articulated in terms of New Zealand history and New Zealand cinema, as does the Parker-Hulme case itself.

Story and history

Today the Parker-Hulme murder is known outside of New Zealand – to the extent that it *is* known at all – as the event that provided the basis for Jackson's 1994 breakthrough film, co-written with his wife, screenwriter Fran Walsh. Prior to 1994, Jackson had been known within New Zealand primarily for a kind of "splatstick" film, represented by *Bad Taste* (1987), *Meet the Feebles* (1989), and *Braindead* (1992). A hybrid combination of comedy and horror, these films synthesised genres that Barry Keith Grant astutely notes "are both rooted in an emphasis on the physical body, both in [their] imagery and in terms of the characteristic physiological response by the spectator."[1] With *Heavenly Creatures*, aspects of horror and comedy would be retained but in a way that catapulted Jackson's work into the international spotlight, not for the first time (his first feature, *Bad Taste*, was given an enthusiastic reception at the Cannes Film Festival in 1988),[2] but in a manner that guaranteed a more sustained visibility and prominence for both him and other New Zealand filmmakers such as Jane Campion and Lee Tamahori, who were emerging in the mid-1990s as well. Today, Jackson is best known as the filmmaker of *The Lord of the Rings* trilogy (2001–2003) and *King Kong* (2005), but *Heavenly Creatures* is key as his breakthrough work and, arguably, still his best work to date.

At the time that they occurred, the Parker-Hulme case and the ensuing trial were notorious and attracted international coverage in the mid-1950s – to no small degree because they co-mingled and sensationalised controversial issues having to do with national, sexual and class issues in a particularly repressive era of cultural negotiation, dislocation and angst. According to scholars Julie Glamuzina and Alison J. Laurie, as well as for Jackson and Walsh, reminders of the case among some New Zealanders of a generation to remember it were painful as late as the mid-1990s, when *Heavenly Creatures* was made, for myriad reasons, among them the cultural angst and shame that the events triggered. As Peter Jackson comments:

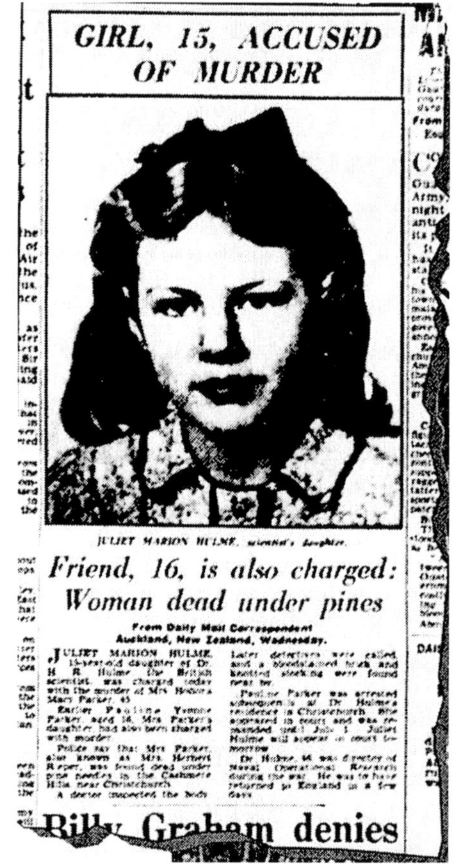

Contemporary newspaper clipping reporting the murder.

> We found that with a lot of the people we interviewed – that even though 50 years had gone by, they were still presenting attitudes of the 1950s: this was some dark, sordid little thing that was best kept quiet and should never be mentioned. Many times we got, "Why on earth would you want to make a film about this? We should just forget about and hope it will somehow disappear."[3]

The shame Jackson describes has been partially read against the backdrop of gender, sexuality, class politics and New Zealand's postcolonial settler relationship to England.[4]

Even the briefest summation of the undisputed facts of the case may suggest why it catalysed a complex series of transcultural reactions to and reimaginings of it. On 24 June 1954, in Christchurch, a 15-year-old English girl, Juliet Hulme, of wealthy, upper middle-class origins, and her working-class New Zealand friend, Pauline Parker, aged 16, lured Pauline's mother on a brief walk. During that walk, they murdered her along an isolated pathway in a wooded park, bludgeoning her to death with 45 blows from a blackjack made from a brick and a stocking belonging to one of the girls. Both Hulme and Parker were arrested within 24 hours of the killing and ultimately confessed to it. The murder of Parker's mother resulted in a trial that was catapulted into the headlines in local, regional, national and international press. The evidence that was introduced into trial incorporated a broad range of material, including testimony from opposing psychiatrists, variously assessing not only the girls' sanity or lack thereof, but their sexual identities as well, with the defence arguing, among other things, that the girls were lesbians – and, therefore, insane according to medical discourses and mores of the time – and thus not guilty by reason of insanity.

In addition, it was revealed in the course of the trial that Hulme's mother, the wife of the rector of Canterbury College and a marriage therapist who had a popular radio program, was involved in an adulterous affair with a male client who had lived at the Hulme home. It was also disclosed that Parker's own parents had never actually been married throughout their long relationship. These revelations added to the sensationalism of the trial and its coverage, as did the introduction into evidence of works of creative fiction penned by the two girls during their friendship, and of excerpts from Pauline Parker's diaries. Motive has never been conclusively determined, though it was certainly guessed at. Indeed, making sense of this matricide – rendering it legible, narratable and coherent, so to speak – has been the endeavour of virtually all commentators, academic or journalistic, since the killing was committed. In the process of interpretation (which is what every retelling of a historical event is, to some degree), there is often a flattening of meaning – a preference of one set of meanings at the expense of another – but one of the remarkable aspects of Jackson's film is its preservation of ambiguity and multivalence of meaning.

I will argue here that, while individual works related to the Parker-Hulme case (of whatever nature – journalistic, novelistic, dramatic or cinematic) may sometimes enact such a flattening, the discursive totality of the Parker-Hulme case is an imbricated and rich one and that the Jackson/Walsh film respects its complexity. For my purposes here, I focus on *Heavenly Creatures* as a point of departure precisely because I regard it as one of the richer individual works about the case and believe that it preserves the multiplicity of meanings and issues raised by the historical Parker-Hulme murder. It does so intentionally and partly, I think, as the result of the extent to which the film participates in, and recombines, the conventions of multiple genres, crossing generic boundaries in order to tell the story in the way that seems most effective to the filmmakers. Indeed, Jackson suggests that such generic border crossings are characteristic of contemporary New Zealand cinema generally:

> What genre a film falls into, how people characterise it, at the end of the day is not that important. In New Zealand we tend to cross genres. In America the film industry is very genre-conscious. If the studio want a horror film [*sic*] then everyone knows what they're talking about and what the ingredients are. It's a marketplace. You're producing a product that has to fit very neatly into a pattern, and this is how it's been going on for 100 years. In New Zealand we don't have that tradition. We're really just a bunch of filmmakers making things that interest us, so we end up muddying the genres [...] That's one of the reasons why, I think, when our films are seen overseas, people regard some of them as being fresh and original. We haven't stuck within one particular genre.[5]

Because *Heavenly Creatures* does not "stick within one particular genre," the narrative space that is created is hybrid, an indeterminate one in which meanings can circulate creatively and suggestively. Indeed, it preserves much of the same kind of indeterminacy as the Parker-Hulme case itself. Jackson's and Walsh's quest for historical accuracy in *Heavenly Creatures* is well documented,[6] but it is their recombination of multiple generic conventions that creates a cinematically complex narrative space that is as memorable as the case they address. A tale of familial set against the backdrop of a repressive 1950s Christchurch, Jackson and Walsh self-consciously both invoke and use modes of melodramatic excess borrowed from film, particularly from the movies and music of Mario Lanza and films by Hollywood's bad-boy director Orson Welles. For example, whether in a largely daylight, outdoor sequence depicting their growing friendship as the girls frolic and discard clothes down to their underwear or in a later sequence in which Juliet and Pauline watch *The Third Man* in a theatre and seem to see its streets and star wherever they turn, ending up at home and in bed in Juliet's room, the film employs a mobile camera and a complex soundtrack that almost literally seem to swing among different points of view and aural and visual generic vocabularies in a cinematic palimpsest. Including scenes depicting the girls' fantasy realm of Borovnia, those vocabularies encompass horror, musicals, historical fantasy, family melodrama and film noir and yet contribute to the construction of a narratively indeterminate space that cannot be comfortably pigeon holed, as I will discuss in a moment.

Jackson and Walsh are not the first nor, I think, will they be the last artists whose creative and speculative imagination has been captured by the Parker-Hulme murder. It has given rise to at least two pulp novels (*Obsession* (Tom Gurr and H. H. Cox, 1958), *The Evil Friendship* (M. E. Kerr/Vin Packer, 1958)), at least three plays (*Minor Murder* (Reginald Denham and Mary Orr, 1967), *Daughters of Heaven* (Michelanne Forster, 1992) and *Where*

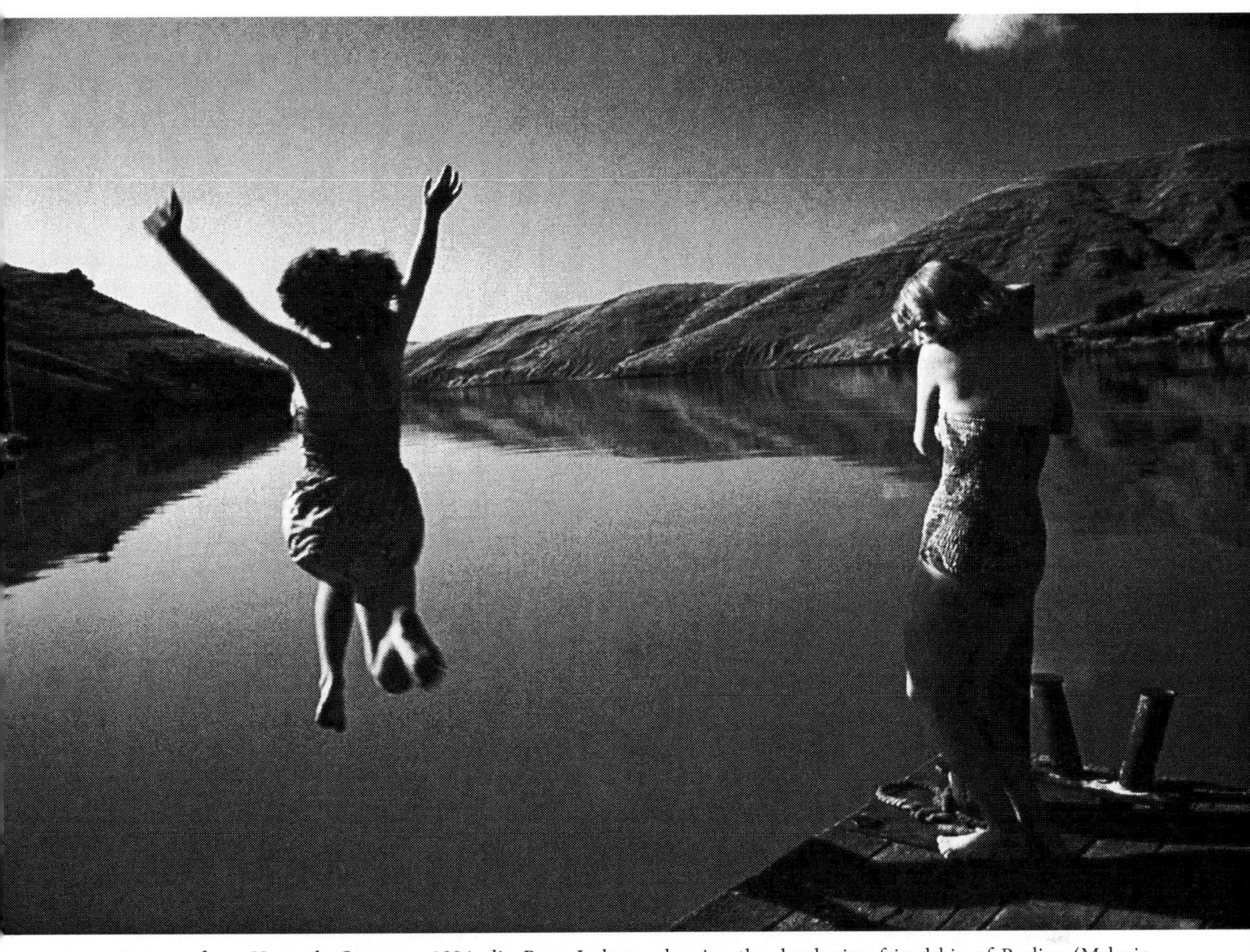

A scene from *Heavenly Creatures*, 1994, dir. Peter Jackson, showing the developing friendship of Pauline (Melanie Lynskey) and Juliet (Kate Winslet). Image courtesy of the Stills Collection, New Zealand Film Archive Ngā Kaitiaki O Ngā Taonga Whitiāhua.

Are They Now? (Cyndi Williams 1996)), and two films, including *Heavenly Creatures* and a lesser-known French film, *Mais ne nous délivrez pas du mal/Don't Deliver Us from Evil* (Joël Séria, 1971). In addition, Jackson's film itself is the source of a great deal of fan research into the Parker-Hulme murder and of related creative works. Some of it is housed on a large, partially group-authored website called *The Fourth World: The Heavenly Creatures Website*, while other examples exist in the even more ephemeral form of fan videos on YouTube. These videos generally consist of footage excerpted from *Heavenly Creatures* and re-edited to the fan's choice of audio or musical tracks. Occasionally, the sound is also excerpted from, and then re-edited to, a different portion of the film, but more often the images are paired with the fan's often whimsical, sometimes brilliantly interpretative choice of songs by both well-known and alternative rock bands.

On the academic front, representations of the Parker-Hulme murder have also been the focus of numerous articles that generally interpret the events through the recurring critical lenses of gender, the maternal, sexuality, postcolonialism and even ethnicity, mostly since the 1990s. For example, in their 1991 book *Parker & Hulme: A Lesbian View*, an excellent ethnographic reading of 1950s New Zealand culture in relation to issues of sexual identity, particularly lesbianism, Julie Glamuzina and Alison J. Laurie note that Port Levy, where Hulme and Parker's vision of their fantasy "Fourth World" first occurred, was the location of a Māori community; the Māori priest whom the authors consulted believed that the girls' vision was grounded not in fantasy but a spiritual experience and that the murder was consistent with that experience.[7] Most, though not all, of this critical work, has appeared since the debut of *Heavenly Creatures*, and relatively little attention has been paid to the constellation and interconnection of discourses across media forms and eras. A partial exception is Glamuzina and Laurie's book, which does devote a chapter to "The Stories" about the murder that circulated in different forms; the authors conclude that "there is little distinction between the writings of journalists, 'pop' crime writers, and medical 'experts.' Each type of writing added to the development of the cautionary tale."[8]

From indeterminate to quantum space

What is interesting to me about this mapping of a historical case across different creative, scholarly discourses and range of media is not so much the conclusions to which individuals come about the Parker-Hulme murder and its motives, but rather the *indeterminate space* which I have already mentioned and to which those mappings, taken collectively, point. It is in those zones of presentation, re-presentation and performance that have grown up around it over time which fascinate, in and of themselves, and which have created a collective performance space that is at once imaginative, memorial, creative and interpretative.

In using the term "indeterminate space" provisionally here, I am recalling the canonical work on classical America film genre by Thomas Schatz as a point of reference.[9] However, I am employing it in an entirely different sense and shifting it to indicate a different kind of space altogether. In formulating a typology of classical Hollywood film genres, Schatz distinguished between genres of determinate and indeterminate space, asserting that settings are ideologically contested and ideologically stable, respectively; in this scheme, western and gangster films, for example, belong to the former, while musicals and family melodrama belong to the latter. According to Schatz's well-known formulation, genres of "indeterminate space" depend "less upon a heavily coded place than on a highly conventionalised value system."[10]

However, my use of the term "indeterminate space" serves, for the moment, to work *against* neat systems of categorisation. *Heavenly Creatures* is most emphatically not a Hollywood or a genre film, classical or otherwise. Indeed, as I have already noted, it works against the neat generic divisions that are common to dominant American cinema. My view is that Peter Jackson and Fran Walsh locate the narrative zones of *Heavenly Creatures* precisely in that indeterminate space that works against, and transgresses, strict generic boundaries, and that this, in part, allows for a complex destabilisation of gender, class, and national and sexual identity. Further, they construct the film at the borders of history, memory and fantasy where the Parker-Hulme case itself is located, and these border-crossings are deliberately emphasised and preserved by the film in the overlap, intrusion or indeterminacy of cinematic space within it, as in the scenes to which I referred above. This space is one which is, in its very nature, ideologically *unstable* – self-consciously fissured by clashing values of national, sexual and class identities – and is represented by the fragmentation of character identities and spaces across the narrative, never even remotely totalised or resolved by the end of the film, nor, I would argue, are they intended to be.

To suggest further what I mean by my use of the term indeterminate space, and in the spirit of additional border crossings, let me briefly consider the interdisciplinary work of theatre scholar David E. R. George. Writing in the mid-1990s at roughly the same time that *Heavenly Creatures* was released, George constructs a thoughtful meditation upon what the world of physics and quantum theory might offer theatre as a way of thinking about how theatre positions itself in relation to representation and lived reality. Like 1950s sociologist Erving Goffman before him (with whose work, however, George ultimately takes issue), George invokes quantum theory as a suggestive analogy, even while cautioning that "one should […] hesitate before claiming [that] […] Quantum Theatre [is] more than a provocative metaphor."[11] Nevertheless, for George, the value of that metaphor lies in quantum physicists' conceptions of the material world as "multiple, plural, parallel,"[12] which he sees as similar to theatre as form and practice. For example, some behaviour in the subatomic world may be measured as light waves or as particles, and how it is measured determines the behaviour's material reality; also, a behaviour of a single particle may not be easily predicted, though a mass of particles may be. Similarly, for George, an actor's lines may be givens, but what that actor does with the lines she is given exists as potential in a quantum sense. For George, then, theatre as form and practice "recognises and enforces a conception of reality as plural and parallel, indeterminate and hypothetical, the co-creation of spectator-players."[13] That potential is the lure for George, for it points "less to the 'single actuality' which matters […] than the alternative which shadows it and the premise of choice behind it."[14]

It is this tantalising prospect of "alterability, potentiality and creative intervention" that George sees in theatre and quantum physics and that I, in turn, see at play in the collective discursive space that constitutes the body of work – historical, creative and academic – that has risen up around the Parker-Hulme event of 1954. Taken together, this space constitutes a kind of unorthodox historiography. In "Feminist Performance as Feminist Historiography," American theatre professor Charlotte Canning identifies herself as "a feminist performance historian and historiographer," and notes that, for her, that identity is linked to the argument she makes "for performance that foregrounds historiographical operations, making physical, gestural, emotional, and agonistic the processes that construct history out of the past." In a remark that reveals the ongoing influence of such historians as Hayden White, she continues, "Concomitantly, I am arguing for history that overtly acknowledges the ways in which it is a performance of the past, but not the past itself."[15] This is precisely what *Heavenly Creatures* does. Canning devotes her attention to theatrical pieces that have been created and performed by artists working implicitly or overtly within a self-conscious tradition that foregrounds the performance of history as process rather than as given. Noting "none of them would typically be labelled a 'history' of its subject [...] [they] would be more conventionally understood as dramatisations, biographies, or autobiographies," she nevertheless proposes that "they might be more provocatively read as historiographical moments that reveal the processes of transforming the past into history and that blur the boundaries between history and dramaturgy."[16] It is precisely this kind of blurring of boundaries and George's notion of quantum space that Jackson's *Heavenly Creatures* creates within its own narrative world. That it preserves those spaces against all attempts to reduce it to a singular iteration of perspective or interpretation is, I think, to the film's credit.

Genre and hybridity

The hybrid generic world of Jackson's early work generally, and of *Heavenly Creatures* specifically, has been noted not only by the director himself but also by multiple scholars and critics. In an early review of the film, Bennett E. Roth notes that "*Heavenly Creatures* becomes a difficult film to categorise according to genre. It is not a murder mystery; it just misses as a psychoanalytic thriller."[17] Barry Keith Grant rightly notes that the generic worlds of horror and comedy intersect in the film as Pauline and Juliet's shared imaginary world of Borovnia intrudes upon the quotidian world of the girls' respective lives: "Jackson blends the two worlds – just as Borovnia existed for Pauline and Juliet [...] Jackson's films tend to mix genres."[18] In a reading of Jackson as a postcolonialist filmmaker, Mary Alemany-Galway sees the film as a "mixture of docu-drama, fantasy film, Gothic horror film, and family melodrama,"[19] suggesting in the process that, under the umbrella of Gothic horror and melodrama, it also participates in conventions of the woman's film. In New Zealand, she asserts, there exists a tradition of women's films which explore the underbelly of heteronormative, Anglo-centric national ideologies of family, the landscape and ethnicity, and she further locates Jackson's film within a feminist tradition (despite its male director), "because it focuses on two female protagonists, and because the script is co-written with Fran Walsh." While the thread of postcolonial themes binds together Alemany-Galway's illuminating exploration of Jackson's work, the rich array of genres she invokes in relation to *Heavenly Creatures* (including the 1990s New Queer Cinema movement and Elizabeth Guzik's reading of the film as a "killer-dyke" narrative) points to its complexity and simultaneous multi-layered meanings.

Some have found the hybrid generic nature of *Heavenly Creatures* confusing rather than rich, a limitation of the film. Roth writes that "the film seems to lack a deeper understanding of the origin of Pauline's hatred of her mother,"[20] while Ribeiro notes, "the film falters slightly in bridging the gap between Pauline and Juliet's leap from emotional desperation at the threat of separation (the Hulmes' breakup precipitating Juliet's relocation to South Africa) to murder."[21] In both instances, these writers see the ambiguity as a misstep on the part of the filmmakers and the lack of legibility of motive as cinematic weakness. However, I would argue that the ambiguity is a marker of a national difference in filmmaking and not a creative misstep. Walsh makes this point in relation to the writing of *The Frighteners* (1996), their foray into American commercial filmmaking after *Heavenly Creatures*:

[Fran Walsh]: One of the things that our "script minder" kept coming up with was: Why are you so oblique about approaching this point? Why don't you just hammer it? We explained that we like a bit of room to move and the audience can get there by themselves. We don't like to be too obviously emotive in terms of the way we manipulate the audience, and for [American studio financiers], that's the goal. If there's any danger of the audience missing the point, they want you to address that.[22]

The clear boundaries between genres in American classical filmmaking to which I referred earlier are traditionally accompanied by equally clear character motivations and distinctions between good and evil, and the absence of such neat divisions or the complication of them often inspires dislike, or at least puzzlement, in an audience accustomed to American commercial films.

Tellingly, Jackson goes on to elaborate on Walsh's point regarding the clarification of points using a specifically spatial metaphor: "[The creators of American films] like to manipulate the audience coming in through the front door. We like to go in through the back door, and let things creep up on an audience."[23] That he chooses to express these narrative and structural difference and ambiguities in spatial terms is, I think, illustrative of exactly how important space is in his films, as an examination of the opening sequence of *Heavenly Creatures* shows. The film begins with footage from a 1950s National Film Unit travelogue about Christchurch, New Zealand. In one canny, deft move, Jackson acknowledges the heretofore one-dimensional view beyond the country's borders of New Zealand as a producer simply of nonfiction films and travelogues and establishes a socio-cultural view of mid-twentieth century Christchurch, the setting of his story. Commencing with an aerial view of the city, the travelogue moves on to reveal a strangely dislocated environment, one which Maureen Molloy describes, in writing about gender and nation in *Heavenly Creatures*, as "New Zealand in location, English in architectural style and social activities – cricket rowing on the Avon, girls in school uniforms."[24] Indeed, the girls in the school uniforms are from the same school that Pauline and Juliet attended, and a number of the historical sites related to the murder are shown in the travelogue. The sense of dislocation in the sequence is the result not only of a settler nation half a world away from its founding country but historical as well: these are emphatically archival images of a world at once familiar as *having taken place* and unfamiliar in their removal in time from a contemporary audience.

An authoritarian, anonymous male voice narrates the travelogue in smooth, reassuring tones and refined accent, against the backdrop of cheerful, lilting music, a travelogue which symptomatically reveals even as it implicitly celebrates the patriarchal norms of gender and class upon which the settler city of Christchurch has been built. Upon multiple viewings of the film and with an awareness of Jackson's own cinematic style that is about to explode upon the scene, an otherwise innocuous moment in the travelogue takes on an almost Hitchcockian air, with hints of David Lynch. "Mothers, fathers, sons, and daughters – all on wheels!" observes the narrator cheerily over an image of a gloved officer directing downtown Christchurch car, bike and pedestrian traffic with economy and precision. Both Hitchcock's depiction of Young Charlie (Teresa Wright) being chastised by the Santa Rosa traffic cop in *Shadow of a Doubt* (1943) and David Lynch's tribute to that scene in an early sequence of *Blue Velvet* (1986) come to mind. These cinematic associations are hardly coincidental: Jackson uses the travelogue to depict a world which believes its ideologies of nation, gender, sexual identity and authority are straightforward, fixed and unshakeable, only to rip off the surface to reveal deep fissures beneath, in the manner of both Hitchcock and Lynch, but in his own unique style.

It is sound that first disrupts this seemingly postcard-perfect view of 1950s Christchurch, and, indeed, sound plays an equally expressive role in creating indeterminate, borderline space as the image. This is particularly true in later fantasy sequences when images of the girls' imagined kingdom of Borovnia are paired with recordings of Mario Lanza's singing. The narrator's voice is drowned out by noise that is at first unidentifiable and then quickly recognisable as the sounds of a low amplified roaring and female screams. At the moment that the sound becomes specific and identifiable, the film cuts away from the mundane, faded images of the travelogue with its largely static camera and into Jackson's own brightly coloured images and peripatetic footage. In a single cut, Jackson not only announces that the image of 1950s Christchurch created by the travelogue is a one-dimensional façade, but the historical cliché about New Zealand as a producer of a narrow kind of filmmaking is equally inadequate, as the ensuing film is about to demonstrate.

From a pedestrian, anonymous, authoritarian and god's eye view of Christchurch, Jackson hurls the viewer into a space that is at once much richer, more subjective and much more disorienting. No god's eye shots here: the post-travelogue portion of the sequence begins with a subjective shot in vivid colour that travels rapidly along a wooded path, branches slapping the camera lens, accompanied by the piercing sounds of continued screaming that bridges the cut from the travelogue. A second shot continues the travelling motion but reveals two girls running and stumbling through the woods, with a third similar tracking shot revealing their bloodied legs in close-up. The fourth shot, in black and white, reveals the same two girls still running in the same direction – but in different clothes, on board the deck of a ship, with soft music replacing the screams. A series of rapid cuts ensues between these two spaces, the sound of music and screams layered and bridging the initial cuts, with the girls themselves, the moving camera and the direction of movement providing common elements. "Mummy!" the girls cry happily, one after the other, in the black and white sequence, at one point sharing a subjective shot as a middle-aged couple on deck turn to face the camera. That shot is followed another subjective shot in colour that emerges from the woods and travels forward to reveal a woman hurrying out of a tea-shop towards the camera, concern on her face. The next shot transitions to a more objective shot of the woman's continued movement, followed by a subjective, hand-held shot from her point of view of the two girls, who come to a halt before her, their faces distraught and covered in blood. "It's Mummy!" shrieks the dark-haired girl. "She's terribly hurt!" Her blonde companion sobs, "Please … help us!" The sequence fades to black with a reverberation on the soundtrack and the following text appears:

> During 1953 and 1954, Pauline Yvonne Parker kept diaries recording her friendship with Juliet Marion Hulme.
> This is their story.
> All diary entries are in Pauline's own words.

At this point, the opening title sequence of the film begins and the story formally commences with its historical and logical starting point, the meeting of the two girls at school.

From the very first shots of the post-travelogue portion of the sequence, issues of narrative legibility, subjectivity and point of view are deliberately emphasised and confused, as was true in the historical Parker-Hulme case. The transition from travelogue to Jackson's footage jarring, and he provides no establishing shot by which viewers can orient themselves. Instead, the point of view initially invoked is that of the screaming, running girls – essentially, their shared point of view, as it is impossible to determine then or retrospectively if the shot "belongs" to Pauline or Juliet. The viewer is thus immediately immersed in the girls' perspective and their shared closeness (which was pilloried by journalistic coverage of the Parker-Hulme case) and related medical discourses on the topic,[25] and that immersion continues through the next few shots. Strictly speaking, they are not point-of-view shots, but the observing camera tracks the girls' progress through the woods with the same dynamism as their running. It is also impossible upon first viewing of the film to determine the status of the shipboard shots that quickly follow and assess the information they seem to provide. Are they flashbacks? Their black and white images might suggest as much. Are they fantasies? This reading, as it turns out, is closer to the mark: the use of black and white links these shots to the fantasies by and about Hollywood commercial filmmaking, for which Juliet and Pauline write reams of fiction hoping that Hollywood will make them into movies. Are the two girls sisters? They both run towards the same middle-aged couple, and both girls cry out, "Mummy!" to the woman standing there. (It is actually Juliet's mother in the black and white footage, that upper-middle-class woman who seems so elegant and refined compared to Pauline's own mother, the wife of a fishmonger and a woman worn down by the hard work of keeping a boarding house to make extra money for her family.) In retrospect, the moment anticipates the later scene at Port Levy in which Mrs Hulme, in a moment of careless fondness, refers to Juliet as her daughter and then to Pauline as her "foster daughter," which Pauline takes to heart. The next edit jerks the viewer from the black and white footage back into the space of the woods through a point-of-view shot, as described above. In the ensuing shots the camera parcels out its remaining subjective shots to the running girls (again, it is impossible to tell which one of the girls) and to the woman emerging from the tea house. Juliet's gasped request, "Please … help us!" is delivered directly to the viewer before the sequence fades to black.

In a film devoted to the story of two girls who were powerfully bound up in a mutually intensely emotional relationship and spent hours co-creating and role-playing across lines of class, gender and ethnicity within entire worlds (the Fourth World), kingdoms (Borovnia) and systems of deities, the deliberate blurring of subjective boundaries preserves the fluidity of identification and identity upon which both Juliet Hulme and Pauline Parker insisted. Jackson's refusal of establishing shots in this sequence is a reaction against the formal and cultural cinematic norms of the travelogue portion; it also underscores and insists upon multiple points of view of a story that, at the time of its occurrence, was recounted primarily by apparatuses of the New Zealand state or its mouthpieces with a purely authoritarian point of view of events and people (i.e., court records, journalistic accounts of the trial, medical witnesses). Only in the years following the murder did an occasional polyvocal novel, play, and or film begin to counter and re-imagine the dominant ideologies expressed in the initial accounts of the Parker-Hulme murder.

The final shot of the sequence concludes with Juliet's direct appeal to the audience: "Please … help us!" That there is no help available for two girls who have since vanished into new lives and old age (Jackson and Walsh were pretty certain of Juliet Hulme's current identity as Anne Perry, the now-successful mystery writer, but had no interest in revealing it) is clear, unless it is to represent the complexities of their situation to a New Zealand-specific audience now granted the gift of hindsight through the film's re-imagining of time and people. Although *Heavenly Creatures* unexpectedly garnered Jackson an international audience, he and Walsh made it for a domestic audience: "The fact is," observes Jackson,

We weren't actually making this film for an international audience. We were very much making it to try and rectify 40 years of misunderstanding about this case within New Zealand. In a way, that was our main motivation for making this film.[26]

It is a bold though not unique move to begin towards the end of the story, but in 1994 the Parker-Hulme murder would still have existed in many New Zealand movie-goers' memories, with a portion of the audience going into the film already well aware that they were about to watch a film about two girls who murdered one of their mothers. Jackson's intent was to create neither a Hollywood style whodunit nor a documentary, but, as the intertitle suggests, an account of the events and relationships leading up to the murder in a way that respected their complexity and even their lack of clarity. "This is their story," the intertitle tells us, indicating that, above all else, it is a story aligned with their subjectivities, however much they and their motivations defied conventional understanding. In an interview conducted with Jackson and Walsh by Tod Lippy, however, one can sense a tension among their commitment to historical accuracy which was part of the team's research, their sense of responsibility to what had been a personal tragedy and a traumatic national event in which both major and minor players are still alive, and also a refusal to engage in the norms of Hollywood-style character development and motivation:

> We felt it was a good time now, while there were still quite a few people alive, to do the interviews and try to get something accurate, for the record. We were also aware of the responsibility we had, because film is such a persuasive medium, and we knew that, unlike any other medium – the newspaper accounts, the play [*sic*] – it can give an audience visual images, which, in a way almost replace the real event, especially if you weren't born at that time [...]. Our intention was to be true to what we understood of the girls' friendship, and the nature of that friendship and the nature of those families from which those two girls came. It was never an attempt to re-create reality. We could never do that, obviously. So we went into those things with the spirit of trying to reflect the situation, rather than reality.[27]

Well aware of the cinematic medium's ability to "almost replace the real event," Jackson anticipated the fact that his film takes on increasing significance as one of the major discourses about the Parker-Hulme case as the number of years since 1954 grows. Thus, it is more than, but it is also, an historical film, despite Jackson's acknowledgement that they could never recreate the historical reality surrounding the Parker-Hulme case. It refuses to settle for unambiguous explanations of the girls' sexual identities and motivation for murder precisely because history has never resolved either issue.

It is a testament to the richness of Jackson and Walsh's preservation of a complex set of historical events and relationships, I think, that the film has given rise to numerous scholarly readings. The arguments of these pieces are various and often divided. To offer only one example, while Deborah Shephard argues that the film articulates a more identifiable feminine perspective than Jackson's earlier work, thanks largely to the influence of his wife and screenwriter Fran Walsh,[28] Maureen Molloy declares that the film "does little to rewrite the 1950s professional and media accounts of the reasons for the murder, except to cast the girls in a more sympathetic light."[29] Malloy thus asserts that the film participates in patriarchal discourses of gender and nation:

> In times of crisis (within the British mode of imperialism) the nation is configured as feminine. It is not surprising therefore, in an age of postcolonialisms and massive economic and social reconfiguration, that themes of matricide should appear in the national narratives.[30]

I believe the film actually leaves those elements open to critique, but in the spirit of Jackson's film itself, I would not insist that it does. Instead, I read that the availability of the film to multiple interpretations within different arenas is a demonstration of one of the ways in which it points to its own indeterminate space and that of the Parker-Hulme murder as well.

At this point I would like to return to theatre scholar David E. R. George's concept of quantum theatre to which I alluded earlier. What George sees as possible for theatre in form and practice, I see as realised in *Heavenly Creatures* specifically, and in the constellation of journalistic coverage, novels, dramas, scholarly work and fan discourse that now makes up the world of Parker-Hulme murder discourse. As I stated above, what George calls quantum theatre "recognises and enforces a conception of reality as plural and parallel, indeterminate and hypothetical, the co-creation of spectator-players."[31] That potential is the lure for George, for it points "less to the 'single actuality' which matters [...] than the alternative which shadows it and the premise of choice behind it."[32] It is this alterity and possibility towards which the collective discourses of the Parker-Hulme case, regardless of medium, point and which, I believe, the single film of *Heavenly Creatures* largely preserves. The "alternative which shadows" the "single actuality" of the murder is what has given rise to so many telling of it, and "the premise of choice" and "co-creation" of spectator-players apply equally not only to the historical figures of Pauline Parker and Juliet Hulme but to the artists, writers and scholars whose own work traverses and creates the indeterminate space surrounding it.

No single work or representation embodies this indeterminate space completely – which is part of my point – but Jackson and Walsh's film comes close in its totality and, in microcosm, in the fantasy space of the Fourth World which intrudes with increasing frequency into the so-called real world constructed within *Heavenly Creatures*, with life-sized Borovnian figures beheading, stabbing, choking and otherwise doing away with those who cross Juliet and Pauline. Similarly, some of the fan spaces that have evolved around *Heavenly Creatures* online to which I alluded earlier seem to match, mirror and otherwise replicate that same space-time of "alterability, potentiality and creative intervention" that George ascribes to quantum theory and to theatre specifically. Together, a world characterised by flux and change is created in which performances of gender, the maternal, sexuality and post-colonialism – part history, part memory, part fantasy – circulate in a play of meanings that preserves complexity in and around the Parker-Hulme case and the constellation of related representational spaces and identities it has generated. As historian Nicole Ward Jouve has written of another murder in a different time and place, "The fascination of murder cases is that they do not stop at the crime itself, the perpetrators, the victims, the immediate surroundings. Every representation or explanation that is offered becomes part of it"[33] – and so it is with the Parker-Hulme murder and its myriad indeterminate spaces.

Notes

1. Barry Keith Grant, *A Cultural Assault: The New Zealand Films of Peter Jackson*, Studies in New Zealand Culture series, 5 (London: Kakapo Books, 1999), 4.
2. Ibid., 10.
3. Tod Lippy, "Writing and Directing *Heavenly Creatures*: A Talk with Frances Walsh and Peter Jackson," *Scenario: The Magazine of Screenwriting Art* 1 (1995): 218.
4. See Julie Glamuzina and Alison J. Laurie, *Parker & Hulme: A Lesbian View* (Ithaca, NY: Firebrand Books, 1991); Maureen Molloy, "Death and the Maiden: The Feminine and Nation in Recent New Zealand Films," *Signs* 35, no. 1 (Chicago: University of Chicago Press, 1999); Elizabeth Guzik, "The Queer Sort of Fandom for *Heavenly Creatures*: The Closeted Indigene, Lesbian Islands, and New Zealand National Cinema," in *Postcolonial and Queer Theories: Intersections and Essays*, ed. John C. Hawley (Westport, CT: Greenwood Press, 2001), 47–61; Davinia Thornley, "Executing the Commoners: Examining Class in *Heavenly Creatures*," in *Film Studies: Women in Contemporary World Cinema*, ed. Alexandra Heidi Karriker (New York: Peter Lang, 2002), 51–68; and Mary Alemany-Galway, "Peter Jackson as a Postcolonial Filmmaker: National Cinema and Hollywood Genres," *Post Script* 25, no. 2 (Winter 2006); http://findarticles.com/p/articles/mi_go1931/is_2_25/ai_n29253112/. Accessed 4 January 2009.
5. Jim Barr and Mary Barr. "NZFX: The Films of Peter Jackson & Fran Walsh," in *Film in Aotearoa New Zealand*, ed. Jonathan Dennis and Jan Bieringa (Wellington: Victoria University Press, 1996), 156.
6. See Lippy, "Writing and Directing *Heavenly Creatures.*"
7. Glamuzina and Laurie, *Parker & Hulme*, 147–48.
8. Ibid., 133.
9. Thomas Schatz, *Hollywood Genres: Formulas, Filmmaking, and the Studio System* (New York: McGraw Hill, 1981).
10. Ibid., 698.
11. David E. R. George, "Quantum Theatre – Potential Theatre: A New Paradigm?" *New Theatre Quarterly* 5 (1989): 174–79.
12. Ibid., 173.
13. Ibid., 174.
14. Ibid.
15. Charlotte Canning, "Feminist Performance as Feminist Historiography," *Theatre Survey* 45, no. 2 (November 2004): 227–33.
16. Ibid., 228.
17. Bennet E. Roth, "*Heavenly Creatures*: Female Adolescence Viewed Darkly," *The Psychoanalytic Review*, Film Notes 82 (1995): 626.
18. Grant, *A Cultural Assault*, 25.
19. Alemany-Galway, "Peter Jackson as a Postcolonial Filmmaker," par. 17.
20. Roth, "*Heavenly Creatures*," 626.

21. Luisa F. Ribiero, "*Heavenly Creatures* by Peter Jackson," *Film Quarterly* 49, no. 1 (Autumn 1996): 33–38, 37.
22. Barr and Barr, "NZFX," 155.
23. Ibid.
24. Molloy, "Death and the Maiden, "4–5.
25. See Glamuzina and Laurie, *Parker & Hulme.*
26. Lippy, "Writing and Directing," 224.
27. Ibid., 218.
28. Deborah Shephard, *Reframing Women: A History of New Zealand Film* (Auckland: Harper Collins Publishers, 2000).
29. Molloy, "Death and the Maiden," 5.
30. Ibid., 7–8.
31. George, "Quantum Theatre," 174.
32. Ibid.
33. Nicole Ward Jouve, "An Eye for an Eye: The Case of the Papin Sisters," in *Moving Targets: Women, Murder and Representation*, ed. Helen Birch (London: Virago Press, 1994), 12.

Chapter 12

Screening Women's Histories: Jane Campion and the New Zealand Heritage Film, from the Biopic to the Female Gothic[1]

Hilary Radner

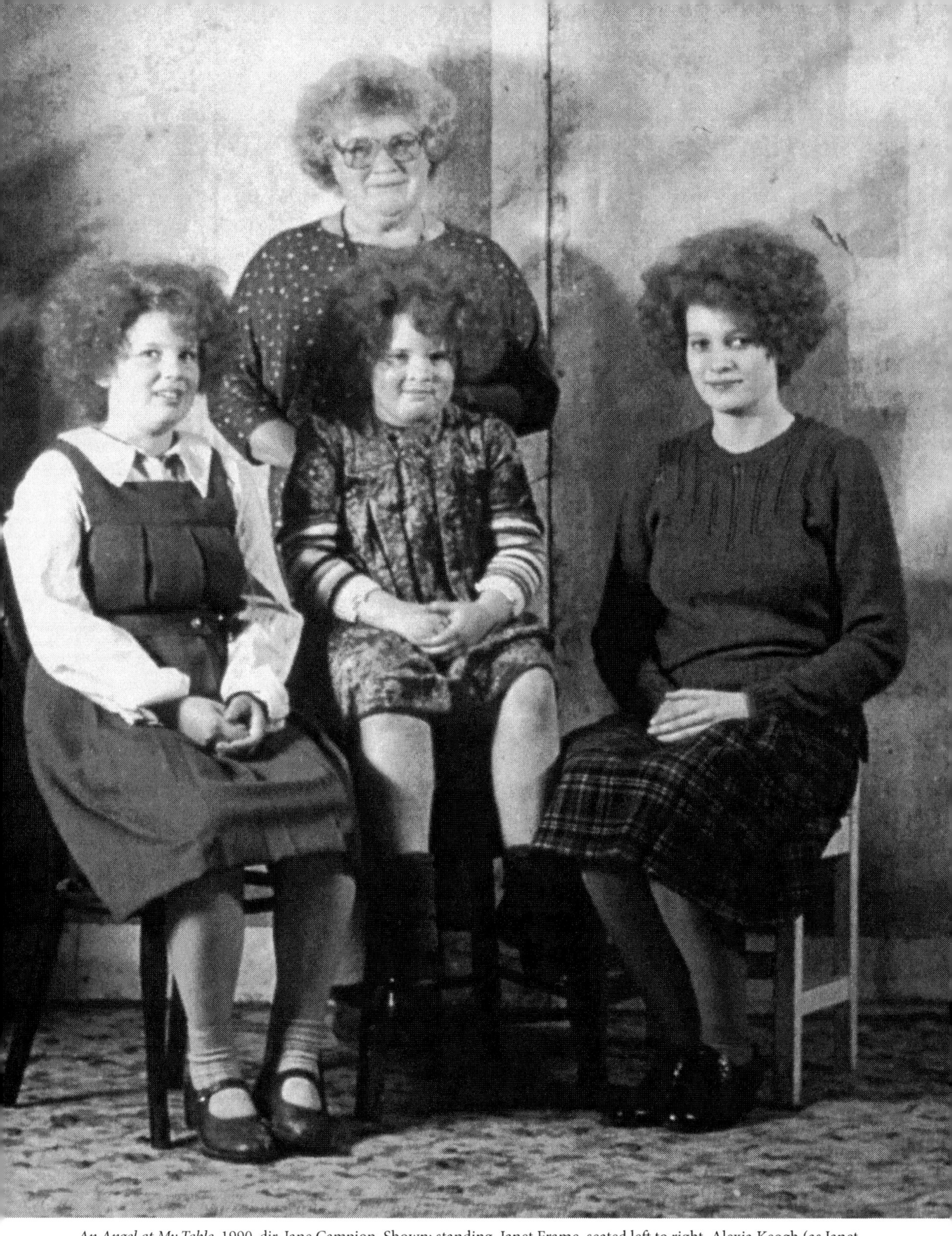

An Angel at My Table, 1990, dir. Jane Campion. Shown: standing, Janet Frame, seated left to right, Alexia Keogh (as Janet Frame as adolescent), Karen Fergusson (as Janet Frame as a child), Kerry Fox (as Janet Frame). Image courtesy of Fine Line Features/Photofest.

History occupies a vexed place in the project of what film scholar Kathleen McHugh calls "global feminism,"[2] which seeks to reclaim what it deems to be the lost stories of great women, while contesting the concept of history itself as privileging the exceptional rather than seeking to recount the lives of ordinary women. Charlotte Macdonald's introduction to *A Woman of Good Character*, an account of single women immigrants to New Zealand in the nineteenth century, lays out these issues in the context of New Zealand history. Thus she notes that the book "has been prompted by a desire to know more about the history of women in New Zealand,"[3] observing that "[r]ecovering the identities and life stories of women who have been 'hidden' from history was a central goal."[4] For Macdonald, these "hidden" women were those who "led the lives of unexceptional people" – in other words, who were typical rather than leaders.[5] For her, as for many of her generation in New Zealand and elsewhere, the goal of the feminist historian has not been to highlight the lives of great women, but to document those unsung and largely unrecognised "unexceptional" women upon whom, in her view, society depended for its stability and continuity.

Not surprisingly, then, films that seek to restore the centrality of women's experience in the New Zealand imagination are influenced by a double need: to express a specifically antipodean feminine experience, and to honour the women of the country's past. More surprisingly, however, are the ways in which the films of the expatriate Jane Campion, New Zealand's prodigal daughter, who has yet to return to the Motherland, also exemplify this national trend.[6] Indeed, the two films that established her international reputation as an *auteur* with a unique and definable vision, *An Angel at My Table* (1991) and *The Piano* (1993), partake of a marked tendency in New Zealand television of the same period, deeply intertwined with the film industry itself, to revisit the national past with a view to defining the woman's place and voice in that history.

Women's histories on the small screen

An Angel at My Table and *The Piano* are two examples (arguably the most high profile) of a group of screen narratives that consider the place of New Zealand women in the nation's history, some broadcast exclusively on television, others enjoying both broadcast and theatrical release, made in the 1980s and early 1990s. As a group, these testify to what New Zealand film historian Bruce Babington calls "the reactivation of a long tradition of female artistic accomplishment – embodied in writers such as Katherine Mansfield, Jean Devanny and Jane Mander."[7] Significantly, Babington also underlines the intimate relationship between film and television in this period, raising questions about "whether a number of films […] should be classified as feature or television films, especially after videotape release further blurred original distinctions."[8] Campion's *An Angel at My Table* clearly raises these issues. Recounting the life of the prominent New Zealand author Janet Frame, drawing on her autobiography, it was one of two important "biographical serials" produced in the early 1990s about women – the other was Gaylene Preston's 1993 *Bread and Roses*, based on the autobiography of the same title by New Zealand activist Sonja Davies – that represent the final flourishing of a cycle of made-for-television narratives about prominent New Zealand women as feminist or proto-feminist cultural heroines. *An Angel at My Table* was co-funded by a number of public institutions, including TVNZ; though it had its début at the Venice Film Festival, it also benefited from pre-sales to ABC Australia and Channel Four in Britain, and was ultimately bought by organisations in 50 countries. Broadcast in July 1991 on TV One in New Zealand in three parts on three consecutive Sunday evenings, it enjoyed a 21-percent audience share, underlining its status as a televisual as well as cinematic narrative.[9]

These hybrid "biopics" (somewhere between television and film) stand out because of the way they highlight a specifically New Zealand feminine sensibility conditioned by the hardship and isolation felt to characterise a national experience that was, at least initially, fundamentally masculine, as expressed in the "Man Alone" theme found in much of the nation's fiction.[10] Film scholar Andrew Spicer underlines that "New Zealand was conceived by migrants to be a 'man's country' where men could prove themselves through hard physical activity, away from the feminising influences of polite society."[11] Similarly, Ian Conrich points to the fact that what he calls New Zealand's "New Wave," the development of New Zealand's film industry subsequent to 1977, was "predominantly testosterone fuelled: the product of a male-dominated. industry in which films offered stories of aggression, stunts, pranks and subversion."[12]

Pamela Jones' *Pioneer Woman*, 1983, received a two-page spread in *The New Zealand Listener* (NZ Listener, 14 May 1983). Courtesy of Hocken Collections Te Uare Taoka o Hākena.

While New Zealand productions were undoubtedly more varied than Conrich's remark might suggest, working against this initial prevailing masculinist tendency was a counter movement identified by Babington: "By 1985 the beginnings of a perceptible feminisation of New Zealand film are observable, not only in subject matter and emphases, but in directing personnel."[13] An important impetus in this "feminisation" was not only feminism itself but also television, which, as a popular medium, was more immediately responsive than perhaps film to what Babington perceived to be "cultural changes" in New Zealand society.[14] New Zealand historian Barbara Brookes described "young women in the 1970s" as "eager to read about women's (imagined unitary) past," seeing in the injustices of the past a source of indignation that fuelled an outpouring of energy into issues such as abortion law reform, the founding of the refuge movement, the attack on sexism in all its manifestations and important legal changes such as the Human Rights Act which, amongst other things, outlawed discrimination on the basis of sex.[15]

Responding to this climate, early made-for-television docudramas, such as *Gone Up North for a While* (Paul Maunder, 1972), addressed social concerns, often women's issues, in this case the predicament of unmarried mothers.[16] This particular broadcast was influential in establishing, in 1972, "the domestic purposes benefit, a support system for single parents that has remained available."[17] *The Governor* (Tony Isaacs, 1977), however, deemed "the most watched and discussed drama of the 1970s,"[18] focused on what Pamela Jones (aka Pamela Meekings-Stewart), television producer, described as "the strongly male administrative side of our history."[19] According to New Zealand television historian Trisha Dunleavy, an interest in screening women's history was inaugurated by the 1983 series *Pioneer Women*. Pamela Jones, the series' producer, saw the project as correcting the male-centred narratives that characterised earlier television historical dramas such as the documentary *Richard John Seddon – Premier* (1973), *The Longest Winter* (1974), as well as *The Governor* – all, not coincidentally, directed by Tony Isaacs – but also responding to a change in New Zealand itself. "Things at that time were just beginning to change, people were just starting to drop that whole thing of call England 'home.' Something was starting to emerge," she opined. She elaborated:

And the more I thought about the whole question of New Zealand identity the more I started to suspect that it may well have been the pioneer women rather than the men who determined who we are. Not only did these women have to go out there and survive – and they showed great stoicism in the face of appalling hardship – but they also had the task of raising a new generation. They were the educators and the keepers of morals.[20]

Six episodes of *Pioneer Women* were produced and aired in 1983, and with three episodes broadcast in 1990.[21]

The subsequent increase in films by, about, and for women resulted in three notable "biopics" produced for television (and usually theatrical release) in this period based on the lives of significant female national figures depicted as cultural heroines, whose talents were

A full-page spread on *It's Lizzie to Those Close*, 1983, dir. David Blyth, in *The New Zealand Listener* (NZ Listener, 24 July 1982). Courtesy of Hocken Collections Te Uare Taoka o Hākena.

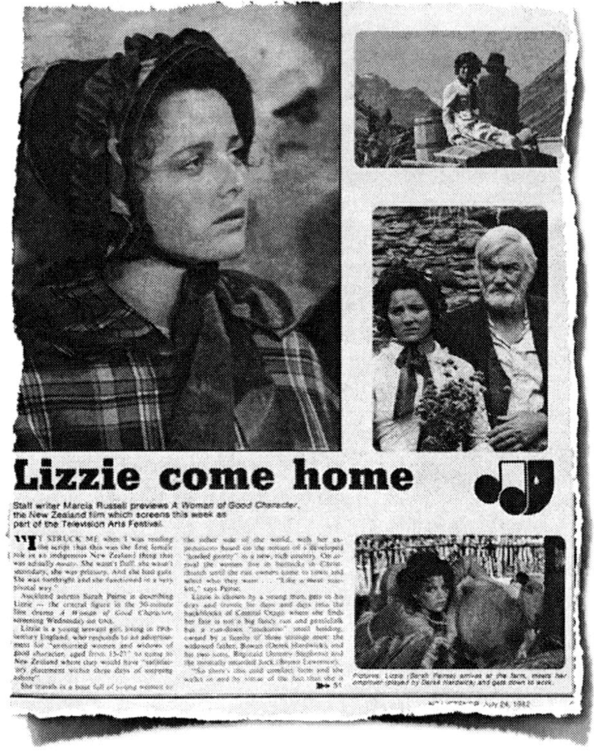

unappreciated and constrained by the social conditions in which they lived: *Iris* (Tony Isaac, 1984), about Iris Wilkinson, who wrote under the pseudonym Robin Hyde; *Sylvia* (Michael Firth, 1985) on Sylvia Ashton-Warner, a novelist and internationally innovative education theorist; and *Leave All Fair* (John Reid, 1985), addressing the life of writer Katherine Mansfield. To this list of films about actual historical figures should be added the film versions of what has been termed the female gothic, about fictional characters, in particular single women, often new immigrants, who suffered at the hands of a society that was a best indifferent and usually hostile.[22] These include the historical drama *It's Lizzie to Those Close* (a.k.a. *A Woman of Good Character*) (David Blyth, 1983),[23] which recounts the experience of a young woman who comes to New Zealand alone seeking work as a "serving girl" and encounters suffering and oppression at the hands of her male employers; the UK/NZ co-produced mini-series *Heart of the High Country* (Sam Pillsbury, 1985), another fictional account of a young woman seeking her fortune in New Zealand; and, finally, *Mesmerized* (Michael Laughlin, 1986), an Australia/New Zealand/UK film co-production staring Jodi Foster that portrays the trials and tribulations of a young orphan in New Zealand forced by circumstance into an arranged marriage. Dunleavy notes that *A Woman of Good Character*, "as the story of an unmarried female immigrant," anticipates Jane Campion's *The Piano*,[24] suggesting the ways in which Campion's auteur production is not unprecedented, but, like *An Angel at My Table*, arises out of a spate of screen narratives that, divided between costume drama and biopic in terms of genre, seek to define the woman's place in New Zealand history at a particular moment in that country's own chronology in which the conceptualisation of a national history was a central concern.

The heritage film in New Zealand

In terms of the "change" noted by Pamela Jones above, New Zealand culture of the 1970s was still struggling with the brutal economic effects of the severing of ties economic ties to Britain, which had brought home to New Zealanders that they were indeed alone – a small country in a global economy controlled by the superpowers – with the concomitant effect that national identity became a significant preoccupation, leading to an increasing sense of New Zealand's autonomy and distinctiveness. An important event in this national maturation process was the screening of the television mini-series, *The Governor*, in 1977. "The six episodes, totalling some 465 minutes of screen time, spanned fifty years of colonial history from 1840 to 1890, including the signing of the Treaty of Waitangi and the land wars of 1860."[25] While *The Governor* deals with the great events of New Zealand history, it also (precisely because it covers such a long span of time and because the television narrative is extended over almost eight hours) offers a broad vision of the New Zealand experiences of the period. Significantly, the programme does not present Sir George Grey (the Governor of the title) as heroic, offering instead a profoundly ambivalent view of the Māori/Pākehā, the indigenous/settler, shared past.

The Governor inaugurated a cycle of what I will call heritage fictions, drawing upon the definition initially articulated by Andrew Higson with regards to English cinema.[26] Higson distinguishes the heritage film from the broader category of the costume drama in terms of the period in which these were made (1980s and 1990s), and also the manner in which this particular set of films highlighted canonical sources, privileged a "museum" aesthetic that conveyed authenticity, and delved into the interior psychic life of its characters (as opposed to the great moments of history), while entering into contemporary debates about issues such as the place of women and the role of sexuality.[27] This group of films also "seemed to articulate a nostalgic and conservative celebration of the values and lifestyles of the privileged classes, and [...] in doing so an England that no longer existed seemed to have been reinvented as something fondly remembered," linked in turn to what he calls "the heritage industry."[28]

While the New Zealand heritage tradition developed contemporaneously with its English counterpart, its characteristics and agenda were quite different, with an emphasis on recovering and establishing a past that anticipates and moves towards the founding of a unified nation, in which the strife between the original Polynesian inhabitants and the European settlers is recognised and healed. The historical films of New Zealand, then, tend to focus on historical events and on Māori/Pākehā confrontation in films such as *Utu* (Geoff Murphy, 1983) and *Twilight of the Gods* (Stewart Main, 1995). A few films such as *Illustrious Energy* (Leon Narbey, 1988), which deals with the experience of Chinese immigrants during the nineteenth-century gold rush, or *Pictures* (Michael Black, 1981), depicting the life to two early Dunedin photographers fascinated by indigenous cultures, seem closer to their European counterparts.

Ultimately, however, what seems most significant is that a very high percentage of New Zealand films are set in the past – often only 20 or 30 years. For example, *Ngati* (Barry Barclay, 1987) and *Mauri* (Merata Mita, 1988), both Māori films describing Māori life, recount narratives that take place in the 1940s and 1950s prior to urban migration, recalling a way of life that was fast disappearing if not already lost. In this sense, New Zealand cinema as a relatively small national cinema that came of age in the late 1970s must be seen as inherently part of the larger process of creating and recognising a cultural heritage. Significantly, the New Zealand Film Commission was established in November 1978, followed by a veritable "boom" in film production.[29]

As New Zealand film reviewer Nicholas Reid remarked in his volume, *A Decade of New Zealand Film*, covering the years 1975–1986: "Many times more feature-films were made in New Zealand between 1977 and 1986 than had been made in the previous eighty years."[30] In this context, he noted that, rather than reflecting a changing New Zealand society in which most of the population are city dwellers, "New Zealand films [...] have come close to perpetuating a dated image of New Zealanders as a sturdy race of laconic country-people."[31] Contextualising this impulse as part of the general drive to create a common past, and a shared sense of myth, highlights how this "image" must be understood not so much as "dated," but as a symptom of the period in which the films were made – that is, one in which the urge to create a shared national history was a significant driving force. The cycle of woman's films discussed above, while being an important expression of this impulse, also diverged from the general thrust of New Zealand heritage culture, with its emphasis on masculinist values and biculturalism, as became increasingly clear with subsequent developments in the film industry.

While the relatively small output of New Zealand films makes it difficult to distinguish a trend that we might call the heritage film, among this group of women-centred films a number suggest the marked influence of the English heritage film and the general influence of the heritage movement itself.[32] Likewise, because New Zealand feature film production emerged as a national force only in the late 1970s,[33] it is not accurate to claim that a new type of costume drama developed in this time period as it did in Britain. It is perhaps more appropriate to say that certain films within the New Zealand corpus exhibit some of the traits associated with the European heritage film, the influence of which was felt in New Zealand as it was elsewhere. Leon Narbey's *Illustrious Energy*, for example, which had been initially conceived as a "docudrama," was converted into a drama when the original concept was refused funding, "drama" being considered a more commercially viable form that would exploit the taste for serious fare that had made the Merchant-Ivory team so successful.[34]

In addition to the television series *The Governor*, two films were fundamental to defining the New Zealand heritage film: *Pictures* and *Utu* – both set in the nineteenth century, and both focusing on the confrontation between Māori and Pākehā, which suggests the importance of "biculturalism" to the creation of a specifically New Zealand history, while suppressing the actual demographics of the current population, which is marked by multiculturalism – a fact reflected in a growing number of films dealing with various ethnic minorities.[35] Despite the increasingly multicultural mix of New Zealand's population, the country's history continues to be largely portrayed as driven by biculturalism as the significant feature of a national allegory. As Reid Perkins, writing in 1996, has pointed out, this tendency derives from "a thematics of the pioneer in relation to the Māori and the land," the "frontier" providing in the words of early twentieth-century New Zealand historian James Cowan, "the poetry of last century's work and endeavouring in New Zealand, as opposed to the more prosaic story of industrial revolution." Perkins elaborates:

> This has been pitched in terms of a Nature/Culture divide: a dichotomy that has structured both endeavours to exploit the imaginative appeal of the romance and adventure inherent in the colonial frontier, as a liminal space poised on the threshold of the wild; and, concomitantly, efforts to identify a distinctive national character, and elaborate a set of criteria by which the descendants of the pioneers could feel legitimised in regarding the land as their own.[36]

This particular vision of the country's history was enhanced by state-supported productions such as *One Hundred Crowded Years* (Government Film Studios, 1940), commissioned for the Tourist and Publicity Department, to commemorate the signing of the Treaty of Waitangi (in which the Māori tribes recognised the sovereignty of the English monarch, then Queen Victoria) and the centennial of the country's founding.[37] Not coincidentally, then, the innovative television series *Pioneer Women*, discussed above as initiating the cycle of screen narratives exploring women's histories in New Zealand, exploited the centrality of the frontier image, while challenging its focus on masculine accomplishment.

Heritage culture and the woman's film

In contradistinction, the spate of films that developed around the experiences of a single woman beginning with *It's Lizzie to Those Close* in 1983, while again partaking in the national myth of frontier origins, also follow on from a classical Hollywood film starring Lana Turner, shot in California while set in nineteenth-century New Zealand, *Green Dolphin Street* (Victor Saville, 1947); these films to a large degree ignore the importance of cultural encounter in order to focus on the trials and tribulation of a woman in search of her destiny, while, nonetheless, emphasising the pioneer qualities of the culture. Reid Perkins commented with regards to *Green Dolphin Street* and its avatars: "[O]ur colonial history has been requisitioned here to meet the genre requirements of a romantic melodrama," one of the many forms taken by what Jeanine Basinger calls the woman's film.[38]

Indeed, in *It's Lizzie to Those Close*, no evidence remains of the Māori as the original inhabitants of what now seems a completely empty and uncivilised South Island, Central Otago landscape. This narrowing of dramatic concern suggests the influence of another facet of the English heritage film: its penchant for melodramas that specifically address a female viewer and her *Bildungsroman*. Within international contexts, the film that best represents these latter influences in New Zealand cinema is Jane Campion's *The Piano*, which to some degree explains its unprecedented success with both New Zealand and global audiences in the 1990s, given that in terms of its sensibility and themes, it corresponded to a set of films – the British heritage films identified by Higson – that were already familiar to the audiences to which *The Piano* appealed.[39] In Higson's words, British heritage films (like *The Piano*) "operate at very much the culturally respectable, quality end of the market," shifting between both "the traditional art house circuit and the mainstream commercial cinemas."[40] Film scholar Deb Verhoeven, in her book-length study of Campion as a director, describes the film as "one of the industry's most profitable crossover films (*The Piano* moving successfully from art cinemas to multiplexes)."[41] Similarly, Raphaëlle Moine hypothesises that what she sees as a "blend of Australasian specificity and the personal exploration of more universal themes and figures" assists the recognition and emergence of Campion as an international auteur.[42] Moine continues:

> Inscription in the category of "international art cinema" increases with *The Piano*, not only because of its financing, its casting, and, of course, retrospectively, its success, but also, and above all, because of its generic anchoring in the "heritage cinema" – a prestige genre in the 1990s that could assure international success for an independent or average production [in terms of budget, author's note].[43]

Importantly, in terms of securing its place as part of the heritage cinema movement, as identified by Moine, *The Piano* was marked by "tension between the visual splendour and narrative meaning" that Higson deemed a defining attribute of the genre, which, while nostalgic in terms of mise-en-scène, also tended to "propose more liberal-humanist visions of social relations, at least at the level of dialogue and narrative theme."[44] In *The Piano*, rather than focusing on problems of cultural encounter by using it as a pretext for the love story (as is the case with Vincent Ward's 2005 *River Queen*), the narrative, like the classic woman's film of Hollywood – such as *Green Dolphin Street* – revolves around the personal dilemmas and emotional and marital strife of the heroine, which are largely a manifestation of her own psyche. As Moine notes, Campion shows "the struggle of a woman searching for psychic autonomy in the quest for her own subjectivity."[45] In other words, she is not at the mercy of historical events as much as she at the mercy of her own internal drives and desires. She, the heroine, is at the centre of her universe. The particular kind of narrative structure associated with the woman's film, character-centred and character-driven, is not only common in English heritage films such as James Ivory's *A Room with a View* (1985) and *Howard's End* (1992), or the Australian *My Brilliant Career* (Gillian Armstrong, 1979), but also informs the parallel cycle of biopics about prominent New Zealand women exemplified by Campion's earlier *An Angel at My Table*.

For Raphaëlle Moine, *An Angel at My Table* marked a significant development in terms of Campion's reputation as a filmmaker. Unlike the earlier *Sweetie* (Jane Campion, 1989), the film combined what she calls "national branding" with the attributes of the woman's film, re-interpreted within a feminist context,[46] linking the film (and Campion's oeuvre) to a series of prestige productions such as *Camille Claudel* (Bruno Nuytten, 1988) or the later *Artemesia* (Agnès Merlet, 1997), which Belén Vidal describes as "films that put under the spotlight women artists at odds with political hierarchies and social conventions."[47] The fact that like the biopics of the 1980s, such as *Sylvia*, the film was an adaptation, based on the three volume autobiography of the esteemed New Zealand writer Janet Frame, added to its value as a "prestige," culturally ambitious film, in sympathy with the heritage genre more generally.[48] Likewise, the biopic format linked the film (and Campion as a director) to earlier feminist-inflected Hollywood successes of the 1980s, such as *Out of Africa* (Sidney Pollack, 1985) based on the life of writer Isak Dinesen/Karen Blixen, played by Meryl Streep. "[O]ne of the decade's biggest productions and most popular films," the movie, in the words of film scholar William J. Palmer, "romanticized the feminist impulse to identity and independence."[49] Other popular female biopics of the 1980s, including *Coal Miner's Daughter* (Michael Apted, 1980), and *Sweet Dreams* (Karel Reisz, 1985), "spotlighted women who overcame social obstacles to fulfil their talents, women forced to depart from the patterns of American life in order to pursue personal dreams."[50] Parallels between these films and Campion's *An Angel at My Table*, suggest how it, like *The Piano*, conformed to an already established "prestige" formula that emphasised a woman's self-realisation as the primary vehicle for narrative development, while providing a national and even exotic mise-en-scène that enhanced the cultural value of the film.

Accordingly, as woman-centred narratives, both *An Angel at My Table* and *The Piano* de-emphasis cultural encounter between Pākehā and Māori, which sets these films apart from many other New Zealand films, while linking them to a group of New Zealand women-centred films and television dramas produced in the previous decade, and to other heritage films produced by other national cinemas, most notably French, British and Australian, as well as Hollywood films such as *Out of Africa*, which in turn follow the patterns established by the woman's film of classical Hollywood.[51] Postmodern and postcolonial scholars have roundly criticised these films for their neo-conservative values more generally – but also more particularly for their emphasis on the problems of a "white" heroine of European origin. For example, Roberta Garret comments:

> While *The Piano* revises certain aspects of the nineteenth-century female-authored text, its Brontësque concern with the subjectivity of a white, lower middle-class woman and her struggle for a stake in the hierarchy of white patriarchal society allows little space for addressing, or rather, re-addressing other subjectivities and histories.[52]

The film, nonetheless, follows the typical plot of the Hollywood woman's film, which centres on an individual woman whose psychological issues drive the plot, external events often serving to manifest her internal traumas. While in the course of the film certain elements of patriarchal authority may be challenged, ultimately the heroine learns to accept the constraints of her existence (which includes patriarchy), thereby achieving a chastened, yet satisfying "happy ending," often signalled through a return to marriage and/or motherhood as the legitimating experiences of a woman's life. Similarly, *An Angel at My Table* generates a narrative in which its heroine must relinquish traditional feminine ambitions, such as marriage and family, in favour of art, supporting a view that femininity is not compatible with art – and while a woman may choose the one or the other, she cannot do so without consequent suffering. Campion's films may challenge certain kinds of conventions about the expression of a woman's desire, emphasising more directly (and anachronistically) her position as an active agent, and her right to end an unrewarding marriage or to choose to be a writer over a mother or wife, while offering a conclusion that nevertheless affirms the heterosexual couple as the socially prescribed founding moment of a woman's life, in keeping with the "liberal-humanist vision" described by Higson.

The female gothic

In the case of *The Piano*, this link is strengthened by its affinities with both the art film and the tradition of the female gothic. For the American film scholar Barbara Klinger, writing in 2006, *The Piano* represents a particularly apt example of the art film that reiterates the female gothic tradition, engaging the viewer through arresting images that evoke "a feminist or quasi-feminist *Bildungsroman*."[53] For Klinger, who describes herself as a "white, middle-class, female subject,"[54] "[t]hese images […] map out the 'before and after' of female identity within systems of domination, embodying the contradictory aspects of this identity as it has been forged across time."[55] Consequently, the film encourages the female viewer to "savour the retelling of a familiar woman's story while finding pleasure in the aesthetic complexity that dramatically renovates the retold tale."[56] As an American, however, Klinger fails to recognise the very different place that the film occupies within the history of other New Zealand screen narratives. Considering *The Piano* in relation to earlier films set in New Zealand, such as the Hollywood *Green Dolphin Street*, or the New Zealand *It's Lizzie to Those Close*, does not invalidate Klinger's view of the film as a particularly eloquent example of the female gothic; however, while *The Piano* may owe its international success to the way it re-tells a specific narrative about female identity, its genesis is also tied to the development of a New Zealand heritage culture, particularly the impulse to bring women's histories to the forefront of the national imagination.

By pointing to the female gothic as a particular type of narrative, Klinger draws attention to a distinctive dimension of New Zealand cinema that led Sam Neill to describe it as "a cinema of unease" in his 1995 film of the same title, referring to the dark vision of the world that marks New Zealand films generally. Similarly, Stacey Abbot declares that, with regards to *It's Lizzie to Those Close*, "the harsh life that awaits Lizzie in this wondrous but lonely setting evokes more than any other film by Blyth, the themes of Kiwi Gothic cinema."[57] While Conrich uses the notion of "Kiwi Gothic" to describe a moody atmosphere or generally negative worldview – "a cinema of isolation and despair in which personal space is threatened by forces that prevent settlement and in which a powerful landscape is seemingly alive"[58] – he also underlines the relations between these films and a literary tradition initiated with the eighteenth-century novels of Ann Radcliffe, which "present a persecuted heroine threatened by a secret, contained in the past."[59] Within a New Zealand context, then, the categorisation of *The Piano* as an example of the female gothic speaks both to the specificity of its New Zealand origins and to its appeal to a global feminist audience, attuned to the politics of literature and culture.

The term "female gothic" was coined by scholar Ellen Moers, as part of a feminist re-assessment of British literature in 1970s, in her analysis of the novels of Radcliffe and the tradition that they inaugurated, as "a coded expression of women's fears of entrapment within the domestic and within the female body, most terrifyingly experienced in childbirth."[60] In turn, feminist film theorists such as Diane Waldman and Mary Ann Doane in the 1980s, applied the term to a cycle of popular women's films based on the "woman-in-jeopardy" formula, produced in the 1940s, in which the threat to the heroine was expressed through mise-en-scène as well as through the narrative itself. These included *Rebecca* (Alfred Hitchcock, 1940), *Suspicion* (Alfred Hitchcock, 1941), *Jane Eyre* (Robert Stevenson, 1944), *Gaslight* (George Cukor, 1944), *Dragonwick* (Joseph Mankiewicz, 1946) and *Under Capricorn* (Alfred Hitchcock, 1949), many of which are also costume dramas. More recently, Helen Hanson has described films such as the 1991 *Sleeping with the Enemy* (Joseph Rubin) as a contemporary re-articulation of the sub-genre,[61] a definition that might be extended to include certain New Zealand films, in particular a number directed by Gaylene Preston, such as *Mr Wrong* (1985) and *Perfect Strangers* (2003). With regards to the cycle of films focusing on a single woman who arrives in New Zealand to make her fortune that includes both *It's Lizzie to Those Close* and *The Piano*, the fact that these films exhibit traits that tie them at once to a canonical literary tradition, that of the gothic, to New Zealand culture and cinema more generally, as well as to a particular sub-genre of the woman's film, the female gothic, enables them to serve the double purpose of highlighting the pioneer dimension of New Zealand's own history while participating in a more globalised discourse about woman and her predicament.

Charlotte Macdonald's research on "single women as immigrant settlers" points to how these film narratives both participate in, and diverge from, the movement to reclaim women's past on the part of historians. While a significant number of single women did immigrate to New Zealand and were encouraged to do so because of a gender imbalance in the country, and while hard work was certainly the norm, it would be unlikely that these women would have encountered the difficulties of Lizzie or Ceci, the heroine of the subsequent mini-series *Heart of the High Country*, whose experiences, her name notwithstanding, replicate those of Lizzie.[62] Even more unlikely in the highly rigid and puritanical milieu of the colony would be the erotic *épanouissement* accorded Ada as the heroine of *The Piano*. Macdonald commented: "Women, like men, came to New Zealand with aspirations which were, in the main, limited and pragmatic." She concluded that it is probably fair to say that these women came to a place in which work was plentiful and better paid (if rather more arduous), where food was readily available and of a higher quality, and where social barriers, if not absent, were less rigid and less extreme than where they had come from.

Nonetheless, Macdonald also points to the fact that "colonial life had greater potential for women to experience isolation and loneliness."[63]

Conclusion

It is undoubtedly the case, then, that these costume dramas, from *It's Lizzie to Those Close to The Piano*, though embroidering and transforming historical fact, do convey some of the emotional reality of a colonial woman's actual experience, while simultaneously entering into contemporary debates about the place of woman and her expectations in current society. Most importantly, in terms of Campion's reputation as a filmmaker, the prevalence of something like the female gothic in her own work, particularly in *The Piano*, illustrates how, in terms of formation and theme, her corpus is marked by developments in the New Zealand film industry. These developments encouraged the two projects that earned her international recognition and allowed her to move from a primarily national mode of production to the position of international art house director, a move which Raphaëlle Moine describes as a "shift toward a transnational discourse [...] and toward essentially international filmic forms."[64]

What I would like to emphasise here is the degree to which Campion's two New Zealand films, *An Angel at My Table* and *The Piano*, participate in a specifically New Zealand project, in which television and film production were interdependent endeavours, during a period when the recovery and representation of New Zealand's history, in particular women's histories, was an important cultural imperative. In the case of *The Piano*, for example, a significant influence was Campion's participation in an earlier project with John Maynard and Bridget Ikin, who had produced *An Angel at My Table*; in this project, which did not come to fruition, Campion worked on an adaptation of a famous New Zealand novel, *The Story of a New Zealand River* by Jane Mander, set in nineteenth-century New Zealand.[65] Her collaboration with Maynard and Ikin demonstrates the degree of her involvement in the New Zealand film scene of the period and also suggests its influence.[66]

Alison Butler describes *The Piano* in *Women's Cinema: The Contested Screen*, underlining its international reception, as "a canonical feminist film which has been widely discussed with two frames of reference: as women's romantic fiction and as a post-colonialist representation of colonial New Zealand."[67] This perspective, while pointing to significant dimensions of the film, fails to recognise the national specificity of its genesis. Recent work on Jane Campion by Annabel Cooper and Alistair Fox has emphasised Campion's cultural debt to contemporary New Zealand, in particular the New Zealand of Campion's childhood and adolescence.

She herself has expressed her gratitude towards Australia for having provided her with the training and milieu that made her a filmmaker;[68] however, little attention has been paid to how two of her most significant films are part of larger trends in New Zealand cinema, especially in terms of their treatment of women's histories and New Zealand cultural heritage more generally, and testify to the influence of this national film industry on her work.

Finally, then, to bring the project of placing Campion within her antipodean context with regard to the middle period of her career to a close, I would like to return to the cycle of female biopics as a uniquely national phenomenon, of which *An Angel at My Table* is a striking, but not anomalous, example.[69] Commonly, the protagonists of these narratives – Iris Wilkinson in *Iris*, Katherine Mansfield in *Leave All Fair*, Sylvia Ashton-Warner in *Sylvia*, Janet Frame in *An Angel at My Table*, Sonja Davies in *Bread and Roses* – find themselves ostracised and isolated in New Zealand society, which causes them (with the exception of Sonja) to leave their country in the hope of finding the sense of self that eludes them at home. Iris and Katherine die tragically abroad; Janet returns, but with an understanding that it is only through her art that she will be at home; while Sylvia achieves respect and renown abroad, she remained unappreciated in her homeland; Sonja remains to fight for peace and civil justice. These narratives depict the creative and talented woman as isolated, unappreciated, and even scorned by her fellow citizens, in a way that recreates a version of the female gothic, in which it is society at large that threatens the female protagonist. Thus, to understand these narratives as histories, we need to understand them not simply as products of the past that they depict, but also of the time in which they were made, a period in which feminism was a redoubtable social force that drew upon emotions as much as facts for its power and influence – a present in which Jane Campion, herself, chose to live in exile rather than to return to her country of origins.

Sylvia Ashton-Warner penned a heart-wrenching plea for understanding in her autobiography, *I Passed This Way*, published in 1979, and on which the biopic *Sylvia* was based, repeating the passage in both introduction and conclusion of the volume:

> Now that I'm far enough and long enough away to look inward on that country, all I can see, still, is the girl spirit of New Zealand standing slight mid-land, her fingers tight on the beginnings of threads, taut from the pull of her ranging birds in the skies overseas. Could she but haul in her exiles, all there together, both buried and living; could she afford her great, the rest of the world might possibly see her and come to learn where she is.[70]

In many ways, Jane Campion's own exile echoes that of earlier New Zealanders, such as Iris Wilkinson, Katherine Mansfield and Sylvia Ashton-Warner herself, who, unlike her predecessors, did live her final days in her own country, but without achieving the recognition she enjoyed abroad – suggesting that New Zealand has yet to write a history, to generate a national allegory, that might encourage its exceptional women to make a place for themselves within the confines of its islands.

Notes

1. Earlier versions of some material included in this chapter appeared in Hilary Radner, "Lettre de Dunedin: Le cinema au 'pays du long nuage blanc,'" *Trafic* 67 (2008): 122–33. I would also like to take this occasion to acknowledge the support of Raymond Bellour, who along with Alistair Fox, encouraged me to write about New Zealand cinema.
2. Kathleen McHugh, *Jane Campion* (Urbana: University of Illinois Press, 2007), 13–17.
3. Charlotte Macdonald, *A Woman of Good Character: Single Women as Immigrant Settles in Nineteenth-Century New Zealand* (Wellington: Allen & Unwin/Historical Branch, 1990), 2. I am indebted to Barbara Brookes for drawing this volume to my attention.
4. Ibid., 9–10.
5. Ibid., 10.
6. For a discussion of the antipodean nature of Campion's heroines. See Annabel Cooper, "On Viewing Jane Campion as an Antipodean," in *Jane Campion: Cinema, Nation, Identity*, ed. Hilary Radner, Alistair Fox and Irène Bessière (Detroit: Wayne State University Press, 2009), 279–304; and Annabel Cooper, "'I Am Isabel, You Know?': The Antipodean Framing of Jane Campion's *Portrait of a Lady*," *M/C Journal* [Online] 11, no. 5 (2008). For a discussion of Jane Campion's links to the larger thematics of New Zealand culture and literature, see Alistair Fox, "Puritanism and the Erotics of Transgression: The New Zealand Influence in Jane Campion's Thematic Imaginary," in *Jane Campion: Cinema, Nation, Identity*, 103–24.
7. Bruce Babington, *A History of the New Zealand Fiction Feature Film* (Manchester: Manchester University Press, 2007), 180.
8. Ibid., 176, n. 2.
9. Trisha Dunleavy, *Ourselves in Primetime: A History of New Zealand Television Drama* (Auckland: Auckland University Press, 2005), 246–49.
10. Philip Matthews, film reviewer for the *NZ Listener*, describes the Man Alone in the following terms:

    > This image is familiar at a deep, almost primal level for New Zealanders. The romantic idea of the New Zealand man in the wilderness, as a kind of feral survivalist or refugee from society, is nearly as old as the colonial nation itself, and it found popular expression in some early New Zealand novels – *Man Alone* (1939) by John Mulgan, who inadvertently gave the tendency a genre name; *A Good Keen Man* (1960) by Barry Crump – while its cinematic apotheosis is still *Smash Palace* (Roger Donaldson, 1981), in which Bruno Lawrence takes to the bush after attracting the hostility of polite society – his wife, the police. ("Fast, Cheap and Out of Control: Three Films from New Zealand's Digital 'Revolution,'" *Senses of Cinema*, March 2004, sensesofcinema.com. Accessed 6 June 2010.

    See also Bruce Babington, "*Man Alone* and Men Together," in *A History of the New Zealand Fiction Feature Film*, 133–36. For an extended discussion of the Man Alone as a national trope within New Zealand literature, see Alistair Fox, *The Ship of Dreams: Masculinity in New Zealand Literature* (Dunedin: University of Otago Press, 2008). See also Alistair Fox, "Inwardness, Insularity and the Man Alone: Postcolonial Anxiety in the New Zealand Novel," *Journal of Postcolonial Writing* 45, no. 3: 263–73.
11. Andrew Spicer, *An Ambivalent Archetype: Masculinity, Performance and the New Zealand Films of Bruno Lawrence* (Studies in New Zealand Culture No. 8) (London: Kakapo Books, 2000), 2.

12. Ian Conrich, "Kiwi Gothic: New Zealand's Cinema of a Perilous Paradise," in *Studies in New Zealand Cinema* (London: Kakapo Books, 2009), 27.

13. Babington, *A History of the New Zealand Fiction Feature Film*, 113.

14. Ibid., 113, 179–80.

15. Barbara Brookes, "A Germaine Moment: Style, Language, and Audience," in *Disputed Histories: Imagining New Zealand's Pasts*, ed. Tony Ballantyne and Brian Moloughney (Dunedin: University of Otago Press, 2006), 210.

16. I want to thank Gabrielle Hine for drawing my attention to this important screen narrative.

17. Trisha Dunleavy, *Ourselves in Primetime: A History of New Zealand Television Drama* (Auckland: Auckland University Press, 2005), 59.

18. Ibid., 95.

19. Pamela Jones quoted in Pamela Stirling, "Unsung Heroines," *NZ Listener* (14 May 1983).

20. Ibid.

21. Dunleavy, *Ourselves in Primetime*, 140, 142.

22. For a succinct overview of the female gothic as a film genre, see Helen Hanson, "From *Suspicion* (1941) to *Deceived* (1991): Gothic Continuities, Feminism and Postfeminism in the Neo-Gothic Film," *Gothic Studies* 9, no. 2 (2007): 20–32.

23. The title of the film on the export script is *Lizzie*. Elizabeth Gowans and David Blyth, *Lizzie: Export Script* (Wellington: New Zealand Film Commission, 1980).

24. Dunleavy, *Ourselves in Primetime*, 154.

25. Duncan Petrie, *Shot in New Zealand: The Art and Craft of the Kiwi Cinematographer* (Auckland: Random House, 2007), 313.

26. While Higson's definition has been the subject of continuing controversy, one that he himself revisits on several occasions, particularly in terms of the later developments in the format, for the purposes of this analysis I will confine myself to his initial definition, since in period it corresponds to the bulk of films that I will be discussing. For a summary of these debates and suggestions for further readings, see James Legott, *Contemporary British Cinema: From Heritage to Horror* (London: Wallflower Press, 2008), 81–82.

27. Andrew Higson, "Re-presenting the National Past: Nostalgia and Pastiche in the Heritage Film," in *Fires Were Started: British Cinema and Thatcherism*, ed. Lester Friedman (Minneapolis: University of Minnesota Press, 1993), 109–29.

28. Andrew Higson, *English Heritage, English Cinema: Costume Drama Since 1980* (Oxford: Oxford University Press, 2003), 12.

29. Nicholas Reid, *A Decade of New Zealand Film: Sleeping Dogs to Came a Hot Friday* (Dunedin: McIndoe, 1986), 11.

30. Ibid.

31. Ibid, 25.

32. This influence is reflected even in children's films such as *Flight of the Albatross* (Werner Meyer, 1993 [1996]), which recounts a very sweet and "clean" romance between a European girl, Sarah, and a Maori boy, Mako, emphasising New Zealand's cultural heritage in terms of landscape and tradition, as well as the Maori/Pakeha encounter as a defining structure. Similarly, the 1992 film, *The Crush* (Alison Maclean), a family melodrama centring on the negative effects of a contemporary femme fatale, Lane, on a father and daughter, goes to great length to include a few natural wonders, in this case the famous geysers and boiling mud pools of Rotorua.

33. Duncan Petrie, *Shot in New Zealand: The Art and Craft of the Kiwi Cinematographer* (Auckland: Random House, 2007), 13.

34. Helen Martin, "Leon Narbey: Art, Politics and the Personal," in *New Zealand Filmmakers*, ed. Ian Conrich and Stuart Murray (Detroit: Wayne State University Press, 2007), 264. Films such as the 2005 *River Queen* and the projected *Behind the Tattooed Face* might be understood as a continuation of this trend. For a discussion of the project *Behind the Tattooed Face*, see Lindsay Shelton, *The Selling of New Zealand Movies* (Wellington: Awa Press, 2005), 185.

35. Films focusing on a contemporary multicultural New Zealand include *Broken English* (Gregor Nicholas, 1996), *Sione's Wedding* [a.k.a. *Samoan Wedding*] (Chris Graham, 2006), *No. 2* (Toa Fraser, 2006) and *Apron Strings* (Sima Urale, 2008).

36. Reid Perkins, "Imag(in)ing Our Past: Colonial New Zealand on Film from *The Birth of New Zealand* to *The Piano*: Part One," *Illusions* 25 (1996): 5.

37. "Tracking Shots: Close Ups on NZ Film History," New Zealand Film Archive, www.filmarchive.org.nz, accessed 5 June 2010. Perkins, "Imag(in)ing Our Past, Part One," 8–9.

38. Perkins, "Imag(in)ing Our Past, Part One," 9. Perkins fleshes out these ideas in more detail in "Imag(in)ing Our Past: Colonial New Zealand on Film: Part Two," *Illusions* 26 (1997): 17–21. For a definition of the woman's film in classical Hollywood, see Jeanine Basinger, *A Woman's View: How Hollywood Spoke to Women, 1930–1960* (Hanover, NH: Wesleyan University Press/University Press of New England, 1993). See in particular "The Genre," 3–23.

39. The relative success of *The Piano* (1993) is signalled by its US box office gross of just over $40 million. As a point of comparison, *Mamma Mia!* (2008), a UK production with Hollywood stars, like *The Piano*, had a US box office gross of over $140 million. *The Piano*, www.the-numbers.com, accessed 2 June 2010. *Mamma Mia!*, www.the-numbers.com, accessed 2 June 2010.

40. Higson, "Re-presenting the National Past," 110.

41. Deb Verhoeven, *Jane Campion* (London: Routledge, 2009), 23.

42. Raphaëlle Moine, "From Antipodean Cinema to International Art Cinema," in *Jane Campion: Cinema, Nation, Identity*, 193.

43. Ibid.

44. Higson, "Re-presenting the National Past," 110.

45. Moine, "From Antipodean Cinema to International Art Cinema," 193.

46. Ibid., 192.

47. Belén Vidal, "Feminist Historiographies and the Woman Artist's Biopic: The Case of *Artemisia*," *Screen* 48, no. 1 (2007): 69.

48. For a detailed discussion of the adaptation of Janet Frame's autobiography, the second volume of which, *An Angel at My Table* provides the film's title, see Lawrence Jones, "'I Can Really See Myself in Her Story': Jane Campion's Adaptation of Janet Frame's *Autobiography*," in *Jane Campion: Cinema, Nation, Identity*, 77–102.

49. William J. Palmer, *The Films of the Eighties: A Social History* (Carbondale: Southern Illinois University, 1993), 277.

50. Ibid., 276.

51. For a definition of the woman's film in classical Hollywood, see Basinger, *A Woman's View*. See in particular "The Genre," 3–23. For a discussion of *The Piano* as a woman's film, see Roberta Garrett, *Postmodern Chick Flicks: The Return of the Woman's Film* (Basingstoke: Palgrave Macmillan, 2007), in particular 126–39. See also Julianne Pidduck, *Contemporary Costume Film: Space, Place and the Past* (London: BFI, 2004).

52. Though Garrett characterises the heroine of *The Piano* as "lower-middle class," in the context of colonial New Zealand, Ada and her husband Alastair Stewart represented a privileged, even "wealthy" group of immigrants. Garrett, *Postmodern Chick Flicks*, 139. For a discussion of

the status of women in nineteenth-century New Zealand, see Macdonald, *A Woman of Good Character*.

53. Barbara Klinger, "The Art Film, Affect and the Female Viewer Revisited," *Screen* 47, no. 1 (2006): 40.
54. Ibid., 39.
55. Ibid., 36.
56. Ibid., 40.
57. Stacey Abbot, "The Horrific Visions of David Blyth," in *New Zealand Filmmakers*, ed. Conrich, 339.
58. Ian Conrich, "New Zealand Cinema," in *Schirmer Encyclopedia of Film*, Vol. 3, ed. Barry Keith Grant (Farmington Hills, MI: Schirmer Reference, 2006), 247–50. The term "Kiwi Gothic" is used broadly to refer to a certain "dark" sensibility that characterizes much of New Zealand culture, especially in the South Island.
59. Conrich, "Kiwi Gothic," 27.
60. Andrew Smith and Diana Wallance, "The Female Gothic: Then and Now," *Gothic Studies* 6, no. 1 (2004): 1.
61. Helen Hanson, "From *Suspicion* (1941) to *Deceived* (1991): Gothic Continuities, Feminism and Postfeminism in the Neo-Gothic Film," *Gothic Studies* 9, no. 2 (2007): 20–32. See also Helen Hanson, *Hollywood Heroines: Women in Film Noir and the Female Gothic Film* (London: I. B. Tauris, 2007).
62. Elizabeth Gowans, who wrote the script for *It's Lizzie to Those Close*, also wrote the novel (and a sequel) on which the series *Heart of the High Country* was based. Ceci's initial experiences in New Zealand, recounted in the first 100 pages of the novel, replicate those of Lizzie. Her little dog is shot when it barks at sheep. She is raped and abandoned by the older brother of the family for whom she works and forcibly married to the father. Finally, with the father's death, she is left, pregnant, to care for the troubled younger brother. Elizabeth Gowans, *Heart of the High Country: A New Zealand Saga* (London; Auckland: Grafton, 1985), 1–100.
63. Macdonald, *A Woman of Good Character*, 2.
64. Moine, "From Antipodean Cinema to International Art Cinema," 200.
65. Jane Mander, *The Story of a New Zealand River* (Auckland: Whitcombe and Tombs, 1938).
66. Alistair Fox discusses the problems posed by this failed project and its consequences, provoking many to feel that Campion had not earned her Oscar for Best Original Screenplay, in "Puritanism and the Erotics of Transgression," 120–21, n. 45. See also Mary Paul, *Her Side of the Story: Readings of Mander, Mansfield and Hyde* (Dunedin: University of Otago Press, 1999). Important to my argument is not whether Jane Campion behaved inappropriately, but rather, the indisputable fact of her involvement with New Zealand film and television culture at a particular moment in her career.
67. Alison Butler, *Women's Cinema: The Contested Screen* (London: Wallflower Press, 2002), 105.
68. Hilary Radner, "'In Extremis': Jane Campion and the Woman's Film," in *Jane Campion: Cinema, Nation, Identity*, 14. See also Kathleen McHugh, *Jane Campion*, 16.
69. Gordon Collier judges that "with *An Angel at My Table*, New Zealand cinema comes of age," with reference specifically to the earlier biopics *Leave All Fair* and *Sylvia*. "Iconic Mythography in New Zealand Film," in *Defining New Idioms and Alternative Forms of Expression*, Cross/cultures, 23, ed. Eckhard Breitinger (Amsterdam: Rodopi, 1996), 217–18.
70. Sylvia Ashton-Warner, *I Passed This Way* (New York: Alfred A. Knopf, 1979), ix, 498.

Chapter 13

The Time and the Place: Music and Costume and the "Affect" of History
in the New Zealand Films of Jane Campion

Estella Tincknell

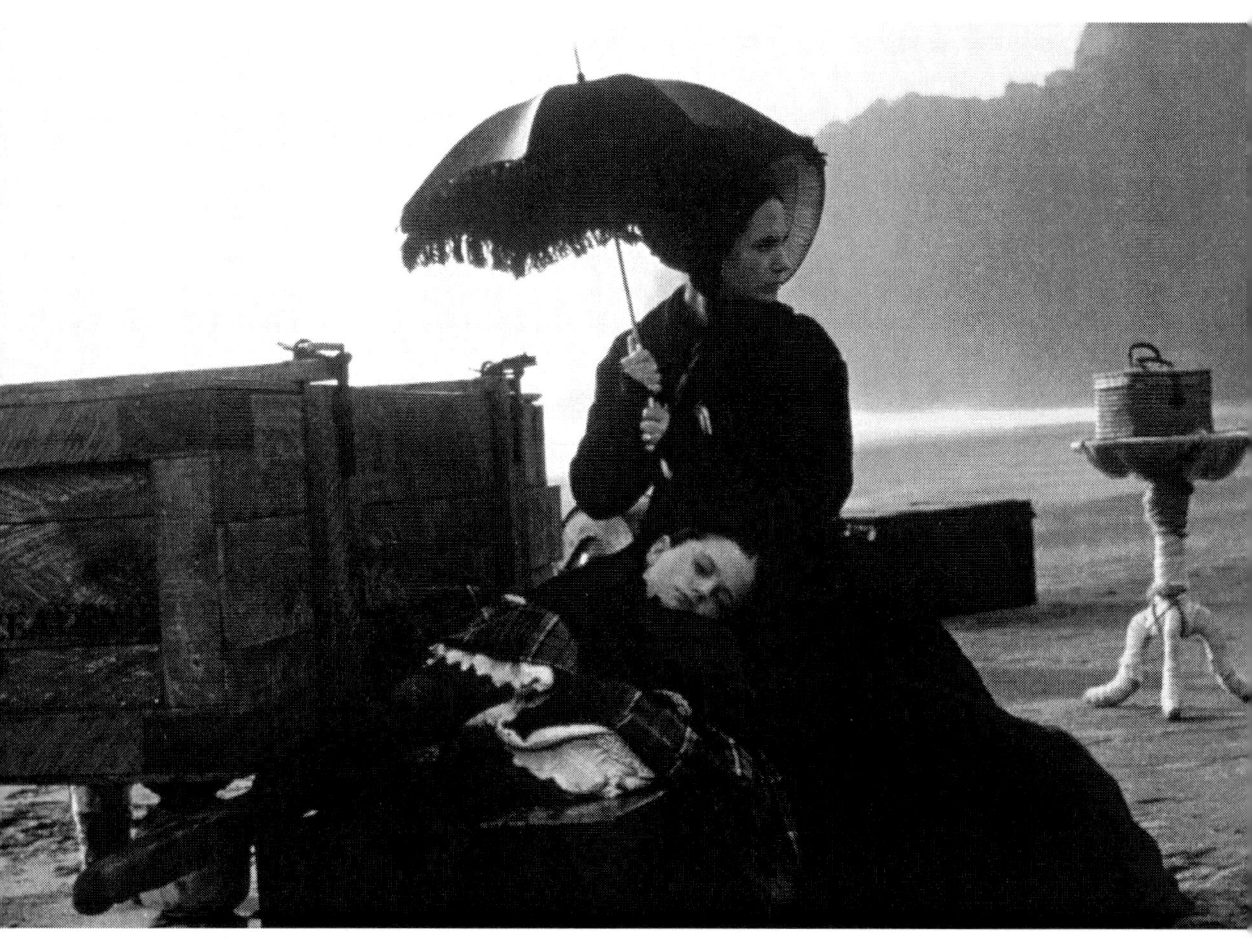

Ada and Flora in *The Piano*, 1993, dir. Jane Campion. Image courtesy of Miramax/Photofest.

Jane Campion's early films have frequently been read and (mis)represented as texts which, because of their focus on the interior lives of their female protagonists, situate femininity outside history. Such accounts overlook the fact that much of Campion's work is marked by a careful *staging* of the past for a contemporary audience in which the material specificities of time and place shape the life experience of her characters in important ways. This is especially true of two films: *An Angel at My Table* (1990) and *The Piano* (1993). Both Janet Frame (Kerry Fox) in the former and Ada McGrath (Holly Hunter) in the latter are located very precisely in temporal and spatial terms, not merely through narrative exposition but also by the powerfully affective means of music and costume. In this chapter I explore this in relation to the films' status as canonical post-feminist texts and (briefly) in the context of the director's most recent and highly acclaimed work, *Bright Star* (2009), a film that makes costume and music absolutely central to the teasing out of history.

Because my focus is on the two films most commonly identified as Campion's "New Zealand" works, it may be useful to begin by identifying how this is constituted. The subject, setting, and production context provide an obvious starting point. But it is the narrative and discursive focus on migration, journeys, landscape, boundaries of sea, sky and land, and on troubled cultural encounters that also defines them as distinctively kiwi texts. Set a century apart, one in the 1850s and the other (mainly) in the 1950s, both feature a narrative structured around journeys to and from the "old" and "new" worlds by women positioned as outsiders, and Ada McGrath's journey to New Zealand in *The Piano* is effectively reversed in Janet Frame's move to Europe and to London in *An Angel at My Table*. The later film sets its heroine within a larger narrative of nineteenth-century colonisation and struggles over land rights; the earlier, *An Angel at My Table*, (Campion's first major international success and originally devised as a television serial), positions her against an emergent national culture in the mid-twentieth century. These are only the most obvious continuities between the two films, however, as we will see.

While the importance of these period settings is widely acknowledged by critics, Campion's understanding of the past has also often been characterised as clouded by a fundamentally ahistorical construction of self and identity. One of the major disputes over the meaning and importance of *The Piano*, for example, has been around its problematic representation of the Māori people. Writers such as Linda Dyson and Anna Neill have argued that the film positions them outside history, "frozen in sacred time" and relegated to the role of noble savage, rather than occupying full historical consciousness and a central place in the temporal narrative.[1] While this liminal textual status is indisputable, I think the underlying premise of the criticism is flawed. As Maria Margaroni points out, *The Piano* actually carefully places both the Māori and their Pākehā colonisers at a transitional *historical* moment, a moment in which the colonial encounter has produced a violent rupture in their relationship to land and to identity, and a moment that will also bring into being the new beginning of a national history.[2] In other words, by setting *The Piano* in the 1850s just a decade after the Treaty of Waitangi, and by establishing clear parallels between the violence enacted upon Ada's body and upon the land by the colonising figure of Alisdair Stewart (Sam Neill), Campion signals a very clear preoccupation with the way in which New Zealand's national story can be told. *An Angel at My Table* is similarly precise in its construction of time and place, carefully evoking the South Island in the 1930s and 1940s and England and Spain in the 1950s in order to situate Janet Frame as an actor *within* history, not simply a commentator upon it.

So, how do these two films *do* history? It is, I think, primarily through their attention to the affective dimensions to the historical – how it feels, sounds, looks, senses – and it is this highly nuanced emphasis and the absence of some of the conventional tropes of the historical epic (such as the overt signalling of major national events that will impact upon the protagonists' lives) that may well lead to the misreading noted above. In this essay, therefore, I will focus on two of the affective elements that are central to the construction of temporal and spatial meaning in these films: music and costume.[3]

A dance to the music of time

All Campion's films make distinctive use of different musical "voices" as an aural textual layer in powerful ways. This involves both the use of especially composed scores and the deployment of popular music and song within the film diegesis as well as on the soundtrack. This mix is not unusual in contemporary cinema (partly because it facilitates the cross-promotion of music brands owned by parent companies), but Campion is not a filmmaker who relies on jukebox soundtracks to do the discursive work of her texts for her. Instead, the musical voices in her films work by a process of cultural layering and sedimentation, a building up of signification through indirect reference and allusion which, although in a minor key (no "great events" or "great men" stride through these narratives), is very carefully documented in historical terms.

For example, Michael Nyman's evocative and lyrical piano score for *The Piano* is both Romantic and Post-romantic in the sense that it refers to but does not wholly embrace Romanticism. It is powerfully referential to the work of Schubert, Brahms and Chopin, evoking a form of musical composition and playing that is identifiably "historical" in its relationship to the mid-nineteenth century Romantic style – "The Attraction of the Peddling Ankle" is based on Chopin's Mazurka Op. 7/I, for example – while also speaking to contemporary tastes. The rhapsodic structure, cyclical themes, dense texture and melodic repetition of the main theme tune of *The Piano*, "The Heart Asks Pleasure First," is characteristic of the Romantic mode as it is found in the work of Schubert and Chopin. It is chromatic, dramatic and, arguably, structurally constitutes a symphonic poem in that it offers in miniature the film's diegesis in a manner that resembles the Romantic sonata, with its developmental schema of expressive thematic harmonies and tensions.[4] In other words, the music is used to articulate the *temporal* and *historical* contexts in which the protagonists are located.

The main musical theme's intensely personal emotionality is also characteristic of the Romantic model in the sense that it is represented as coming directly from the heart rather than from a composer's pen, as is its articulation of the idea of an essential self whose interior core is being expressed. But it is also a meta-textual commentary on Romanticism: deploying the compositional register, style and idiom of the Romantic score while also maintaining a cultural distance from the genre's conventions. This distance is also mediated by the score's relationship to the context of performance and reception – particularly the knowledge that we have as an audience that this is not an "authentic" piece of nineteenth-century music but a kind of musical pastiche in which the more extreme characteristics of Romanticism have been intensified and exaggerated through repetition, and in order to signal their historicised status.

Even so, Pwyll ap Sion points to the high level of integration between music and image within *The Piano* through the particular use made of Nyman's music, which "draws the viewer closer, encouraging a direct engagement with its sounds." Ap Sion observes *The Piano*'s apparent reversal of music's usual diegetic role "on the margins" of a film text, whether as soundtrack or score; it is, instead, central to the film and plays a crucial discursive role in the production of meaning.[5] Indeed, piano playing (and the piano itself) occupies as pivotal a place in *The Piano* as that taken by the individual or paired performance of song and dance in the film musical; it is both expressive of a specific set of emotions that cannot otherwise be articulated, and it works to develop plot and character. However, ap Sion also notes that this integrative approach is differentially organised within *The Piano*. The solo piano playing is diegetically located, while the orchestral score on the soundtrack is not. This difference is crucial to the discursive function of the music as historical signifier: "the [orchestral score] occupies a more illustrative role," signifying the landscape, the Scottish settler community and the role played by Māori within it.[6]

Importantly, it is the *social* dimension to the soundtrack score – the communal character of the orchestra and orchestration – that overtly suggests the social-historical and which has one kind of role in the construction of period, while the solo performance on the piano emphasises the personal and individualised, and has a different relationship to the historical. The actual piano theme, then, represents Ada's interior self and it is through this that Romantic authenticity is both foregrounded and re-mediated by the film.

While the musical score of *The Piano* taken as a whole offers a subtle commentary on these historical relations, the character of Ada can be specifically cast as "authentic" in her romantic subjectivity because she has been situated within a period (the mid-nineteenth century) when the idea of an essential self as the privileged locus of identity had become culturally hegemonic. As a *woman* claiming that subjectivity, however, she remains limited in her access to expressivity. Playing the piano, for Ada, means "performance [becomes] a means of empowerment,"[7] but this can only be achieved with difficulty because of the problematic position femininity occupies within the public realm, a position which the film's own post-feminist perspective brings into relief.

The piano itself, in fact, constitutes the most eloquent "voice" to which she has recourse for much of the film, so that the relationship between body, performance, self and object is thoroughly entwined in a way that resembles the relationship the feminist theorist Donna Haraway identifies when she talks of the cyborg as a radical fusion of the organic and technological, and in which the "extended self" is a source of empowerment and pleasure.[8] For Ada, the difficulty of "speaking the self" as a woman is mediated by the piano's "cyborgian" eloquence. Her rapture when playing the instrument is therefore highly culturally specific to the film's period location, not transcendentally timeless, although the *representation* of such rapture as an overt articulation of feminine consciousness is itself only made possible by contemporary post-feminist culture.

Furthermore, the fact that it is a piano that facilitates Ada's romanticism to become her substitute voice is equally specific to the temporal, since it is only in the nineteenth century, with the industrialised manufacture of musical instruments and the development of a new middle-class market for "respectable" and family-orientated entertainment, that it becomes a domestic and largely feminised object, associated with the bourgeois home. The middle-class Ada's intense emotional attachment to and skilful playing of her piano, then, would have been impossible a hundred years earlier in 1750 and improbable a century later in 1950. Even so, the residual association of the piano with sensitive femininity is still persuasive, so that the film's representation of this instrument as the fetishised object of Ada's repressed desire is somehow entirely comprehensible to a modern audience. Imagine what a very different (possibly more radical) film this would have been if it had been titled *The Trumpet.*[9]

In this way, like the representation of Māori, far from presenting a woman "out of her time" or her place as some critics have suggested, the film's depiction of Ada's sensibility seems entirely consonant with early and mid-nineteenth-century Romantic femininity, especially the femininity voiced in the emergent literary culture of the period in the writings of the Brontës and Emily Dickinson. Ada is a thoroughly "Victorian" woman, not merely because she has been oppressed by patriarchy (which is not in itself specific to the nineteenth century, after all), but because of the *character* of her resistance to patriarchy, which is, unlike the film itself, fundamentally Romantic rather than political. Like Jane Eyre and Cathy Earnshaw, she is a woman whose very desire for the sublime is a symptom of her historical positioning. Yet this positioning is itself refracted through the lens of a postfeminist emphasis on social empowerment and sexual self-determination.

The use of the Romantic style of music also situates *The Piano* within time and place through its invocation of the genre of the melodrama. Other critics have noted the film's narrative continuity with the woman's film, with its traditional emphasis on mother–daughter relations, the ruptured family, private emotion and a "psychic" level of truth. There are two further levels of sedimentary meaning at play here, however. One is the direct and central relationship between music and drama in the very conception of the genre in its early theatrical form, in which dialogue was rhythmically spoken to a musical accompaniment – "melo" + "drama" – and signified the heightened emotions of specific characters. The genre's development and refinement as a film style within Classical Hollywood in texts such as *Stella Dallas* (King Vidor, 1937) and *Written on the Wind* (Douglas Sirk, 1956) cemented the Romantic connection between intensity of feeling, specifically feminine moral dilemmas and a lushly orchestrated and densely textured musical score. The pivotal role of *The Piano*'s score in expressing Ada's innermost feelings is, then, of a piece with the way the film knowingly references the film melodrama in its representational gestures. *The Piano* also references the conventions of Victorian theatrical melodrama, both directly in the diegetic performance of the gothic tale *Bluebeard's Castle*, which was a successful popular piece during the mid-Victorian period, and indirectly in the film's own staging of a love triangle that will culminate in violence. These references thus situate *The Piano* very specifically within a recognisable set of cultural traditions, as well as within a particular historical context of colonial anxiety and incipient violence.

Campion's attention to the specificity of music as an historical and historicised cultural practice is also a feature of the way deceptively simple folksongs are integrated into the textual structure of *An Angel at My Table* so that the social locatedness of Janet Frame's childhood is powerfully evoked. Don McGlashan's music reworks folk styles and melodies to suggest both New Zealand's Anglo-Celtic cultural heritage and, in the main theme tune's mournful singularity, the country's geographical isolation in the context of the global depression of the 1930s. Robert Burns's original poem on which this signature song is based, "Duncan Gray," has a demotic lyric and a theme of melancholic wandering which, as Suzette Henke points out, becomes a leitmotif throughout the film from the opening credits onwards.[10] The song seems to look both backwards and forwards simultaneously, invoking at once an "old" world of Celtic mysticism and a new one of seaborne adventure and uncertainty. Part Three, for example, begins with a flashback to the three young Frame girls seated on a windy cliff-top looking out to sea singing the song, clearly presaging Janet's imminent journey to Europe and her uneasy abandonment of childhood and its privations to face new forms of social torture.

While the score for *An Angel at My Table* makes extensive use of thematic variations on this haunting melody, played on recorders, guitar, xylophone, whistles, the triangle and piano accordion, it is important to note that these are all *modern* folk instruments, not "traditional" in an ancient sense, but products of a modernised folk community, and one which is no longer rooted in European soil. The main melodic theme, therefore, articulates this relationship between "old" and "new" identities and also the social and communal, in ways that echo but do not replicate the use of *The Piano*'s orchestral score. Instead, the folk music is complemented by a series of classical piano pieces, as well as by orchestral and solo performances, which represent Janet's intense interior life while also suggesting her desire for order and quietude.

These selections also work to situate Janet within the cultural environment of post-war Dunedin while offering a powerful mediation of her interior life. In the pivotal scene where she runs from her classroom as a novice primary school teacher, unable to cope with a school inspector's visit, it is Kathleen Ferrier's 1949 recording of Schubert's "An Die Musik" which saturates the soundtrack – a moment which manages to present Janet's torment as both universally recognisable and as historically located. Ferrier's deep contralto, with its extraordinary melancholic timbre, resonant as it is of post-war Britain's awakening from cultural austerity, places Janet within the specific context of the musical tastes available within a colonial culture in the early 1950s. Indeed, Ferrier's "Britishness" works to both locate and dislocate Janet: the latter's cultural references and store of cultural capital are drawn from a home that isn't home. And Ferrier's voice carries with it a whole range of powerful connotations: of the possibilities available to an "ordinary" woman who, like Janet, aspires to high culture; of the heightened affectivity that Lieder articulates and which is mirrored in Janet's own writing; and of an emergent bridge between the emotional constrictions of Frame's working-class origins (signified by the folk style) and a new potential for expressivity. Furthermore, the eerie disembodied-ness of this voice as it soars over the images of Janet's despair powerfully connotes the disembodied status of Frame's relationship to her "self."

In the last scenes, when Janet has finally found safety, serenity and focus, and is ensconced in a tiny caravan at the side of her sister's house where she can write in peace, the film ends with her trying out "the Twist" in the dusk alone and unpartnered, to the tinny sounds of a transistor radio. The twist to this twist is that it's a New Zealand version: it's by Herma Keil and the Keil Isles, a group whose fame never went much beyond the antipodes. But that is entirely appropriate. This move away from folk to rock and roll (another kind of folk music) comes as Janet finds contentment in her writing and is able to face her future – and modernity – full on. That this is marked in the film by a very clearly located bit of musical history which unequivocally places Janet in the early 1960s without actually having to spell it out is a fitting conclusion to the consistently subtle process by which historical locatedness is evoked musically throughout *An Angel at My Table*.

Costuming her place

The conventions of costuming in cinema are habitually linked to the realist film's deployment of two key premises: verisimilitude and expressiveness. Verisimilitude can simply take the form of fidelity to a genre's costume conventions (such as the gangster's sharp suit or the cowboy's hat and spurs), or it can be understood as closeness to everyday life, so that costuming guarantees the indexical "truth" of a film's depiction. When it comes to films set in the past, however, the costuming of period is also a way of establishing a claim to historical credibility. The more "pictorialist" heritage cinema texts (such as the Merchant-Ivory literary adaptations of the 1980s) heavily foreground this period detail, tending to fetishise individual objects – *things* rather than events or ideas – to authenticate their depiction of the past.[11] Yet because heritage pictorialism too often renders the past picturesque it also recuperates it, so that in such films costume stands in for "pastness" while the material social relations involved are rendered unproblematic. The bonnet especially carries these meanings: its iconic status signifies nostalgia for an apparently stable past and for a femininity whose relationship to social inequality has either become obscure and therefore available for sentimentalisation (exemplified by the glut of Jane Austen television adaptations in the 2000s), or which is marked by grotesquerie[12]. These polarisations, pleasurable though they may be in terms of a visual aesthetic, also construct the past as essentially and immutably "other."

Campion's work operates against this tendency of the heritage film. Interestingly, given the overt literary associations of both these films, she avoids these obvious generic ploys, so that both *The Piano* and *An Angel at My Table* occupy but do not pastiche a specific historical moment. She pays great attention to naturalistic detail but reworks it to eschew heritage cinema's clichés, an approach especially distinctive in the way costume is used in both film texts. If anything, as a consequence these films constitute a form of anti-heritage cinema, as does Campion's version of *Portrait of a Lady* (1996) and *Bright Star*. In each case, the aesthetic tropes of art cinema are deployed to distance the film from heritage pictorialism and its fetishisation of individual objects, substituting a more restrained, formalistic style. Yet the *expressive* role of costume to produce meaning beyond plot or story is also important.[13] Like the use of music, costumes in these "period" films express an interior self that extends outwards into the habitus, the lived reality, of everyday life. In Campion's most recent work, *Bright Star*, for example, it is the texture – the materiality – of clothing, of *cloth*, which is astonishingly "felt" in this extended fashion.[14]

Refuting the costume drama's prettification, then, Ada's black bonnet in *The Piano* starkly frames her white face with its dark eyes, outwardly signifying an austere intensity that does not conform to conventional 1990s models of beauty or to the Austen cult's nostalgia for an imagined past. Similarly, Janet's print dresses and blouses in *Angel* do not flatter her figure, but instead elaborate her physical awkwardness and therefore her internalised struggles to deal with her own flesh.

Stella Bruzzi has argued for a complex distinction between Campion's uses of costume in these films, identifying a difference between the construction of community through emblematic historical figures such as Janet Frame herself in *An Angel at My Table* and the use of costume to express the gendering of sexual fetishisation in *The Piano*. In the latter, she observes, the crinoline functions as an elaborately constructed garment that emphasises what it conceals, over-determining the woman's body as an object of desire through its overtly restrictive mechanisms. For Bruzzi, the sexualisation of costume in historical melodrama becomes a way of acknowledging female fetishism.[15] But this is to ignore the "real" existence of the crinoline as a material object with its own history, and it is also to remove the human characters from what is a highly specific, even if it is a fictionalised, historical context.

I therefore want to argue that in *The Piano* the crinoline becomes a very precise way of locating the woman as historical subject. There can be few garments loaded with a greater and more obvious kind of cultural-historical baggage than the crinoline, after all, and fewer still which serve as the nexus for a web of historical and cultural signifiers. It is not necessary to have a detailed knowledge of the history of western clothing and fashion to recognise the crinoline as the archetypal "Victorian" woman's dress and its widely deployed symbolic function in post-Victorian culture as a sign of female oppression. When our culture seeks to represent subjugation by patriarchy, it reaches for the crinoline as the equivalent of Chinese foot binding. When it wants to find examples of the awkward collision between mechanisation, fashion and an emergent consumer fetishism (never mind the sexual kind) within modernity (as in Veblen's work), it also reaches for the crinoline. So, it carries some very specifically historicised symbolic functions here, even if they are over-simplified.[16]

Yet the crinoline has alternative meanings attached to it, also located in the mid-nineteenth century, also developed retrospectively, this time in relation to the feminine romance. In the form of Scarlett O'Hara's ball gown in another "woman's film," *Gone with the Wind* (Victor Fleming, 1939), for example, it is cast as the epitome of a romantic/Romantic femininity that is self-determining and determined, resistant rather than subservient to excessive patriarchy and to those "Victorian values" of domestic servitude. Indeed, in terms of historical verisimilitude, this is exactly the way in which the crinoline was represented in the fashion culture of the 1850s and 1860s when it first appeared, as Elizabeth Wilson has pointed out – as a defiantly modern feminine gesture against the killjoys who found an interest in clothes frivolous and absurd. This one garment carries all of these meanings and others, too; it is a deeply contradictory piece of clothing. [17]

So, Campion's expressive deployment of Ada's crinoline in *The Piano* is highly astute. It de-familiarises those associations noted above and uncouples the crinoline from its own "costume" heritage. Instead, the garment figures as both restrictive and enabling; it is used as a kind of tent to offer night-time shelter from the storm for Ada and her daughter at the beginning of the film; yet its cage-like structure makes it easily caught on the branches of the trees surrounding their cabin, thus enabling Stewart to violently capture Ada towards the climax; through its weight it helps to tether her to the piano at the moment of her near drowning and "rebirth"; and it is the very symbol of Ada's modernity in her embrace of a new femininity at the end. In all of this, far from casting femininity or indeed the story as timeless, Campion presents Ada as a very precisely historically located figure, whose struggles and dilemmas are specific to her time and place in colonial New Zealand in 1850.

In *An Angel at My Table* it is hair ribbons and hand-knitted Fair Isle sweaters – those complex signifiers of a Celtic heritage and of the pre-war period – which connote a desperate, failed attempt at respectability by the "poor and smelly" Frames in the 1930s. The time and place of a New Zealand still looking to Great Britain for much of its cultural identity is powerfully evoked by such sartorial details. The young Janet's frayed jumper and single school skirt, her sisters' greying vests and knickers and brother's flannel shorts and Wellington boots for shoes, are central to situating the family within a depression context. But their vibrant clashing clothing colours also reverberate with the New Zealand landscape itself, offering flashes of brightness that suggest an incipient refusal of the dreary and the mundane. Janet's sister, Isabel, is consistently clad in startlingly vivid colours; her bright red beret, appliquéd pinafore and crocheted sweaters echoing the intensity of the natural scene around her as well as working to signal her extrovert personality and status as a leader within the family. In contrast, Janet's muted pink and blue embroidered blouses and ill-matched garments express her suppressed emotions and an as yet unfulfilled poeticism.

When Janet finally arrives in Ibiza in the second stage of her voyage of self-discovery, her floral dresses and frayed and bulky knits, worn uneasily on her voluptuous body, at first identify her abjection, setting her awkwardly apart from the largely male, middle class and cosmopolitan Anglo-American bohemian clique already living there. With their linen shirts and casually rolled up trousers, they exemplify a social ease and sense of entitlement that Janet struggles to attain. It is also Janet's unfashionability, her habitus of provincial and respectable taste, which locates her within a narrowly defined set of cultural expectations about femininity. Once she has begun to blossom in the heat of a love affair with a fellow poet, Janet's frumpy tea-dresses at least start to match her cardis, but her taste remains figured as profoundly lacking in style or flair. It is only when Janet has begun to discover her voice as a writer that she also finds a way of comfortably inhabiting her body and her clothes.

This move to a more confident and expressive sense of self is most powerfully foregrounded in the penultimate scenes set in literary London at the point when Janet has begun to acquire a reputation as a writer. Invited to a soirée at her agent's house to meet the novelist Alan Sillitoe and his wife, Janet arrives soaked through from the London rain in her thin and inadequate clothing. She is ushered into a comfortable bedroom and offered a sophisticated black cocktail dress to wear while her own cotton day frock dries out. Nothing expresses the social awkwardness she feels as economically as this brief exchange of clothing, but also her growing self-confidence and ability to carry off the temporary glamour she has been offered – just. In this brief scene the possibility of a future as a successful writer is presented, recast, refused and remodelled. Janet's literary world will not involve cocktail dresses or even cocktails, but it has been a necessary encounter that enables her to reject these worldly symbols. Such scenes also locate her within a crucial moment in British and commonwealth post-war literary culture, a moment in which writers such as Frame – and indeed Sillitoe – from backgrounds very different to those of the dominant literary class, were able to gain access to the literary sphere for the first time.

The place of costume and of music in these two films, then, is pivotal. Against the grain of the literary adaptation or heritage text they present a nuanced, complex approach to representing the past, one that acknowledges the centrality of affect to the construction of the historical subject. These modes of representation evoke a sense of place and of time in ways which cannot be articulated through expositionary dialogue or scene-setting, and are fundamental to Campion's careful, considered treatment of character and relationships. *Bright Star*, the director's most recent film at the time of writing, is exemplary in this respect in its lyrical attentiveness to and its affective evocation of the materiality of the early nineteenth century. Its use of chamber-style music centred on a limited number of instruments powerfully bridges sensibility and cognition to capture the atmosphere of nineteenth-century domestic life and culture, while the costumes not only express character in the sense of a distinctive individual (in particular the flamboyantly creative dressmaking of Fanny Brawne, played by Abby Cornish) but also express the social relationships that inflect that individual's identity. Rather than being ahistorical, as is sometimes claimed, then, both *The Piano* and *An Angel at My Table* deliberately engage with the specificities of time and place to recreate a fully historicised, and a richly affective, version of the past.

Notes

1. See Linda Dyson, "The Return of the Repressed? Whiteness, Femininity and Colonialism in *The Piano*," *Screen* 36, no. 3 (1995): 267–76; and Anna Neill, "A Land Without a Past: Dreamtime and Nation in *The Piano*," in *Piano Lessons: Approaches to* The Piano, ed. Felicity Coombs and Suzanne Gemmell (London: John Libbey), 136–47.

2. M. Margaroni, "Jane Campion's Selling of the Mother/Land: Restaging the Crisis of the Postcolonial Subject," *Camera Obscura* 53, no. 2 (2003): 92–124, esp. 109.

3. Jane Campion has described how she took care to costume the Maori characters in *The Piano* in line with records from the late-nineteenth-century which showed top hats being worn along with blankets, *kete* and *piupiu* by Maori at that time. Jane Campion quoted in *The New Zealand Herald* (16 September 1993, section 3:1.). Also, in *Cinema Papers*, 93 (May 1993): 6, Campion talks of her interest in a photo history of Maori and contemporary photographs as "a graphic visual metaphor of how Maori culture was assimilated by European culture." These references are recorded in Mary Paul, *Her Side of the Story: Readings of Mander, Mansfield, and Hyde* (Dunedin: Otago University Press, 1999), 75, 95.

4. The sonata form in classical music consists of three elements – exposition, development and recapitulation – which are organised into three or four movements characterised by a dramatic and "psychological" form of musical expression. The romantic sonata (roughly dominant between 1820 and the early 1900s, and developed by Brahms, Liszt and later Mahler) further emphasised this emotional dimension, seeking to create movement and 'texture' through the use of different but closely connected harmonic themes and melodies that would structure the various parts of the composition via repetition and expressive variation while retaining formal coherence.

5. Pwyll ap Sion, *The Music of Michael Nyman* (Aldershot and Burlington VT: Ashgate Publishing Ltd., 2007), 181.

6. Ibid., 173.

7. Ibid., 182.

8. Donna Haraway, *Simians, Cyborgs and Women: The Reinvention of Nature* (London: Free Association Books, 1991), *passim*. Haraway's argument is grounded in her feminist refusal of dualistic and essentialist accounts of gender difference and her recognition that "femininity" is produced discursively. The "cyborg" self is the consequence of the relationship between the human being and the machine in which identity is extended and transformed beyond the assumed boundaries of the stable, autonomous subject. Although Haraway's argument relates specifically to twentieth-century post-war technologies and what may be called post-modern culture, I think it can be applied here in recognition that the textual "consciousness" of *The Piano* is characterised by a post-modern and post-feminist refraction of the period in which the film is set.

9. Indeed, Krin Gabbard has discussed the peculiarly phallic meanings associated with the trumpet and with the jazz trumpeter on screen in his essay, "Signifyin(g) the Phallus: *Mo' Better Blues* and Representations of the Jazz Trumpet," in *Representing Jazz*, ed. K. Gabbard (Durham, NC: Duke University Press, 1995), 104–30.

10. Suzette A. Henke, "Jane Campion Frames Janet Frame: A Portrait of the Artist as a Young New Zealand Poet," *Biography* 23, no. 4 (2000): 651–69.

11. See John Hill, *British Cinema in the 1980s* (Oxford: Oxford University Press, 1999): Claire Monk, "The British 'Heritage Film' and Its Critics," *Critical Survey* 7, no. 2 (1995): 16–24; and Claire Monk, "Sexuality and the Heritage Film," *Sight and Sound* 5, no. 10 (1995): 32–34.

12. The latter is a feature found in some television classic novel adaptations, such as the BBC's 2008 version of *Little Dorritt*: all grimy stays, grubby bonnets and lank hair.

13. See Jane Gaines, "Costume and Narrative: How Dress tells the Woman's Story," in *Fabrications: Costume and the Female Body*, ed. Jane Gaines and Charlotte Herzog (London and New York: Routledge, 1990), 180–288.

14. Having noted this, it must also be acknowledged that *Bright Star* offers a rhapsody of prettiness in its visual style, from its lyrically photographed fields of bluebells and butterflies to its intense close-ups of Ben Whishaw and Abbie Cornish's lips, eyes and fingers as they embrace.

15. Stella Bruzzi, *Undressing Cinema: Clothing and Identity in the Movies* (London and New York: Routledge, 1997), 63.

16. See Thorstein Veblen, *Theory of the Leisure Class: An Economic Study of Institutions* (London: Unwin, 1925).

17. See Elizabeth Wilson's book, *Adorned in Dreams: Fashion and Modernity* (London: Virago, 1985) for more on this.

Chapter 14

Mining for Forgotten Gold: Leon Narbey's *Illustrious Energy* (1987)

Bruce Babington

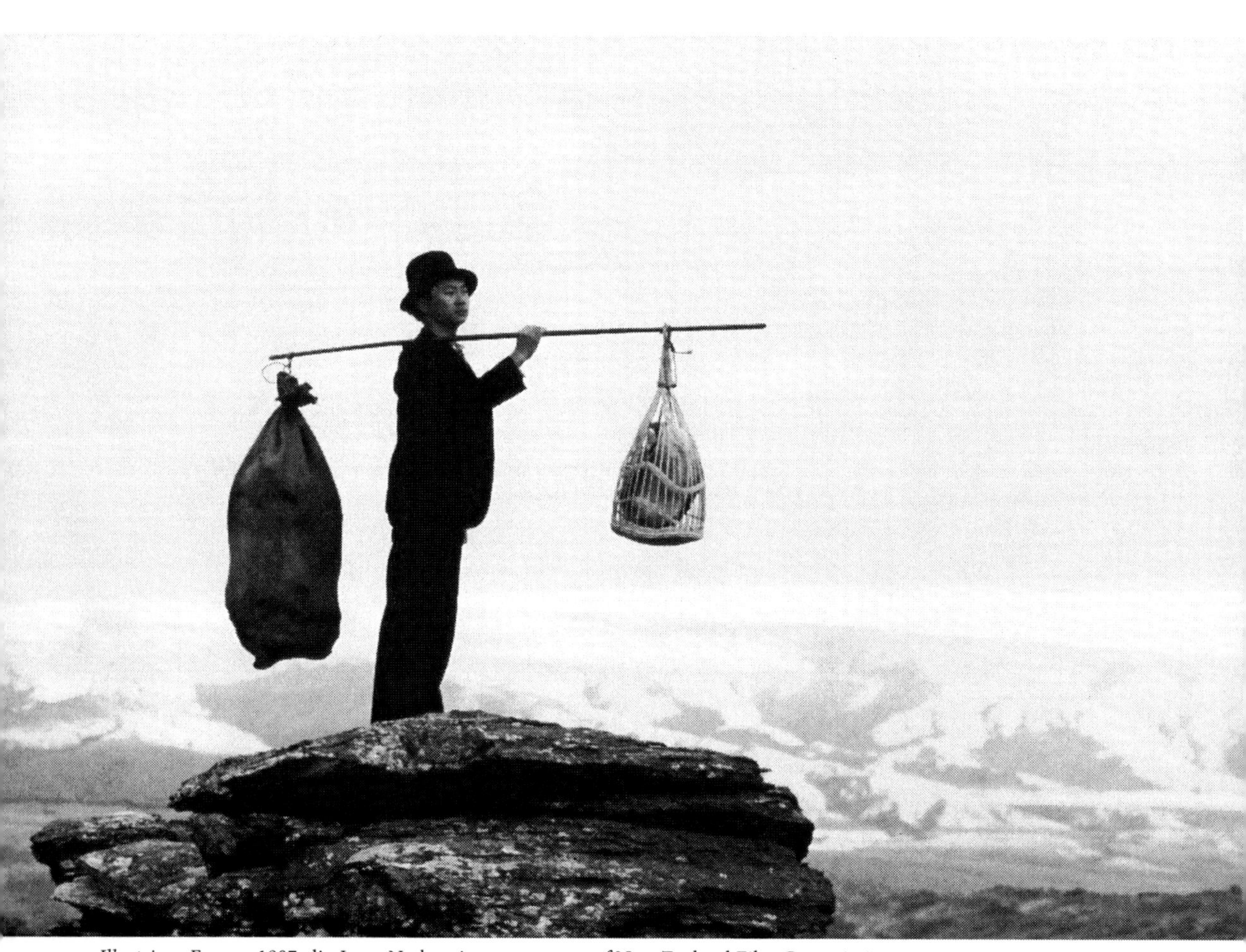

Illustrious Energy, 1987, dir. Leon Narbey, image courtesy of New Zealand Film Commission.

A belated centrality

Articles and interviews in the New Zealand periodical *Illusions* (no. 40, Winter, 2008), marking *Illustrious Energy's* twentieth anniversary, have advanced this previously all but obscured (but indubitably good) object of New Zealand cinema to a belated centrality. As befits a film whose subject is the largely overlooked – at the time of its 1987 release – history of the small fraction of the mid-nineteenth-century Cantonese diaspora which reached the Otago goldfields in 1866, *Illustrious Energy* has its own history of neglect, the result of the collapse of its producers, Mirage Films, just after its release, and its passing into American hands. This author, like the *Illusions* contributors, eventually found a copy of the Film Commission videotape, released on the back of the film's eight *Listener* Film and Television awards (including best director) which Narbey says was made from a TVNZ one-inch tape recording, imperfect with its cropped right and left hand sides, but otherwise adequate.[1]

Twenty years later, the renewed critical interest in the film is bound up with a complex of factors. First, the major influx of Chinese immigrants from the late 1980s on spectacularly reversed historical antipathy to Asian, especially Chinese, immigration, resulting in a present-day ethnic Chinese population of 100,000 – 2 per cent of the total, up from only 19,000 in 1986, just before the government drive to attract Chinese immigrants' perceived business skills. In the 1896 census, just after the film is set, the total Chinese population was only 3773 men and 86 women (including 148 "European Chinese," presumably mixed race offspring).[2] Second, influenced by this change, Chinese diasporic history became studied in New Zealand, as elsewhere. In New Zealand, this still continuing burst of excavatory writing was part of a concentration on immigrant minorities' histories just beginning when the film was made. Narbey and his co-writer Martin Edmond note their debt to the journals and photographs of the Rev. Alexander Don (1857–1934), the director of the Presbyterian Chinese mission, who is the one historical (as distinct from invented representative) character impersonated in the film, and Narbey adds their consultation of then recent publications by James Ng, Charles Sedgewick and Neville Ritchie, an archaeologist who had studied the Chinese goldfield sites.[3] Third, in the wake of the gigantification of New Zealand film in the *Lord of the Rings* era, the large number of offshore productions and big budgets created through international co-production in the new century, *Illustrious Energy* stands as an exemplary instance of successful small-scale feature filmmaking, wary of immediate market pressures and the forces of global homogeneity. Asked how *Illustrious*

Energy might be made today, Narbey, expressing a preference for the smaller scale and intimate, replied sardonically that "today we would have to have the spectacle of 10,000 gold miners on the flats with wide shots coming in and there would be a much bigger love interest or the conflict would be much bigger."[4] Fourth, Narbey's extensive career as director of photography on such films as *Rain of the Children* (Vincent Ward, 2008), *The Price of Milk* (Harry Sinclair, 2000), *Whale Rider* (Niki Caro, 2002), *Desperate Remedies* (Peter Wells and Stewart Main, 1993) and *Velvet Dreams* (Sima Urale, 1997) points to the visual interests which give *Illustrious Energy* a special place in a cinema not generally notable for visual complexity, something taken up in some of the *Illusions* pieces' emphasis on its treatment of landscape. Fifth, the filmmakers' combination of intellectual scrupulousness and vivacious invention makes *Illustrious Energy* required viewing for any serious thinking about filmic approaches to New Zealand's national past.

East by South

East by South, a recent collection of essays on Australasian perceptions of China and the Chinese, while covering New Zealand literature's connections (the young Mansfield's glancing underworld interest in "Ole Underwood," the malign stereotypes in John A. Lee's *Children of the Poor*, Robin Hyde's and James Bertram's travel writing, and even Jack Boddy's opera *Rewi Alley*), says nothing about filmic representations.[5] Of these, there are, in a field even smaller than the literary one, five that are notable.[6] In Hayward's *My Lady of the Cave* (1922), a lowlife Chinese commits suicide by jumping over a cliff, his stereotyped Chinglish ridiculed in subtitles ("Polis, polis, allee chance gone. I no hang"), drawing an onlooker's comment, "That'll save the hangman's job – been dodging the police for knifing a gumdigger." The moment, invoking contemporary popular sinophobia, depicts the Chinese as laughable, criminal and a danger to New Zealand. In an alternative world of 1908, the pioneer New Zealand filmmaker, Colin McKenzie, the imagined subject of Peter Jackson's and Costa Botes's mockumentary, *Forgotten Silver* (1993), created the world's first sound film, *The Warrior Season*, hiring the cheapest actors available, local Chinese. The extract shown is of a goldfield battle – not between whites and Chinese (the Australasian pattern), but between feuding Chinese, with close-ups of a pan used for sifting gold possibly alluding to *Illustrious Energy*. The primary joke is of a cinematic genius so obsessed with technical innovation that he forgets the audience will find the actors' unsubtitled Cantonese incomprehensible, thus dooming the film to abject failure. The early Jackson's many floutings of contemporary New Zealand's puritan residue of extreme political correctness hardly need detailing, with this one gaining laughter from, and in part perhaps at, linguistically blinkered attitudes that the Chinese language sounds ridiculous. However interpreted, Jackson's use falls into the category of Chinese as comic, with a touch of the criminal.[7]

This last is also found in Peter Wells's and Stewart Main's *Desperate Remedies* (1993) a different kind of invented history, anachronistically employing, for its fantasy Auckland circa 1840, a palimpsest of periods and styles that memorably creates a brief doubled chinoiserie (Grey's Avenue Gothic?), both sinister and beautiful when Jennifer Ward-Lealand visits Cliff Curtis in the extravagantly wrought mise-en-scène of an opium den. Such marginal representations underline the lack of filmic interest in the small New Zealand Chinese population. However, in *Broken English* (Gregor Nicholas, 1996), made after the 1980s immigration changes, and centring on non-traditional immigrants, the Croatian heroine, Nina, becomes involved in an illegal marriage business, arranging to marry a young Chinese male for a fee to enable him to stay in New Zealand. When Nina pushes Jasmin, a shady entrepreneurial Chinese, to up her $12,000 fee, she reminds her that it is "hard to find girls to marry these Chinese guys." Though their portrayal is not unfriendly, the Chinese couple, Wu and Clara, tend to the comic, especially in their strenuous attempts to produce a "small kiwi" to seal their desired New Zealandness. The film displays a certain ambivalence to the new large-scale Chinese immigration, balancing qualified affirmation with less positive undertones, especially when Nina and Eddie (her Māori boyfriend) find Clara and Wu with their possessions on the balcony of Nina's flat, ready to take up shared residence. *Kung Fu Vampire Killer* (Phil Davison, 2002), a low-budget horror film, which harks back to *Illustrious Energy*'s period in finding an indigenous horror plot in an undead Chinese vampire unwisely wakened from Dunedin's past, enacts an ingenious if roughly made local version of Freud's "return of the repressed."

An example of omission rather than commission, repression rather than its return, occurs in *Once Were Warriors* (Lee Tamahori, 1994). In Alan Duff's source novel, Jake Heke's gross antipathy towards "the Slit-eyes," the takeaway owners he sees as cheating and despising Māori, utilises a version of the nineteenth- and early twentieth-century fear of the abstemious hardworking Chinese, qualities paradoxically co-existing with the usual accusations of depravity and criminality. As Jake comments, their shop is "open seven days all year the cunts don't even close on Christmas day."[8] The passage's sense of danger comes from it being thought by a Māori, fracturing bonds which some historians have emphasised linking Māori and Chinese, between whom marriages were recorded (often, it is suggested, between Chinese market gardeners and Māori employees), as two minorities discriminated against by the Pākehā majority.[9] Though Jake's disdain is racist and irrational, in its crude way it might be seen to shadow some recent Māori objections to the scale of the new immigration as endangering the Māori position in a state envisaged in its Waitangi founding as bicultural rather than multicultural.[10] The film deletes this passage and its implications, an omission exhibiting a sensitivity to New Zealand's historic sinophobia, but arguably dubious in its evasion of complexity and conflict.

The lovely bones

Illustrious Energy's cinematic contexts set it apart as the only feature film in which immigrant Chinese experience moves to the centre as one among various pioneering histories.

Significantly, the film was made at a time when the old Australasian animus against Chinese was largely absent, the small local community being regarded as a "model minority,"[11] and before negative reactions to multicultural engineering made themselves felt among the happier manifestations of the changes.

Two early sequences in *Illustrious Energy* uncover meanings important to the narrative as it develops. In the first, three Chinese, the alluvial gold miners Chan and Kim (Chan's elderly father-in-law), and their friend and sponsor, Wong, dig into the barren Central Otago landscape to exhume the bones of Kim's old friend, Tong. In the second, mirroring, sequence the miners perform a different excavation, pickaxing rocks which they laboriously transport to the nearby river, hoping that when the pounded detritus is washed away they will be left with nuggets of gold. These two diggings, with their different material and spiritual objectives, besides also introducing the film's concern with landscape, trope the filmmakers' own unearthing of the largely hidden history the film restages, an archaeology retrieving its own forgotten gold, and revivifying buried bones.

In 1895, nearly 30 years after the Chinese miners arrived in the already heavily worked Otago goldfields, Chan (Shaun Bao) and Kim (Harry or Ha-lei Yip) seem to be the last still prospecting. The only other miners seen are one group of whites equipped with superior pressure hose technology. The cooperative Chinese work gangs with their common purses now defunct, Chan and Kim live isolated lives, regulated by backbreaking work, their goal finding enough gold to pay their debts and fares back home as well as enough profit to justify their long sojourn in New Zealand. Their rationale for being in the "Sun Gum San" (New Gold Hill) of New Zealand is emphasised by the letter from home that Wong (Peter Chin) gives Chan asking for money for the mother in law's medicine. Chan later tells Miss Li, the woman who becomes his lover, that he has previously been in Ballarat and Bendigo, as Kim presumably has too, the old man saying it is 27 years since he has seen his wife and that he cannot remember her face. As the much younger man, Chan possibly joined his relative later, leaving behind his wife who was six months pregnant with a son he has never seen; but time has taken its toll on him too: as he confesses to Miss Li, "I'm tired, tired of trying to remember."

Kim may not remember his wife's face, but his orientation is wholly towards the past. He speaks touchingly to Tong's bones, calling him "old friend" and assuring him he has not been forgotten. Though Chan is far from immune to memory's pull – as the film's most focalised character, he is the only one given direct (though interestingly distorted) visualised memories – his low-keyed quarrel with Kim suggests the generational differences typical of diasporic sub-societies, with the old holding to inherited patterns, the young diverging from them. Chan's statement to Li suggests memory as burden rather than solace, with the desire to return home increasingly less his and more a filial duty owed to Kim. The film's middle section – Chan's visit to town to pay debts and get provisions – is structured around alternating sequences juxtaposing Chan's outward looking interests, even where they lead him into trouble, with Kim back at the home, closed, resistant to all contact with the "white devils." In one memorable shot, Kim is shown lying rigidly paranoiac in bed grasping a huge machete, his prejudices paralleling, though with more excuse, the local sinophobia.

In the persuasive terms used by Bickleen Ng Fong to theorise diasporic experience, Kim is a type of "the sojourner" whose "essential characteristic" is "that he clings to the culture of his own ethnic group in contrast to the bi-cultural complex of the marginal man."[12] As Manying Ip adds, "Oral history evidence also shows that these men cared little about which country they were in, as long as the place offered them a means of living,"[13] in this different from the "marginal man" attempting to adapt to the new environment from its edges, a dichotomy enacted in diasporic sub-cultures generally.

Kim's position as absolute "sojourner," encouraged by his age, was almost inevitable in late nineteenth-century New Zealand, not only because of its anti Chinese legislation, including heavy poll taxes and refusal of naturalisation (for which the Prime Minister formally apologised in 2002), and anti-Chinese feeling orchestrated from the highest levels by major politicians such as Sir George Grey (a major Governor of New Zealand), Richard Seddon (the populist Prime Minister, 1893–1906), William Pember Reeves (politician, historian and poet) and Sir Apirana Ngata (a major twentieth-century Māori politician), evident where the gang of adolescents attacks Chan, singing "Ching Chong Chinaman," where thugs beat him up outside the circus, and pursue him on his way home, and in the hostile looks he receives from the town's blacksmith and the white miners. However, the Cantonese diaspora's sending away of men without women in order to encourage payments back home and ultimate return generally precluded ideas of permanent settling. These two intertwining factors led to what has been described as "an isolated, ageing, poverty-stricken group of people stranded in an alien land."[14]

Wong is Kim's opposite, a successful "marginal" man, combining aspects of actual entrepreneurs like (Choie) Charles Sew Hoy (1837–1901)[15] in Dunedin, William Kwok in Wellington and Thomas Wong Doo in Auckland, and of the few recorded instances of Chinese marrying white women.[16] Having sold his claim to Chan and Kim, Wong has moved into an expansive orchard business which he combines with money lending and staking immigrants, part social and patriotic service, and part capitalist enterprise. Hence his complex relationship with Chan, part friend, part sponsor, giving rise to Chan's flash of resentment, when Wong says he never asks for the money owed him, in his reply that "You never let us forget it." Wong, while retaining relationships with his compatriots, has successfully adapted into the new culture, as much as the extremely marginalised can, most obviously through marriage with a white woman. When Chan meets Wong's wife and their two offspring, indubitably Chinese but dressed as middle-class Victorian children, he looks soulfully at the sailor-suited boy, thinking of his unseen son, though that son must now be a young man. The marriage seems well-adapted, with Wong's wife fitting none of the usual denigratory stereotypes of women who married Chinese, but more like what Vincent Pyke, a Clyde Warden, described:

The Chinese interpreter, John Alloo has an Irish wife, and they live together very happily – have a fine family of boys and girls, who are well educated and speak and write English well. In Victoria, such marriages are very common and, and generally turn out well.[17]

However, hidden marital tensions are revealed when Wong's wife (Heather Bolton), having sympathised with Chan's distant wife, comments, "she's certainly had a widow's time of it," and asks him if Wong also has family, meaning a wife and children in Canton. When Chan replies that she must ask him herself, she says, "I can't, there are things he won't tell me." It seems likely that Wong has, more ruthlessly than Chan could ever do, shucked off his domestic past in his drive to establish himself in the colony as husband, father and successful businessman.

Poised uncertainly between Kim's commitment to the lost home and Wong's successful adaptation to a new one, Chan is both similar to and different from the historical character whom the filmmakers note as his inspiration, the unfortunate "Illustrious Energy" (preserved in the film's title) recorded in the Rev. Don's journals. Like him, Chan is a miner, but ultimately a survivor, not a victim. He doesn't go mad, isn't confined in an asylum, and isn't literally a poet like "Illustrious Energy," whose manuscripts were discovered in his room.[18] He does, however, inherit a poetic sensibility from him ("plum blossom fall and old man die"), and when asked to sing for his supper at the circus, he recites Li Po's poem "Drinking with a Friend in the Mountains," causing the boss to call him "our friend, the poet." Drawn to knowledge, his mind moves outwards, as two related moments show. Discussing the comet, he is impressed by the friendly surveyor's dismissal of Kim's claim that it portends bad luck as "superstition," repeating the word wonderingly, and later employing it when denying the afterlife to the Rev. Don (Peter Hayden) in their religious debate.

Chan spends much of the narrative physically on the move – towards the town (a composite of Clyde and Cromwell), within the town and its environs, returning home, and finally, after Kim's death, setting out again. This mobility is paralleled by his interior traversing between intellectual worlds, as when the surveyor asks him what he thinks about the comet and persists past Chan's conventional replies "the old man says" and "Chinese say," until his "what do *you* say?" draws from Chan "I see the sky. I feel the earth. I walk between," which can be read, after two wholly tradition-bound rejoinders, as an inflection of tradition and innovation, oriental and western views, into a personally felt definition. It is presumably this intellectual flexibility that leads Miss Li to misidentify him as coming from a big city.

In the last third of the film, Chan encounters Miss Li and the circus and is offered a job, which he has to refuse because of obligations to Kim. While he is away, Kim hides their recently multiplied savings (enough for both to return to China) somewhere in the landscape, but dies suddenly, leaving Chan unable to find them.

The narrative, now centred on Chan, resists unambiguous resolution. He buries Kim, then burns the letter from home, which suggests that, with the savings lost, he knows he is unlikely to return, leaving no alternative but New Zealand, a life which Wong, despite local prejudices, has some reason to regard optimistically. "It's a good country," he says. "There's a place for you – here." But is this freedom or entrapment for Chan? Two creatures owned by Chan suggest both alternatives. The goose he carries with him trapped in a basket-like container, but also the cricket, a recurring visual and aural presence, closely identified with Chan, both being fighters and singer/reciters, shown coming out of its cage which Chan opens to let it escape when he finally leaves the homestead. Will Chan, now also released, return to the circus? The suggestion may be yes, but the film resists closing on him being welcomed by Miss Li and the multicultural counter family, ending instead with unfinished journeying. Though the tone is not unoptimistic – with the landscape in morning sunshine, Chan walking briskly, Jan Preston's music underwriting these elements – the ending might be compared with that of Frank Sargeson's earlier, famous short story, "The Making of a New Zealander" (1939), with its suggestions of a long adaptive process: "And Nick was saying he was a New Zealander. But he knew he wasn't a New Zealander. And he knew he wasn't Dalmatian any more."[19]

The film begins with Tong's bones being exhumed for return, alluding to the diasporic Chinese custom of sending home the bones of those who died while sojourning, through burial societies which arranged transport on "corpse ships," the best known local example of which, the SS Ventnor, sank off Hokianga in 1902 with the remains of 499 Chinese on board (including Charles Sew Hoy, who died, like Tong and Kim, before returning). The fate of some of the remains lost with the Ventnor has recently been clarified, with a party of their New Zealand Chinese descendants visiting Mitimiti, where local Māori reburied them after they drifted ashore, gaining the thanks of the relatives, and providing another curious inflection of Māori-Chinese relationships. (The search for the remains were also dramatised in a play by a New Zealand Chinese, Renee Liang, *The Bone Feeder*, staged in Auckland in 2009.)[20] Will Kim's bones be finally returned, his exhumation several years on being a last duty owed by Chan? Where will Chan's bones lie eventually, depending, if not on accident, on whether he defines home as Canton, New Zealand or Australasia? (If he joined the Australian circus for any length of time, that would take him back to Australia, only returning to New Zealand on tour; on the other hand, Sew Hoy, as adapted as any nineteenth-century Chinese could be to New Zealand, still chose return to Canton, reminding us of the complexities of migration and allegiance, then, as now.) Around the time the film is set in, one of the few major nineteenth-century New Zealand poems appeared, Arthur H. Adams's "The Dwellings of Our Dead" (quoted by Rudall Hayward in a funerary scene in his 1927 *The Te Kooti Trail*).[21] Adams's poem is about corpses and bones, where they wish to lie, and where the burgeoning nation wishes them to lie. Its extraordinariness – what makes it more than an impressive but conventional elegy for the dead "brave white and braver brown" of the New Zealand Wars – resides in the tension between the poem's nationalist desire to claim the immigrant dead as the nation's founding mortalities and these dead's posthumous "despair" (in the context of this essay, one might say, like Kim's) at being separated from their (though in this case very English) home envisaged in terms of a grey-walled, beech tree-shaded country churchyard.

Pasco's circus and "the wonderful Miss Li"

Both of Narbey's and Edmond's features, *Illustrious Energy* and the later *The Footstep Man* (1992), involve historical reconstruction, a process, if self-conscious, involving a double perspective – the contemporary viewer and the historical viewed. This self-conscious bi-temporality is explicit within *The Footstep Man*, where 1990s New Zealand filmmakers work on the post-production of a film, *Monsieur Henri*, set in Toulouse Lautrec's Paris, with Sam, the sound effects man of the title, and Vida, the director, interpreting the film in conflicting ways through their own psychological needs and identifications with the characters. *Illustrious Energy* has no such explicit double time frame (what one might call *The French Lieutenant's Woman* effect after the influential Reisz/Pinter 1991 collaboration from the John Fowles novel) and eschews the other more overt strategies by which historical films often underline past-present relations – for example, the prologue in which the past comes to light for present interpreters, or, more allusively, the play with deliberate anachronism that creates past/present parallels, as with the relation between the 1870s and 1980s in *Utu* (Geoff Murphy, 1983). In *Illustrious Energy* such doubleness is always implicit – generally in the presumptions of the film's address that the audience no longer shares old prejudices, and that the Chinese are part of the country's pioneer history, and particularly depending on detail readable with reference to the present being undisruptive of the sense of an authentic past valued by Narbey and Edmond, as their painstaking research indicates. For instance, when Chan looks through the surveyor's theodolite, nothing breaks with historically verifiable detail (surveying was going on in Central Otago from 1857). Chan is clearly fascinated by the surveyor (Desmond Kelly) and his theodolite, for earlier he approached the surveyors' camp, but rather than going up to it, turned away, his curiosity obvious but unfulfilled. Later, travelling towards the township, he sees the theodolite unattended, and looks through it, gaining the upside-down view of the landscape given by the old-fashioned instrument, which is transformed into a travelling shot as he adjusts it. Given the similarity of the theodolite to the camera view, even, with the travelling shot, to a moving picture camera, the surveyor, with his sympathy for Chan (not shared by his younger partner, who mutters "he's only a Chinaman. Give 'em an inch and they'll take a mile"), acts by extension as a surrogate for the contemporary film director himself, a retrospective sympathy for the outsider dominating his own mode of "surveying." In this sense, the theodolite's inverted image also suggests the changed view that later history brings (cf. the military photo taken near the beginning of *Utu*) – rhymed with the earlier significant moment when Chan, lying on the ground, stares at the upside down image of the overhanging cliff. Notably, in their refusal to paint an unrelieved picture of prejudice and to place the viewer too condescendingly above the past, the filmmakers do not allow the modern surveyor/ filmmaker to be the only sympathiser – as well, there are a little girl who smiles at Chan from the hotel entrance before her mother calls her away, Wong's wife, the Reverend Don with his commitment to the Chinese immigrants, and the members of Pasco's Circus.

Like his meeting with the surveyor and his theodolite, Chan's encounter with the circus touring the small Central Otago townships is historically plausible. Circuses were a major nineteenth-century entertainment in Australia (Miss Li tells Chan that the circus as well as she is Australian), playing to widely distributed populations, including the gold towns which provided early audiences, with some extending the Australasian circuit to New Zealand, which is how Pasco's Circus happens to be in central Otago. Though major international circuses such as Cooper & Bailey's and Chiarini's toured New Zealand in the late 1870s, most of the touring circuses were Australian family companies like Fitzgeralds' and Wirth's.[22] However, though important, this is not the whole story, for though sanctioned by historical fact, the circus and Miss Li narratives at points subtly engage the implicit double temporality of the film, and, further, without overtly breaking its realism, occasionally move into something close to magic realism.

Miss Li introduces Chan to the multicultural circus, the mixed makeup of which, dictated by the international currency and exchange of circus skills, was a contemporary fact, with a study of Fitzgerald Bros, who made trans-Tasman tours from 1894 on, revealing a multicultural and multiracial community with aboriginals as well as performers from Germany, Japan, Java, England and United States, to compare with Pasco's "family" which includes a Chinese, the Afro-American male who helps Chan after he's been attacked, a gypsyish looking woman (whose appearance suggest Central European or South American origin), as well as a number of dwarves.[23] For all its magical, utopian elements and artistic genesis in Narbey's love of Fellini,[24] this representation of the circus has roots in reality, for it was at the time a small multicultural society in which ethnic and racial difference were not feared but welcomed, a microcosm of what the larger society's attitude might ideally be. (This utopianism, though, is tempered by realism in that such considerations mean nothing to the thugs who attack Chan during the show). The circus is a white Australian concern, reflecting social realities, but its bluff white Australian boss is thoughtful, unprejudiced and kind, delivering his dinner table admonition to the acrobats as a joke at which they and the rest of the company laugh, and publicly welcoming Chan as a visitor from "the flowery land," an interesting phrase in that it was frequently used, like the word "celestials," by sinophobic journalism with hostile irony, something wholly missing from Pasco's pleasant greeting. Australia's nineteenth century sinophobia (motivated by its north's closeness to Asia, by the large number of Chinese in Queensland and the Northern Territory, and orchestrated by *The Bulletin* and some of its most distinguished writers as a major constituent of growing nationalism) was more virulent than New Zealand's, which was, in many ways, a lesser imitation of Australia's. However, Australia, after the Greek and Italian immigration of the 1940s and 1950s, loosened its attitude to Asian, especially Chinese, immigration ahead of New Zealand, instituting a consciously multicultural agenda which New Zealand followed a few years later, and which is the contemporary context of the film.

"The wonderful Miss Li"

The brevity and unfinishedness of the love plot that Narbey sardonically imagined being made "much bigger" in 2008 is at one with the film's insistence on staging history through low-keyed happenings, suggesting political meanings while avoiding overtly political incidents (such as one might imagine in an alternative, less subtle scenario – a goldfields anti-Chinese riot ("the spectacle of 10,000 goldminers on the flats"), Seddon electioneering sinophobically, or, slightly temporally and geographically transposed, Lionel Terry's notorious shooting of the old ex-miner Joe Kum in Haining Street, Wellington, in 1905 as a protest against the Yellow Peril. Chan meets Li (Geeling Ng) very late in the film, and there is only one shot of them together in bed in a sequence mostly concentrated on land and skyscapes. Yet, for all this discretion, hovering over the representative details of her biography – Chinese father driven away by Australian minefield riots, English dancer mother bringing her up in Melbourne – an aura of magic attends her. "For your mystification and pleasure" intones the ringmaster to the Thompson's Farm audience; "Would you welcome the wonderful Miss Li," repeating the phrase "the wonderful Miss Li." At her entry in a turquoise oriental gown, Chan is plucked from the audience to take a passive role as she weaves traditional sleight-of-hand around him. Bewildered by this, he staggers off, after which she disrobes to show a revealing turquoise and black basque and moves into her exotic fire dance and fire-eating finale, watched fixedly by Chan until the thugs attack him.

Her earlier eruption into Chan's life has its magical aspects, too. Walking through the township, he is drawn to the Pasco's Circus poster dominated by a representation of the fire-eating Li. Then, next day, walking home, he is knocked down by her carriage while crossing a bridge, an accident which leads him to the circus and spending the night with her. However, exceeding this serendipity, the strangest element is that before he has actually encountered her (except through the poster), Li figures powerfully in the first of the two visions in which he sees his wife and the son he has never met. These complex moments, fleeting but rich in implication, dramatise Chan's desires and anxieties, staging a moment where (perhaps conjoined in the complex contractions of dreamwork with his mother and himself as child), his wife calls out to him a lip-readable, almost audible "Where are you?" Both visions enact a condensation in which Li merges with the wife (/mother?), more explicable in the second instance, Chan's dream, which occurs (though with a rationally inexplicable synchronicity), at the moment of Kim's death, because of the couple's recent intimacy. The opium-induced first vision in the gambling den, which occurs as a white prostitute and two Chinese try to push him into sex with her, presumably in order to rob him, seems uncanny, even magical, since Chan has only ever seen Li in the circus poster, suggesting an extraordinary force in her reaching out through the roughest portrait. For Chan, desire and guilt coalesce – desire for Li and what she signifies, and duty and nostalgia for the wife and son, joining past and future. The wife's "Where are you?" melds psychic and geographical meanings: Where are you when I need you? Where are you (in your thoughts), in Canton or New Zealand, with the wife or another woman?

It is symptomatic of Chan's readiness to modulate traditional ways that the woman who attracts him is identified with the dangerous eating of fire. She is also the first modern woman he has met, modern in her ambiguous border crossing, feminine (appearing as a kind of oriental *ewig weibliche* in her circus act), but dressing, when she goes ahead of the circus, in a man's black suit and hat. She is also self-defining, claiming that she is not Chinese but "Australian" (at a time when Australia was for many a whiteness defined against Chineseness), using the term as a kind of mantra of liberation, even rather oddly suggesting that she wears men's clothes because she is Australian. She is thus a more extraordinary version of Wong's self-determination, with her refusal of the median term "Chinese Australian," and with a perhaps similar ruthlessness shown in her apparent lack of concern about her parents. Her unconventionality is further marked by her sleeping with Chan on the day she meets him, even though she knows he is married. It is fitting then that when she meets him, she "literally sweep[s] Chan off his feet,"[25] knocking him down, in a reversal of the ubiquitous "meet cute" in which the man bumps into the woman or knocks over something she is carrying. Given her association with the modern, it is fitting that this meeting happens on a bridge clearly late nineteenth-century modern in its Victorian engineering, as distinct from the primitive modes of crossing ravines and rivers seen in the rest of the film. A beguiling character, shifting between the realism of most of the film and symbolic and even magical meanings, Miss Li, like Wong, offers meanings and possibilities that play into the more complexly felt dilemmas of place, allegiance and future that Chan faces as he walks towards the future in the film's closing moments, dilemmas which, through their historical specificity, still resonate for present audiences attuned to the complexities of identity in a global and glocal world.

Notes

1. Duncan Petrie, "'The Rhythm of the Process': An Interview with Leon Narbey," *Illusions* 40 (2008): 4–8.
2. Bickleen Ng Fong, *The Chinese in New Zealand: A Study in Assimilation* (Hong Kong: Hong Kong University Press, 1959), 33. James Belich, using Fong's statistics, writes that between 1871 and 1920 15,500 Chinese entered New Zealand, but almost all returned home (*Paradise Reforged* (London: Allen Lane/Penguin, 2001), 21–22).
3. "Notes from the Director," 32nd London Film Festival, 1988. See also Laurence Simmons, "'That Rare Thing a Film that is also a Work of Art': Laurence Simmons interviews Martin Edmond," *Illusions* 40 (2008): 21–24. On Don, see James Ng, "Don, Rev. Alexander," *Online Dictionary of New Zealand Biography*, http://vuw.dnzbgovt.nz/dnzb/.
4. Petrie, "The Rhythm of the Process," 8.
5. Charles Ferrall, Paul Millar and Karen Smith (eds), *East By South: China in the Australasian Imagination* (Wellington: Victoria University Press, 2005).
6. This discussion is centred on feature films, but the New Zealand Film Archive holds two short documentaries on the Chinese miners, *Chinaman's Gold* (Alan Brady, 1981) and *The Missing Miners* (Alex Clark, 2006). Narbey's earlier filmic connections with China can be traced in the three documentaries he photographed in China for the director Geoff Steven: *Gung Ho – Rewi Alley and China* (1979), *The Humble Force* (1979), and *China's Patriot Army* (1980). Like Narbey's, Rudall Hayward's short documentaries were about China rather than Chinese in New Zealand: *New China* (1958), *Wonders of China* (1958), and *Rewi Alley Interview* (1960). All three are in the Archive, though the uncatalogued *Children of the Goldrush: Arrowtown Centenary* (1962), unseen by this author, probably refers to the Chinese miners.

7. Minor Chinese characters appear in Jackson's *King Kong* (2005) where Lobo Chan plays Choy, the ship's cook, and in *The Lovely Bones* (2009), where Nikki Soo plays Holly.

8. Alan Duff, *Once Were Warriors* (Auckland: Vintage, 1990), 82.

9. On Chinese-Maori relations and marriages, see Manying Ip, "Chinese Immigrants and Transnationals in New Zealand: A Fortress Opened," in *The Chinese Diaspora: Space, Place, Mobility and Identity*, ed. Laurence J. C. Ma and Carolyn Cartier (Lanham, MD: Rowman and Littlefield, 2003), 339–58, esp. 355.

10. Ranginui Walker, "Immigration Policy and the Political Economy of New Zealand," in *Immigration and National Identity in New Zealand: One People, Two Peoples, Many Peoples?* ed. S. W. Greif (Palmerston North: Dunmore Press, 1995), 282–301.

11. Brenda Allen, "Identity and Cultural Salience in *Illustrious Energy*," *Illusions* 40 (2008): 9–13, esp. 10.

12. Bickleen Ng Fong, *The Chinese in New Zealand: A Study in Assimilation* (Hong Kong: Hong Kong University Press, 1959), 4ff. The "marginal man" is borrowed from Everett V. Stonequist, via R. E. Park, and "The sojourner" from Paul C. P. Siu.

13. Manying Ip, "Chinese New Zealanders: Old Settlers and New Immigrants," in *Immigration and National Identity in New Zealand*, 161–200, esp. 161.

14. Ibid., 169.

15. James Ng, "Sew Hoy, Charles," *Online Dictionary of New Zealand Biography*, http://vuw.dnzbgovt.nz/dnzb/. See also P. S. Butler, *Opium and Gold* (Martinborough: Alister Taylor, 1974), 109.

16. Writing of the goldmining era, Fong notes only four cases of Chinese- non-Chinese intermarriage in Dunedin, "two Chinese with white wives, one with a half-caste Maori wife, and a Chinese woman with a white husband." Fong, *The Chinese in New Zealand*, 105.

17. Quoted in *Opium and Gold*, 57–58. Butler also records many anti-Chinese statements of the time, 54–58.

18. Ibid., 47.

19. Frank Sargeson, "The Making of a New Zealander," *Collected Stories* (Auckland: Blackwood and Janet Paul, 1974), 116.

20. On the sinking of the S.S. Ventnor and the reburial of some of the bones in local *urupa*, see www.kamirawhanau.com/stories/ss_ventnor_revisited and http://nla.gov.au/nla.news-article 9590889. On the sending back of bones from the USA, see Pan Lyan, *Sons of the Yellow Emperor: A History of the Chinese Diaspora* (New York: Kodanshe International, 1994), 55. On Renee Liang's play, see "New Play Explores Early Kiwi-Chinese Heritage," http://www.scoop.co.nz/stories/CU0909/SOO226.htm.

21. *The Collected Verses of Arthur H. Adams* (Melbourne: Whitcombe and Tombs , 1913), 53–55.

22. For material on nineteenth-century Australian circuses, see Mark St Leon, *Spangles and Sawdust: The Circus in Australia* (Melbourne: Greenhouse Publications, 1983); and www.edencircus.com/News%20press.htm; http://www.pennygaff.com.au/heritage.html; http://circushistory.org/publications.htm; and http://www.gov.au/pub/nlasnews/2006/apr06/story.

23. Gillian Arrighi, "Roll up to the Circus," www.nla.gov.au/pub/nlanews/2006/apr06/story-3.

24. Petrie, "The Rhythm of the Process," 8.

25. Allen, "Identity and Cultural Salience," 12.

Filmography

Primary films discussed

***Broken Barrier* (1952)**

Directors: Roger Mirams and John O'Shea
Writer: John O'Shea
Cinematographer: Roger Mirams
Producers: Roger Mirams and John O'Shea
Production company: Pacific Films
Cast (chief characters): Kay Ngarimu (Rawi), Terence Bayler (Tom), Mira Hape (Kiri), Bill Merito (Johnny), George Ormond (Alec), Lily Te Nahu (Maata), Dorothy Tansley (Mrs Sullivan) and F. W. French (Mr. Sullivan)
Running time: 71 minutes.

***The Bush Cinderella* (1928)**

Director: Rudall Hayward
Writer: Henry Hayward
Cinematographer: Rudall Hayward
Producer: Rudall Hayward
Production company: Rudall Hayward
Cast (chief characters): Dale Austen (Margaret Cameron/Mary Cameron), Walter Gray (Andrew Cameron), Tony Firth (Sergeant Bennett), Allan Cornish (the Doctor), Ernest Yandall (Michael Myrgadroyd) and Fred Chatwin (the Detective).
Running time: 84 minutes.

The Chant of Jimmie Blacksmith (1978)

Director: Fred Schepisi
Writer: Fred Schepisi (novel by Thomas Kenneally)
Cinematographer: Ian Baker
Producers: Fred Schepisi and Roy Stevens
Production companies: The Film House and Victoria Films
Cast (chief characters): Tommy Lewis (Jimmie Blacksmith), Freddy Reynolds (Mort Blacksmith), Ray Barrett (Farrell), Jack Thompson (Rev. Neville), Angela Punch McGregor (Gilda Marshall), Steve Dodds (Tabidgi), Peter Carroll (McCready), Ruth Cracknell (Mrs Heather Newby), Don Crosby (Newby), Elizabeth Alexander (Petra Graf), Peter Sumner (Dowie Steed), Tim Robertson (Healey), Ray Meagher (Dud Edmonds), Brian Anderson (Hyberry) and Jane Harders (Mrs Healey)
Running time: 120 minutes.

Crooked Earth (2001)

Director: Sam Pillsbury
Writers (in alphabetical order): Karin Altmann, Michael Brindley, Greg McGee, Waihoroi Shortland and Gavin Strawhan
Cinematography: David Gribble
Producer: Robin Scholes
Production company:
Cast (chief characters): Temuera Morrison (Will Bastion), Jaime Passier-Armstrong (Ripeka Bastion), Lawrence Makoare (Kahu Bastion), Quinton Hita (Api), Nancy Brunning (Marama), Sydney Jackson (Pettigrew) and George Henare (Tipene)
Running time: 95 minutes.

A Daughter of Dunedin (1928)

Director: Rudall Hayward
Writer: Rudall Hayward
Cinematographer: Rudall Hayward
Producer: Rudall Hayward
Production company: Rudall Hayward
Cast (chief characters): Dale Austen (School teacher), Norman Scurr (Freddy Fishface) and "Tiff" Bennett (Bill Cowcockeye)
Running time: 35 minutes.

Desperate Remedies (1993)

Directors: Peter Wells and Stewart Main
Writers: Peter Wells and Stewart Main
Cinematographer: Leon Narbey
Producer: James Wallace
Production company: NZ Film
Cast (chief characters): Jennifer Ward-Lealand (Dorothea), Kevin Smith (Lawrence Hayes), Lisa Chappell (Anne Cooper), Cliff Curtis (Fraser) and Michael Hurst (William Poyser)
Running time: 92 minutes.

The Feathers of Peace (2000)

Director: Barry Barclay
Writer: Barry Barclay
Cinematographers: Michael O'Connor and Bretton Richards (with John Miller as Still Photographer)
Producers: Ruth Kaupua-Panapa and Don Selwyn
Production company: He Taonga Films
Cast (chief characters): Sonny Kirikiri (Riwai), Calvin Tuteao (Hiriwanu Tapu), John Callen (Freeman), Michael Lawrence (Broughton), Star Gossage (Waiteka), Alan De Malmanche (Judge Rogan/Interviewer), Lawrence Makoare (Pemako), David Stott (Johnstone), William Davis (Pomare), Patrick Wilson (Johannes Engst), Ray Bishop (Meremere), Graheme Moran (Henry Halse), Eryn Wilson (Cooper Maines), Michael Holt (Bishop Selwyn), Mick Innes (Captain Harewood), Roimata Taimana (Koche), Lionel Waaka (Catechist Tamihana), Peter Tait (Will Sanders), John Paekau (Practical Farmer), Max Auld (Ewing), Ngamaru Raerino (Rakatau Katike), Rakai Karaitiana (Young Assistant), David Mercer (Surgeons Assistant), Prince Davis (Eel Worker), Herena Wood (Moemoe), Gina Emery (Farming Wife), Tama Davis (Pumipi), Pineaha Murray (Horomona), Piri Davis (Pohatu), Piripi Daniels (Te Wetini), Manu Korewha (Toenga Te Poki), Jason Greenwood (Surgeon), Antonio Maioha (Ngati Tama Warrior), Steven Smith (Tamakaroro) Michael Morissey and John Brazier (Interviewers) and Joanna Paul (Voice Over Commentary)
Running time: 82 minutes.

Greenstone (1999)

Director: Chris Bailey (with Jim Goddard)
Writers: Stephen Lowe, Greg McGee and Dean Parker
Cinematographer: Allen Guilford

Producer: Chris Bailey

Production company: Communicado

Cast (chief characters): Richard Coyle (Sir Geoffrey), Norman Forsey (Captain Barnes), George Henare (Te Manahau), Te Paki Cherrington (Te Hau), Tungia Baker (Whetu), Simone Kessell (Marama), Matthew Rhys (Sam), Andy Anderson (Lamont), Norman Fairley (Manager), Tim Balme (Father Michael), Mandie Gillette (Siobhan), Alison Wall (Lady Evelyn), Anna Mcphail (Queen Victoria), Christopher Cooke (Prince Albert), Bruce Hopkins (Soldier), Renee Brennan (Jane), Willa O'Neill (Elizabeth), Olivia Skinner (Emma), Stuart Turner (Elyot Barlow), Chris Bailey (Bosun), Peter Bailey(Neptune) and Bruce Hopkins (Lord Halford)

Running time: 343 minutes (eight episodes of approximately 42 minutes).

Heavenly Creatures (1994)

Director: Peter Jackson

Writers: Frances Walsh and Peter Jackson

Cinematographer: Alun Bollinger

Producer: Jim Booth

Production company: Wingnut Films

Cast (chief characters): Melanie Lynskey (Pauline), Kate Winslet (Juliet), Sarah Pierse (Honora), Diana Kent (Hilda), Clive Merrison (Henry), Simon OConnor (Herbet), Jed Brophy (John/Nicholas), Peter Elliott (Bill Perry), Gilbert Goldie (Dr Bennett), Geoffrey Heath (Rev Norris), Kirsty Ferry (Wendy), Jonathan Hulme (Ben Skjellerup), Moreen Easen (Miss Stewart), Elizabeth Moody (Miss Waller) and Liz Mullane (Mrs Collins)

Running time: 105 minutes.

Illustrious Energy (1988)

Director: Leon Narbey

Writers: Martin Edmond and Leon Narbey

Cinematographer: Alan Locke

Producers: Don Reynolds and Chris Hampson

Production company: Mirage Entertainment

Cast (chief characters): Shaun Bao (Chan), Harry Ip (Kim), Peter Chin (Wong), Geeling (Li), Desmond Kelly (Surveyor), Heather Bolton (Mrs Wong), Peter Hayden (Reverend Don) and David Telford (Stan Pasco)

Running time: 95 minutes.

Iris (1984)

Director: Tony Isaac
Writer: Keith Aberdein
Cinematographers: James Bartle and Howard Anderson
Producers: John Barnett and Tony Isaac
Production company: Endeavour Productions/Aotea Enterprises
Cast (chief characters): Helen Morse (Iris Wilkinson), Phillip Holder and John Bach
Running time: 90 minutes.

It's Lizzie to Those Close (1983) (*see* **A Woman of Good Character***)*

Journey for Three (1950)

Director: Michael Forlong
Writer: Michael Forlong
Cinematographer: Randall Beattie
Producer: Stanhope Andrews
Production company: New Zealand National Film Unit
Cast (chief characters): Margaret McNulty (Margaret Allen), Stewart Pilkington (Harry White), Elizabeth Armstrong (Cassie McLeod) and Francis Renner (The Foreman)
Running time: 40 minutes.

The Killing of Kane (1971)

Director: Warren Dibble
Writer: Warren Dibble
Cinematographer: Waynne Williams
Producer: Chris Thompson
Production company: New Zealand Broadcasting Corporation
Cast (chief characters): Alan Jervis (Charles Kane), Napi Waaka (Tītokowaru), Peter Vere-Jones (Kimble Bent), Anthony Groser (Lt Col T. McDonnell) and Ray Henwood (Major Hunter)
Running time: 51 minutes.

Leave All Fair (1985)

Director: John Reid
Writers: Stanley Harper, Maurice Pons, Jean Betts and John Reid
Cinematographer: Bernard Lutic
Producer: John O'Shea
Production company: Pacific Films
Cast (chief characters): John Gielgud (John Middleton Murry), Jane Birkin (Marie Taylor/
   Katherine Mansfield) and Feodor Atkine (André de Sarry)
Running time: 90 minutes.

Mauri (1988)

Director: Merata Mita
Writer: Merata Mita
Cinematographer: Graeme Cowley
Producer: Merata Mita
Production company: Awatea Films
Cast (chief characters): Anzac Wallace (Rewi Rapana), Eva Rickard (Kara), James Heyward
   (Steve), Susan D. Ramari Pail (Ramari), Sonny Waru (Hemi), Rangimarie Delamere
   (Awatea), Willie Raana (Willie Rapana) and Geoff Muphy (Mr. Semmens)
Running time: 99 minutes.

My Lady of the Cave (1922)

Director: Rudall Hayward
Writer: Rudall Hayward
Cinematographer: Frank Stewart
Producer: Rudall Hayward
Production company: Bay of Plenty Films
Cast (chief characters): Hazel West (Beryl) and Bob Ramsey (Gordon Campbell)
Running time: 71 minutes.

The New Zealand Wars (1998)

Director: Tainui Stephens
Writer: James Belich
Cinematographer: Richard Long

Producer: Colin McRae
Production company: Landmark Productions
Presenter: James Belich
Running time: 250 minutes (five episodes at 50 minutes).

Ngati (1987)

Director: Barry Barclay
Writer: Tama Poata
Cinematographer: Rory O'Shea
Producer: John O'Shea
Production company: Pacific Films
Cast (chief characters): Tutu Ngarimu Tamati (Uncle Eru), Ngawai Harrison (Hine), Wi Kuki Kaa (Iwi), Oliver Jones (Ropata), Judy McIntosh (Jenny Bennet), Iranui Haig (Nanny Huia), Tawai Moana (Nanny Ngaropi), Michael Tibble (Tione), Ross Girven (Greg Shaw), Connie Pewhairangi (Sally), Norman Fletcher (Dr Paul Bennet), Lucki Renata (Dike), Kiri McCorkindale (Sue) and Paki Cherrington (Mac)
Running time: 88 minutes.

Once Were Warriors (1994)

Director: Lee Tamahori
Writer: Riwia Brown (novel by Alan Duff)
Cinematographer: Stuart Dryburgh
Producer: Robin Scholes
Production company: Communicado
Cast (chief characters): Rena Owen (Beth), Temuera Morrison (Jake), Mamaengaroa Kerr-Bell (Grace), Julian (Sonny) Arahanga (Nig), Taungaroa Emile (Boogie), Rachael Morris (Polly), Joseph Kairua (Huata), Cliff Curtis (Bully), Shannon Williams (Toot) and Pete Smith (Dooley)
Running time: 102 minutes.

The Piano (1993)

Director: Jane Campion
Writer: Jane Campion
Cinematographer: Stuart Dryburgh
Producers: Jan Chapman, Alain Depardieu and Mark Turnbull

Production companies: New South Wales Film and Television Office, Jan Chapman Productions, CIBY 2000 and Australian Film Commission

Cast (chief characters): Holly Hunter (Ada), Harvey Keitel (Baines), Sam Neill (Stewart), Anna Paquin (Flora), Kerry Walker (Aunt Morag), Genevieve Lemon (Nessie), Tungia Baker (Hira), Te Whatanui Skipwith (Chief Nihe), Pete Smith (Hone) and Cliff Curtis (Mana)

Running time: 120 minutes.

Pictures (1981)

Director: Michael Black

Writers: Robert Lord and John O'Shea (idea by Michael Black)

Cinematographer: Rory O'Shea

Producer: John O'Shea

Production company: Pacific Films

Cast (chief characters): Kevin J. Wilson (Alfred Burton), Peter Vere-Jones (Walter Burton), Helen Moulder (Lydia Burton), Elizabeth Coulter (Helen Burton), Terence Bayler (John Rochfort), Matiu Mareikuira (Ngatai) and Ken Blackburn (James Gilchrist)

Running time: 87 minutes.

Rabbit Proof Fence (2002)

Director: Phillip Noyce

Writer: Christine Olsen (novel by Doris Pilkington)

Cinematographer: Christopher Doyle

Producers: Phillip Noyce, Christine Olsen and Joan Winter

Production companies: Rumbalara Films, Australian Film Commission, Australian Film Finance Corporation and Showtime Australia

Cast (chief characters): Everlyn Sampi (Molly Craig), Tianna Sansbury (Daisy Craig Kadibill), Laura Monaghan (Gracie Fields), David Gulpilil (Moodoo), Ningali Lawford (Maud), Myarn Lawford (Molly's Grandmother), Deborah Mailman (Mavis), Jason Clarke (Constable Riggs), Kenneth Branagh (A. O. Neville), Natasha Wanganeen (Nina), Garry McDonald (Mr. Neal), Roy Billing (Police Inspector), Lorna Leslie (Miss Thomas) and Celine O'Leary (Miss Jessop)

Running time: 94 minutes.

Rewi's Last Stand (1925)

Director: Rudall Hayward
Writer: Rudall Hayward (based on the narratives of James Cowan)
Cinematographer: Frank Stewart
Producer: Rudall Hayward
Production company: Maori War Films
Cast (chief characters): Frank Remo (Dr Wake), Nola Casselli (Cecily Wake), M. Millington (Miss Jessica Wake), Eric Yates (Colonel Grieg), Edmund Finney (Kenneth Gordon), Fred Mills (Colonel Dobby), Cadia Taine (Mrs Wake), Wightman McCombe (Sir George Grey), Chief Mita (Hitiri Paerata), H. J. Bentley (Cabinet Minister), Mr. Alexis (Von Tempsky), Chas Archer (General Cameron), W. Surrell (Lieutenant Colonel McDonnell) and Tina Hunt (Takiri)
Running time: 34 minutes.

Rewi's Last Stand/The Last Stand (1940)

Director: Rudall Hayward
Writer: Rudall Hayward
Cinematographer: Rudall Hayward (with Edwin Coubray and Jay McCarthy)
Producer: Rudall Hayward
Production company: Equity British Films
Cast (chief characters): Te Miha (Ariana), Stanley Knight (Ben Horton), Leo Pilcher (Robert Beaumont), Selwyn Wood (Rev. Morgan), Phoebe Clarke (Mrs Morgan), Tom Moisley (Old Tom), Henare Toka (Tama te Heu Heu) and Rauriti te Huia (Rewi Maniapoto).
Running time: 93 minutes.

River Queen (2005)

Director: Vincent Ward
Writers: Vincent Ward, Toa Fraser and Kely Lyons
Cinematographer: Alun Bollinger
Producers: Chris Auty and Don Reynolds
Production companies: Silverscreen Films and The Film Consortium
Cast (chief characters): Samantha Morton (Sarah O'Brien), Kiefer Sutherland (Doyle), Cliff Curtis (Wiremu), Temuera Morrison (Te Kai Poi), Anton Lesser (Baine), Rawiri Pene (Boy), Stephen Rea (Francis) and Wi Kuki Kaa (Old Rangi)
Running time: 94 minutes.

The Te Kooti Trail (1927)

Director: Rudall Hayward
Writers: Rudall Hayward and Frank Bodle
Cinematographers: Rudall Hayward and Oswald Calwell
Producer: Rudall Hayward
Production company: Whakatane Films
Cast (chief characters): Jasper Clader (Rev J Winslow), Billie Andreasson (Alice Winslow), Arthur Lord (Eric Mantell), Eric Yandall (Geoffrey Mantell), Edward Armitage (Sir Richard Mantell), Te Pairi Tu Te Rangi (Te Kooti), H. Redmond (Jean Guerrin), Mary Kingi (Erihapeti), Tina Hunt (Monika), A. P. (Patiti) Warbrick (Taranahi), J. Tennant (Barney O'Halloran), J. Warner (Jules Vidoux), Tom McDermott (Gilbert Mair), Arapeta Tuati (Te Rangihiroa) and Tipene Hotene (Baker McLean)
Running time: 103 minutes.

Ten Canoes (2006)

Directors: Rolf de Heer and Peter Djigirr
Writer: Rolf de Heer
Cinematographer: Ian Jones
Producers: Rolf de Heer and Julie Ryan
Production companies: Adelaide Film Festival, Fandango, Special Broadcasting Service and Vertigo
Cast (chief characters): Crusoe Kurddal (Ridjimiraril), Jamie Gulpilil (Dayindi/Yeeralparil), Richard Birrinbirrin (Birrinbirrin), Peter Minygululu (Minygululu), Frances Djulibing (Nowalingu), David Gulpilil (The Storyteller), Sonia Djarrabalminym (Banalandju), Cassandra Malangarri Baker (Munandjarra) and Philip Gudthaykudthay (The Sorcerer)
Running time: 90 minutes.

Utu (1983)

Director: Geoff Murphy
Writers: Geoff Murphy and Keith Aberdein
Cinematographer: Graeme Crowley
Producers: Don Blakeney, Kerry Robinson and David Carson-Parker
Production company: Utu Productions
Cast (chief characters): Anzac Wallace (Te Wheke), Bruno Lawrence (Williamson), Wi Kuki Kaa (Wiremu), Kelly Johnson (Lieutenant Scott) and Tania Brisowe (Kura)
Running time: 116 minutes (original version), 100 minutes (revised version).

***Whale Rider* (2002)**

Director: Niki Caro
Writer: Niki Caro (novel by Witi Ihimaera)
Cinematographer: Leon Narbey
Producers: Tim Sanders, John Barnett and Frank Hubner
Production company: South Pacific Pictures
Cast (chief characters): Keisha Castle-Hughes (Paikea), Rawiri Patene (Koro), Vicky Haughton (Nanny Flowers), Cliff Curtis (Porourangi), Grant Roa (Uncle Rawiri), Mana Taumaunu (Hemi), Rachel House (Shilo), Tauṅgaroa Emile (Willie), Tammy Davis (Dog), Mabel Wharekawa-Burt (Maka), Rawinia Clarke (Miro), Tahei Simpson (Miss Parata), Roimata Taimana (Hemi's Dad), Elizabth Skeen (Rehua), Tyrone White (Jake), Taupua Whakataka-Brightwell (Ropata), Tenia McClutchie-Mita (Wiremu), Peter Patuwai (Bubba), Rutene Spooner (Parekura), Riccardo Davis (Maui) and Apiata Whangaparita-Apanui (Henare)
Running time: 97 minutes.

***A Woman of Good Character* (1980) (also known as *It's Lizzie to Those Close* in an extended version of 74 minutes released in 1983)**

Director: David Blyth
Writer: Elizabeth Gowan
Cinematographer: John Earnshaw
Producer/Designer: Graham McLean
Production company: Filmcraft
Cast (chief characters): Sarah Peirse (Lizzie), Jeremy Stephens, Derek Hardwick, Bruno Lawrence, Martyn Sanderson and Ian Watkins
Running time: 50 minutes.

Other films cited

Adventures of Dot, The (dir. Cyril J. Sharpe, 1928)
Adventures in Maoriland: The Making of Hei Tiki (dir. Geoff Stevens, 1985)
Aguirre: The Wrath of God (*Aguirre der Zorn Gottes*) (dir. Werner Herzog, 1972)
Among the Cinders (dir. Rolf Hädrick, 1983)
An Angel at My Table (dir. Jane Campion, 1990)
Apocalypse Now (dir. Francis Ford Coppola, 1979)
Apron Strings (dir. Sima Urale, 2008)
Aroha: A Story of the Maori People (dir. Michael Furlong, 1951)

Artemesia (dir. Agnès Merlet, 1997)
Bad Blood (dir. Mike Newell, 1982)
Bad Taste (dir. Peter Jackson, 1987)
Bar Harbour (dir. Margaret Cram Showalter, 1936)
Battle of Elderbush Gulch, The (dir. D. W. Griffith, 1913)
Bettie of Blenheim (dir. Lee Hill, 1928)
Beyond Reasonable Doubt (dir. John Laing, 1980)
Birth of a Nation, The (dir. D. W. Griffith, 1915)
Birth of New Zealand, The (dir. Harrington Reynolds, 1922)
Black Robe, The (dir. Bruce Beresford, 1991)
Blue Velvet (dir. David Lynch, 1986)
Bondage of Barbara, The (dir. Emmett J. Flynn, 1919)
Boy (dir. Taika Waititi, 2010)
Braindead (dir. Peter Jackson, 1992)
Bread and Roses (dir. Gaylene Preston, 1993)
Brideshead Revisited [television series] (dirs Charles Sturridge and Michael Lindsay-Hogg, 1981)
Bright Star (dir. Jane Campion, 2009)
Bright Victory (dir. Mark Robson, 1951)
Broken English (dir. Gregor Nicholas, 1996)
Camille Claudel (dir. Bruno Nuytten, 1988)
Casablanca (dir. Michael Curtiz, 1942)
Centenary of Cinema Trailer (dir. John O'Shea, 1996)
Children of the Goldrush: Arrowtown Centenary (dir. Rudall Hayward, 1962)
Chinaman's Gold (dir. Alan Brady, 1981)
China's Patriot Army (dir. Geoff Steven, 1980)
Chunuk Bair (dir. Dale G. Bradley, 1991)
Coal Miner's Daughter (dir. Michael Apted, 1983)
Comata, the Sioux (dir. D. W. Griffith, 1909)
Constance (dir. Bruce Morrison, 1984)
Cover Story [Episode 10, television series] (dir. Mike Smith, 1996)
Crush, The (dir. Alison Maclean, 1992)
Daughter of a Sheep Rancher, The (dir. unknown, 1913)
Daughter of Australia, A (dir. Lawson Harris, 1922)
Daughter of Christchurch, A (dir. Rudall Hayward, 1928)
Daughter of Dawn, The (dir. Norbert A. Myles, 1920)
Daughter of Dixie, The (dir. unknown, 1911/1916)
Daughter of Invercargill, A (dir. Rudall Hayward, 1928)
Daughter of Masterton, A (dir. Rudall Hayward, 1928/1929)
Daughter of the West, A (dir. William Bertram, 1918)
Daughter of the Wilderness, A (dir. Walter Edwin, 1913)

Dil Hai Tumhaara (*My Heart Is Yours*) (dir. Kundan Shah, 2002)
Dragonwick (dir. Joseph Mankiewicz, 1946)
First Two Years at School, The (dir. Margaret S. Thompson, 1950)
Fitzcarraldo (dir. Werner Herzog, 1982)
Flight of the Albatross (dir. Werner Meyer, 1993 [1996])
Footstep Man, The (dir. Leon Narbey, 1992)
Forgotten Silver [television] (dirs Costa Botes and Peter Jackson, 1995)
Frances of Fielding (dir. Lee Hill, 1928)
French Lieutenant's Woman (dir. Karel Reisz, 1981)
Frighteners, The (dir. Peter Jackson, 1996)
Frontier of Dreams. [Episode 3, "When Worlds Collide," Television Series] (dir. Howard Taylor, 2005)
Gaslight (dir. George Cukor, 1944)
Gentleman's Agreement (dir. Elia Kazan, 1948)
Germany, Year Zero (dir. Roberto Rossellini, 1948)
Gone up North for a While (dir. Paul Maunder, 1972)
Gone with the Wind (dir. Victor Fleming, 1939)
Governor, The (dir. Tony Isaacs, 1977)
Green Dolphin Street (dir. Victor Saville, 1947)
Groundhog Day (dir. Harold Ramis, 1993)
Gung Ho – Rewi Alley and China (dir. Geoff Steven, 1979)
Heart of the High Country [mini series] (dir. Sam Pillsbury, 1985)
Hei Tiki (dir. Alexander Marky, 1935)
Hinemoa (dir. Gaston Méliès, 1912)
Hinemoa (dir. George Tarr, 1914)
Home by Christmas (dir. Gaylene Preston, 2010)
Home of the Brave (dir. Mark Robson, 1949)
Howard's End (dir. James Ivory, 1992)
How Chief Te Ponga Won His Bride (dir. Gaston Méliès, 1913)
Humble Force, The (dir. Geoff Steven, 1979)
In the Mood for Love (dir. Wong Kar Wai, 2000)
Jane Eyre (dir. Robert Stevenson, 1944)
Josephine Barker Story, The (dir. Brian Gibson, 1991)
Kannapolis N. C. (dir. H. C. Waters, 1941)
King Kong (dir. Peter Jackson, 2005)
Kingpin (dir. Mike Walker, 1985)
Kung Fu Vampire Killer (dir. Phil Davison, 2002)
Last of the Mohicans, The (dir. Michael Mann, 1992)
Last Samurai, The (dir. Edward Zwick, 2003)
Last Tattoo, The (dir. John Reid, 1994)

Little Dorritt [television series] (dirs Adam Smith, Dearbhla Walsh and Diarmuid Lawrence, 2008)

Longest Winter, The (dir. Tony Isaacs, 1974)

Lord of the Rings: The Fellowship of the Ring (dir. Peter Jackson, 2001)

Lord of the Rings: The Two Towers (dir. Peter Jackson, 2002)

Lord of the Rings: The Return of the King (dir. Peter Jackson, 2003)

Lost Boundaries (dir. Alfred L. Werker, 1949)

Loved by a Maori Chieftess (dir. Gaston Méliès, 1913)

Lovely Bones, The (dir. Peter Jackson, 2009)

Mais ne nous délivrez pas du mal (*Don't Deliver Us from Evil*) (dir. Joël Séria, 1971)

Making Utu [documentary featurette] (dir. Gaylene Preston, 1982),

Mamma Mia! (dir. Phyllida Lloyd, 2008)

Mary Stuart (*Marie Stuart*) (dir. Albert Capellani, 1908)

Mary of Morton (dir. Lee Hill, 1928)

Massacre, The (dir. D. W. Griffith, 1914)

Meet New Zealand (dir. Michael Forlong, 1949)

Meet the Feebles (dir. Peter Jackson, 1989)

Mesmerized (dir. Michael Laughlin, 1986)

Missing Miners, The (dir. Alex Clark, 2006)

Mission, The (dir. Roland Joffé, 1986)

Mr Wrong (dir. Gaylene Preston, 1985)

My Brilliant Career (dir. Gillian Armstrong, 1979)

Nellie of Nelson (dir. Lee Hill, 1928)

New China (dir. Rudall Hayward, 1958)

New Zealand Now Number Seven: Bushman (prod. New Zealand National Film Unit, 1952)

New Zealand Cinema: The Past Decade [television documentary] (prod. Kaleidoscope 1987).

No. 2 (dir. Toa Fraser, 2006)

Olive of Orange (William R. Reed and Dal Clausen, 1928)

One Hundred Crowded Years (dir. H. H. Bridgeman, 1940)

Out of Africa (dir. Sidney Pollack, 1985)

Out of the Blue (dir. Robert Sarkies, 2006)

Passage to India, A (dir. David Lean, 1984)

Patsy of Palmerston (dir. Rudall Hayward, 1928)

Perfect Strangers (dir. Gaylene Preston, 2003)

Picnic at Hanging Rock (dir. Peter Weir, 1975)

Pictorial 23: Pumicelands (dir. John Feeney, 1954)

Pinky (dir. Elia Kazan, 1949)

Pioneer Women [television series] (dir. Pamela Jones, 1983)

Portrait of a Lady (dir. Jane Campion, 1996)

Price of Milk, The (dir. Harry Sinclair, 2000)

Priscilla of Parkes (William R. Reed and Dal Clausen, 1928)
The Quiet Earth (dir. Geoff Murphy, 1985)
Rain of the Children (dir. Vincent Ward, 2008)
Rebecca (dir. Alfred Hitchcock, 1940)
Rewi Alley Interview (dir. Rudall Hayward, 1960)
Richard John Seddon, Premier (dir. Tony Isaacs, 1973)
Roi s'amuse, Le (dirs Albert Capellani and Michel Carré, 1909)
Romance of Hine-moa, The (dir. Gustav Pauli, 1926 [1927])
Rome, Open City (*Roma, città aperta*) (dir. Roberto Rossellini, 1945)
Room with a View, A (dir. James Ivory, 1985)
Rua, Te (dir. Barry Barclay, 1992)
Sampson and Delilah (dir. Warwick Thornton, 2009)
Searchers, The (dir. John Ford, 1956)
Shadow of a Doubt (dir. Alfred Hitchcock, 1943)
Shortland Street [television series] (prod. South Pacific Pictures, 1992–)
Simba (dir. Brian Desmond Hurst, 1955)
Sione's Wedding (a.k.a. *Samoan Wedding*) (dir. Chris Graham, 2006)
Sleeping Dogs (dir. Roger Donaldson, 1977)
Sleeping with the Enemy (dir. Joseph Rubin, 1991)
Starlight Hotel (dir. Sam Pillsbury, 1987)
Stella Dallas (dir. King Vidor, 1937)
Suspicion (dir. Alfred Hitchcock, 1941)
Sweet Dreams (dir. Karel Reisz, 1985)
Sweetie (dir. Jane Campion, 1989)
Tama Tu. (dir. Taika Waititi, 2004)
Tam of Tamworth (dir. William R. Reed and Dal Clausen, 1928)
Tangata Whai Rawa O Weneti, Te (dir. Don Selwyn, 2002)
Tangata Whenua [television series] (prod. Pacific Films, 1974)
Tuberculosis and the Maori People of the Wairoa District (prod. New Zealand National Film Unit, 1952)
Twilight of the Gods (*Te Keremutunga o Nga Atua*) (dir. Stewart Main, 1995)
Under Capricorn (dir. Alfred Hitchcock, 1949)
Valley Settlers, The (dir. Michael Forlong, 1951)
Velvet Dreams (dir. Vincenzo Salviani, 1988)
Vertical Limit (dir. Martin Campbell, 2000)
Waimate Conspiracy, The (dir. Stefan Harris, 2006)
Weekly Review 332: Hokianga… Backblock Medical Service [Newsreel] (prod. New Zealand Film Unit, 1948)
Weekly Review 346: Rhythm and Movement [Newsreel] (prod. New Zealand Film Unit, 1948)
Wild and Woolly Women (dir. Roy Clement, 1917)
Winifred of Wanganui (dir. Rudall Hayward, 1928)

Without a Paddle (dir. Steven Brill, 2004)
Woman Suffers, The (dir. Raymond Longford, 1918)
Wonders of China (dir. Rudall Hayward, 1958)
World's Fastest Indian, The (dir. Roger Donaldson, 2005)
Written on the Wind (dir. Douglas Sirk, 1956)

Bibliography

Abbot, Stacey. "The Horrific Visions of David Blyth," in *New Zealand Filmmakers*, ed. Ian Conrich and Stuart Murray, 336–48. Detroit: Wayne State University Press, 2007.

Abel, Richard. *The Ciné Goes to Town: French Cinema, 1896–1914*. Berkeley and Los Angeles: University of California Press, 1998.

Adams, Arthur H. *The Collected Verses of Arthur H. Adams*. Melbourne: Whitcombe and Tombs Limited, 1913.

Alemany-Galway, Mary. "Peter Jackson as a Postcolonial Filmmaker: National Cinema and Hollywood Genres." *Post Script*. 25, no. 2 (Winter 2006). <http://findarticles.com/p/articles/mi_go1931/is_2_25/ai_n29253112/>. Accessed 4 January 2009.

Allen, Brenda. "Identity and Cultural Salience in *Illustrious Energy*." *Illusions* 40 (2008): 9–13.

Anderson, Mona. *A River Rules My Life*. Wellington: A. H. and A. W. Reed, 1963.

Ap Sion, Pwyll. *The Music of Michael Nyman*. Aldershot and Burlington VT: Ashgate Publishing, 2007.

Arrighi, Gillian. "Roll up to the Circus." *National Library of Australia News*. <www.nla.gov.au/pub/nlanews/2006/apr06/story-3>. Accessed 15 November 2009.

Ashton-Warner, Sylvia. *I Passed This Way*. New York: Alfred A. Knopf, 1979.

Aumont, Jacques. *The Image*. Trans. Claire Pajackowska. London: British Film Institute, 1997.

Awatere, Donna. *Maori Sovereignty*. 1982; reprint. Auckland: Broadsheet Magazine, 1984.

Babington, Bruce. *A History of the New Zealand Fiction Feature Film*. Manchester: Manchester University Press, 2007.

Ballara, Angela. *Proud to be White? A Survey of Pakeha Prejudice in New Zealand*. Auckland: Heinemann, 1986.

Barclay, Barry. "Amongst Landscapes." In *Film in Aotearoa New Zealand, Film in Aotearoa New Zealand*, ed. Jonathan Dennis and Jan Bieringa, 116–29. Wellington: Victoria University Press, 1992.

——. "Celebrating Fourth Cinema." *Illusions* 35 (Winter 2003): 7–11.

——. "An Open Letter to John Barnett from Barry Barclay." *OnFilm* (February 2003): 11–14.

Barr, Jim and Mary Barr. "NZFX: The Films of Peter Jackson & Fran Walsh." In *Film in Aotearoa New Zealand*, ed. Jonathan Dennis and Jan Bieringa, 150–60. Wellington: Victoria University Press, 1996.

Barraclough, Geoffrey. *An Introduction to Contemporary History*. London: C. A. Watts, 1964.

Basinger, Jeanine. *A Woman's View: How Hollywood Spoke to Women, 1930–1960*. Hanover, New Hampshire: Wesleyan University Press/University Press of New England, 1993.

Belich, James. "Titokowaru's War and Its Place in New Zealand History." MA diss., Victoria University of Wellington, 1979.

——. "The New Zealand Wars 1845–70: An Analysis of Their History and Interpretation." PhD diss., Oxford University, 1982.

——. *The New Zealand Wars and the Interpretation of Racial Conflict*. Auckland: Auckland University Press; Oxford: Oxford University Press, 1986.

——. *The New Zealand Wars*. Auckland: Penguin, 1988.

——. *"I Shall Not Die": Titokowaru's War, New Zealand, 1868–9*. Wellington: Allen & Unwin/Port Nicholson Press, 1989.

——. *Paradise Reforged: A History of the New Zealanders from the 1880s to the Year 2000*. Honolulu: University of Hawai'i Press, 2001; London and Auckland: Allen Lane, The Penguin Press, 2001.

——. *Replenishing the Earth: The Settler Revolution and the Rise of the Anglo World, 1783–1939*. Oxford University Press, 2009.

Bell, Avril. "Bifurcation or Entanglement? Settler Identity and Biculturalism in Aotearoa New Zealand." *Continuum: Journal of Media & Culture Studies* 20, no. 2 (2006): 253–268.

Bentley, Trevor. *Cannibal Jack: The Life & Times of Jacky Marmon, a Pākehā-Māori*. North Shore: Penguin, 2010.

Binney, Judith. *Redemption Songs: A Life of Te Kooti Arikirangi Te Turuki*. Auckland: Auckland University Press, 1995.

——, Gillian Chaplin, and Craig Wallace. *Mihaia: The Prophet Rua Kenana and His Community at Maungapohatu*. Wellington: Oxford University Press, 1979.

Blythe, Martin. *Naming the Other: Images of the Maori in New Zealand Film and Television*. Metuchen, N. J., and London: The Scarecrow Press, 1994.

Boast, R. P. "New Zealand Maori Council v Attorney-General: The Case of the Century?." *New Zealand Law Journal* (August 1987): 240–45.

Bogle, Donald. *Blacks in American Films & Television; An Illustrated Encyclopedia* (Simon and Schuster) <http://www.tcm.com/thismonth/article.jsp?cid=133215>. Accessed 21 July 2010.

Bracken, Thomas. *Musings in Maoriland*. Dunedin: Arthur T. Keirle, 1890.

Braithwaite, Errol. *The Evil Day*. London & Auckland: Collins, 1967.

Brittenden, Wayne. *The Celluloid Circus: The Heyday of the New Zealand Picture. Theatre*. Auckland: Godwit, 2008.

Brookes, Barbara, Annabel Cooper and Robin Law, eds. *Sites of Gender: Women, Men and Modernity in Southern Dunedin, 1890–1939*. Auckland: Auckland University Press, 2003.

——. "A Germaine Moment: Style, Language, and Audience." In *Disputed Histories: Imagining New Zealand's Pasts*, ed. Tony Ballantyne, Brian Moloughney, 191–214. Dunedin, New Zealand: University of Otago Press, 2006.

——. "Health Education Film and the Maori: *Tuberculosis and the Maori People of the Wairoa District (1952)*." *Health and History* 8, no. 2 (2006): 45–68.

——. "Gender, Work and Fears of a "Hybrid Race" in 1920s New Zealand." *Gender and History* 19, no. 3 (2007): 201–18.

Brown, John Macmillan. *Peoples & Problems of the Pacific*. 2 vols. London: T. Fisher Unwin, 1927.

Brown, Kevin M. "Re-presenting the 'Obvious': An Analysis of the film 'The Chant of Jimmie Blacksmith'." In Andrew Markus and Radha Rasmussen, eds. *Prejudice in the Public Arena: Racism*. Melbourne: Monash University, 1987.

Bruno, Frank. *Black Noon at Ngutu*. R. Hale: London, 1960.

Bruzzi, Stella. *Undressing Cinema: Clothing and Identity in the Movies*. London and New York: Routledge, 1997.

Burgoyne, Robert. *Film Nation: Hollywood Looks at U.S. History*. Minneapolis and London: University of Minnesota Press, 1997.

——. *The Hollywood Historical Film*. Malden, MA: Blackwell, 2008.

Butler, Alison. *Women's Cinema: The Contested Screen*. London: Wallflower Press, 2002.

Butler, Ivan. "Pictures." Review of *Pictures*, directed by Michael Black. *Films and Filming* 338 (1982): 34–5.

Butler, P. S. *Opium and Gold*. Martinborough: Alister Taylor, 1974.

Callister, Paul. "Ethnicity Measures, Intermarriage and Social Policy." *Ministry of Social Development*. <http://www.msd.govt.nz/about-msd-and-our-work/publications-resources/journals-and-magazines/social-policy-journal/spj23/ethnicity-measures-intermarriage-and-social-policy-pages109-140.html>. Accessed 21 July 2010.

Campbell, Russell. "The Ideology of the Social Consciousness Movie: Three films of Darryl F. Zanuck." *Quarterly Review of Film Studies* 3 no. 1 (1978): 49–71.

——. "In Order that They May Become Civilised: Pakeha Ideology in *Rewi's Last Stand*, *Broken Barrier* and *Utu*." *Illusions* 1 (Summer 1986): 4–15.

Canning, Charlotte. "Feminist Performance as Feminist Historiography." *Theatre Survey* 45, no. 2 (November 2004): 227–33.

Carter, Ian and Nick Perry. "Rembrandt in Gumboots: Rural Imagery in New Zealand Television Advertisements." In Jock Phillips, ed. *Te Whenua Te Iwi: The Land and the People*, 61–72. Wellington: Allen & Unwin/Port Nicholson Press, 1987.

Césaire, Aimé. *Discourse on Colonialism*. Trans. Joan Pinkham. New York, Monthly Review Press, 1972.

Chapman, James. *Past and Present: National Identity and the British Historical Film*. London: I. B. Tauris, 2005.

Churchman, Geoffrey D. ed. *Celluloid Dreams: A Century of Film in New Zealand*. Wellington: Transpress New Zealand, 1997.

Clelland-Stokes, Sacha. *Representing Aboriginality: A Post-Colonial Analysis of the Key Trends of Representing Aboriginality in South African, Australia and Aotearoa/ New Zealand Film*. Hojbjerg: Intervention Press: 2007.

Clifford, James. "Indigenous Articulations." *Contemporary Pacific* 13, no. 2 (Fall 2001): 468–89.

Collier, Gordon. "Iconic Mythography: The Mediation of Cross-Cultural and Literary Topoi in the New Zealand Film." In *Defining New Idioms and Alternative Forms of Expression*, ed. Eckhard Breitlinger, 205–19. Amsterdam and Atlanta, GA: Rodopi, 1996.

Collins, Felicity and Davis, Therese. *Australian Cinema after Mabo*. Cambridge: Cambridge University Press, 2004.

Coney, Sandra. *Standing in the Sunshine: A History of New Zealand Women Since they Won the Vote*. Auckland: Penguin, 1993.

Conor, Liz. *The Spectacular Modern Woman: Feminine Visibility in the 1920s*. Bloomington and Indianapolis: Indiana University Press, 2004.

Conrich, Ian ."New Zealand Cinema." In *Schirmer Encyclopedia of Film*, volume 3, ed. Barry Keith Grant, 247–250. Farmington Hills, Michigan: Schirmer Reference, 2006.

——. *Studies in New Zealand Cinema*. London: Kakapo Books, 2009.

Cook, David A. *A History of Narrative Cinema*, 2nd edition. New York: Norton, 1990.

Cooper, Annabel. "'I Am Isabel, You Know?': The Antipodean Framing of Jane Campion's *Portrait of a Lady*." *M/C Journal* [online] 11, no. 5 (2008), <http://journal.media-culture.org.au/index.php/mcjournal/article/viewArticle/99>. Accessed 9 February 2009.

——. "On Viewing Jane Campion as an Antipodean." In *Jane Campion: Cinema, Nation, Identity*, ed. Hilary Radner, Alistair Fox and Irène Bessière, 279–304. Detroit: Wayne State University Press, 2009.

——. "Another Take on 'Who's We, White Man?' Addressing Pākehā in the New Zealand Wars." *European Journal of Cultural Studies* 14, no. 3 (2011).

Courtney, Susan. *Hollywood Fantasies of Miscegenation: Spectacular Narratives of Gender and Race, 1903–1967*. Princeton N.J., Princeton University Press, 2005.

Cowan, James. *The Adventures of Kimble Bent: A Story of Wildlife in the New Zealand Bush*. London: Whitcombe and Tombs, 1911; Capper Press, 1975; Wellington: New Zealand Electronic Text Centre, 2008. <http://www.nzetc.org/tm/scholarly/tei-CowKimb.html>. Accessed 8 February 2009.

——. *The New Zealand Wars: A History of the Māori Campaigns and the Pioneering Period*, 2 Vols. 1922; reprint. New York: AMS Press, 1969; Wellington: P. D. Hasselberg, Government Printer, 1983.

Craig, Cairns. "Rooms Without a View." *Sight and Sound* 1, no. 2 (1991): 10–13.

Craven, Peter. "Introduction." In David Malouf, "Made in England: Australia's British Inheritance." *Quarterly Essay* Issue 12, iii-viii. Melbourne: Black Inc, 2003.

Crofts, Stephen. "Foreign Tunes? Gender and Nationality in Four Countries' Reception of *The Piano*." In *Jane Campion's The Piano*, ed. Harriet Margolis, 135–61. Cambridge, New York, Melbourne: Cambridge University Press, 2000.

da Souza, Pascale. "*Maoritanga* in *Whale Rider* and *Once Were Warriors*: A Problematic Rebirth through Female Leaders." *Studies in Australasian Cinema* 1, no. 1 (2007): 15–27.

Davis, Natalie Zemon. *Slaves on Screen: Film and Historical Vision*. Cambridge, M.A.: Harvard University Press, 2000.

Davis, Therese. "Remembering our Ancestors: Cross-cultural Collaboration and the Mediation of Aboriginal Culture and History in *Ten Canoes* (Rolf de Heer, 2006)." *Studies in Australasian Cinema* 1, no. 1 (2007): 5–14.

Dawson, Graham. *Soldier Heroes: British Adventure, Empire and the Imagining of Masculinities*. London: Routledge, 1994.

Denham, Reginald and Mary Orr. *Minor Murder: A Crime Play in Two Acts*. New York, NY: Dramatists Play Service, 1967.

Dennis, Jonathan. "A Time Line." In *Film in Aotearoa New Zealand*, ed. Jonathan Dennis and Jan Bieringa, 2nd edition, 199–235. Wellington: Victoria University Press, 1996.

Dermody, Susan and Elizabeth Jacka. *The Screening of Australia: Anatomy of a National Cinema*, volume 2. Sydney: Currency Press, 1988.

Derrida, Jacques. *The Post Card: From Socrates to Freud and Beyond*. Trans. Alan Bass. Chicago: University of Chicago Press, 1987.

Dobie, Madeleine. "Gender and the Heritage Genre: Popular Feminism Turns to History." In *Jane Austen and Co.: Remaking the Past in Contemporary Culture*, ed. Suzanne R. Pucci and James Thompson, 247–60. Albany: State University of New York Press, 2003.

Duff, Alan. *Once Were Warriors*. Tandem Press, Auckland: 1990.

Dunleavy, Trisha. *Ourselves in Primetime: A History of New Zealand Television Drama*. Auckland, New Zealand: Auckland University Press, 2005.

Dunningham, Margaret M. "Broken Barrier." *Landfall* (1952): 326–27.

Durie, E. T. "Will the Settlers Settle? Cultural Conciliation and Law." *Otago Law Review* 8, no. 4 (1996): 449–65.

Dyer, Richard. *White*. London and New York: Routledge, 1997.

——. "White." In *Film and Theory: An Anthology*, ed. Robert Stam and Toby Miller, 733–51. Oxford: Blackwell, 2000.

Dyson, Linda. "The Return of the Repressed? Whiteness, Femininity and Colonialism in *The Piano*." *Screen* 36, no. 3 (1995): 267–76.

Edwards, S. R. "Docudrama from the Twenties: Rudall Hayward, Whakatane, and the Te Kooti Trail." *Historical Review, Bay of Plenty Journal of History* 41, no. 2 (November 1993): 58–65.

Edwards, Sam and Stuart Murray. "A Rough Island Story: The Film Life of Rudall Charles Hayward." In *New Zealand Filmmakers*, ed. Ian Conrich and Stuart Murray, 35–53. Detroit: Wayne State University Press, 2007.

Ellison, Ralph. *Shadow and Act*. London: Secker and Warburg. 1967; reprinted from *The Reporter*, 6 December 1949.

Evans, Patrick. *The Long Forgetting: Post-Colonial Literary Culture in New Zealand*. Christchurch: Canterbury University Press, 2007.

Fairburn, Miles. "Is There a Good Case for New Zealand Exceptionalism." In *Disputed Histories: Imagining New Zealand's Pasts*, ed. Tony Ballantyne and Brian Moloughney, 143–67. Dunedin: Otago University Press, 2006.

Fanon, Franz. *The Wretched of the Earth*. 1965; reprint. Harmondsworth: Penguin Books, 1967.

——. *Black Skin, White Mask*. London: Pluto, 1986.

Fay, Charles R. *Imperial Economy and its Place in the Formation of Economic Doctrine, 1600–1932*. Oxford: Oxford University Press, 1934.

Ferrall, Charles, Paul Millar and Karen Smith. *East By South: China in the Australasian Imagination*. Wellington: Victoria University Press, 2005.

Ferro, Marc. *Cinema and History*. Trans. Naomi Greene. Detroit: Wayne State University Press, 1988.

Fong, Bickleen Ng. *The Chinese in New Zealand: A Study in Assimilation*. Hong Kong: Hong Kong University Press, 1959.

Foucault, Michel. *The Archaeology of Knowledge*. Trans. A. M. Sheridan Smith. New York: Pantheon Books, 1972.

Fox, Alistair. *The Ship of Dreams: Masculinity in Contemporary New Zealand Fiction*. Dunedin: Otago University Press, 2008.

——. "Inwardness, Insularity, and the Man Alone: Postcolonial Anxiety in the New Zealand Novel." *Journal of Postcolonial Writing* 45, no. 3 (2009): 263–73.

——. "Puritanism and the Erotics of Transgression: The New Zealand Influence in Jane Campion's Thematic Imaginary." In *Jane Campion: Cinema, Nation, Identity*, ed. Hilary Radner, Alistair Fox, and Irène Bessière, 103–22. Detroit: Wayne State University Press, 2009.

Frame, Janet. *A State of Siege*. 1966; reprint. Sydney: Angus & Robertson/Sirius Paperback, 1982.

Fryer, Roland G. "Guess Who's Been Coming to Dinner? Trends in Interracial Marriage over the 20th Century." *Journal of Economic Perspectives* 21, no. 2 (2007): 71–90.

Gaines, Jane. "Costume and Narrative: How Dress Tells the Woman's Story." In *Fabrications: Costume and the Female Body*, ed. Jane Gaines and Charlotte Herzog, 180–211. London and New York: Routledge, 1990.

Garrett, Roberta. *Postmodern Chick Flicks: The Return of the Woman's Film*. Basingstoke: Palgrave Macmillan, 2007.

George, David E. R. "Quantum Theatre - Potential Theatre: A New Paradigm?" *New Theatre Quarterly* 5 (1989): 174–79.

Gibbons, Peter. "Cultural Colonisation and National Identity." *New Zealand Journal of History*, 36, no. 1 (2002): 5–17.

Gilroy, Paul. *There Ain't No Black in the Union Jack*. London: Hutchinson, 1987.

Glamuzina, Julie and Alison J. Laurie. *Parker & Hulme: A Lesbian View*. Ithaca, New York: Firebrand Books, 1991.

Goffman, Erving. *The Presentation of Self in Everyday Life*. New York: Anchor, 1959.

Goldson, Annie. "Piano Lessons." In *Film in Aotearoa New Zealand*, ed. Jonathan Dennis and Jan Bieringa, 2nd edition, 195–8. Wellington: Victoria University Press, 1996.

Gordimer, Nadine. "Relevance and Commitment (1979)." In *The Essential Gesture: Writing, Politics and Places*, ed. Stephen Clingman, 133–43. New York: Alfred A. Knopf, 1988.

——. "Where Do Whites Fit In? (1959)." In *The Essential Gesture: Writing, Politics and Places*, ed. Stephen Clingman, 31–7. New York: Alfred A. Knopf, 1988.

Gowans, Elizabeth. *Heart of the High Country: A New Zealand Saga*. London; Auckland: Grafton, 1985.

Grant, Barry Keith. *A Cultural Assault: The New Zealand Films of Peter Jackson*. London: Kakapo Books, 1999.

Grant, Nick. "Backyard Glitz." Interview with Toa Fraser. *Onfilm* 23, no. 1 (December 2005): 28–9.

——. "Not Drowning, Waving." Interview with Vincent Ward. *Onfilm* 23, no. 1 (December 2005): 22–4.

Greer, Germaine. *Whitefella Jump Up: The Shortest Way to Nationhood (Quarterly Essay)*. 2003; reprint. London: Profile Books, 2004.

Griffin, J. and Bob Cline. "Circus History Publications." *Circus Historical Society*. 2002–2009. <http://circushistory.org/publications.htm>. Accessed 15 November 2009.

Grindon, Leger. *Shadows on the Past: Studies in the Historical Fiction Film*. Philadelphia: Temple University Press, 1994.

Gudgeon, Thomas W. *Reminiscences of the War in New Zealand*. London: Sampson Low, Marston, Searle and Rivington, 1879.

Gurr, Tom and H. H. Cox. *Obsession*. London: Frederick Muller Ltd. 1958.

Guzik, Elizabeth. "The Queer Sort of Fandom for *Heavenly Creatures*: The Closeted Indigene, Lesbian Islands, and New Zealand National Cinema." In *Postcolonial and Queer Theories: Intersections and Essays*, ed. John C. Hawley, 47–61. Westport: Greenwood Press, 2001.

Hall, Stuart. Interview with Julie Drew. In *Race, Rhetoric, and the Postcolonial*, ed. Gary A. Olson and Lynn Worsham, 207–39. Albany: State University of New York Press, 1999.

Hamby, Louise. "Thomson Times and *Ten Canoes* (de Heer and Djigirr, 2006)." *Studies in Australasian Cinema* 1, no. 2 (2007): 127–46.

Hamer, Paul. "A Quarter-century of the Waitangi Tribunal: Responding to the Challenge." In *The Waitangi Tribunal: Te Roopu Whakaman i te Tiriti o Waitangi*, ed. Janine Hayward and Nicola R. Wheen, 3–14. Wellington: Bridget Williams Books, 2004.

Hanson, Allan and Louise Hanson. *Counterpoint in Maori Culture*. London & Boston: Routledge & Kegan Paul, 1983.

Hanson, Helen. "From *Suspicion* (1941) to *Deceived* (1991): Gothic Continuities, Feminism and Postfeminism in the Neo-Gothic Film." *Gothic Studies* 9, no. 2 (2007): 20–32.

——. *Hollywood Heroines: Women in Film Noir and the Female Gothic Film*. London: I. B. Tauris, 2007.

Harari, Roberto. *Lacan's Seminar on Anxiety: An Introduction*. Trans. Jane C. Lamb-Ruiz. New York: Other Press, 2001.

Haraway, Donna. *Simians, Cyborgs and Women: The Reinvention of Nature*. London: Free Association Books, 1991.

Harre, John. *Maori and Pakeha: A Study of Mixed Marriages in New Zealand*. London: Pall Mall Press, 1966.

Hedges, Chris. *American Fascists: The Christian Right and the War on America*. 2007; reprint. London: Vintage Books, 2008.

Higson, Andrew. *English Heritage, English Cinema: Costume Drama since 1980*. Oxford: Oxford University Press, 2003.

Hill, John. *British Cinema in the 1980s*. Oxford: OUP, 1999.

Hilliard, Chris. *The Bookmen's Dominion: Cultural Life in New Zealand 1920–1950*. Auckland: Auckland University Press, 2006.

Hokowhitu, Brendan. "Tackling Māori Masculinity: A Colonial Genealogy of Savagery and Sport." *The Contemporary Pacific* 16, no. 2 (2004): 259–84.

——. "The Death of Koro Paka: 'Traditional' Māori Patriarchy." *The Contemporary Pacific* 20, no. 1 (2008): 115–41.

Hutchings, Megan. *Long Journey for Sevenpence: Assisted Immigration to New Zealand from the United Kingdom, 1947–1975*. Wellington: Victoria University Press in association with Historical Branch, Department of Internal Affairs, 1999.

Ihimaera Witi. *The Whale Rider*. Auckland: Heinemann: 1987.

Ip, Manying. "Chinese New Zealanders: Old Settlers and New Immigrants." In *Immigration and National Identity in New Zealand: One People? Two Peoples? Many Peoples?* Ed. S. W. Greif, 161–200. Palmerston North: The Dunmore Press, 1995.

——. "Chinese Immigrants and Transnationals in New Zealand: A Fortress Opened." In *The Chinese Diaspora: Space, Place, Mobility and Identity*, ed. Laurence J. C. Ma and Carolyn Cartier, 339–58. Lanham: Rowman and Littlefield, 2003.

Jameson, Fredric. *Postmodernism, or, the Cultural Logic of Late Capitalism*. Durham, NC: Duke University Press, 1991.

Jeffords, Susan. *The Remasculinization of America: Gender and the Vietnam War*. Bloomington: Indiana University Press, 1989.

Jensen, Kai. *Whole Men: The Masculine Tradition in New Zealand Literature*. Auckland: Auckland University Press, 1996.

Johansen, J.Prytz. *The Maori and His Religion in Its Non-Ritualistic Aspects: With a Danish Summary*. Copenhagen: Ejnar Munksgaard, 1954.

Johnson, Colin. "Chauvel and the centring of the Aboriginal male in Australian film." *Continuum: The Australian Journal of Media and Culture* 1, no.1 (1987) [online] <http://wwwmcc.murdoch.edu.au/ReadingRoom/1.1/Johnson.html>. Accessed 26 June 2010.

Jones, Lawrence. *Barbed Wire and Mirrors: Essays on New Zealand Prose*. Dunedin: University of Otago Press, 1990.

——. *Picking Up the Traces: The Making of a New Zealand Literary Culture 1932–1945*. Wellington: Victoria University Press, 2003.

——. "'I can really see myself in her story': Jane Campion's Adaptation of Janet Frame's *Autobiography*." In *Jane Campion: Cinema, Nation, Identity*, ed. Hilary Radner, Alistair Fox, Irène Bessière, 77–102. Detroit: Wayne State University Press, 2009.

Jones, Stan. "Siting *Whale Rider*: A Survey of its Reception in a European Context." *British Review of New Zealand Studies* 14 (2003/2004): 61–83.

Joseph, Philip A. *Constitutional and Administrative Law in New Zealand*. Sydney: The Law Book Co., 1993.

Jouve, Nicole Ward. "An Eye for an Eye: The Case of the Papin Sisters." In *Moving Targets: Women, Murder and Representation*, ed. Helen Birch, 7–31. London: Virago Press, 1994.

Kaplan, E. Ann. *Trauma Culture: The Politics of Terror and Loss in Media and Literature*. New Brunswick, N.J. Rutgers University Press, 2005.

Keenan, Danny ed. *Terror in Our Midst? Searching for Terror in Aotearoa/New Zealand*. Wellington: Huia, 2008.

Keneally, Thomas. *The Chant of Jimmie Blacksmith*. Angus and Robertson: Sydney 1972.

Keown, Michelle. "'He Iwi Kotahi Tatou'?: Nationalism and Cultural Identity in Maori Film." In *Contemporary New Zealand Cinema: From New Wave to Blockbuster*, ed. Ian Conrich and Stuart Murray, 197–210. London and New York: I. B. Tauris, 2008.

Kerr, M. E./Vin Packer. *The Evil Friendship*. Gold Medal Press, 1958.

King, Michael. *Moriori: A People Rediscovered*. Auckland: Viking, 1989.

——. *The Penguin History of New Zealand*. Auckland: Penguin Books, 2004.

Klinger, Barbara. "The Art Film, Affect and the Female Viewer Revisited." *Screen* 47, no. 1 (2006): 19–41.

Lamb, Jonathan. "A Sublime Moment Off Poverty Bay, 9 October 1769." In *Dirty Silence: Aspects of Language and Literature in New Zealand*, ed. Graham McGregor and Mark Williams, 97–115. Auckland: Oxford University Press, 1991.

——. "The Idea of Utopia in the European Settlement of New Zealand." In *Quicksands: Foundational Histories in Australia and Aotearoa New Zealand*, ed. Klaus Neumann, Nicholas Thomas and Hilary Eriksen, 79–98. Sydney: UNSW Press, 1999.

Landy, Marcia, ed. *The Historical Film: History and Memory in Media*. New Brunswick, New Jersey: Rutgers University Press, 2000.

Langton, Marcia. *Well, I Heard It on the Radio and I Saw It on the Television: An Essay for the Australian Film Commission on the Politics and Aesthetics of Filmmaking by and about Aboriginal People and Things*. Sydney: Australian Film Commission, 1983.

Lascelles, David. *80 Turbulent Years: The Paramount Theatre Wellington 1917–1997*. Wellington: Millwood Press, 1997.

Law, Robin, Hugh Campbell and John Dolan eds. *Masculinities in Aotearoa/New Zealand*. Palmerston North: Dunmore Press, 1999.

Lawn, Jennifer and Bronwyn Beatty. "Getting to Wellywood: National Branding and the Globalisation of the New Zealand Film Industry." *Postscript: Essays in Film and the Humanities* 24, no. 2 (2004–2005):124–43.

Lawson, Alan. "The Anxious Proximities of Settler (Post)Colonial Relations." In *Literary Theory: An Anthology*, ed. Julie Rivkin and Michael Ryan, 1210–1223. Oxford and Malden, Massachusetts: Blackwell, 1998.

——. "Proximities: From Asymptote to Zeugma." In *Postcolonising the Commonwealth: Studies in Literature and Culture*, ed. Rowland Smith, 19–39. Ontario: Wilfred Laurier University Press, 2000.

Lealand, Geoff. *A Foreign Egg in Our Nest? American Popular Culture in New Zealand*. Wellington: Victoria University Press, 1988.

Legott, James. *Contemporary British Cinema: From Heritage to Horror*. London: Wallflower Press, 2008.

Limbrick, Peter. "The Australian Western, or A Settler Colonial Cinema par excellence," *Cinema Journal* 46, no. 4 (Summer 2007): 68–95.

——. *Making Settler Cinemas: Film and Colonial Encounters in the United States, Australia, and New Zealand*. New York: Palgrave Macmillan, 2010.

Lippy, Tod. "Writing and Directing *Heavenly Creatures*: A Talk with Frances Walsh and Peter Jackson." *Scenario: The Magazine of Screenwriting Art* 1 (1995): 217–224.

Lyan, Pan. *Sons of the Yellow Emperor: A History of the Chinese Diaspora*. New York: Kodanshe International, 1994.

Maaka, Roger and Augie Fleras. *The Politics of Indigeneity: Challenging the State in Canada and Aotearoa*. Dunedin: University of Otago, 2005.

Macassey, Olivia. "Torn Stitches of the Heart: Post-imperial Trauma and Colonial Heritage Romance Cinema, 1979–2005." PhD diss., University of Auckland, 2009.

Macdonald, Charlotte. *A Woman of Good Character: Single Women as Immigrant Settles in Nineteenth-century New Zealand.* Wellington, New Zealand: Allen & Unwin/Historical Branch, 1990.

Macdonald, Myra. *Exploring Media Discourse.* Oxford: Arnold, 2003.

McDonnell, Brian. "Images of Aotearoa: Rural and Urban Settings in NZ Films." *Alternative Cinema* (Spring/Summer 1984–5): 5–7.

McHugh, Kathleen. *Jane Campion.* Urbana: University of Illinois Press, 2007.

McHugh, P. G. "Australasian Narratives of Constitutional Foundation." In *Quicksands: Foundational Histories in Australia and Aotearoa New Zealand,* ed. Klaus Neumann, Nicholas Thomas and Hilary Eriksen. 98–115. Sydney: UNSW Press, 1999.

McKee, A. "Films vs real life: Communicating Aboriginality in Cinema and Television." *UTS Review* 3, no. 1 (1997): 160–82.

McKenna, Mark. "Metaphors of Light and Darkness: The Politics of 'Black Armband' History." *Melbourne Journal of Politics: The Reconciliation Issue* 25 (1998): 67–84.

McQueen, Harvey, ed. The *New Place: The Poetry of Settlement in New Zealand 1852–1914.* Wellington: Victoria University Press, 1993.

Mander, Jane. *The Story of a New Zealand River.* London: The Bodley Head, 1920; Auckland, New Zealand: Whitcombe and Tombs, 1938.

Manthorne, Katherine E., with John W. Coffey. *The Landscapes of Louis Rémy Mignot.* Raleigh: North Carolina Museum of Art, 1996.

Margaroni, M. "Jane Campion's Selling of the Mother/Land: Restaging the Crisis of the Postcolonial Subject." *Camera Obscura* 53, no. 2 (2003): 92–124.

Margolis, Harriet. "Indigenous Star: Can *Mana* and Authentic Community Survive International Co-Productions?" *Quarterly Review of Film and Video* 19, no. 1 (2002): 15–29.

Martin, Helen and Sam Edwards. *New Zealand Film 1912–1996.* Auckland: Oxford University Press, 1997.

Martin, Helen. "Leon Narbey: Art, Politics and the Personal." In *New Zealand Filmmakers,* ed. Ian Conrich, Stuart Murray, 256–72. Detroit: Wayne State University Press, 2007.

Mason, Bruce. "Notes." *Landfall* 6, no. 4 (1952): 259–60.

Matthews, Philip. "Fast, Cheap and Out of Control: Three Films from New Zealand's Digital 'Revolution.'" *Senses of Cinema* March 2004.< www.sensesofcinema.com>. Accessed 6 June 2010.

May, Sue. "River Queen: The Making of the Film on the Whanganui River" [pamphlet]. Wanganui: Whanganui Inc., 2005.

Maybury-Lewis, David. *Indigenous Peoples, Ethnic Groups, and the State.* Boston and London: Allyn and Bacon, 1997.

Mayer, Geoff and Keith Beattie. *The Cinema of Australia and New Zealand.* London: Wallflower Press, 2007.

Mikalsen, Ron. "*Kingpin*: Can There Be Only One?" *Illusions* 5 (1987): 11–22.

Miller, Arthur. "Uneasy About the Germans: After the Wall." In *Echoes Down the Corridor: Collected Essays 1944–2000,* ed. Steven R. Centola, 222–29. New York: Penguin Books, 2001.

Miller, Jacques-Alain. "Introduction to Reading Jacques Lacan's Seminar *Anxiety.*" Trans. Barbara P. Fulks. *Lacanian Ink* 26 (2005): 8–70.

Mirams, Gordon. *Speaking Candidly: Films and People in New Zealand.* Hamilton, NZ: Paul's, 1945.

Mishra, Vijay and Bob Hodge. "What was Postcolonialism?" *New Literary History* 36 (2005): 375–402.

Mita, Merata. "The Soul and the Image." In *Film in Aotearoa New Zealand,* ed. Jonathan Dennis and Jan Bieringa, 36–54. Wellington: Victoria University Press, 1992; 2nd edition, 36–53. Wellington: Victoria University Press, 1996.

Moine, Raphaëlle. "From Antipodean Cinema to International Art Cinema." In *Jane Campion: Cinema, Nation, Identity*, ed. Hilary Radner, Alistair Fox and Irène Bessière, 189–204. Detroit: Wayne State University Press, 2009

Molloy, Maureen. "Death and the Maiden: The Feminine and Nation in Recent New Zealand Films." *Signs* 35, no. 1, 153–162. Chicago: University of Chicago Press, 1999.

Monk, Claire. "The British 'Heritage Film' and Its Critics." *Critical Survey* 7, no. 2 (1995): 16–24.

——. "Sexuality and the Heritage Film." *Sight and Sound* 5, no. 10 (1995): 32–4.

—— and Amy Sargeant, eds. *British Historical Cinema: The History, Heritage and Costume Film*. London and New York: Routledge, 2002.

Moore, Catriona and Stephen Muecke. "Racism and the Representation of Aborigines in Film." *Australian Journal of Cultural Studies* 2, no. 1 (1984): 35–63.

Mulgan, John. *Man Alone*. London: Selwyn Blount: 1939.

Mulgan, Richard. "Citizenship and Legitimacy in Post-colonial Australia." In *Citizenship and Indigenous Australians: Changing Conceptions and Possibilities*, ed. Nicholas Peterson and Will Sanders, 179–95. Cambridge: Cambridge University Press, 1998.

Murdoch, Iris. *Metaphysics as a Guide to Morals*. 1992; reprint. London: Vintage/Random House, 2003.

Murphy, Geoff. "The End of the Beginning." In *Film in Aotearoa New Zealand*, ed. Jonathan Dennis and Jan Bieringa, 2nd edition, 130–49. Wellington: Victoria University Press, 1996.

Murray, Jenny. "Review: The New Zealand Wars." *Historical News* 56 (1988): 13–15.

Murray, Stuart. *Images of Dignity: Barry Barclay and Fourth Cinema*. Wellington: Huia Publishers, 2008.

——. "Precarious Adulthood: Communal Anxieties in 1980s Film." In *Contemporary New Zealand Cinema: From New Wave to Blockbuster*, ed. Ian Conrich and Stuart Murray, 169–181. London and New York: I. B. Tauris, 2008.

—— and Ian Conrich. "Introduction." In *New Zealand Filmmakers*, ed. Ian Conrich and Stuart Murray, 1–14. Detroit: Wayne State University Press, 2007.

Najita, Susan Y. *Decolonizing Cultures in the Pacific: Reading History and Trauma in Contemporary Fiction*. New York & London: Routledge Research in Postcolonial Literatures, 2006; reprint. 2008.

Neill, Anna. "A Land without a Past: Dreamtime and Nation in *The Piano*." In *Piano Lessons: Approaches to* The Piano, ed. Felicity Coombs and Suzanne Gemmell, 136–47. London: John Libbey, 1999.

Ng, James. "Don, Rev. Alexander." *Online Dictionary of New Zealand Biography*. <http://vuw.dnzbgovt. nz/dnzb/>. Accessed 20 October 2009.

——. "Sew Hoy, Charles." *Online Dictionary of New Zealand Biography*. <http://vuw.dnzbgovt.nz/ dnzb/>. Accessed 23 October 2009.

Nickel, John. "Disabling African American Men: Liberalism and Race Message Films," *Cinema Journal* 44, no. 1 (2004): 25–48.

Novitz, David. "On Culture and Cultural Identity." In *Culture and Identity in New Zealand*. Wellington: GP Books, 1989.

O'Regan, Tom. *Australian National Cinema*. London and New York: Routledge, 1996.

O'Riley, Michael F. "Postcolonial Haunting: Anxiety, Affect and the Situated Encounter." *Postcolonial Text* 3, no. 4 (2007): 1–15.

Orr, Bridget. "Birth of a Nation? From *Utu* to *The Piano*." In *Piano Lessons: Approaches to* The Piano, ed. Felicity Coombs and Suzanne Gemmell, 148–60. London: John Libbey, 1999.

O'Shea, John. "Saraband for Blind Critics." *Design Review* 2, no. 6 (May-June 1950), <http://www. nzetc.org/tm/scholarly/tei-Arc02_06DesR-t1-body-d7.html>. Accessed 21 July 2010.

——. *Don't Let it Get You*. Wellington: Victoria University Press, 1999.

Palmer, William J. *The Films of the Eighties: A Social History*. Carbondale: Southern Illinois University, 1993.

Perkins, Reid. "Imag(in)ing Our Past: Colonial New Zealand on Film from *The Birth of New Zealand* to *The Piano*: Part One," *Illusions* 25 (Winter 1996): 4–10.

——. "Imag(in)ing our Colonial Past: Colonial New Zealand Films from *The Birth of New Zealand* to *The Piano: Part Two*" *Illusions* 26 (Winter 1997): 17–21.

——. "Cinema in a Settler Society: Brand New Zealand". In *Cinema at the Periphery*, ed. Diane Iordanova, David Maryin and Bélen Vidal, 67–83. Detroit: Wayne State University Press, 2010.

Petrie, Duncan. *Shot in New Zealand: The Art and Craft of the Kiwi Cinematographer*. Auckland: Random House NZ, 2007.

——. "'The Rhythm of the Process': An Interview with Leon Narbey." *Illusions* 40 (2008): 4–8.

Phillips, J. O. C. *A Man's Country?: The Image of the Pakeha Male, A History*. Auckland: Penguin Books, 1996.

Pidduck, Julianne. *Contemporary Costume Film: Space, Place, and the Past*. London: BFI Publishing, 2004.

Pihama, Leonie. "Repositioning Maori Representation: Contextualising *Once Were Warriors*." In *Film in Aotearoa New Zealand*, ed. Jonathan Dennis and Jan Bieringa, 2nd edition, 191–2. Wellington: Victoria University Press, 1996.

Pilkington, Doris. *Rabbit-Proof Fence*. Miramax Books/Hyperion: New York, 2002 [1996].

Pocock, J. G. A. "Burke and the Ancient Constitution." *Historical Journal* 3 (1960): 125–

Polan, Dana. *Jane Campion*. London: BFI, 2001.

Pollock, Jacob. "'We Don't Want Your Racist Tour': The 1981 Springbok Tour and the Anxiety of Settlement in Aotearoa/New Zealand." *Graduate Journal of Asia-Pacific Studies* 2, no. 1 (2004): 32–43.

Pound, Francis. *Frames on the Land: Early Landscape Painting in New Zealand*. Auckland: Collins, 1993.

——. *The Invention of New Zealand: Art and National Identity, 1930–1970*. Auckland: Auckland University Press, 2009.

Prentice, Chris. "Riding the Whale? Postcolonialism and Globalization in Whale Rider." In *Global Fissures: Postcolonial Fusions*, ed. Clara A.B. Joseph and Janet Wilson, 247–68. Cross Cultures 85. Amsterdam and New York: Rodopi, 2006.

Radner, Hilary. "*'In Extremis*': Jane Campion and the Woman's Film." In *Jane Campion: Cinema, Nation, Identity*, ed. Hilary Radner, Alistair Fox and Irène Bessière, 3–24. Detroit: Wayne State University Press, 2009.

——. "Lettre de Dunedin: Le cinéma au 'pays du long nuage blanc.'" *Trafic* 67 (2008): 122–33.

Rangihau, John. "Being Maori." In *Te Ao Hurihuri, The World Moves On: Aspects of Maoritanga*, ed. Michael King, 220–23. Auckland: Hicks Smith/Methven, 1977.

Read, Lynette. "*Feathers of Peace*: Lynette Read Interviews Barry Barclay." *Illusions* 31 (2000/2001): 2–6.

——. "National Identity and the Films of Vincent Ward." *Metro Magazine* 148 (Spring 2006): 124–31.

Reade, Eric. *History and Heartburn: The Saga of Australian Film, 1896–1978*. Brunswick, N.J.: Associated University Presses, 1981.

Reid, Nicholas. *A Decade of New Zealand Film:* Sleeping Dogs *to* Came a Hot Friday. Dunedin: John McIndoe, 1986.

Ribeiro, Luisa F. "Heavenly Creatures." Review of *Heavenly Creatures*, directed by Peter Jackson. *Film Quarterly*, 49, no. 1 (Autumn 1996): 33–8.

Ritchie, James. *Becoming Bicultural*. Wellington: Huia Publishers/Daphne Brasell Associates Press, 1992.

Robinson, J. Dennis. "The Making of 'Lost Boundaries.'" *Seacoast New Hampshire* (1997). <http://www.seacoastnh.com/louis/lostfilm.html>. Accessed 21 July 2010.

Rogin, Michael. "'Democracy and Burnt Cork': The End of Blackface, the Beginning of Civil Rights." *Representations* 46 (1994): 1–34.

Roth, Bennet E. "*Heavenly Creatures*: Female Adolescence Viewed Darkly." *The Psychoanalytic Review* 82 (1995): 624–27.

Rygiel, John. "Circus Rolls On." *Eden Bros Good Time Circus.* <www.edencircus.com/News%20press.htm>. Accessed 15 November 2009.

St Leon, Mark. *Spangles and Sawdust: The Circus in Australia.* Melbourne: Greenhouse, Publications, 1983.

Salecl, Renata. *On Anxiety.* London and New York: Routledge, 2004.

Sargeson, Frank. *Collected Stories.* Auckland: Blackwood and Janet Paul, 1974.

Schatz, Thomas. *Hollywood Genres: Formulas, Filmmaking, and the Studios.* New York: McGraw Hill, 1981.

——. *Boom & Bust: The American Cinema in the 1940s (History of the American Cinema).* New York: University of California Press, 1997.

Scott, Dick. *Ask That Mountain: The Story of Parihaka.* Auckland: Heinemann/Southern Cross, 1975.

Shadbolt, Maurice. *Monday's Warriors.* Auckland: Hodder & Stoughton, 1990.

Sheldon, Karan and Dwight Swanson. "The Movie Queen: Northeast Historic Film." In *Mining the Home Movie: Excavations in Histories and Memories*, ed. Karen L. Ishizuka and Patricia R. Zimmerman, 185–90. Berkeley: University of California Press, 2008.

Shelton, Lindsay. *The Selling of New Zealand Movies.* Wellington, New Zealand: Awa Press, 2005.

Shephard, Deborah. *Reframing Women: A History of New Zealand Film.* Auckland: Harper Collins Publishers, 2000.

Shepherdson, Charles. "Foreword." In *Lacan's Seminar on Anxiety: An Introduction*, by Roberto Harari, ix-lxiii. New York: Other Press, 2001.

Shortland, Edward. *Traditions and Superstitions of the New Zealanders.* London: Longman, Brown, 1854.

Sigley, Simon. "Film Culture: Its Development in New Zealand, 1929–1972." PhD diss., University of Auckland, 2004.

——. "How the Road to Life (1931) Became the Road to Ruin: the Case of the Wellington Film Society in 1933." *New Zealand Journal of History* 42, no. 2 (2008): 195–215.

Simmons, Laurence. "*Broken Barrier*: Mimesis and Mimicry." *Landfall* 185 (1993): 131–36.

——. "Casting Aside Old Nets: John O'Shea's First Fight Against Racism." *Illusions* 33 (Autumn 2002): 8–16.

——. "'That Rare Thing, a Film that is also a Work of Art': Laurence Simmons Interviews Martin Edmond." *Illusions* 40 (2008): 21–24.

Simpson, Tony. *Te Riri Pakeha/the White Man's Anger.* Martinborough: Alister Taylor, 1979.

Sinclair, Keith. *The Origins of the Maori Wars*, 2nd edition. Wellington: New Zealand University Press, 1961.

Singh, Sunny. "Writing Against History: Seizing Subjecthood for the Aborigine Narrative." In *New Zealand and Australia. Narrative, History and Representation*, ed. Sue Ryan Fazilleau, 111–33. Studies in New Zealand Culture 10. Nottingham: Kakapo Books, 2008.

Smith, Andrew and Diana Wallance. "The Female Gothic: Then and Now." *Gothic Studies* 6, no. 1 (2004): 1–7.

Smith, Jean. "Self and Experience in Maori Culture." In *Indigenous Psychology and the Anthropology of the Self*, ed. Paul Heelas and Andrew Lock, 145–59. London: Academic Press Inc., 1981.

Smith, Philippa Mein. *A Concise History of New Zealand*. Cambridge: Cambridge University Press, 2005.

Smither, Roger. "'Watch the Picture Carefully, and See If You Can Identify Anyone:' Recognition in Factual Film of the First World War Period." *Film History* 14, no. 3/4 (2002): 390–404.

Søland, Birgitte. *Becoming Modern: Young Women and the Reconstruction of Womanhood in the 1920s*. Princeton and Oxford: Princeton University Press, 2000.

Sontag, Susan. *Against Interpretation*. London: Vintage Books, 1994; reprint. 2001.

Spicer, Andrew. *An Ambivalent Archetype: Masculinity, Performance and the New Zealand Films of Bruno Lawrence*. London: Kakapo Books. 2000.

Spivak, Gayatri C. *Outside in the Teaching Machine*. London: Routledge, 1993.

Spoonley, Paul. *Mata Toa: The Life and Times of Ranginui Walker*. Auckland: Penguin Group, 2009.

Stables, Kate. "Films: River Queen." *Sight and Sound* 18, no. 4 (April 2008): 75–6.

Stafford, Jane and Mark Williams. *Maoriland: New Zealand Literature 1872–1914*. Wellington: Victoria University Press, 2006.

Stea, David and Ben Wisner. "Introduction: The Fourth World." *Antipode: A Radical Journal of Geography* 16, no 2 (1984): 3–4.

Stenhouse, John. "God, the Devil and Gender." In *Sites of Gender: Women, Men and Modernity in Southern Dunedin, 1890–1939*, ed. Barbara Brookes, Annabel Cooper and Robin Law, 313–47. Auckland: Auckland University Press, 2003.

Stewart, Stephanie Elaine. "Movies of a Local People and a Usable Past: Mill Town Treasures and Transcendent Views, 1936–1942." *The Moving Image* 7, no. 1 (2007): 51–77.

Streible, Dan. "Filmmakers and Amateur Casts: A Homemade 'Our Gang', 1926." *Film History* 15, no. 2 (2003): 177–92.

Stirling, Pamela. "Unsung Heroines." *NZ Listener*, 14 May 1983.

Strub, Whitney. "Black and White and Banned all Over: Race, Censorship and Obscenity in Postwar Memphis," *Journal of Social History*, 40, no. 3 (2007): 685–715.

Sturm, Terry. "Thomas Keneally and Australian Racism: *The Chant of Jimmie Blacksmith*." *Southerly* 33 (1973): 261–74.

Sugars, Cynthia. "(Dis)Inheriting the Nation: Contemporary Canadian Memoirs and the Anxiety of Origins." In *Moveable Margins: The Shifting Spaces of Canadian Literature*, ed. Chelva Kanaganayakam, 177–203. Ontario: TSAR, 2005.

Szazsy, Mira. "After all, I am partly Māori, partly Dalmatian, but first of all I am a New Zealander." *Ethnography* 6, no. 4 (2005): 517–42.

Thomas, Julian. "A History of Beginnings." In *Quicksands: Foundational Histories in Australia and Aotearoa New Zealand*, ed. Klaus Neumann, Nicholas Thomas and Hilary Eriksen, 115–33. Sydney: UNSW Press, 1999.

Thompson, Kirsten Moana. "*Once Were Warriors*: New Zealand's First Indigenous Blockbuster." In *Movie Bockbusters*, ed. Julian Streeper, 230–41. London: Routledge, 2003.

Thornley, Davinia. "White, Brown or 'Coffee'?: Revisioning Race in Tamahori's *Once Were Warrior*." *Film Criticism* 25, no. 3 (Spring 2001): 22–36.

——. "Executing the Commoners: Examining Class in *Heavenly Creatures*." In *Film Studies: Women in Contemporary World Cinema*, ed. Alexandra Heidi Karriker, 51–68. New York: Peter Lang, 2002.

Tredell, Nicolas ed. *Cinemas of the Mind: A Critical History of Film Theory*. Duxford, Cambridge: Icon Books, 2002.

Turner, Graeme. *National Fictions: Literature, Film and the Construction of Australian Narrative*. Sydney: Allen & Unwin, 1986.

——. "Art Directing History: The Period Film." In *The Australian Screen*, ed. Albert Moran and Tom O'Regan, 99–117. Ringwood: Penguin, 1989.

——. "Breaking the Frame: The Representation of Aborigines in Australian Film." In *Aboriginal Culture Today*, ed. A. Rutherford. Special issue of *Kunapipi* 10, no. 1 & 2 (1988): 134–45.

Turner, Stephen. "Settlement as Forgetting." *Quicksands: Foundational Histories in Australia and Aotearoa New Zealand*, ed. Klaus Neumann, Nicholas Thomas and Hilary Eriksen, 20–39. Sydney: UNSW Press, 1999.

Tzioumakis, Yannis. *American Independent Cinema: An Introduction*. New Brunswick: Rutgers University Press, 2006.

Veblen, Thorstein. *Theory of the Leisure Class: An Economic Study of Institutions*. London: Unwin, 1925.

Veracini, Lorenzo. "Historylessness: Australia as a Settler Colonial Collective." *Postcolonial Studies* 10, no. 3 (2007): 271–85.

Verhoeven, Deb. *Jane Campion*. London: Routledge, 2009.

Vidal, Belén. "Feminist Historiographies and the Woman Artist's Biopic: the Case of *Artemisia*." *Screen* 48, no. 1 (2007): 69–90.

Walker, Ranginui. "Graveyard or Seedbed," "Korero." *New Zealand Listener*, 8 April 1989: 31.

——. "Immigration Policy and the Political Economy of New Zealand." In *Immigration and National Identity in New Zealand: One People, Two Peoples, Many Peoples?*, ed. S. W.Greif, 282–301 (Palmerston North: The Dunmore Press, 1995).

——. *Ka Whawhai Tonu Mātou: Struggle Without End*. Auckland: Penguin, 2004.

Walker, R. J. "Maori Identity." In *Culture and Identity in New Zealand*, ed. David Novitz and Bill Willmott, 35–52. Wellington: GP Books, 1989.

Walsh G.P. "Governor, Jimmy (1875–1901)." *Australian Dictionary of Biography*, (online edition). <http://www.adb.online.anu.edu.au/biogs/A090063b.htm>. Accessed 1 June 2010.

Wanhalla, Angela. *In/visible sight: The Mixed Descent Families of Southern New Zealand*. Wellington: Bridget Williams Books, 2009.

Wards, Ian. *The Shadow of the Land: A Study of British Policy and Racial Conflict in New Zealand 1832–1852*. Wellington: Historical Publications Branch, Department of Internal Affairs, 1968.

Wartenburg, Thomas E. *Unlikely Couples: Movie Romance as Social Criticism*. Boulder: Westview Press, 1999.

Watson, Chris. "*Frances of Fielding* (Lee Hill, 1928) - A Community Comedy: New Zealand's Populist Answer to Hollywood." *Screening the Past* 8 (1999), <http://www.latrobe.edu.au/screeningthepast/firstrelease/fr1199/cwfr8c.htm>. Accessed 14 August 2010.

Weber, Samuel. *Return to Freud: Jacques Lacan's Dislocation of Psychoanalysis*. Trans. Michael Levine. Cambridge, New York: Cambridge University Press, 1991.

Wells, Peter. "Pictures." *The New Zealand Listener*, 18 June 1983, 30–2.

——. *Frock Attack! Wig Wars! Strategic Camp in* Desperate Remedies. Auckland: Centre for Film, Television and Media Studies, University of Auckland, 1997.

——. *Iridescence*. Auckland, New Zealand: Random House, 2003.

Westerwood, Elan. *Maoriana*. Ed. David S. Westerwood. Dunedin: Whitcombe & Tombs, [ca. 1916].

White, Hayden. *Tropics of Discourse: Essays in Cultural Criticism*. Baltimore: Johns Hopkins University Press, 1978.

Whitmore, George S. *The Last Maori War in New Zealand under the Self-Reliant Policy*. London: Sampson Low, Marston & Company, 1902.

Williams, H.W. *A Dictionary of the Maori Language*, 7th Edition. Wellington: Government Printer, 1985.

Wilson, Janet. "Intertextual Strategies: Reinventing the Myths of Aotearoa in Contemporary New Zealand Fiction." In *Across the Lines: Intertextuality and Transcultural Communication in the New Literatures in English*, ed. Wolfgang Kloos (Amsterdam: Rodopi, 1998), 271–90.

——. "Reconsidering Fred Schepisi's The Chant of Jimmie Blacksmith (1978): The Screen Adaptation of Thomas Keneally's novel (1972)." *Studies in Australasian Cinema* 1, no. 2 (2007): 191–207.

Winks, Robin W. "On Decolonization and Informal Empire." *The American Historical Review* 81, no. 3 (June 1976): 540–56.

Wollen, Tana. "Over Our Shoulders: Nostalgic Screen Fictions for the 1980s." In *Enterprise and Heritage*, ed. John Corner and Sylvia Harvey, 178–93. London: Routledge, 1991.

Wong, Tim. "Out of the Mist." *Landfall* 211 (April 2006): 171–78.

Wood, Houston. *Native Features: Indigenous Films from Around the World*. New York and London: Continuum, 2008.

Wright, Matthew. *Two Peoples, One Land: The New Zealand Wars*. Auckland: Reed, 2006.

Yska, Redmer. *All Shook Up: the Flash Bodgie and the Rise of the New Zealand Teenager in the Fifties*. Auckland: Penguin Books, 1993.

Zamora, Lois Parkinson. *The Usable Past: The Imagination of History in Recent Fiction of the Americas*. Cambridge: Cambridge University Press, 1997.

Contributors

Bruce Babington is Professor Emeritus of Film at Newcastle University. His research interests include New Zealand cinema and television, British and Hollywood film and New Zealand literature. He is the author or editor of numerous books, including *A History of the New Zealand Fiction Feature Film* (2007), *Blue Skies and Silver Linings: Aspects of the Hollywood Musical* (1985), *Affairs to Remember: The Hollywood Comedy of the Sexes* (co-editor, 1989), *Biblical Epics* (co-editor, 1993), *Launder and Gilliat* (co-editor, 2001), *British Stars and Stardom* (editor, 2000) and *The Trouble with Men: Masculinities in European and Hollywood Cinema* (co-editor, 2004). He was given the Jonathan Dennis award for his contribution to New Zealand Film History for 2006–2008.

Barbara Brookes is Professor of History at the University of Otago. Her research interests include gender relations in New Zealand, and the history of health and disease in New Zealand and Britain. Her book *Abortion in England, 1900–1967* (1988) appeared in the Wellcome Institute Series in the History of Medicine, and she is the co-editor of a number of essay collections, including *At Home in New Zealand: History, Houses and People* (2000), *Communities of Women: Historical Perspectives* (2002) and *Sites of Gender* (2003). Currently, she is writing a general history of women in New Zealand.

Annabel Cooper is Associate Professor in the Department of Anthropology, Gender and Sociology at the University of Otago, New Zealand. Her research has focused on the cultural history of gender in New Zealand, and has included work on identity, memory, place and war. Her essays have appeared in journals such as *Gender, Place and Culture*, and in the anthology "On Viewing Jane Campion as an Antipodean," in (eds.), *Jane Campion: Cinema, Nation, Identity*, ed. Hilary Radner, Alistair Fox and Irene Bessiere (2009). Her current project is entitled "The Pākehā Wars: A Genealogy of Memory and Identity."

Alistair Fox holds a personal chair in the Department of English, and is Director of the Centre for Research on National Identity at the University of Otago. He has written extensively on humanism, politics and reform in early modern England, and more recently on post-colonial literature and the formation of New Zealand cultural identity. His books include

Thomas More: History and Providence (1982), *Utopia: An Elusive Vision* (1993), *Politics and Literature in the Reigns of Henry VII and Henry VIII* (1989), *The English Renaissance: Identity and Representation in Elizabethan England* (1997) and *The Ship of Dreams: Masculinity in Contemporary New Zealand Fiction* (2007). His publications on cinema include *Jane Campion: Cinema, Nation, Identity,* co-edited with Hilary Radner and Irène Bessière (2009), and a translation of Raphaëlle Moine, *Les genres du cinema* as *Cinema Genre* (2008). His latest book is *Jane Campion: Authorship, Personal Cinema* (2011).

Barry Keith Grant is Professor of Film Studies and Popular Culture at Brock University, St Catherines, Ontario, Canada. He is the general editor of the Contemporary Approaches to Film and Television Series for Wayne State University Press and the New Approaches to Film Genre series for Wiley-Blackwell. His many books include *100 Documentaries* (with Jim Hillier, 2009), *Film Genre: From Iconography to Ideology* (2007), *The Film Studies Dictionary* (with Steve Blandford and Jim Hillier (2001)), *Voyages of Discovery: The Cinema of Frederick Wiseman* (Urbana and Chicago: University of Illinois Press, 1992), *Film Genre Reader 3* (2003) and *The Dread of Difference: Gender and the Horror Film* (1996). The general editor of the four-volume *Schirmer Encyclopedia of Film* (2007), his most recent books are a monograph on Invasion of the Body Snatchers for the BFI's "Film Classics" series, and Shadows of Doubt: Negotiations of Masculinity in American Genre Films (2011).

Bruce Harding is a researcher in the Ngāi Tahu Research Centre and Research Associate in the Macmillan Brown Centre for Pacific Studies, University of Canterbury. He is also Curator of the Ngaio Marsh House (Christchurch) and has lectured on New Zealand literature (Maori and Pasifika) at the University of Canterbury, and his research interests cohere around explorations of New Zealand's cultural identity. He publishes on writers and cinematographers within this kaupapa.

Jeanette Hoorn is Professor of Visual Cultures in the Cinema Program in the School of Culture and Communication at the University of Melbourne. Her most recent books are *Reframing Darwin: Evolution and Art and Australia* (2009) and *Australian Pastoral: The Making of a White Landscape, Fremantle Arts Press* (2007). She is currently preparing the exhibition "Reframing Darwin: Evolution and Art and Australia," to be exhibited at the Ian Potter Museum of Art, University of Melbourne, August–December 2009, and "Reframing Darwin: Evolution at the Baillieue Library, and Darwin for Kids," University of Melbourne.

Cherie Lacey gained an MA in English literature from Victoria University of Wellington, before completing a PhD in film at the University of Auckland. Foregrounding a Lacanian approach to cultural narratives, Cherie has published on the topics of writing and madness, ordinary psychosis and the psychoanalysis of colonial phenomena. She is currently teaching in the department of Film, Television and Media Studies at the Department of Auckland.

Olivia Macassey completed her PhD in the Department of Film, Television and Media at the University of Auckland in 2009. Her thesis is on the intersection of colonial heritage romance film and trauma. She is currently Lecturer in the School of English Film Theatre and Media Studies at Victoria University of Wellington.

Alison L. McKee is Assistant Professor in the Department of Television, Radio, Film and Theatre at San José State University in California, where she teaches film history, theory and criticism. Her research interests encompass film, gender, identity and politics. She is currently writing a book about the Parker-Hulme murder and the assorted cultural representations of the case across different media and decades.

Harriet Margolis is the editor of *Jane Campion's The Piano* (2000). She has published internationally on self-directed stereotypes, feminism and film, semiotics, film theory and women's romance novels. Co-editor of *Studying the Event Film: The Lord of the Rings* (2008), she is currently co-editing with Alexis Krasilovsky a book on camerawomen from around the world.

Hilary Radner is the foundation professor of Film and Media Studies in the Department of Media, Film & Communication Studies at the University of Otago. She is the author of *Shopping Around* (1995), co-editor of *Film Theory Goes to the Movies* (1993), *Constructing the New Consumer Society* (1997), *Swinging Single* (1999) and the special issue, "Strange Localities: Utopias, Intellectuals, and National Identities in the 21st Century," *Portal: Journal of Multidisciplinary International Studies* 2:2 (2005). Her latest books are *Jane Campion: Cinema, Nation, Identity*, co-edited with Alistair Fox and Irène Bessière (2009) and *Neo-Feminist Cinema: Girly Films, Chick Flicks, and Consumer Culture* (2010).

Simon Sigley is Lecturer in Media Studies in the School of Social and Cultural Studies at Massey University (Auckland) where he co-ordinates Media Practice and New Zealand Cinema. His major current research project is a cultural history of New Zealand's National Film Unit (1941–1990). He is an experienced screen media practitioner, has worked in a variety of programme formats in France and New Zealand and creates multiple platform stories on a Mac. His essay, "How the Road to Life (1931) Became the Road to Ruin: the Case of the Wellington Film Society in 1933," published in the *New Zealand Journal of History* (2008), was awarded a prize by the Film and History Association of Australia and New Zealand for the best article published on a topic relating to film history.

Michelle Smith has a PhD from the University of Melbourne, and holds a position in the School of Communication and Creative Arts at Deakin University. She has worked on the development of the "female Crusoe" genre from the eighteenth century to the twentieth century, and is conducting research on social Darwinism, masculinity and Edgar Rice Burroughs' *Tarzan of the Apes*.

Estella Tincknell is Reader in Media and Cultural Studies at the University of the West of England. She is the author of *Mediating the Family: Gender, Culture and Representation* (2005) and the forthcoming *Re-visioning Jane Campion: Angels, Voices, Demons* (2012), and co-editor of *Film's Musical Moments* (2006) and *New Zealand Fictions: Literature and Film* (2008). The editor of the journal *The Soundtrack*, she has contributed to such journals as *Feminist Media Studies, Journal of European Cultural Studies, Journal of Popular Film and Television* and *The Bulletin of New Zealand Studies* and such volumes as *Popular Music and Television in Britain* (2011), *Revisioning 007: James Bond and Casino Royale* (2010), *Horror Zone: The Cultural Experience of Contemporary Horror Cinema* (2009), *Textual Infidelities: Adaptation in Contemporary Culture* (2009), *Reality Television: A Reader* (2003) and *New Zealand: A Pastoral Paradise?* (2000).

Janet Wilson is Professor of English and Postcolonial Studies at the University of Northampton, UK. From 1988 to 1998 she taught in the Department of English at the University of Otago. She is Editor of the *Journal of Postcolonial Writing* and (2008–2011) Chair of the European Association for Commonwealth Language and Literature Studies (EACLALS). Recent publications include *The Gorse Blooms Pale, Dan Davin's Southland Stories* (2007), *Fleur Adcock* (2007) and (as co-editor) *Rerouting the Postcolonial: New Directions for the New Millennium* (2010). She is currently editing two volumes of essays on Katherine Mansfield, preparing a study of adaptation in New Zealand and Australian feature films 1978–2008, and a monograph on Katherine Mansfield as colonial traveller-writer.

Index